Lecture Notes in Computer Science 11894

More information about this series at http://www.springer.com/series/7409

Ching-Hsien Hsu · Sondès Kallel ·
Kun-Chan Lan · Zibin Zheng (Eds.)

Internet of Vehicles

Technologies and Services Toward Smart Cities

6th International Conference, IOV 2019
Kaohsiung, Taiwan, November 18–21, 2019
Proceedings

 Springer

Editors
Ching-Hsien Hsu
Chung Hua University
Hsinchu, Taiwan

Kun-Chan Lan
China Medical University
Tainan, Taiwan

Sondès Kallel
Saint-Quentin-en-Yvelines
Université de Versailles
Versailles Cedex, France

Zibin Zheng ⓘ
Sun Yat-sen University
Guangzhou, China

ISSN 0302-9743   ISSN 1611-3349   (electronic)
Lecture Notes in Computer Science
ISBN 978-3-030-38650-4   ISBN 978-3-030-38651-1   (eBook)
https://doi.org/10.1007/978-3-030-38651-1

LNCS Sublibrary: SL3 – Information Systems and Applications, incl. Internet/Web, and HCI

This Springer imprint is published by the registered company Springer Nature Switzerland AG
The registered company address is: Gewerbestrasse 11, 6330 Cham, Switzerland

Preface

This volume contains the proceedings of IOV/SC2 2019, the 6th International Conference on Internet of Vehicles and the 9th International Symposium on Cloud and Service Computing, which was held in Kaohsiung, Taiwan, during November 18–21, 2019.

In the era of the Internet of Things, Internet of Vehicles (IOV) plays an important role in constructing smart cities as well as in establishing smart industrial environments according to the Industry 4.0 paradigm. Smart cities are complex integrated network systems, which connect different people within automotives, different automotives, and different environmental objects in cities. In the industrial environments, IOV focuses on providing new efficient solutions with digital intervehicular data transfer and overall communications. Yet, IOV is different from telematics, vehicle ad-hoc networks, and intelligent transportation, in which vehicles, like phones, can run within the whole network and obtain various services by swarm intelligent computing with people, vehicles, and environments.

This year, the technical program of IOV/SC2 2019 attracted submissions from 20 countries/regions. In the first stage, all papers submitted were screened for their relevance and general submission requirements. These manuscripts then underwent a rigorous peer-review process with at least three reviewers, coordinated by the international Program Committee. The Program Committee accepted a total of 32 high-quality papers. As all previous meetings in the IOV/SC2 series, the conference was intended to play an important role for researchers and industry practitioners to exchange information regarding advancements in the state of art and practice of IOV/Cloud architectures, protocols, services, and applications. It was also intended to identify emerging research topics and define the future directions of IOV/Cloud Computing and its related areas such as Internet supported autonomous driving. We believe that this volume not only presents novel and interesting ideas but also will stimulate interesting discussions from the participants and inspire new ideas that will be submitted and presented at further conferences in this series.

The organization of a conference is hard work. It would not have been possible without the exceptional commitment of many expert volunteers. We would like to take this opportunity to extend our sincere thanks to all the authors, keynote speakers, TPC members, and reviewers. Special thanks go to the entire Local Arrangement Committee for their help in making this conference a success. We would also like to express our gratitude to all the organizations that supported our efforts to bring the conference to fruition. We are grateful to Springer for publishing the underlying proceedings.

Finally, we hope that the participants not only enjoyed the technical program during this prestigious conference, but also discovered many historical attractions in

Kaohsiung in order to make their stay unforgettable. Thank you for your participation in this fruitful and enjoyable IOV/SC2 2019 conference!

November 2019

Ching-Hsien Hsu
Sondès Kallel
Zibin Zheng
Kun-Chan Lan

Organization

International Conference on Internet of Vehicles (IOV 2019)

Honorary Chair

Jeffrey J. P. Tsai   Asia University, Taiwan

General Chairs

Chung-Ming Huang   National Cheng Kung University, Taiwan
Andrzej M. J. Skulimowski   AGH University of Science and Technology, Poland

Program Chairs

Kun-Chan Lan   National Cheng Kung University, Taiwan
Lyes Khoukhi   University of Technology of Troyes, France

Workshop Chair

Li Liu   Chongqing University, China

Demo/Poster Chair

Kuan-Chou Lai   National Taichung University of Education, Taiwan

Award Chair

Hui-Huang Hsu   Tamkang University, Taiwan

Publicity Chairs

Daxin Tian   Beihang University, China
William Liu   Auckland University of Technology, New Zealand
Carson Leung   University of Manitoba, Canada
Min-Xiao Chen   National Dong Hua University, Taiwan

Publication Chair

Sondes Khemiri-Kallel   Université Versailles Saint-Quentin-en-Yvelines,
                               France

Advisory Committee

Mohammad Obaidat   Monmouth University, USA
Chu-sing Yang   National Cheng Kung University, Taiwan
Feng Xia   Dalian University of Technology, China
Raouf Boutaba   University of Waterloo, Canada
Peng Cheng   Zhejiang University, China

Hsiao-Hwa Chen	National Cheng Kung University, Taiwan
Sajal Das	Missouri University of Science and Technology, USA
Yao-Nan Lien	Asia University, Taiwan

Steering Committee

Mohammed Atiquzzaman	University of Oklahoma, USA
Jiannong Cao	The Hong Kong Polytechnic University, Hong Kong, China
Robert Hsu	Asia University, Taiwan
Victor C. Leung	The University of British Columbia, Canada
Shangguang Wang	BUPT, China
Reinhard Klette	Auckland University of Technology, New Zealand

Technical Program Committee

José Santa Lozano	Polytechnic University of Cartagena, Spain
George Yannis	National Technical University of Athens, Greece
Anis Laouiti	Télécom SudParis, France
Deyun Gao	Beijing Jiaotong University, China
Hassan Al-Muhairi	Khalifa University, UAE
Jozef Wozniak	Gdansk University of Technology, Poland
Kayhan Ghafoor	Cihan University-Erbil, Iraq
Manuel Ricardo	Universidade do Porto, Porto
Mario Freire	University of Beira Interior, Portugal
Michal Hoeft	Gdańsk University of Technology, Poland
Nai-Wei Lo	National Taiwan University of Science and Technology, Taiwan
Pascal Lorenz	University of Upper Alsace, France
Fernando J. Velez	Portugal
Rui Cruz	Universidade de Lisboa, Portugal
Anand Nayyar	Duy Tang University, Vietnam
Scott Trent	IBM Research, Japan
Tianhua Xu	University College London, UK
Wuyi Yue	Konan University, Japan
Xiangjie Kong	Dalian University of Technology, China
Yair Wiseman	Bar-ilan University, Israel
Zsolt Saffer	Budapest University of Technology and Economics, Hungary
Tzung-Shi Chen	National University of Tainan, Taiwan
Ignacio Soto	Universidad Carlos III de Madrid, Spain
Razvan Stanica	INSA Lyon, France
Winston Seah	Victoria University of Wellington, New Zealand
Luca Reggiani	Politecnico di Milano, Italy
Carlos Calafate	Universitat Politècnica de València, Spain
Natarajan Meghanathan	Jackson State University, USA
Shujun Li	University of Kent, UK

Sokratis Katsikas	Norwegian University of Science and Technology, Norway
Miguel López-Benítez	The University of Liverpool, UK
Lingxi Li	Purdue School of Engineering and Technology, USA
Baris Fidan	University of Waterloo, Canada
Bastian Bloessl	Trinity College Dublin, Ireland
Khoukhi Lyes	Université de Technologie de Troyes, France
Sun Hung-Min	National Tsing Hua University, Taiwan
Masip Xavier	Universitat Politècnica de Catalunya, BarcelonaTech, Spain
Sheng-Wei Wang	Fo Guang University, Taiwan
Lo Shou-Chih	National Dong Hwa University, Taiwan
Santos Alexandre	Universidade do Minho, Portugal
Jana Dittmann	Otto von Guericke University of Magdeburg, Germany
Chang Yao-Chung	National Taitung University, Taiwan
Wang Jenq-Haur	National Taiwan University, Taiwan
Hyytiä Esa	Mechanical Engineering and Computer Science, Iceland
Giacomo Verticale	Politecnico di Milano, Italy
Chen Thomas	University of London, UK
Wolfinger Bernd	University of Hamburg, Germany
Parrein Benoît	Polytech Nantes, France
Tadeusiewicz Ryszard	AGH University of Science and Technology, Poland
Uppal Momin	Lahore University of Management Sciences, Pakistan
Chen Mu-Song	Da-Yeh University, Taiwan
Chelouah Rachid	École Internationale des Sciences du Traitement de lnformation (EISTI), France
Wuyi Yue	Konan University, Japan
Ing-Ray Chen	Virginia Tech, USA
Tara Yahiya	University of Kurdistan Hewlêr, Iraq

International Symposium on Cloud and Service Computing (SC2 2019)

Honorary Chair

Jeffrey J. P. Tsai	Asia University, Taiwan

General Chairs

Pangfeng Liu	National Taiwan University, Taiwan
Patrick C. K. Hung	University of Ontario Institute of Technology, Canada

General Executive Chair

Chung-Nan Lee	National Sun Yat-Sen University, Taiwan

Program Chairs

Chao-Tung Yang   Tunghai University, Taiwan
Zibin Zheng   Sun Yat-Sen University, China

Workshop Chair

Zhikui Chen   Dalian University of Technology, China

Demo/Poster Chair

Wen-Hua Liao   Tatung University, Taiwan

Award Chair

Yue-Shan Chang   National Taipei University, Taiwan

Publicity Chairs

Mianxiong Dong   Muroran Institute of Technology, Japan
Yuri Demchenko   University of Amsterdam, The Netherlands
Richard Lomotey   Penn State University, USA
Sheng-Lung Peng   National Dong Hua University, Taiwan

Publication Chair

Li-Hsing Yen   National Chiao Tung University, Taiwan

Advisory Committee

Anna Kobusinska   Poznan University of Technology, Poland
Shu Tao   IBM Research, USA
Shian-Shyong Tseng   Asia University, Taiwan
Shangguang Wang   BUPT, China
Lizhe Wang   China University of Geosciences, China
Saeid Abolfazli   University of Malaya, Malaysia
Pascal Bouvry   University of Luxembourg, Luxembourg
Keqin Li   State University of New York, USA
Ren-Hung Hwang   National Chung Cheng University, Taiwan
Daqing Zhang   Institut Mines-Télécom/Télécom SudParis, France
Chung-Nan Lee   National Sun Yat-Sen University, Taiwan
Michael Sheng   Macquarie University, Australia
Hong Shen   University of Adelaide, Australia

Steering Committee

Hamid Arabnia   University of Georgia, USA
Rajkumar Buyya   University of Melbourne, Australia
Chung-Ta King   National Tsing Hua University, Taiwan
Robert Hsu   Asia University, Taiwan
H. J. Siegel   Colorado State University, USA

Philip Yu   University of Illinois at Chicago, USA
Christophe Cérin   Université Paris 13, France
Omer Rana   Cardiff University, UK

Technical Program Committee

Mohammad Shojafar   University of Padua, Italy
Che-Rung Lee   National Tsing Hua University, Taiwan
Chau Yuen   Singapore University of Technology and Design,
                             Singapore
Fenfang Xie   Sun Yat-sen University, China
Nicolas Bernard   University of Luxembourg, Luxembourg
Xiang Zhao   National University of Defense Technology, China
Fuu-Cheng Jiang   National Chung-Hsing University, Taiwan
Satheesh Abimannan   VIT University, India
Tyng-Yeu Liang   National Kaohsiung University of Applied Sciences,
                             Taiwan
Chuan Chen   Sun Yat-sen University, China
Weili Chen   Sun Yat-sen University, China
Zhe Chen   Northeastern University, China
Jiajing Wu   Sun Yat-sen University, China
Pritam Shah   DSI Bangalore, India
Wuu Yang   National Chiao Tung University, Taiwan
Che-Wei Chang   National Chung Shan Institute of Science
                             and Technology, Taiwan
Byungchul Tak   Kyungpook National University, South Korea
Ramin Yahyapour   GWDG - University of Göttingen, Germany
You-Chiun Wang   National Sun Yat-sen University, Taiwan
Chuan-Ming Liu   National Taipei University of Technology, Taiwan
Eddy Caron   ENS-Lyon, Inria, LIP, France
Xavier Masip   Universitat Politècnica de Catalunya, Spain
Lung-Pin Chen   Tunghai University, Taiwan
Anna Sikora   Universitat Autònoma de Barcelona, Spain
Danilo Pelusi   University of Teramo, Italy
Jenq-Haur Wang   National Taipei University of Technology, Taiwan
Luca Reggiani   Politecnico di Milano, Italy
Domenico Ciuonzo   University of Naples Federico II, Italy
Luca Caviglione   CNR-IMATI, Italy
Christian Prehofer   Technical University of Munich, Germany
Kuan-Chou Lai   National Taichung University of Education, Taiwan
Amir H. Alavi   University of Missouri, USA
Weihai Yu   Norway
Jana Dittmann   University of Magdeburg, Germany
Fabrice Huet   Université Côte d'Azur, CNRS, I3S, France
I-Chen Wu   National Chiao Tung University, Taiwan
Georgios Kambourakis   University of the Aegean, Greece

Contents

A Novel Protocol for Information Dissemination in Vehicular Networks

Ravi Tomar$^{(\boxtimes)}$ ⓘ, Hanumat G. Sastry ⓘ, and Manish Prateek ⓘ

School of Computer Science, University of Petroleum and Energy Studies,
Dehradun, India
ravitomar7@gmail.com

Abstract. The Vehicular Ad Hoc Networks (VANETs) are rapidly emerging as we are moving towards autonomous and self-driving vehicles. Network hardware efficiency is growing day by day. However, optimal algorithms play a vital role in the effective utilization of the network. The need for supporting algorithm is vital. Cooperative network behavior is highly suitable for VANETs in comparison to infrastructure-based networks. The cooperation for active information exchange between vehicles is a prime requirement to provide safe, secure, and smoother experience on roads. Broadcasting is always the best way to disseminate information among all neighboring nodes in this kind of networks. However, broadcasting in VANET has multiple issues such as broadcast storm problem, network partition problem, network contention. The benefits of broadcasting inspire the presented research work and propose a solution as Priority Based Efficient Information Dissemination Protocol (PBEID). The work utilizes probability-based and density-based information dissemination using conventional broadcasting. The work has been compared with popular techniques for information dissemination and has been statistically proven significant.

Keywords: VANETs · PBEID · Information dissemination

1 Introduction

The Vehicular Ad-Hoc Networks (VANETs) are the self-organizing networks; vehicles act as nodes to exchange useful information [1]. VANET has evolved from Mobile Ad-Hoc Network (MANET) but differs mainly due to the high mobility of nodes [2]. VANETs have the capability to cater to various services towards vehicles such as assisting in blind crossing, route computation in real-time, avoiding intersection collision, passing red lights without stopping, managing speed at curves, detection of traffic signal violation, providing multimedia services, dissemination of safety or emergency messages, assisting in highway merging, etc. However, there are situations where one can utilize infrastructure to cater to different needs, such as Infotainment services and Traffic Control. For the two scenarios, communication between nodes is classified into two major types Vehicle to Vehicle (V2V) and Vehicle to Infrastructure (V2I) [3]. V2V focus only on communication between the vehicles and forming the Ad-hoc network on the go. While V2I rely on infrastructure to communicate with vehicles. The Vehicle to Vehicle (V2V) communication also known as cooperative

© Springer Nature Switzerland AG 2020
C.-H. Hsu et al. (Eds.): IOV 2019, LNCS 11894, pp. 1–14, 2020.
https://doi.org/10.1007/978-3-030-38651-1_1

communication [4]. To enable cooperative communication, a Dedicated Short-Range Communication (DSRC) spectrum of 75 MHz (5.85 to 5.925 GHz) is allotted by the U.S. Federal Communication Commission [1]. The spectrum contains seven channels of 10 MHz wide each and have 1 Control Channel (CCH) and 6 Service Channel (SCH). To create a cooperative awareness among all nodes in the network small periodic packets are exchanged, and the process is known as beaconing, these packets contain necessary information such as speed, position, and direction of a vehicle. The beaconing process is always done on CCH while non-critical messages are transferred through SCH. The IEEE 802.11p also specifies the Medium Access Control (MAC) protocol for single-channel operation [5].

The information dissemination in V2V can be achieved in two ways, by single-hop broadcasting or by multi-hop broadcasting. In single-hop broadcasting, the vehicle sends the information packet to its nearby neighbours only i.e., to those vehicles which are in its one-hop neighbourhood. The vehicle carrying information packet will roam around with the information and periodically will transmit the packet in its one-hop neighbourhood. On the other hand, in the case of multi-hop broadcasting, the vehicle sends its on-board information to others by using the means of flooding. The flooding is the technique to broadcast the packet to all the vehicles in its range of transmission. [6] This type of broadcasting of message leads to many problems, out of which two are of prime attention. One is the broadcast storm problem [7] where each vehicle is rebroadcasting the packets which lead to redundant packets in the network which cause an increased level of packet collisions and thereby the throughput of the network is considerably reduced. The second problem is the network disconnection [8] problem, which occurs due to the mobility of vehicles. However, when it comes to safety messages, broadcasting is always preferred as it helps to effectively disseminate relevant information to the maximum number of vehicles possible in the shortest interval of time.

Three models can be classified into existing VANET dissemination techniques: push, pull, and hybrid. In the Push model, the data is pushed as it is generated or periodically in the network, and the pull model demands data on need basis [9]. The hybrid model makes use of both. The pull model is mostly preferred in case of safety applications while the pull model is suited in delay-tolerant applications such as knowing traffic status, finding a restaurant nearby, etc.

There is no standard approach to access the performance of data dissemination in VANETs due to its mobility and real-world scenario. The challenge is to find a very detailed level traffic scenario and driving behavior data to perform analysis on an algorithm. The techniques are verified through simulations and mathematical modeling.

Thus, we propose our PBEID protocol, which works upon prioritization of messages and then dynamically calculates the density of nodes, the delay between rebroadcast and probability to rebroadcast. The protocol uses neighbor knowledge to calculate density and distance information to prune neighbors, uses Store carry forward (SCF) approach to maximize dissemination, uses the probability-based delay to become opportunistic. This paper is further classified into 7 sections, Sect. 2 explains the related work, Sect. 3 provides a novel protocol for information dissemination, followed by Sect. 4 explaining the working of the proposed protocol. Sections 5 and 6 discuss the simulation and results and finally, Sect. 7 concludes the paper and future directions.

2   Related Work

Broadcasting refers to merely sending a message to all receivers within the network. Once received, every vehicle is supposed to rebroadcast the packet as long as every vehicle has received that packet at least once when they have participated in that particular network. This mechanism is called as flooding, and it works very reliably in sparse environments where the vehicle density is low. On the other hand, when it comes to broadcasting a message in a denser environment, the numbers of average collisions increase significantly, and it leads to the broadcast storm problem [7]. The redundant packet collision also leads to the hidden terminal problem [8] at times. Chen et al. in [10] provides a summary of broadcast techniques used for dissemination of critical messages in emergency scenarios. Various techniques have been proposed in selecting the most suitable node to rebroadcast the message, and this is the critical area where a lot more has to be done. As there exists no technique which suffices the requirement of all type of networks. Here we discuss a few techniques which are used for controlling the rebroadcast.

– **Probability-based rebroadcast:** In probability-based protocols, every vehicle which receives an information packet will decide whether to re-broadcast the same packet or not. The decision is taken based on probability-based functions. These protocols use the value of probability in such a way so as reduce the medium contention and the number of packet collision. Though, when these protocols are used in sparse environments, there always lies a possibility that some of the vehicles may not receive the data packet. An adaptive probabilistic protocol [11] proposes a higher rebroadcast probability for the areas which are dense in terms of vehicle density, and conversely, it proposes a lower rebroadcast priority for the areas where vehicle density is low, i.e., sparse areas. Other types of probability-based algorithms include weighted p-persistent algorithm, slotted 1-persistent algorithm, slotted p-persistent algorithm [7].
– **Counter-based rebroadcast:** In this type of broadcasting protocols, the vehicle decides its rebroadcast priority based on a counter which tells the vehicle as in how many times it has received the same packet. Whenever a vehicle receives an information packet for the very first time, it will wait for 't' time units and then broadcast it to all the neighbors. However, when a vehicle crosses the threshold value, then the rebroadcasting process is canceled by the vehicle as it implies that the message has already been broadcasted by some other vehicle in the network. However, in the case where the threshold value is not crossed, and the timer expires, then the packet is rebroadcasted instantly to increase the covering range of the information packet. The dynamic counter-based protocol has been proposed in [12] where authors have used a different value of threshold which varies corresponding to the number of vehicles present on the road segment. So, a vehicle present in a denser area will be having a smaller value of the threshold, and conversely, a vehicle present in a sparse area will have a comparatively higher threshold. Counter based technique has been integrated with Probability-based techniques in [13], the author proposed that a probability distribution-based function will choose a value, and in parallel, a counter will also be managed. When the counter value has been

reached, the rebroadcasting is cancelled as it implies that already the message has been broadcasted too many times in the network.

- **Distance-based rebroadcast:** In distance-based protocols, the decision of when to broadcast a packet depends upon the distance between the two vehicles, i.e., transmitter and receiver. Hence vehicles located at a greater distance will have a higher threshold value—the high dependency of these protocols on threshold results in a variable degree of performance. In [14], the authors have proposed to let the vehicles wait for x seconds before taking on the broadcasted process for a packet. The value of time interval is dependent on the distance between the two vehicles, i.e., the transmitting vehicle and the receiving vehicle. The work in [15] aims at selecting the next relay vehicle based on distance as well as on the communication range of that road segment. In this work, the vehicle which is located in the farthest segment of the road will be getting the highest rebroadcasting priority.
- **Neighbour knowledge-based rebroadcast:** Protocols based on neighbor knowledge use factors such as position, and movement of their neighbors to decide whether a vehicle is an excellent candidate to serve as the next relay vehicle or not. In cases of sparse networks, such algorithms may yield more unsatisfactory results due to less or no availability of neighbor data. Connected Dominating Sets are used to propose an algorithm to reduce the number of redundant transmissions by the authors in [16, 17]. While using CDS, a graph is generated depicting available nodes and using this graph, a minimum number of vehicles are selected for the rebroadcast process to achieve 100% coverage of the road segment.
- **Opportunistic based rebroadcast:** As the name suggests, opportunity-based protocols work on the opportunities which are available using inheritance in the broadcast process. Hence, the vehicle residing in the farthest location will have a higher priority for broadcast and will also lead to more excellent coverage in a comparatively shorter period. The authors in [18] have assigned the shortest waiting delay to the vehicles which are residing in the farthest locations so that they can broadcast the message instantly leading to faster delivery of packets to maximum vehicles.
- **Delay-Based rebroadcast:** In the delay-based protocol, as the name suggests, the delay is selected for each node wishing to rebroadcast the message. The delay may be static or may come from an intelligent system. In [19] author proposed a static delay-based protocol to ensure low delay and high reliability. The author has assigned a 0.5 ms delay for the farthest node, 1 ms for the second farthest node, 1.5 ms for the third farthest node and so on till ten farthest nodes with a delay of 5 ms. This approach used neighbor knowledge and Delay based.

3 Proposed Protocol

This section explains the proposed novel protocol for efficient information dissemination over VANET. This protocol has been developed to maximize the radio channel utilization and message transmission to maximum nodes in minimum time. Network density and message priority are the significant factors which influence the information dissemination. Various research studies have focused on message classification to prioritize crucial information for effective dissemination, and this approach has given encouraging results [20, 21]. This protocol works in three stages, at first stage the message will be generated and prioritized along with direction, in second stage message will be received by nodes in the vicinity, and every receiving node will compute density, delay, and probability to rebroadcast and finally, in the third stage the algorithm decides to broadcast the message or not. This protocol is fully compatible with IEEE 802.11p standards [22].

3.1 Message Prioritization

The message generation node determines the message priority and direction of the message to be disseminated. Broadcast is generally done circularly whereas mostly messages are direction-specific, e.g. Ambulance information must be forwarded in forwarding direction while sudden brake or accident information needs to be disseminated in backward direction. Keeping the above two parameters this work classify the message propagation direction along with the priority of message. So, the messages are classified into five classes where each class can identify the priority and direction of message. Each class corresponds to a broadcast policy. Table 1 shows priority and direction with example of use case. Figures 1, 2 and 3 depicts the scenario for all classes.

Table 1. Class of message based on priority and direction

Class	Priority	Direction	Example
1	High	Backward	Accident, sudden brake, bad road
2	High	Forward	Ambulance, fire vehicle
3	Medium	Backward	Traffic updates, infotainment
4	Medium	Forward	Other infotainment
5	Low	Both	General broadcast

- Class 1 message indicates an emergency message which needs to be disseminated in a backward direction, e.g., Accident, Sudden Brake detection. These messages are of zero tolerance and should be disseminated as early as possible to all the following vehicles.
- Class 2 message indicates an emergency vehicle trying to overtake vehicles in front, and this message needs to be disseminated in the forward direction, e.g., Ambulance, Fire Vehicle. These messages are also of high priority and should be disseminated as early as possible to all ahead vehicles.

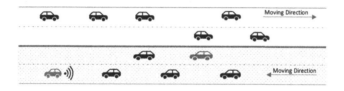

Fig. 1. Class 1 & Class 3 message, backward broadcast

- Class 3 message indicates a medium message, and this message needs to be disseminated in a backward direction, e.g., Traffic Updates, Infotainment Applications. These messages are of medium priority and possess less critical information.
- Class 4 message indicates a medium message, and this message needs to be disseminated in the forward direction, e.g., Traffic Updates, Infotainment Applications. These messages are of medium priority and possess less critical information. The primary purpose is to share traffic information among nodes and finally updating this information to traffic monitoring applications.

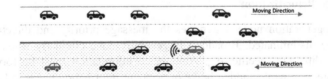

Fig. 2. Class 2 & 4 message, forward broadcast

- Class 5 message indicates a general message, e.g., point of interest, advertisement service, weather information, etc. These messages are of low priority and can be disseminated separately (with permissible latency), Fig. 3 depicts the scenario. Our protocol makes use of V2I approach to disseminate such kind of messages. Broadcast policy this class of messages has already been proposed in our work [23].

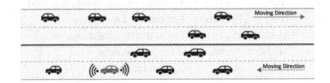

Fig. 3. Class 5 message, general broadcast

3.2 Density of Nodes

Density is calculated by counting neighbors of a node within its coverage. However, this is not possible in real life due to obstacles and interference in the signal. So, we calculate density by counting the number of nodes in neighbor who can communicate. Denser the network more is the traffic. Hence, we need to adjust rebroadcasting parameter, as the density changes. To calculate the density in proposed work we make use of beaconing [24]. With the help of beaconing each node maintains list of its two-hop neighbors containing information such as speed, distance, and coordinates. The list contains unique entry for each neighbor, only additional information changes on receiving new packet. So, it does not lengthen the list of addresses for the concerned packet. The table is pruned based on distance threshold of communication range. The count of one-hop neighbors (h_0) and two-hop neighbor (h_1) is used to calculating density using this Eq. (1), where α is a density constant.

$$density = \frac{\alpha * h_0 + (1 - \alpha) * h_1}{2} \tag{1}$$

Choosing the value of α: The value of α is between 0 to 1 and is dependent on its one-hop and two-hop neighbors. We can understand from Eq. (2), that if α is kept near to the lower side than the impact of one-hop neighbor decreases and impact of two-hop neighbor increases. So, we classify the system as if $h_0 < h_1$, the scenario is sparse, and we need probability to rebroadcast to be high, which results in lower delay. Similarly, if $h_0 > h_1$, the scenario is dense, and we need probability to rebroadcast to be less which would eventually create higher delay. If $h_0 = h_1$ we can take any value of alpha between $0 < \alpha < 1$, as the value of α has no impact on density in this case.

3.3 Rebroadcasting Probability (P_{rb})

The probability calculated based on the density of the network, this indicates whether the packet needs to be rebroadcasted or not, we have carried multiple experiments to determine and found 0.3 as the suitable value beyond which a packet should be rebroadcasted. The P_{rb} is calculated using the Eq. (2) where density is calculated from Eq. (1), and Nodes are the number of vehicles in the network.

$$P_{rb} = 1 - \frac{density}{Nodes} \tag{2}$$

3.4 Delay Between Rebroadcast (D_{rb})

The delay between rebroadcast is the waiting time before rebroadcasting the packet; this value needs to be set such that the farthest node should rebroadcast as early as possible. So, we calculate this delay using the range of communication medium, distance to initiator and Probability to rebroadcast. The D_{rb} is calculated using Eq. (3).

$$delay(D_{rb}) = \left(\frac{Range - distance}{Range * Prb} \right) milliseconds \tag{3}$$

3.5 Number of Rebroadcast (N_{rb})

This parameter is used to ensure a failsafe system, as broadcasting does not have an acknowledgment mechanism. So, if the packet is received many times, then a delay of 1 ms is added to the previously scheduled message, and the value of N_{rb} is decremented by 1. This delay ensures the packet to broadcast at least once and if anytime during the scheduled phase the N_{rb} value becomes 0 or negative all scheduled broadcast message are canceled.

3.6   MaxDistance to Broadcast (M_{db})

The Maximum distance to rebroadcast defines the area of coverage, if the packet has reached this value, then no further dissemination is done. This work considers the value of M_{db} to be maximum.

4   Working of the Protocol

The overall protocol contains four procedures which are explained below, the pseudocode for the protocol is provided in Algorithm 1, and the flow chart of the received packet is depicted in Fig. 4.

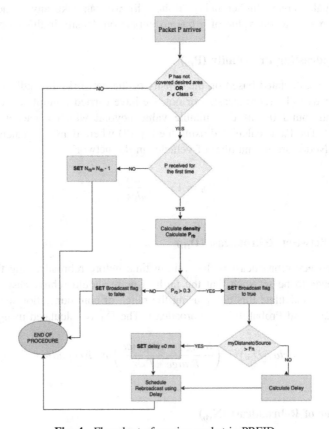

Fig. 4. Flowchart of receive packet in PBEID

4.1   Generate Packet

The message generation node will decide the priority and direction of the message and assigns suitable class from the defined Table 1. The source node looks up for its farthest neighbor in the data collected through the beaconing process. The new packet will be generated with this additional information to broadcast over the network. The rest of the flow continues with the receiving vehicles and is explained in next section.

4.2 Receive Packet

At every receiving node, receive packet procedure will be executed. The packet receiving node contains the information about itself and its neighboring nodes through beaconing process. The class 5 messages will be handled by V2I approach explained already in [23]. In case if the packet has already covered the desired area, then the packet will be rejected. Further, the node compares its moving direction with the intended direction of the message to be disseminated. If it is false, this indicates that this node will not participate further in the dissemination of this message, so the algorithm marks rebroadcast flag as false, and the algorithm ends. However, If it is true then node will participate in further information dissemination, and it checks whether the packet has been received for the first time or has also been received previously. If the packet has been received previously the N_{rb} value is decremented by 1, and a static delay is added to packet so that rebroadcast procedure can decide. If this packet has been received for the first time then the density and probability to rebroadcast are calculated. Based on different simulations performed we found that 0.3 value of P_{rb} is appropriate to reject the rebroadcast of message. So, if P_{rb} is greater than 0.3 then rebroadcast flag is set to true and delay to rebroadcast is calculated. At this point we also check if the node processing the message is farther from the Fn value set by source node, the delay is set to 0 ms to catalyze the dissemination. Finally, the packet along with delay is passed to the rebroadcast procedure which will actually rebroadcast the packet whenever the scheduled time event occurs. The rebroadcast procedure is explained in the next section.

4.3 Rebroadcast

All the rebroadcast are scheduled by receive packet procedure and also the value of N_{rb}. This procedure checks for rebroadcast flag and value of N_{rb} before rebroadcasting. If the rebroadcast flag is false or N_{rb} value is zero or negative it cancels the rebroadcast. Otherwise, it checks for class and broadcast the packet on CCH/SCH accordingly. In the case of class 1 and 2, it also adapts store carry forward approach so that message is disseminated even in the case of hidden node problem.

5 Simulation

5.1 System Model

In our model, we are using the realistic road map, extracted from OpenStreetMap [25], the city environment of 3×2.5 km has been taken for analysis, which commonly has high-density vehicle moving around on a city road and also a lot of intersection and junctions are available in the city. We define a curved road segment which merges onto a two-lane highway. The curved road and buildings helped us to see the effect of Signal loss in DSRC. The work is focused on V2V communication, and hence, no Roadside Unit or V2I is considered. We identified the following four parameters which affect the information dissemination in VANET. The parameters that need to be optimized for different needs of application are Rebroadcasting Probability (P_{rb}), Number of Rebroadcast (N_{rb}), Delay between Rebroadcast (D_{rb}) and Maximum Hop Count (MHC).

5.2 Simulation Setup and Parameters Used

The Simulation is carried out in OMNET++ [26] and VEINS [27] framework. The mobility model is generated through SUMO. The parameters for the simulation are described in Table 2. The mobility model is generated for variable vehicles running on a curved road with random speed. The model is realistic due to the random speed. The simple obstacle model is used to depict real-world condition. An accident message is introduced in the network at time 400 s during the simulation. The objective is to disseminate this message to maximum nodes in minimum time. The simulation is executed for total of 450 s. The mobility model and the network parameters are kept constant for all the five-algorithm implementation.

Table 2. Simulation parameters

Parameter	Value
Field	City: 3000 m × 2500 m
Simulation duration	450 s
Scheduled accident	(Randomly near 400 s)
Transmission range	300 m
Beaconing interval	3 s
Mobility	Fixed path
Vehicle speed	Random with (acceleration = 2.6 m/s, maxSpeed = 14 m/s)
Average speed	13.41 m/s
Number of nodes	30, 50, 70, 90, 110, 130, 150
Data packet size	512 byte
MAC protocol	IEEE 802.11p

6   Result and Discussion

In this section, we present the detailed graphical and statistical analysis to evaluate the significance of the proposed PBEID protocol. The proposed PBEID protocol is compared with the standard information dissemination techniques as Flooding [28], Probability-based [11, 29], Distance-Based [30] and Counter Based [12, 13]. The performance of PBEID is evaluated based on the following metrics [31].

– **Propagation Time:** The propagation time is defined as the difference of time between the packet generation at the source node and reception of first message at the last node. Minimizing this value makes an algorithm efficient.

- **Reachability:** The Reachability or Full Reception Ratio is defined as the number of nodes receiving the message irrespective of the time taken. All nodes should receive the message.
- **Number of Retransmission:** The total number of Packet Generated or retransmission is the number of packets generated on all nodes during the retransmission of the packet. Generating a higher number of rebroadcasts creates network contention and broadcast storm problem. So, this should be minimized to make a congestion-free network.
- **Number of collisions:** the number of collisions is dependent on the total number of retransmissions done if higher retransmission is done then higher packet would generate in the network and there are chances of getting more packet collision which will affect overall performance of network.

Any single parameter cannot decide the optimal algorithm, e.g., as a best-case, we need 100% reachability in minimum time using the minimum network resources and minimum collisions.

6.1   Evaluating the Propagation Time

The propagation time is the parameter which is most useful when we talk about the critical messages. The propagation time is the time taken by a message to be delivered to the last accessible node in the network. Figure 5 shows the performance of PBEID protocol against different techniques in sparse to the dense network environment. The propagation time is calculated using Eq. (4). We can observe that PBEID protocol is consistently performing well in almost all the scenarios. Only the distance-based approach is outperforming the PBEID protocol with very little difference.

$$PT = ReceiveMsgTime - InitTime \tag{4}$$

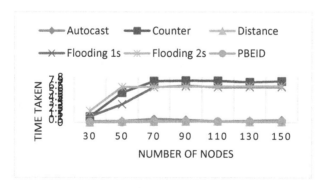

Fig. 5. Number of nodes vs. propagation in time

6.2 Reachability

The reachability refers to the overall coverage of the message, and it is always expected that message covers the entire network for which it was intended. The reachability is affected by many parameters such as collision, blind node, network contention, etc. The Reachability is calculated using Eq. (5).

$$\text{Reachablity} = \frac{\text{Number Vehicle Received}}{\text{Total Vehicles in Network}} \tag{5}$$

In Fig. 6, we can see that PBEID is performing best in contrast to all other algorithms.

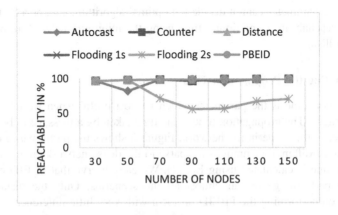

Fig. 6. Number of nodes vs. reachability in percentage

7 Conclusion and Future Work

In this work, we have explained various techniques available for information dissemination in VANETs. We identified and explained the necessary parameters to optimize the information dissemination such as density bases and prioritization. Based on these findings, we proposed a priority-based efficient information dissemination technique (PBEID). All the discussed existing and proposed algorithm are implemented in VEINS [27], and the exhaustive comparison is made. The simulation is carried out based on different scenarios from sparse to dense. Based on graphical analysis we could see that performance of PBEID is performing well if we look all values holistically. So, to better understand our results in future work we plan to perform statistical test on the data collected through simulation and to observe that our results are significant and not by chance. As future work, we will analyze the performance of PBEID in more complex scenarios and on more parameters. Our primary interest is to study the behavior of our protocol when there are multiple messages in the network. More work will be carried out in the making α adaptive to calculate density in a real scenario. With these findings, we may conclude further that PBEID will work in more complex scenarios.

References

1. Jiang, D., Delgrossi, L.: IEEE 802.11p: towards an international standard for wireless access in vehicular environments. In: IEEE Vehicular Technology Conference, pp. 2036–2040 (2008)
2. Liang, W., Li, Z., Zhang, H., Wang, S., Bie, R.: Vehicular ad hoc networks: architectures, research issues, methodologies, challenges, and trends. Int. J. Distrib. Sensor Netw. **2015**(8), 745303 (2015)
3. Andrews, S.: Vehicle-to-vehicle (V2V) and vehicle-to- infrastructure (V2I) communications and cooperative driving. In: Eskandarian, A. (ed.) Handbook of Intelligent Vehicles, vol. 2, pp. 1121–1144. Springer, London (2012). https://doi.org/10.1007/978-0-85729-085-4_46
4. Willke, T., Tientrakool, P., Maxemchuk, N.: A survey of inter-vehicle communication protocols and their applications. IEEE Commun. Surv. Tutorials **11**(2), 3–20 (2009)
5. IEEE, "IEEE Std 802.11-2016 (Revision of IEEE Std 802.11-2012): IEEE Standard for Information technology–Telecommunications and information exchange between systems Local and metropolitan area networks–Specific requirements - Part 11: Wireless LAN Medium Acce," IEEE Std 802.11-2016 (Revision of IEEE Std 802.11-2012), p. 3534 (2016)
6. Panichpapiboon, S., Pattara-Atikom, W.: A review of information dissemination protocols for vehicular ad hoc networks. IEEE Commun. Surv. Tutorials **14**(3), 784–798 (2012)
7. Wisitpongphan, N., Tonguz, O.K., Parikh, J.S., Mudalige, P., Bai, F., Sadekar, V.: Broadcast storm mitigation techniques in vehicular ad hoc networks. IEEE Wirel. Commun. **14**(6), 84–94 (2007)
8. Jin, Z., Yan, N., Li, B.: Reliable on-demand geographic routing protocol resolving network disconnection for VANET. In: Proceedings - 5th International Conference on Wireless Communications, Networking and Mobile Computing, WiCOM 2009, pp. 1–4 (2009)
9. Nadeem, T., Shankar, P., Iftode, L.: A comparative study of data dissemination models for VANETs. In: 2006 3rd Annual International Conference on Mobile and Ubiquitous Systems: Networking and Services, MobiQuitous, pp. 1–10 (2006)
10. Chen, R., Jin, W.L., Regan, A.: Broadcasting safety information in vehicular networks: issues and approaches. IEEE Netw. **24**(1), 20–25 (2010)
11. Mylonas, Y., Lestas, M., Pitsillides, A., Ioannou, P., Papadopoulou, V.: Speed adaptive probabilistic flooding for vehicular ad hoc networks. IEEE Trans. Veh. Technol. **64**(5), 1973–1990 (2015)
12. Mohammed, A., Ould-Khaoua, M., Mackenzie, L.M., Abdulai, J.D.: Dynamic probabilistic counter-based broadcasting in mobile Ad hoc networks. In: ICAST 2009 - 2nd International Conference on Adaptive Science and Technology, pp. 120–127 (2009)
13. Yassein, M.B., Nimer, S.F., Al-Dubai, A.Y.: A new dynamic counter-based broadcasting scheme for mobile ad hoc networks. Simul. Model. Practice Theory **19**(1), 553–563 (2011)
14. Li, D., Huang, H., Li, X., Li, M., Tang, F.: A distance-based directional broadcast protocol for urban vehicular ad hoc network. In: 2007 International Conference on Wireless Communications, Networking and Mobile Computing, WiCOM 2007, pp. 1520–1523 (2007)
15. Korkmaz, G., Ekici, E., Ozguner, F.: Black-burst-based multihop broadcast protocols for vehicular networks. IEEE Trans. Veh. Technol. **56**(5), 3159–3167 (2007)
16. Ros, F.J., Ruiz, P.M., Stojmenovic, I.: Reliable and efficient broadcasting in vehicular ad Hoc networks. In: IEEE Vehicular Technology Conference, pp. 1–5 (2009)
17. Na Nakorn, K., Rojviboonchai, K.: Non-GPS data dissemination for VANET. Int. J. Distrib. Sens. Netw. **2014** (2014)

18. Li, M., Zeng, K., Lou, W.: Opportunistic broadcast of event-driven warning messages in Vehicular Ad Hoc Networks with lossy links. Comput. Netw. **55**(10), 2443–2464 (2011)
19. Gonzalez, S., Ramos, V.: Preset delay broadcast: a protocol for fast information dissemination in vehicular ad hoc networks (VANETs). Eurasip J. Wirel. Commun. Netw. **2016**(1), 117 (2016)
20. Amadeo, M., Campolo, C., Molinaro, A.: Priority-based content delivery in the internet of vehicles through named data networking. J. Sens. Actuator Netw. **5**(4), 17 (2016)
21. Yang, J., Fei, Z.: Broadcasting with prediction and selective forwarding in vehicular networks. Int. J. Distrib. Sens. Netw. **2013**(12), 309041 (2013)
22. Huang, C.M., Yang, C.C., De Huang, H.: An effective channel utilization scheme for IEEE 1609.4 protocol. In: Proceedings of the 4th International Conference on Ubiquitous Information Technologies and Applications, ICUT 2009, pp. 1–6 (2009)
23. Tomar, R., Prateek, M., Sastry, H.G.: A novel approach to multicast in VANET using MQTT. Ada User J. **38**(4), 231–235 (2017)
24. Tomar, R., Prateek, M., Sastry, H.G.: Analysis of beaconing performance in IEEE 802.11p on vehicular ad-hoc environment. In: 2017 4th IEEE Uttar Pradesh Section INternational Conference on Electrical, COmputer and Electronica (UPCON) GLA University, Mathira, 26–28 October 2017, vol. 2018, pp. 692–696 (2017)
25. OpenStreetMap. https://www.openstreetmap.org/#map=18/30.32427/78.04188. Accessed 16 May 2019
26. OMNETPP. https://omnetpp.org/software/2017/12/12/omnet-5-2-1-released
27. Sommer, C., German, R., Dressler, F.: Bidirectionally coupled network and road simulation for improved IVC analysis. IEEE Trans. Mob. Comput. **10**(1), 3–15 (2011)
28. Tseng, Y.C., Ni, S.Y., Chen, Y.S., Sheu, J.P.: The broadcast storm problem in a mobile ad hoc network. Wirel. Netw. **8**(2–3), 153–167 (2002)
29. Kumar, S., Mehfuz, S.: Intelligent probabilistic broadcasting in mobile ad hoc network: a PSO approach. J. Reliab. Intell. Environ. **2**(2), 107–115 (2016)
30. Hall, R.J.: An improved geocast for mobile ad hoc networks. IEEE Trans. Mob. Comput. **10**(2), 254–266 (2011)
31. Oliveira, R., Montez, C., Boukerche, A., Wangham, M.S.: Reliable data dissemination protocol for VANET traffic safety applications. Ad Hoc Netw. **63**, 30–44 (2017)

Uplink Access Control in Narrowband IoT

Ren-Hung Hwang$^{(\boxtimes)}$, Min-Chun Peng, and Bo-Hao Tu

National Chung Cheng University, Chaiyi, Taiwan
rhhwang@cs.ccu.edu.tw

Abstract. In order to provide low-power wide area network (LPWAN) services, 3GPP adopted the Narrow-Band Internet of Things (NB-IoT) standard in 2016. NB-IoT is expected to become the transmission communication standard for providing a large number of IoT devices in 5G networks. However, development of NB-IoT is still in its earlier stage and encounters several challenges. First, NB-IoT is designed for machine type communication. Generally, connection and transmission delays are not the primary consideration for this type of communication. Thus, it is not able to meet different delay requirements of different types of IoT applications. For example, for life-threatening or life-saving applications, they would require very high reliable and low latency transmission of emergency messages. Secondly, when a user equipment wants to associate to a NB-IoT network, it must synchronize with the regional base station (eNB) through the random access channel (RACH) procedure. A large number of IoT devices will cause a big challenge to the RACH procedure. Therefore, in this paper, we aim to improve the RACH procedure to handle a large number of IoT devices without affecting the transmission delay of emergent messages. We propose a Dynamic RACH Resource Allocation (DRRA) scheme which integrates with resource allocation scheme and Access Class Barring (ACB) scheme to improve the delay and throughput of the RACH procedure. Our simulation results show that the proposed DRRA scheme is able to achieve higher access success rate, higher system throughput, and low transmission delay for emergent message as compared to the original RACH procedure.

Keywords: NB-IoT · RACH · LPWAN · IoT

1 Introduction

Internet of Things (IoT) is one of the booming technologies in recent years. IoT industries, such as smart meter, smart grid, smart city, and healthcare, is expected to grow radiantly in next 10 years. Wireless communication technologies play a key role in meeting the flexible and ubiquitous communication demand of IoT devices. In particular, because the wide deployment scope and limited battery life of IoT devices, several Low-Power WAN (LPWAN) technologies have been developed to fit the demand of long distance but small data volume transmission. Among them, NB-IoT proposed by 3GPP becomes the most promising LPWAN technology due to its reliable infrastructure and licensed communication band [1].

© Springer Nature Switzerland AG 2020
C.-H. Hsu et al. (Eds.): IOV 2019, LNCS 11894, pp. 15–27, 2020.
https://doi.org/10.1007/978-3-030-38651-1_2

In the NB-IoT network, devices need to perform a Random Access (RA) procedure [2] to communicate with an eNB before data transmission using preambles. There are two types of RA procedures, contention-based and contention-free. They use different set of preambles. The contention-based RA procedure is initiated by devices and used when the devices have demands for accessing the network. On the other hand, contention-free RA procedure is initiated by eNB and assign dedicated preamble to device directly. In most cases, devices need to perform contention-based RA procedure when first attached to an eNB. Only after the RA procedure, devices can achieve the uplink frequency synchronization and access the NB-IoT network. There are four steps in the contention-based RA procedure.

Step1. Random Access Preamble (MSG1)
The resource allocation in the frequency domain is a set of starting preambles. Preambles are carried in the Physical Random Access Channel (PRACH) which is a part of an uplink resource of a NB-IoT network. Each starting preamble is equivalent to the first NB-IoT PRACH (NPRACH) symbol group and associated with a specific 3.75 kHz tone. The set of starting preambles is determined by a subcarrier offset and a number of spanned subcarriers. The time-domain allocation is defined by a periodicity, a starting time with the period, and the number of repetitions associated with the NPRACH resource. Allocation of the PRACH in a subframe is determined by the prach-ConfigIndex of System Information Block 2 (SIB2) announced by an eNB [3]. Devices then randomly choose one preamble for contention-based RA procedure and send it to the eNB. If a device does not receive the Random Access Response (RAR) in a RAR window, its contention for RA is failed.

Step2. Random Access Response (MSG2)
When an eNB receives a preamble from a device, a RAR message is sent to the device. The RAR consists of the preamble index, uplink time synchronization, uplink grant, and Temporary Cell-Radio Network Temporary Identifier (TC-RNTI). Once a device succeeds in the RA procedure, its TC-RNTI is changed to C-RNTI. During this step, it is possible that more than one device selects the same preamble. In this situation, if the preamble can be received correctly, a RAR will be replied and the contention is solved in Step 4. However, due to the signal collision, the eNB is more likely not able to receive the preamble. In this study, we assume that when more than one device sends the same preamble, the RA will fail due to collision.

Step3. Scheduled Transmission (MSG3)
When a device receives a RAR, it replies with a MSG3 to the eNB. The uplink resource allocated in the RAR is used to transmit the MSG3, which consists of the device ID and the RRC connection request.

Step4. Contention Resolution (MSG4)
When an eNB receives a MSG3, it has to decide which devices succeed in the contention. The eNB transmits the MSG4 to devices that send the MSG3. The MSG4 consists of the device ID and the RRC connection setup. If a device finds that the device ID in the MSG4 is itself, its contention succeeds. The TC-RNTI of the device changes to C-RNTI and the status changes to RRC_CONNECTED. Otherwise, the device knows its contention failed and starts the RA procedure all over again.

In order to achieve maximum energy loss of 144 dB, 154 dB, and 164 dB against Maximum Coupling Loss (MCL), there are three coverage levels in NB-IoT. The system information sets the specifications for each CE Level, such as the period in which the channel appears, the position of the channel on the frequency axis, the position of the channel on the time axis, the number of subcarriers used by the channel, and the maximum number of retries for the preamble. The base station will determine the threshold of the two reference signals (Reference Signal Received Power, RSRP). The transmission device will find out which CE level it is based on the measured RSRP. UE will perform random access procedure with corresponding NPRACH configuration.

Although in reality, there are many types of IoT devices and applications with very different traffic characteristics and QoS requirements, such as transmission delay and reliability, differentiating the RACH procedure for different types of IoT devices has received very little attention in the literature. In this study, we classify NB-IoT devices (applications) into two categories, the emergency transmission type and the regular transmission type. As the number of NB-IoT devices grow rapidly, it is a big challenge to guarantee the emergency transmission type device to connect to the eNB with a high successful rate and short delay. We aim to design the RACH procedure to handle a large number of IoT devices without affecting the transmission delay of emergent messages. We propose a Dynamic RACH Resource Allocation (DRRA) scheme which integrates with resource allocation scheme and ACB scheme to improve the delay and throughput of the RACH procedure. As compared to the enhanced RA procedure proposed by 3GPP [4], our simulation results show that the proposed DRRA scheme is able to achieve higher access success rate, higher system throughput, and extremely low transmission delay for emergent message.

The remainder of this paper is organized as follows. Section 2 surveys state-of-the-art works on NB-IoT RACH procedure. Section 3 presents the proposed Dynamic RACH Resource Allocation (DRRA), including the Resource Allocation scheme, and the Access Class Barring (ACB) scheme. Simulation results are shown in Sect. 4. Finally, conclusions and future research are given in Sect. 5.

2 Related Works

Surveys on recent advances in NB-IoT standards, key technologies and open issues can be found in [5–7]. Quite a few recent works on NB-IoT RACH procedure focused on efficient power consumption issues [8]. Performance modeling on the standard RACH procedure is done in [9]. The authors in [10] proposed a method to determine the required number of preambles for a target RA request arrival rate, but details of the RACH procedure, such as retransmission, were ignored. Preamble repetition was analyzed using stochastic geometry from physical signal aspect in [11] which showed little improvement in a heavy traffic scenario. Authors in [12] also showed that fewer repetitions with more retransmissions can yield higher successful RA probability. Thus, in this work, we will focus on the effect of retransmission.

In general, six basic mechanisms were proposed by 3GPP to enhance the RACH procedure [4], include ACB, separate RACH resource for MTC, dynamic allocation of

RACH resources, MTC specific backoff, slotted access, and pull based scheme. Most of the previous works studied how to improve the RACH procedure from one of the above mechanisms. Different from previous works, in this paper, we combine the first three mechanisms to enhance the RACH procedure with goals to provide large number of simultaneous IoT devices access and low delay transmission of emergency messages.

3 Dynamic RACH Resource Allocation (DRRA) Scheme

3.1 System Overview

In this section, a system architecture overview is given of the proposed DRRA. The following assumptions are made.

- eNBs are aware of preamble collisions
  It is assumed that eNBs are aware of the collisions of the preambles when they happened, and will not reply RAR to those devices.
- Service types and classes
  It is assumed that a device collects the same service type of data. There are two service types with different delay and reliability requirements (see Table 1).

Table 1. Types of IoT devices (applications).

Type	Data type	Application
Type A	Emergent data	Life-threatening or life-saving applications (e.g., alarms)
Type B	Regular data	Environmental sensing data (e.g., smart meter)

Figure 1 shows the overview of the DRRA scheme. Before a device accesses a NB-IoT network, it receives a SIB2 from an eNB, which allocates the RACH resource based on the traffic condition in the previous frame. With the RACH resource allocation, the device attempts to transmit a preamble in a RA-slot. In a heavy traffic load condition, an ACB scheme is triggered. The device has to follow the ACB policy before sending a preamble. The ACB policy sets a probability and the device can only send a preamble according to this probability.

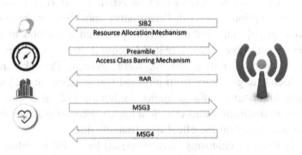

Fig. 1. Architecture of the DRRA scheme

3.2   RACH Resource Allocation Scheme

The DRRA scheme aims to control two types of the RACH resources. One is the number of preambles in a RA-slot, and the other is the number of RA-slots in a frame. They are adjusted to reflect the traffic load to guarantee high successful access probability.

In a NB-IoT network, an eNB broadcasts the prach-ConfigIndex in the SIB2, which then allows the eNB to adjust the number of RA-slots in a frame. In addition to the RACH resource adjustment, the eNB can also control the distribution of preambles for different service classes. As a result, the devices are aware of which preambles they can choose and when to begin the RA procedure.

Table 2 shows the notations used in the DRRA scheme. Arrival rates of Type A and Type B devices are assumed to follow Poisson process.

Table 2. Notations used in the DRRA scheme.

Notation	Meanings
$N_{Preamble}$	Number of contention-based preambles in a RA-Slot
N_{TypeA}	Number of preambles allocated for Type A devices in a RA-Slot
N_{TypeB}	Number of preambles allocated for Type B devices in a RA-Slot
λ_{TypeA}	Estimated arrival rate of Type A devices per preamble in a frame
λ_{TypeB}	Estimated arrival rate of Type B devices per preamble in a frame
X_0	No. of preambles for Type A devices which is not selected by any device
X_1	No. of preambles for Type A devices which is selected by only one device
Y_0	No. of preambles for Type B devices which is not selected by any device
Y_1	No. of preambles for Type B devices which is selected by only one device
$P_{b,TypeA}$	Estimated blocking probability of Type A devices (i.e., prob. of failed RA)
$P_{b,TypeB}$	Estimated blocking probability of Type B devices
$P_{b,TypeA}^G$	Guarantee blocking probability of Type A devices
$P_{b,TypeB}^G$	Guarantee blocking probability of Type B devices

In order to estimate the arrival rate of these two types of devices, the eNB keeps track the number of preambles that are not used by any devices (X_0, Y_0) and only one device (X_1, Y_1). Following the Poisson distribution, arrival rate per preamble of Type A (B) can be estimated from $X_0(Y_0)$ and $X_1(Y_1)$ by following equations, respectively.

$$e^{-\lambda_{TypeA}} = \frac{X_0}{N_{TypeA}} \tag{1}$$

$$\lambda_{TypeA} e^{-\lambda_{TypeA}} = \frac{X_1}{N_{TypeA}} \tag{2}$$

$$e^{-\lambda_{TypeB}} = \frac{Y_0}{N_{TypeB}} \tag{3}$$

$$\lambda_{TypeB} e^{-\lambda_{TypeB}} = \frac{Y_1}{N_{TypeB}} \tag{4}$$

λ_{TypeA} can be derived either from (1) or (2). In this work, λ_{TypeA} is estimated by taking the average of the values from (1) and (2) if both of them yield valid values. Similarly, λ_{TypeB} is calculated in the same way. The blocking probabilities of Type A and Type B devices can then be estimated by using (5) and (6) where $P_A = (\lambda_{TypeA})e^{-(\lambda_{TypeA})}$ and $P_B = (\lambda_{TypeB})e^{-(\lambda_{TypeB})}$.

$$P_{b,TypeA} = 1 - \frac{\sum_{i=1}^{N_{TypeA}} \binom{N_{TypeA}}{i} \times i \times P_A^i \times (1 - P_A)^{N_{TypeA}-i}}{\lambda_{TypeA}} \tag{5}$$

$$P_{b,TypeB} = 1 - \frac{\sum_{i=1}^{N_{TypeB}} \binom{N_{TypeB}}{i} \times i \times P_B^i \times (1 - P_B)^{N_{TypeB}-i}}{\lambda_{TypeB}} \tag{6}$$

They are compared with the predefined guaranteed blocking probabilities of $P_{b,TypeA}^G$ and $P_{b,TypeB}^G$ to determine as to whether the traffic load is too heavy or not. If the traffic load is too heavy, the RACH resource and preamble distribution are adjusted to give priority to guarantee the blocking probability of type A devices. The new values of N'_{TypeA}, and N'_{TypeB} will be used to calculate the updated arrival rates (per preamble), λ'_{TypeA} and λ'_{TypeB}, based on Eqs. (7) and (8).

$$\lambda'_{TypeA} = \frac{\lambda_{TypeA} * N_{TypeA}}{N'_{TypeA}} \tag{7}$$

$$\lambda'_{TypeB} = \frac{\lambda_{TypeB} * N_{TypeB}}{N'_{TypeB}} \tag{8}$$

With the new arrival rates and number of allocated preambles, new blocking probability is calculated again using Eqs. (5) and (6). This process is repeated until suitable N'_{TypeA}, and N'_{TypeB} are found. Algorithm 1 shows the pseudo code of the RACH Resource Allocation Scheme. In Algorithm 1, when traffic load is low, lines (4)–(9) reallocate preambles to both types of devices according to their arrival rates. On the other hand, if the traffic load is high, lines (10)–(17) increases the preambles allocated to type A traffic first which guarantees the transmission of emergent messages. Finally, lines (19)–(30) adjusts the number of preambles allocated to type B under the constraint of available preamble left over. Notably, if the traffic load is extremely high, we will run out of preambles and cannot guarantee the probability of success probability of RA for either type. In this case, we will need to apply Access Class Barring

Scheme proposed in the next section to restrain the arrival rate of IoT devices. In the future work, we will also consider the option of adding RACH resources on non-anchor carriers.

Algorithm 1 RACH Resource Allocation Scheme

---

input $X_0, X_1, Y_0, Y_1, N_{TypeA}, N_{TypeB}, P^G_{b,TypeA}, P^G_{b,TypeB}$

output new N_{TypeA}, N_{TypeB}

1: **Begin**

2: Calculate λ_{TypeA} and λ_{TypeB} based on $X_0 \cdot X_1$ by (1),(2), (3),(4)

3: Calculate $P_{b,TypeA}$ and $P_{b,TypeB}$ based on (5), (6)

4: **if** $P_{b,TypeA} \le P^G_{b,TypeA}$ **&&** $P_{b,TypeB} \le P^G_{b,TypeB}$ // traffic load is light

5:    $\alpha = \lambda_{TypeA}/(\lambda_{TypeA} + \lambda_{TypeB})$ //proportional share the extra RACH resources

6:    $N_{TypeA} = N_{TypeA} + floor(\alpha \times (N_{Preamble} - N_{TypeA} - N_{TypeB}))$ //floor function

7:    $N_{TypeB} = N_{Preamble} - N_{TypeA}$ and exit the algorithm

8: **else if** $P_{b,TypeA} > P^G_{b,TypeA}$ // give priority to increase N_{TypeA}

9:    Find the smallest N'_{TypeA} such that $N_{TypeA} \le N'_{TypeA} \le N_{Preamble}$ and $P'_{b,TypeA} \le$
     $P^G_{b,TypeA}$ where λ'_{TypeA} and $P'_{b,TypeA}$ are calculated by (7) and (5) (use λ'_{TypeA})

10:    **if** $P'_{b,TypeA} > P^G_{b,TypeA}$ when $N'_{TypeA} = N_{Preamble}$ //not sufficient preambles

11:      $N_{TypeA} = N_{Preamble}$ and $N_{TypeB} = 0$ and exit the algorithm

12:    **else**

13:      $N_{TypeA} = N'_{TypeA}$

14:    **endif**

15: **endif**

16: // **final check with** N_{TypeB}

17: **if** $P_{b,TypeB} \le P^G_{b,TypeB}$ **&&** $N_{TypeB} \le (N_{Preamble} - N_{TypeA})$ //reduce N_{TypeB}

18:    **repeat steps 5-7**

19: **else** //increase N_{TypeB} **under the constraint that** $N_{TypeB} \le (N_{Preamble} - N_{TypeA})$

20:    Find the smallest N'_{TypeB} such that $N'_{TypeB} \le (N_{Preamble} - N_{TypeA})$ and $P'_{b,TypeB} \le$
     $P^G_{b,TypeB}$ where λ'_{TypeB} and $P'_{b,TypeB}$ are calculated by (8) and (6)

21:    **if** $P'_{b,TypeB} > P^G_{b,TypeB}$ when $N'_{TypeB} = (N_{Preamble} - N_{TypeA})$ //not sufficient preambles

22:      $N_{TypeB} = (N_{Preamble} - N_{TypeA})$

23:    **else**

24:      $N_{TypeB} = N'_{TypeB}$

25:      **repeat steps 5-7**

26:    **endif**

27: **endif**

28: **end** //end of algorithm

3.3   Access Class Barring (ACB) Scheme

The ACB scheme is adopted to restrain the RA requests. Since we expect the number of type A devices will be relatively small and they provide life-saving applications, the proposed ACB scheme only applies to the type B devices. In the ACB scheme, an ACB barring factor is set to control devices to perform the RA procedure. A device generates a random number and if the number higher than the ACB barring factor, it has to give up this trial and restart the RA procedure later.

Next, the detail steps of the proposed ACB scheme are presented. Initially, the number of RA requests in a frame sent from type B devices is $\lambda_{TypeB} * N_{TypeB}$. After setting up an ACB barring factor, the arrival rate of type B devices is reduced to $(\lambda_{TypeB} \cdot \rho_{ACB})$ and the blocking probability can then be calculated by Eq. (6).

The goal of the ACB scheme is to find a suitable ACB barring factor such that the number of RA requests is expected to lower than the system capacity, which is one arrival per preamble. Thus, given current per preamble arrival rate of type B device, λ_{TypeB}, the ACB barring factor is set according to following equation.

$$\rho_{ACB} = \begin{cases} \frac{1}{\lambda_{TypeB}}, & \text{if } \lambda_{TypeB} > 1 \\ 1, & \text{if } \lambda_{TypeB} \leq 1 \end{cases} \tag{9}$$

4 Performance Evaluation

Performance is evaluated via simulations which are written in C language.

4.1 Simulation Parameters and Performance Metrics

We follow the same parameter settings proposed in [6], as shown Table 3.

Table 3. Simulation parameter setting.

CE level	Subcarrier	Repetition	Periodicity
CE0	48	1	40 ms
CE1	24	2	80 ms
CE2	24	4	160 ms

$P_{b,TypeA}^{G}$ is set to 0.01 and $P_{b,TypeA}^{G}$ is set to 0.1 unless otherwise stated. Simulation time is 10 min and each simulation is performed 30 times to obtained average performance metric and 95% confidence interval. The confidence interval is very small, thus not shown in following results.

The following metrics are used to evaluate the performance of a RACH scheme.

- Access success probability: it is the average successful probability of a RA request per RACH period.
- Average access delay: it is the average access delay given a RA request is successful.
- Average throughput: it is the average number of successful RA requests per RACH period.

In the following simulation experiments, we will compare the performance of three schemes: the original scheme proposed in 3GPP NB-IoT without ACB, the ACB scheme proposed in [13] which is designed to cope with massive IoT devices, and our DRRA scheme.

4.2   Simulation Case 1: Single CE Level

In the first simulation case, we valid the basic features of the DRRA scheme. We assume there are only CE level 0 devices, and the MaxTry parameter is set to 5. The MaxTry parameter defines how many times a device will retry the RA procedure after failures. Preamble is randomly reselected when a device performs a retry. The arrival rate of CE level 0 devices varies from 10 to 30. For each arrival rate, half of them are type A devices.

Figure 2 shows the average access probability of three schemes. When arrival rate is higher than 20, the system becomes congested. As we can observed from Fig. 2, ACB scheme outperforms the other two schemes when traffic load is light. The rationale is that the ACB scheme restrain the arrival rate even the system is not overloaded. Figure 3 confirms this situation as the average throughput of the ACB scheme is lower than the other two schemes. When the system becomes overloaded with RA requests, the proposed DRRA outperforms the other two schemes both in access success probability and average throughput. This confirms that the proposed DRRA scheme is able to adapt to traffic load better than the other two schemes. Notably, even when the arrival rate is 30, the DRRA scheme is still able to yield a very high throughput.

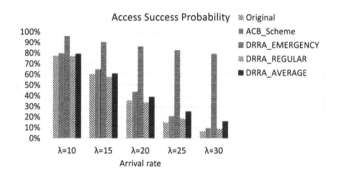

Fig. 2. Average access success probability of three schemes

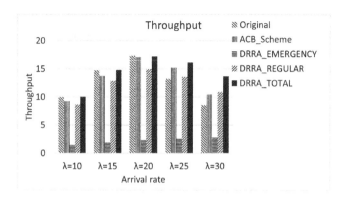

Fig. 3. Average throughput of three schemes

Figure 4 compares the average access delay of three schemes. As the DRRA scheme gives priority to type A devices, emergent data is able to be sent in a very short delay. This shows the superior feature of the proposed DRRA scheme. For type B devices, when the traffic load is high, the DRRA scheme also yields smaller delay that the other two schemes.

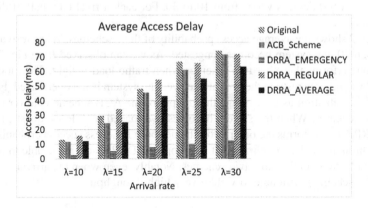

Fig. 4. Average access delay of three schemes

4.3   Simulation Case 2: Three CE Levels

In the second simulation case, we simulate IoT devices distributed in 3 CE levels. Five sets of arrival rates are simulated, they are (11, 3.5, 2.5), (13, 4, 3), (15, 4.5, 3.25), (17, 5, 3.5), (19, 5.5, 4), where three numbers in each set are the RA request arrival rates of devices of three CE levels, respectively. In this simulation, we show that the MaxTry affects the performance of the RACH procedure significantly. On one hand, increase the MaxTry will increase the chances of RA trials. On the other hand, increase the MaxTry will also increase the traffic load which results in higher chance of collision and unsuccess access probability.

Figure 5 shows the effect of MaxTry on the average throughput of devices of CE level 0. As we can see that the throughput increases as the MaxTry increases initially. However, when the MaxTry is too large, e.g., 7, the throughput decreases as the MaxTry increases, especially for scenario 5 where the traffic load is high.

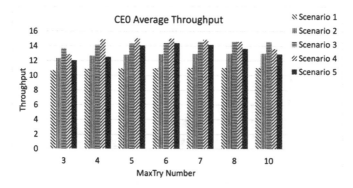

Fig. 5. Effect of MaxTry on throughput of CE level 0 devices

When the RA request of a CE level 0 device failed after MaxTry times, the device will change its CE level to 1 and continue the RACH procedure. If it failed on this level again, it will increase its CE level to 2. Figures 6 and 7 show the effect of MaxTry on the average throughput of CE level 1 and 2, respectively. The MaxTry affects the throughput of these two levels significantly. Only a small number of MaxTry can increase the throughput of CE level 1. For CE level 2, the average throughput decreases as the MaxTry increases, for most of the scenarios.

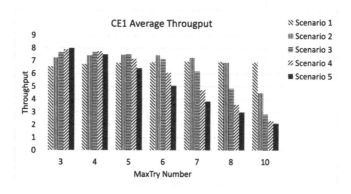

Fig. 6. Effect of MaxTry on throughput of CE level 1 devices

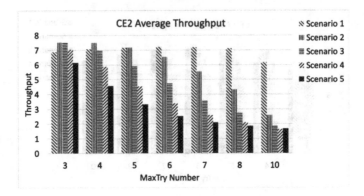

Fig. 7. Effect of MaxTry on throughput of CE level 2 devices

5 Conclusion and Future Works

In this paper, we proposed a Dynamic RACH Resource Allocation (DRRA) scheme which integrates with resource allocation scheme and ACB scheme to improve the performance of the RACH procedure. The DRRA scheme classify devices into two types and gives priority to devices that need to send emergent messages, e.g., life-saving alarm messages. Our simulation results show that the DRRA scheme can cope with large RA request rates and yield better throughput and delay than existing schemes. In particular, even under extremely high RA request rate, emergent devices can still have high throughput and low delay.

Several mechanisms can be integrated into the DRRA scheme and requires further study. When the RACH resources of anchor carrier are not enough to accommodate the RA requests, allocating RACH resources on non-anchor carrier has been proposed by 3GPP [5] which requires further investigation. Adjusting backoff timer can also alleviate the bursty traffic load. Repetition number is similar to the MaxTry, may increase access success probability, but consume more resources. More importantly, if collision happens, no matter how many repetitions will not help to avoid collision. Thus, how to perform repetition also requires further study. Finally, we are also investigating the effect of different traffic arrival models, such as MMPP which can capture more bursty arrival pattern. We believe the proposed DRRA can cope with MMPP arrival process better than other schemes.

References

1. Popli, S., Jha, R.K., Jain, S.: A survey on energy efficient narrowband internet of things (NBIoT): architecture, application and challenges. IEEE Access **7**, 16739–16776 (2019)
2. 3GPP: NB-IoT—Random access design. 3GPP TSG-RAN1 #83 R1-157424, Ericsson, Stockholm, Sweden (2015)
3. 3GPP: Evolved universal terrestrial radio access; radio resource control protocol. 3GPP TS 36.331 specification v13.4.0 (2017)

4. 3GPP. RAN improvements for machine-type communications. 3GPP TR 37.868 v11.0.0 (2011)
5. Ratasuk, R., Mangalvedhe, N., Xiong, Z., Robert, M., Bhatoolaul, D.: Enhancements of narrowband IoT in 3GPP Rel-14 and Rel-15. In: IEEE Conference on Standards for Communications and Networking (CSCN). IEEE, Helsinki (2017)
6. Wang, Y.-P.E., et al.: A primer on 3GPP narrowband internet of things. IEEE Commun. Mag. **55**(3), 127–133 (2017)
7. Feltrin, L., Tsoukaneri, G., Condoluci, M., Buratti, C., Mahmoodi, T., Dohler, M.: Narrowband IoT: a survey on downlink and uplink perspectives. IEEE Wirel. Commun. **26**(1), 78–86 (2019)
8. Bello, H., Jian, X., Wei, Y., Chen, M.: Energy-delay evaluation and optimization for NB-IoT PSM with periodic uplink reporting. IEEE Access **7**, 3074–3081 (2019)
9. Harwahyu, R., Cheng, R.-G., Wei, C.-H., Sari, R.F.: Optimization of random access channel in NB-IoT. IEEE Internet Things J. **5**(1), 391–402 (2018)
10. Azari, A., Hossain, M.I., Markendahl, J.I.: RACH dimensioning for reliable MTC over cellular networks. In: Vehicular Technology Conference, IEEE, Sydney (2017)
11. Jiang, N., Deng, Y., Condoluci, M., Guo, W., Nallanathan, A., Dohler, M.: RACH preamble repetition in NB-IoT network. IEEE Commun. Lett. **22**(6), 1244–1247 (2018)
12. Harwahyu, R., Cheng, R.-G., Tsai, W.-J., Hwang, J.-K., Bianchi, G.: Repetitions versus retransmissions: trade-off in configuring NB-IoT random access channels. IEEE Internet Things J. **6**(2), 3796–3805 (2019)
13. Leyva-Mayorga, I., Rodriguez-Hernandez, M.A., Pla, V., Martinez-Bauset, J., Tello-Oquendo, L.: Adaptive access Type Barring for efficient mMTC. Comput. Netw. **149**, 252–264 (2019)

Dynamic Path Planning Method Based on Cluster Queuing Communication in VANET

Mengdi Du[1,3], Shuisheng Lin[1,3(✉)], Chunbo Luo[1,2,3], Liang Zhou[1,3], and Haifen Yang[1,3]

[1] School of Information and Communication Engineering, University of Electronic Science and Technology of China, Chengdu, China
dumengdi@std.uestc.edu.cn,
{sslin,c.luo,zlzl,yanghf}@uestc.edu.cn
[2] University of Exeter, Exeter, UK
[3] National College of Ireland, Mayor Square, IFSC, Dublin 1, Dublin, Ireland

Abstract. Large-scale personnel vehicles choose and update the optimal path in real time under congested scenarios, which is of great significance for people to travel and balance traffic network traffic. Based on the regularity of people's work, it is important to make full use of traffic history data flow to establish optimal path planning. Our work studies the road network traffic congestion model based on historical and real-time traffic data flow to predict the roads that may be congested. Through the clustered queue communication mechanism and queue-based shunting, our work provides real-time optimal path planning for large-scale vehicles at the same time, and uniform road network traffic capacity. Our work simulated in the UESTC scenario to verify the improvement our work offers and the future potential performance.

Keywords: Queue-based shunting · Path planning · VANET

1 Introduction

Traffic jam is a common problem in many cities, particulary during rush hour. One of the current research priorities focuses on how to quickly provide an optimal route for vehicles under congested scenario with the assistance of vehicular ad-hoc network (VANET) [1,2].

In order to find a fast real-time route when occurs to sudden congestion, Wu et al. [3] proposed a dynamic path selection algorithm to avoid congestion. Guo et al. [4] proposed a TTE (traveling time estimation) compared path planning algorithm to avoid congested streets. Amr et al. [5] calculate the quality of routes based on the fuzzy model and recommend the optimal one. Souza et al. proposed a path planning algorithm CHIMERA [6] to avoid congestion by the degree of congestion. Processing all vehicles to request reroute and obtain the real-time

© Springer Nature Switzerland AG 2020
C.-H. Hsu et al. (Eds.): IOV 2019, LNCS 11894, pp. 28–36, 2020.
https://doi.org/10.1007/978-3-030-38651-1_3

traffic condition rely on VANET to unremittingly exchange information result in high real-time data processing cost.

Our work adopted queue-based shunting under cluster queuing communication to divert the traffic flow instead of avoid congestion, which can reduce the possibility of new congestion problems, so as to cope with the planning route of large-scale vehicles at the same time in large areas. Historical traffic data is applied to relieve congestion modeling pressure and information obtain pressure, and cluster head vehicles is applied to detect the congestion to prevent continually requesting re-planning paths, which can reduce the process cost. Hence our work improve the efficiency of path planning and alleviate traffic congestion.

2   Transportation Network System Model

2.1   Network System Model

The urban road network model mainly includes vehicles equipped with onboard unit (OBU), and roadside units (RSUs) deployed at road intersections to form a self-organizing network.

Road network $G = (N, E)$ includes road segment $w_i(t)$ and intersection collection N. A road segment with the adjacent two intersections x_i to y_i, $x_i, y_i \in N$ is represented as

$$w_i(t) = \{w(x_i, y_i)|x_i, y_i \in N, w \in E\} \tag{1}$$

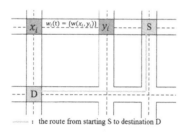

: the route from starting S to destination D

Fig. 1. Abstracted road network

As shown in Fig. 1, according to the basic path selection strategy from Section IV(A), the initial optimal path from s to d can be expressed as:

$$p(t) = \{w_1(t), w_2(t), w_3(t), ..., w_n(t)|t \in R\} \tag{2}$$

2.2   Real-Time Congestion Model

For populated areas, most of the vehicles have regular driving routes, which is why urban traffic especially some important roads, are regularly and periodically blocked. Based on this situation, our work establish a road network traffic congestion model for urban areas based on historical traffic data, and be updated continuously according to the real-time traffic data provided by the RSUs and the OBUs, to estimate the road traffic flow and predict road congestion.

Established congestion model D with enough historical data, D contains the average vehicle density den_{avg}, threshold α, and a set of streets that are determined to be congested and their ID and congestion value.

$$D = \{den_{avg}, \alpha, [edgeID_1, len_1, den_1], \ldots, [edgeID_i, len_i, den_i]\} \quad (3)$$

The number of vehicles on the road is $N(t)$, the average speed of a vehicle is $v_k(t)$ then the traffic flow on the road is $r_k(t)$.

$$r_k(t) = \frac{N(t)}{\frac{\sum_k v_k(t)}{k}} \quad (4)$$

Suppose that for a time Δt, the current road length L_k. The vehicle density of the road is den_k, which can be obtained from (4).

$$den_k = \frac{L_k}{r_k(t)} = \frac{L_k \sum_k v_k(t)}{kN(t)} \quad (5)$$

Equation (5) is modeled as inversely proportional to road traffic conditions. Therefore, crowded roads have a higher den_k than free-flowing roads.

For the initial establishment of the congestion model, a threshold α is set. α comes from historical information of all streets. $\bar{den}_{all}$ is taken as the average value of all streets's vehicle density. The average value of $\bar{den}_{front}$ is taken for half of the streets with higher den values.

$$\alpha = \frac{\bar{den}_{front}}{\bar{den}_{all}} - 1 \quad (6)$$

Every street from historical data will be judged by (7). If (7) is workable, add this street in the inital congetion model.

$$\frac{den_k(t)}{den_{avg}} - 1 > \alpha \quad (7)$$

The congestion model is updated with real-time traffic information at regular intervals, or each time the cluster head vehicle travels to a new road.

At regular intervals, all roads will be judged by (8), if (8) is established, it is determined that the current road is congested.

$$\frac{den_k(t_0 + \Delta t) - den_k(t_0)}{den_k(t_0)} = \frac{den_k(t_0 + \Delta t)}{den_k(t_0)} - 1 > \alpha \quad (8)$$

Each time the cluster head vehicle travels to a new road, the average driving speed $\bar{v}$ of the cluster head vehicle in the past Δs time on the current road is acquired, and compares with the average driving speed $\bar{v}_s$ of the previous $n\Delta s$ time. A formula for the comparison of the threshold α can be obtained:

$$\frac{\bar{v}_s}{\bar{v}} - 1 = \frac{\frac{\sum_0^{n\Delta s} \sum_k v_k(t)}{nk\Delta s}}{\frac{\sum_0^{\Delta s} \sum_k v_k(t)}{k\Delta s}} - 1 = \frac{\sum_0^{n\Delta s} \sum_k v_k(t)}{n \sum_0^{\Delta s} \sum_k v_k(t)} - 1 > \alpha \qquad (9)$$

If (9) is established, then the current street will be updated into the congestion model.

3   Cluster Queuing Communication Mechanism

N random cluster head vehicles are selected in the road network. The scheme for establishing and updating the congestion model is as follows:

Step 1: The congestion model establishment scheme is: Establish an initial road network traffic congestion model with enough historical information. After that, all the traffic and vehicle information in the road network is stored and the vehicle density of all the roads is recalculated at intervals. Then a congestion threshold α is obtained, and the congestion threshold is used to judge whether the road is congested. When a road is judged to be congested, it is determined that the road is in a blocked state before the next recalculation of the congestion threshold. The congestion model filters and adds existing traffic congestion models, and the stored information will be discarded after calculation.

Step 2: The congestion model update scheme is: after the congestion model (including the set of streets determined to be congested, and the congestion value of the street) is established, it will be updated according to historical traffic information at regular intervals, or each time the cluster vehicle travels to a new road. When the cluster vehicle travels to a new road, calculate the average driving speed of the cluster vehicle in the past time, and compare with the current average driving speed, then the congestion degree of the current street can be obtained and update the congestion model. The establishment of the clustering queue as shown in Fig. 2 below.

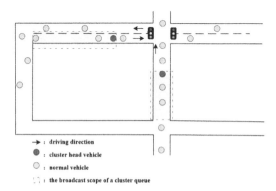

→ : driving direction
● : cluster head vehicle
○ : normal vehicle
⌐ ⌐ : the broadcast scope of a cluster queue

Fig. 2. The establishment of the clustering queue

4   Real-Time Path Planning

In this section, a real-time path planning algorithm based on the road network traffic congestion model and the clustered queuing communication mechanism is proposed.

In our work, this strategy provides a basic path selection strategy of selecting the optimal path for all real-time conditions mentioned above, which mainly applies to the situation when planing the initial route and encountering congestion, it is necessary to re-select a path to compare with the selected path in the previous round of comparison.

Our work aims to find a path $p(t)$ that allows the vehicle from s to d with the shortest time, based on the algorithm of Contraction Hierarchies, which can be derived as:

Input: $G = \{N, E\}$, $N(t)$, MA,SE

Subject to: $v_k(t) \leq 90$ kilometer per hour

Objective: $T = \sum_i^{w_i(t)\in p(t)} \frac{w_i(t)}{v_i(t)} + \sum_j o_j(t)$

The road can be divided into the main road collection MA, the secondary road collection SE according to the width of the road. When selecting the optimal path, the main road is selected first, and then the secondary road is selected.

A path is selected from the main road collection MA, $\dot{p}(t) = \{w_1(t), w_2(t), w_3(t)...w_n(t)|w_n(t) \in MA\}$. The adjacent points of the intersections of the selected roads is found, which belong to the secondary road collection SE. If there are $A \in MA$, $A \in w_1(t)$, A has two adjacent points B, C, and $B, C \in SE$, $B, C \in w_2(t)$. If $A \in w_2(t)$, then $w_1(t)$ does not need to be updated; if $A \notin w_2(t)$, and $w_1(t) < w_2(t)$, then $w_1(t)$ in $\dot{p}(t)$ updated to $w_2(t)$.

At the beginning of the vehicle's traveling, an inital optimal route $p_0(t)$ is planned. When the vehicle is about to drive to a congested street, replan a path $\bar{p}(t)$ according to the optimal path selection method in Section IV(A). The travel time $\bar{T}$ and T_0 of the routes $\bar{p}(t)$ and $p_0(t)$ are calculated. If the travel time of original selected route is less than the alternate route $\bar{T} \geq T_0$, the vehicle is still in accordance with the original selected route $p_0(t)$ forward; if the alternate route travel time is less than the original selected route $\bar{T} < T_0$, the vehicle follows the new route $\bar{p}(t)$. As shown in Fig. 3 below.

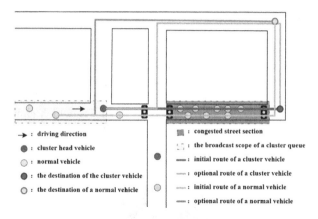

Fig. 3. Route selection

The sketch of the proposed real-time path planning algorithm is summarized in Algorithm 1.

Algorithm 1. The real-time path planning algorithm

1: BEGAIN
2: Input: G, D, random clusters, s, d, $vehmsg^i$, $edgemsg^i$, $p_0(t)$, T_0
3: **for** d and s **do**
4:    find $T = \sum_i^{w_i(t) \in p(t)} \frac{w_i(t)}{v_i(t)} + \sum_j o_j(t)$
5: **end for**
6: **while** not arrive d **do**
7:   **for** d **do**
8:     Select $w_i(t) = \{w(x_i, y_i)) | x_i, y_i \in N, w \in MA, min\{(2)\}$
9:     **if** $\exists \bar{w}(x_j, y_j) \in SE$,and $x_i, y_i = x_j, y_j, w(x_i, y_i) > w(x_j, y_j)$ **then**
10:       Make $\bar{w}(x_j, y_j)$ replace $w(x_i, y_i)$ in $min\{(2)\}$
11:     **end if**
12:   **end for**
13:   **if** vehicle $\in$ cluster and $edge^i \neq edge^{i-1}$ **then**
14:     Get $r \in E$ and $r \in p_0(t)$ and $r = edge^{i+1}$
15:     **if** $r \in D$ **then**
16:       Build (14) and broadcast
17:     **end if**
18:     **for** $vehicle \in Q_N^{ND}(T)$ **do**
19:       Select $min\{\bar{p}(t) = \{w_1(t), w_2(t)...w_n(t)\}\}$, $\bar{T}$
20:       **if** $\bar{T} \geq T_0$ **then**
21:         $p_0(t)$
22:       **else**
23:         $\bar{p}(t)$
24:       **end if**
25:     **end for**
26:   **end if**
27: **end while**

---

5 Simulation

Our simulation works on a real scenario latitude of 30.8122 to 30.7235 and a longitude of 103.8876 to 103.9961 of UESTC (the University of Electronic Science and Technology of Chengdu) about 31.225 square kilometers is simulated to verify the future potential performance obviously. In UESTC scenario, 1000/3000/5000/10000 vehicles are placed within 1.5 h, which causes huge traffic jam to obeserve the performance of our work. Our work simulate in SUMO (Simulation of Urban Mobility) as shown in the Fig. 4 below.

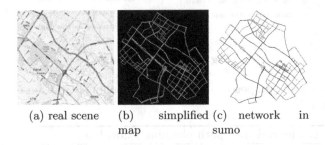

(a) real scene   (b)   simplified (c) network   in
                  map   sumo

Fig. 4. Illustration of simulation scenario

Our work compares with the well-known routing algorithms A* (astar) and Contraction Hierarchies (CH) to determine new path and both have the environmental awareness provided by VANET.

The simulation time is approximately equal to 166.6 min–933 min of the real time. All vehicles are generated from random locations and disappear from random locations. Random accidents like vehicle collisions and vehicle breakdowns are set up in simulation, which can cause real-time traffic congestion and in line with the real situation.

Our work mainly uses the average travel time of all vehicles to reach the destination and the average vehicle density in the road network as experimental results. The simulation results expressed as percentage that improved by using the strategy compared with the strategy of avoiding congestion.

When there are few vehicles, it is still guarantee the path optimization efficiency similar to the strategy of avoiding congestion. Optimized the average travel time of 37.64% and optimized the vehicle density of 9.88% during the simulation time. It can be predicted that as the amount of vehicles in the road network increases and the simulation time increases, the optimization ratio will be higher.

Figure 5(a) shows that this strategy provide a better route for vehicles in the road network, which greatly reduces the travel time of all vehicles, optimized the average travel time up to 37.64%, and allows the vehicle to reach its destination faster. Figure 5(b) shows that this strategy reduces the real-time capacity of all

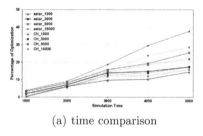

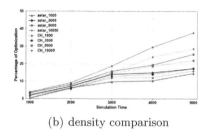

(a) time comparison   (b) density comparison

Fig. 5. Experimental results. (a) shows the result of optimization percentage of the average travel time of all vehicles to reach the destination. (b) shows the result of optimization percentage of the average road density in the road network. The label means which basic algorithm and the amount of vehicle our work choose for strategy of avoiding congestion in simulation, and the strategy in our work choose the same amount with the congestion avoiding strategy.

streets in the road network, optimized the vehicle density up to 9.88%, and can optimize the vehicle capacity problem of the street to some extent.

The simulation result shows that the our strategy can improves the efficiency of path planning and eases the traffic congestion of the road network, and verify the future potential.

6   Conclusion

The current intelligent transportation field is committed to enhance vehicle assistance and path planning capabilities, and to improve traffic efficiency in congested scenarios. In our work, congestion model is established benefits from the sensing and communication capabilities of the VANET, and it can predict the future congestion and assist rerouting decision. Proposed clustered queuing communication mechanism can divert vehicles by queue-type shunt to prevent new congestion. Our work realize the rapid response for the sudden traffic accidents with the proposed real-time path planning algorithm. Using the Luxembourg traffic scenario, the extensive evaluations validate that our work provides a more efficient path and alleviate road network congestion.

References

1. Wang, Y., Zheng, J., Mitton, N.: Delivery delay analysis for roadside unit deployment in vehicular Ad Hoc networks with intermittent connectivity. IEEE Trans. Veh. Technol. **65**, 8591–8602 (2016)
2. Zhu, M., et al.: Public vehicles for future urban transportation. IEEE Trans. Intell. Transp. Syst. **17**(12), 3344–3353 (2016)
3. Wu, S., Li, D., Zhang, G., Guo, C., Qi, L.: Density-based dynamic revision path planning in urban area via VANET. In: Huang, X.-L. (ed.) MLICOM 2016. LNICST, vol. 183, pp. 129–138. Springer, Cham (2017). https://doi.org/10.1007/978-3-319-52730-7_13

4. Guo, C., Li, D., Zhang, G., Zhai, M.: Real-time path planning in urban area via VANET-assisted traffic information Sharing. IEEE Trans. Veh. Technol. 1 (2018)
5. El-Wakeel, A.S., Noureldin, A., et al.: iDriveSense: dynamic route planning involving roads quality information. In: IEEE Global Communications Conference (GLOBE-COM) (2018)
6. De Souza, A.M., et al.: Real-time path planning to prevent traffic jam through an intelligent transportation system. In: Computers & Communication IEEE (2016)
7. Akabane, A.T., Gomes, R.L., Pazzi, R.W., Madeira, E.R., Villas, L.A.: Apolo: a mobility pattern analysis approach to improve urban mobility. In: GLOBECOM 2017–2017 IEEE Global Communications Conference, pp. 1–6 (2017)
8. Codeca, L., Frank, R. and Engel, T.: Luxembourg sumo traffic scenario: 24 hours of mobility for vehicular networking research. In: Proceedings of the 7th IEEE Vehicular Networking Conference, pp. 1–8 (2015)

Performance Evaluation of Citywide Intersections Traffic Control Algorithm inVANETs-Based

Sarah Hasan[✉] and Mourad Elhadef

College of Engineering, Abu Dhabi University, Abu Dhabi, UAE
1003299@students.adu.ac.ae

Abstract. The massive improvement in wireless communications pertains a real time and accurate delivery of information, which makes it possible to remotely control and manage a wide number of applications and services. The ability to connect to mobile and fast-moving nodes can aid in providing or obtaining information from vehicles that in turn provides a diverse picking in the development of vehicular communications and control. This includes all type of vehicular communications such as Vehicle to Infrastructure (V2I) and the Vehicle-to-Vehicle (V2V) communications. In this paper, we try to enhance traffic flow at intersections by simulating an improved VANET-based control algorithm. The study focuses on the flow of traffic across multiple adjacent intersections in a city where each intersection is equipped with a Roadside Unit (RSU). We believe that the communication between RSU at a given intersection and nearby vehicles, RSU and other surrounding RSUs (RSU2RSU) will affect the flow of the vehicles positively. We also consider the need to minimize the required time to cross an intersection particularly if a vehicle is an emergency vehicle.

Keywords: Vehicular ad-hoc networks · Intersection traffic control · Smart city · Intelligent transportation system · Internet of vehicles

1 Introduction

The overwhelmed city roads are a priority to study and analyze to improve the flow in the streets. One of the most important areas in traffic control is managing the flow at intersections. Traffic lights are the oldest form of traffic control at intersections. In their earlier version, traffic lights implement a prefixed time interval, which can lead to a delay especially if the green light is open for an empty street. The newer version of the prefixed time interval can be customized based on the load of a street and timing of the day or any other preset condition. This means that the timing for each intersection must be set separately nevertheless it also cannot perform well in case of change in the traffic flow due to any reason such as weather or holidays. The modern traffic lights implement an intelligent time-intervals by modifying the timing when the road load or condition changes. This type of traffic lights is known as reactive as it reacts to the new road condition and adjust the crossing time. The reaction is based on the collected road information by using different devices such as microwave detectors, loop detectors,

© Springer Nature Switzerland AG 2020
C.-H. Hsu et al. (Eds.): IOV 2019, LNCS 11894, pp. 37–46, 2020.
https://doi.org/10.1007/978-3-030-38651-1_4

radars and laser beams, geomagnetic vehicle detectors, and video/image detectors. The main problem of reactive-traffic lights is the high cost of purchasing, fixing and maintaining the devices [1–4]. The modern intersections traffic control is based on using wireless communication technologies such as the IEEE802.11p standard and the IEEE1609.4 which tolerates Multi-Channel Operations with Wireless Access in Vehicular Environments (WAVE) [5]. The standardization of vehicular communication makes it easier to provide centralized-based and distributed-based traffic management. In the case of the intersection control, vehicles mostly communicate with RSU or/and with other vehicles to receive instructions [6–9]. Figure 1 summarizes some of the contributions in the area of intersection control [10–15]:

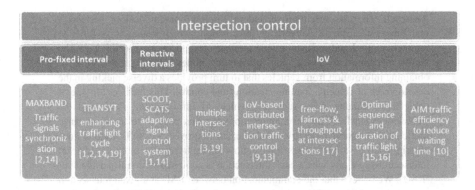

Fig. 1. Advancements in intersection control

To contribute to the development of intersections traffic control, we tested and improved the centralized intersection algorithm for controlling traffic at intersections by using VANET- based communications (V2I and RSU2RSU) in a citywide level. Our work is a continues improvement to the centralized algorithm in [16] which is based on a study suggested by [8]. We extended the scope of the study to include multiple number of RSUs in a citywide level to guarantee an efficient mutual exclusion; increase throughput; prioritize emergency and public transportations. The paper is organized as follow. Section 2 states preliminary elaboration of the inVANETs-based intersection control algorithm. Section 3 describes the model of the enhanced inVANETs-based intersection control algorithm in citywide. Section 4 provides the simulation results. Section 5 concludes and presents the future research directions.

2 Preliminary

The adapted system model is an adjusted version of the intersection control proposed by [8] and improved by [16]. The flow of the algorithm adheres to the mutual exclusion (MUTEX) where vehicles compete for the critical section, which is the intersection, or the core area (CA). Vehicles in a specific lane/s can access the CA as a group and lock the rest of the vehicles in conflicting lanes from entering the CA based on FCFS approach. In the centralized algorithm in [8], the RSU is responsible for managing the entrance to the CA. Based on a request message received from the vehicles; the RSU can only permit the vehicle/s based on FCFS and a locking logic which can affect safety, fairness and liveness properties as the RSU can only give permission to cross the intersection but not denying it [8]. In this case, if an accident happened, the vehicles that were given the permission will continue having a state of crossing forever; cause collision; affect the liveness of the CA; and will cause junction bottleneck. To overcome issues found in [8], [16] suggested an adapted approach to resolve the safety problem and the liveness by changing the used locking schema and by adjusting the algorithm to set a timer to avoid starvation. The change in the locking schema is as in the Table 1 (Fig. 2):

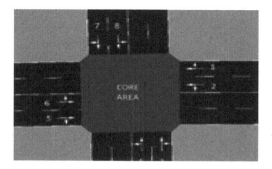

Fig. 2. 4-Way traffic intersection

Table 1. New locking schema

Lanes	1	2	3	4	5	6	7	8
Lanes to be Locked	1, 6, 8	2, 4, 7	2, 3, 8	1, 4, 6	2, 4, 5	3, 6, 8	4, 6, 7	2, 5, 8

3 inVANETs-Based Intersection Traffic Control Algorithm in Citywide

The study follows the same locking schema as in [16]; nevertheless, we will implement it in two adjacent intersections in Abu Dhabi city. We extended the scope of the study to include multiple number of RSUs in a citywide level to guarantee an efficient mutual exclusion; increase throughput; prioritize emergency and public transportations. The inVANETs-based intersection control algorithm in a citywide has 2 main tasks; the vehicleTask and the controllerTask. The vehicleTask main states are IDLE, the vehicle is within the reach of the CA; WAITING, the vehicle sent a "request" to cross the CA and waits for the RSU's respond; QUEUING, the vehicle received the permission to cross the CA; CROSSING, the position of the vehicles is inside the CA; URGENT, request with higher priority to enter the CA; and DELAYED, vehicle lost the right of accessing the CA due to time-out, lane changed or urgent request.

The previously referred to states are triggered either by entering the CA or by receiving a message from the RSU. Figures 3 and 4 are the state machine of the vehicles' tasks and the controllers' tasks.

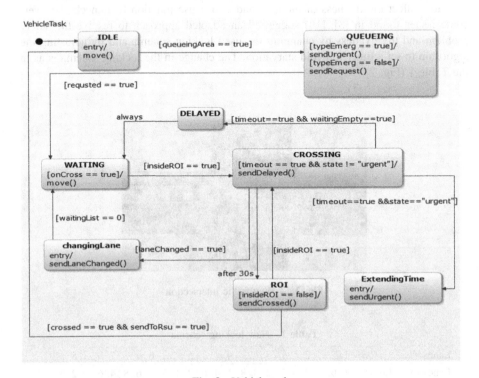

Fig. 3. Vehicle task

The desired scenario between the *vehicleTask* and the *controllerTask* is as follow. Vehicles arrives to the waiting area and sends a "request" message to the RSU. As soon as the RSU sends a replay to permit crossing, the vehicle crosses the CA. If the vehicle got the "cross" message and crossed the CA, the vehicle must send a "crossed" message to notify the RSU so the RSU removes it from the crossing list. There are other scenarios like when a vehicle changes its lane to a conflicting lane; or when a vehicle did not receive the "cross" message. In the cases of changed lane, the vehicle must inform the RSU about its current state by sending "newlane" or by sending the request message again. The vehicle then must wait for the RSU's replay. In each case, the RSU must check for the availability of the CA. If the CA is empty or the CA is accessible by a vehicle/s in a concurrent lane then the RSU will allow the vehicle/s to cross; otherwise, the vehicle/s must wait for a specific time. In case of exceeding the expected required time to cross the CA, the RSU must check if there is a conflicting waiting vehicle. If there is a conflicting waiting vehicle, the RSU sends "delayed" to stop the vehicles in the current crossing list form crossing the CA and to allow vehicles in the waiting list to fairly access the CA. In case of arrival of emergency vehicle, the algorithm proposes a mechanism to prioritize emergency vehicle in all cases. In this case, when the emergency vehicle sends an "urgentMsg" message, the RSU first checks if the CA is available. If not available, the RSU sends a "delayed" message to all vehicles conflicting with the emergency vehicle. The emergency vehicle can ask for extending crossing time if could not cross during the expected time by sending "emerExtendTime" message. If the vehicle crossed the intersection, it will send "emerCrossed", but its state will remain Urgent until it reaches to its destination. In case of "urgentMsg" request from multiple emergency vehicles from conflicting lanes, the access to the CA is given based on the expected arrival time. If the expected arrival time is the same, then emergency vehicles will be served based on FCFS. The algorithm also gives the highest level of priority to the emergency vehicles then to public transportations over personal vehicles. For a better controlling schema, the information collected from vehicles such as speed, direction, and throughput will be shared and sent to other RSUs. This information will be used to predict the status of the road with Fuzzy Logic [17–20]. As well as, it will use Dijkstra algorithm to find the shortest path to a pre-set destination. The RSU will evaluate the results from both algorithms and the decision will be propagated to the vehicle/s. Similar approach was pointed by other researchers such as [21, 22].

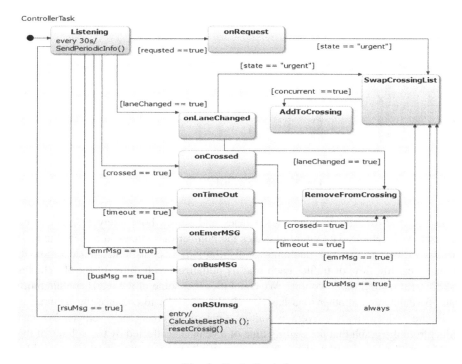

Fig. 4. Controller task

4   Simulation Results

The test consists of 2 intersections, 600 m apart from each other. Each intersection has 4 roadways with the same priority to have the right of way to access the CA based on the locking mechanism and FCFS to optimally traverse the CA. Each road consists of 2 lanes where the right lane can move forward or turn right; the left lane can move straight or left with maximum speed of 20 m/s. Each intersection has RSU to control the flow of the vehicles to the CA. The RSU receives request message/s from the vehicle/s and can allow or deny the request. The performed simulation adapted 2 different sets of 5 groups of volumes of vehicles. Each set is meant to study the effect of volume change; existence of emergency vehicle; RSUs exchanged messages to inspect the required time for a vehicle to cross the CA. The simulation is based on an open source framework (Veins) and a network simulator (Omnet++), a road traffic simulator (SUMO) and open street map (OSM). The framework uses the IEEE-802.11p and IEEE 1609.4 standards [23]. The feasibility of the algorithm to control the intersection was proved by [24] from a centralized perspective and by [9] from a distributed perspective. It was proven that the algorithm meets the fairness property for it allows various queue length and it fairly switches between the conflicting lanes. It was also proven that the waiting time is in a manageable range even when the queue length is long though it performs better with small queue length. The study [9, 24] also verified that the algorithm maintain high level of the throughput comparing to the tested results in [8]. The locking schema utilized the access to the CA and maintained high level of safety [16].

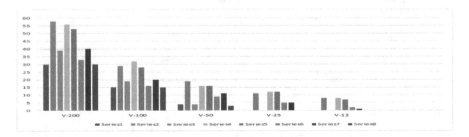

Fig. 5. Vehicle's load distribution

In Fig. 5 illustrates the load of the lanes and shows how likely a lane can be traversed by a vehicle. The figure indicates the number of vehicles in a road (the road consists of two lanes) and randomness distribution was taken in consideration to simulate real-life flow of traffic. Each road is initialized with different set of vehicles and different overall traffic volume. We can notice that some of the roads contain more than 50 vehicle and another road has no vehicles, in order to enhance the accuracy.

Figure 7 illustrates the average waiting time of an emergency vehicle. We can deduct from the graph that the waiting time of a vehicle is affected by the volume of the traffic as well as by whether the vehicle has a privilege (emergency vehicle or public transportation) or not. The waiting time will mostly decrease if the traffic load is low

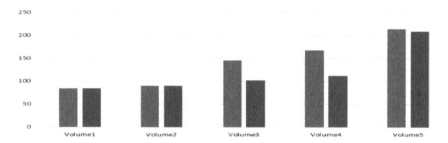

Fig. 6. Average waiting time

and the "request" is from an urgent vehicle. Saying that we need to consider Fig. 6 to get a better understating of the vehicle waiting time. The graph illustrates not only the waiting time for the urgent vehicle but also the waiting time of all the vehicles. In contrast to the emergency's vehicle waiting time, it is likely that the overall waiting time will increase when accompanied with urgent request. As giving the permission to an urgent vehicle could mean a "delay" for the normal vehicles which is an acceptable when considering the importance of giving the right of way to emergency. Also, the increase in traffic will rise the waiting time in all the scenarios as in the graph. The increased waiting time will decrease the overall throughput as the traffic increases.

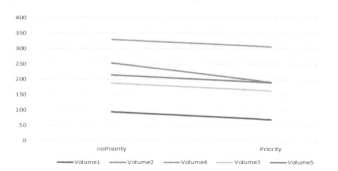

Fig. 7. Emergency average waiting time

This is verified in Fig. 8 we can tell as the traffic load decreases, higher number of vehicles cross the CA per second. In the (T-12) scenarios where the traffic load is at its lowest volume, the number of vehicles passes the CA is 2 vehicle/s at least. This means if the crossing time of an intersection is set to be 1 min, around 30 vehicles/m to 50 vehicles/m can cross the CA if considering the drivers' attitude, spacing between vehicles and if the car starts moving from speed of 0/m and accelerates up.

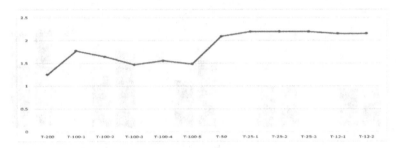

Fig. 8. Throughput

The number of the passed vehicles in (T-200) scenario is reduced to the half. Several reasons can justify this decreased affect like the swapping between conflicting lanes consumes more time to accelerate from stopping state; high chance of requesting the CA by urgent vehicle which means sending "delay" to the conflicting crossing lanes. Last but not least, Fig. 9 illustrates the number of messages sent or received by one of the controlling RSUs. We can notice that the number of request messages increase as the traffic load increases. If the load of the traffic is low or moderate, the increase in the number of cross messages will be associated with the increase in the number of request messages. Otherwise when the traffic load is very high, cross messages amount will be affected by the number of delay messages and the rsu messages. This is because when a vehicle is given the permission to access the CA, then due to a message from RSU, timeout, or emergency vehicle, the vehicle will go back to the WAITING state and will wait until it receives the cross-message from the RSU when a preset duration is met.

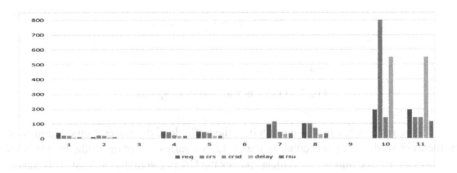

Fig. 9. Type and amount of sent messages

5 Conclusion

In this paper, we elaborate in depth about the enhanced intersection control algorithm suggested by [16] and improved by [8] and uses inVANET communications. We provide a performance evaluation for a suggested algorithm that claims its efficiency and ability to handle intersections control. We tested number of different properties of traffic like different load of traffic; prioritized emergency vehicles; and the effect of the waiting time on the overall flow of the traffic. Based on these enquiries we set the simulation scenarios. The implementation of the algorithm evaluates the scenarios across 2 adjacent intersections, each has its own controller unit. The RSUs were communicating to inform each other about the traffic load moving between them. Also, in some cases, the RSUs sends information to the next RSU hub to inform it if an emergency vehicle is approaching so it can reschedule the CA availability when the emergency vehicles arrives. Based on the result we can deduce that the overall performance is satisfactory especially in normal load flow. However, when the traffic volume increases or when an emergency vehicle approached, we noticed that the waiting time increases as well. The algorithm favors the emergency vehicle and provide a quick access to serve it. Future investigations will study the feasibility with more numbers of vehicles where RSUs are able to find the best path for a given destination. We believe this will improve the overall flow and will solve the delay for the vehicles. Best path can be assumed based on Fuzzy logic and Dijkstra algorithm.

References

1. Su, Y., Cai, H., Shi, J.: An improved realistic mobility model and mechanism for VANET based on SUMO and NS3 collaborative simulations. In: 20th IEEE International Conference on Parallel and Distributed Systems (ICPADS), Hsinchu, pp. 900–905 (2014)
2. Saini, T., Zahoor, S., Bedekar, M., Atote, B., Panicker, S.: Optimization of signal behavior through dynamic traffic control. proposed algorithm with traffic profiling. In: 2nd International Conference on Contemporary Computing and Informatics, pp. 598–602 (2016)
3. Chen, L.W., Chang, C.C.: Cooperative traffic control with green wave coordination for multiple intersections based on the internet of vehicles. IEEE Trans. Syst. Man Cybern.: Syst. **47**(7), 1321–1335 (2017)
4. Ma, D., Luo, X., Li, W., Jin, S., Guo, W., Wang, D.: Traffic demand estimation for lane groups at signal-controlled intersections using travel times from video-imaging detectors. IET Intell. Transp. Syst. **11**(4), 222–229 (2017)
5. Research and Innovative Technology Administration: Telecommunications and Information Exchange Between Systems - Local and Metropolitan Area Networks - Specific Requirements - Part 2: Logical Link Control. ISO 8802-2 IEEE 802.2, 1st (1989)
6. Benslimane, A., Taleb, T., Sivaraj, R.: Dynamic clustering-based adaptive mobile gateway management in integrated VANET-3G heterogeneous wireless networks. IEEE J. Commun. **29**(3), 559–570 (2011)
7. Zheng, B., Lin, C.W., Liang, H., Shiraishi, S., Li, W., Zhu, Q.: Delay-aware design, analysis and verification of intelligent intersection management. In: IEEE International Conference on Smart Computing, Hong Kong, pp. 1–8 (2017)
8. Wu, W., Zhang, W., Luo, A., Cao, J.: Distributed mutual exclusion algorithms for intersection traffic control. IEEE Trans. Parallel Distrib. Syst. **26**(1), 65–74 (2015)
9. Saeed, I., Elhadef, M.: Performance evaluation of an IoV-based intersection traffic control approach. In: IEEE Conference on IoT, Green Computing and Communications, Cyber, Physical and Social Computing, Smart Data, Blockchain, Computer and Information Technology, Congress on Cybermatics, Canada, pp. 1777–1784 (2018)

10. Bedekar, M., Atote, B., Panicker, S.: Centralized approach towards intelligent traffic signal control. In: International Conference on ICT for Competitive Strategies, p. 63 (2016)
11. Zhao, Y.F., Wang, F.Y., Gao, H., Zhu, F.H., Lv, Y.S., Ye, P.J.: Content-based recommendation for traffic signal control. In: IEEE 18th International Conference on Intelligent Transportation Systems, Las Palmas, pp. 1183–1188 (2015)
12. Pasin, M., Scheuermann, B., Moura, R.F.D.: VANET-based intersection control with a throughput/fairness tradeoff. In: 8th IFIP Wireless and Mobile Networking Conference, pp. 208–215 (2015)
13. Baselt, D., Knorr, F., Scheuermann, B., Schreckenberg, M., Mauve, M.: Merging lanes – fairness through communication. Veh. Commun. **1**(2), 97–104 (2014)
14. Burdett, R., Casey, B., Becker, K.H.: Optimising offsets and bandwidths in vehicle traffic networks. ANZIAM J. **55**, 77–108 (2014)
15. Hasan, S., Elhadef, M.: A citywide distributed inVANETs-based protocol for managing traffic. In: Park, J., Loia, V., Choo, K.K., Yi, G. (eds.) MUE/FutureTech-2018. LNEE, vol. 518, pp. 117–124. Springer, Singapore (2019). https://doi.org/10.1007/978-981-13-1328-8_15
16. Elhadef, M.: An adaptable inVANETs-based intersection traffic control algorithm. In: IEEE International Conference on Computer and Information Technology; Ubiquitous Computing and Communications; Dependable, Autonomic and Secure Computing; Pervasive Intelligence, pp. 2387–2392 (2015)
17. Pi, S., Sun, B.: Fuzzy controllers based multipath routing algorithm in MANET. In: International Conference on Applied Physics and Industrial Engineering, pp. 1178–1185 (2012)
18. Upadhayay, S., Sharma, M.: Performance evaluation of fuzzy routing algorithms for a new fuzzy mixed metric approach. Int. J. Comput. Sci. Netw. Secur. **8**(4), 21–28 (2008)
19. Doja, M., Alam, B., Sharma, V.: Analysis of reactive routing protocol using fuzzy inference system. In: AASRI Conference on Parallel and Distributed Computing Systems, pp. 164–169 (2013)
20. Gajjar, S., Sarkar, M., Dasgupta, K.: FAMACRO: fuzzy and ant colony optimization basedMAC/routing cross-layer protocol for wireless sensor networks. In: International Conference on Information and Communication Technologies, vol. 8, pp. 1014–1021 (2015)
21. Ganda, J.: Simulation of routing option by using two layers fuzzy logic and Dijkstra's algorithm in MATLAB 7.0. J. Electr. Electron. Eng. **1**(1), 11–18 (2016)
22. Biswas, S.: Fuzzy real time Dijkstra's algorithm. Int. J. Comput. Intell. Res. **13**(4), 631–6404 (2017)
23. veins.car2x.org. http://veins.car2x.org/features/. Accessed 17 June 2019
24. Tabaza, H., Elhadef, M., Saeed, I.: Performance evaluation of an adaptable invanets-based traffic control. In: ICT Conferences, Society, and Human Beings, Porto (2019)

Task Planning with Manual Intervention Using Improved JSHOP2 Planner

Liancheng Tao[✉], Qibo Sun, Jinglin Li, Ao Zhou,
and Shangguang Wang

State Key Laboratory of Networking and Switching Technology,
Beijing University of Posts and Telecommunications, Beijing, China
tllccc@163.com

Abstract. In real-world task planning, such as automatic vehicles dispatch, often face the arrival of new tasks and uncertain factors in the process of task execution. As a typical implementation of Hierarchical Task Network (HTN) planning, JSHOP2 planner is suitable for complex task planning. Given the fact that JSHOP2 planner fails to get planning results in the global level when facing uncertain factors, an improved JSHOP2 planner is proposed to solve this problem. The improved JSHOP2 planner with manual intervention supplements the planning result and eliminates the impact of uncertain factors with the help of human experience. In addition, we conducted comparative experiments based on improved planner. The simulation results show the effectiveness and the ability to emergency response of improved planner.

Keywords: HTN planning · Task planning · JSHOP2

1 Introduction

As we known, a complex task, such as vehicles dispatch, often consists of a great quantity of atomic tasks. Task planning is essential to ensure the effective execution of different tasks. It depends on resource allocation, state change, path selection and so on. The factors involved in planning are numerous, and wide-ranging. Furthermore, task planning faces the impact of uncertain factors, causing it to be a complicated topic. According to the specific planning target, how to choose the optimal decomposition path for a specified target is a crucial problem.

Hierarchical Task Network (HTN) planning follows the idea of AI planning, and has been widely used in various task planning systems. As a typical implementation of HTN planning, JSHOP2 can effectively model specific domain knowledge and come up with complete and valid plan lists. However, when JSHOP2 is planning, (1) each path selection for target decomposition only depends on whether it meets the current resource needs, ignoring the global impact; (2) it is assumed that all resources are determined to be unchanged and always available during planning. However, the planning result is hoped to be a global optimal solution based on actual situation. At the same time, uncertain factors will bring unexpected changes in state of resources during planning process, affecting planning results that have been obtained.

© Springer Nature Switzerland AG 2020
C.-H. Hsu et al. (Eds.): IOV 2019, LNCS 11894, pp. 47–55, 2020.
https://doi.org/10.1007/978-3-030-38651-1_5

Considering the characteristics of JSHOP2, we introduce manual intervention and solve the above problems with improved JSHOP2. Manual intervention complements each path selection according to global optimization and human perception. Furthermore, it helps to deal with uncertain factors and eliminate the impact they have brought. The improved JSHOP2 can keep in control when facing uncertain factors, and generate final plan lists as the global optimal solution.

This paper is organized as follows. The next section reviews related works on task planning using JSHOP2. In Sect. 3 we will explain why manual intervention needs to be introduced. The principle of improved JSHOP2 planner is elaborated in Sect. 4. Section 5 illustrates the relative experiments and their results. We conclude with a summary and a discussion of future work in Sect. 6.

2   Related Works

Since the launch of JSHOP2, there have been a number of contributions on task planning. Researchers employed or improved the JSHOP2 planner in various fields.

Sirin et al. [1] used SHOP2 to do automatic Web service composition. They successfully describe an approach to translate process models of Web services into sets of SHOP2 methods and operators. However, this approach makes a difference with lots of hypothesis and restriction and cannot work with extra uncertain factors. Alami et al. [2] proposed a framework that promotes human-robot interaction with HTN planning. They hope to develop schemes that consider human preferences above the framework. It is a pity that this framework is not implemented on physical experiments. Sohrabi et al. [3] combined the control of knowledge domain specified by HTN with user's preferences. In the meantime, they proposed a language based on HTN planner to evaluate the satisfaction of preferences during planning. However, it cannot handle temporally extended constraints in SHOP2, such as unexpectedly changed occurs. Compared with other papers based on JSHOP2, our aim is to improve the ability of JSHOP2 to treat uncertain factors in task planning process. Furthermore, the introduction of manual intervention helps JSHOP2 to generate plan lists from the global optimization perspective.

3   Improved JSHOP2 Planner with Manual Intervention

This section describes two reasons for introducing manual intervention during the JSHOP2 planning process.

3.1   Global Optimal Solution

The JSHOP2 planner is a state-based and pre-ordered HTN planner that contains two significant files: the problem domain file and the knowledge domain file. The problem domain file is written with a specific language that JSHOP2 can recognize. It records the known status and resource information on current task scenario. The knowledge domain file is written with the same language as the problem domain file. It records the methods of decomposing various tasks when meeting different conditions. The JSHOP2 planner completes the task-autonomous planning process in specific domain under the guidance of the above two files.

The JSHOP2 planner succeeds in decomposing a task according to the planning algorithm combing with current task state and conditional satisfaction. The general syntax has the following form:

$$(: method\ h\ [name_1]\ L_1T_1\ [name_2]\ L_2T_2 \ldots [name_n]\ L_nT_n)$$

where h is the current task, each L_i is a condition list, each T_i is a subtask list.

When satisfying condition list L_i, h is decomposed into the corresponding subtask list T_i, representing a task decomposition. During the task planning process, each subtask decomposition is only related to the current task state and conditional satisfaction. The scheme of optimizing to decompose subtasks is in terms of current task, that is, the local optimal solution, not the global optimal solution. Manual intervention is a supplement to the JSHOP2 planning algorithm while ensuring that the planning result is a global optimal solution. When the decision information described in knowledge domain file is not comprehensive enough to cover all situations that occur during the planning process, we profit task planning with human perception through manual intervention, assisting the decision-making process to generate more accurate and reasonable planned result. For example, if an aircraft is used to collect specified images, the aircraft generally captures regional information in a wide range. It has no idea of when to collect key images from multiple dimensions, so it is necessary for the scout to make a judgment based on the collected images, and issue specific instructions to guide the following planning process.

The JSHOP2 planner retains the decision-making and intelligence to self-planning after the introduction of manual intervention. In the meantime, it can dynamically adjust the planning result. JSHOP2 hands over part of decision-making authority to operators to ensure the global optimization of planning result.

3.2   Uncertain Factors

The original JSHOP2 planner uses a deterministic planning algorithm as its planning algorithm. This algorithm decomposes tasks according to the hierarchical relationship of tasks with the help of environmental information and resource information obtained. It is assumed that current state remains unchanged during the hierarchical decomposition process. The state can only be updated by decomposed result. As executing one of the JSHOP2 default operators:

An operator has the following form:

$$(: operator\ h\ P\ D\ A)$$

where h is the name of the operator, P is a condition list, D is a deleted condition list after executing this operator, A is an added condition list after executing this operator.

The JSHOP2 planner updates status through changing A and D in the operator, and requires P remaining unchanged during executing h. However, a variety of uncertain factors may occur in the actual planning process. The source of uncertain factors can be internal or external to the system. Also taking the aircraft collecting images as an example, internal uncertainties such as the failure of some components of the power system, which causes this aircraft fails to take off normally. External uncertainties such as the temporary weather change affect the quality of captured images. Due to the uncertainty, variability, complexity and dynamics of uncertain factors, the task planning system works with many uncertainties. The decision-making process is complex and uncertain. Introducing manual intervention can effectively cope with accidents and weaken the negative effect of uncertain factors.

With the help of manual intervention, humans can flexibly deal with uncertain factors and take the advantage of human experience to handle emergencies. JSHOP2 can maintain in control when the external state is unknown and it lacks of autonomic perception, which avoids the inconsistency between the planning result and the actual situation.

4 Principle and Improvement

We modify the source code to make JSHOP2 support manual intervention and return final plan lists. JSHOP2 itself defines complete templates of different operators to help to find a plan. Users add the domain description and the domain knowledge on specific domain combined with templates. After compiled, constants are stored in order while variables are stored in index. All contents are stored as java files. The optimization of JSHOP2 takes place after compiling, which is shown in Fig. 1.

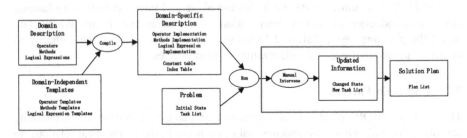

Fig. 1. Planning process of JSHOP2

Keeping JSHOP2 automatic planning to generate a complete plan list, we make additional function, as single step planning. Any step is interruptible in planning process and can perform manual intervention. The system identifies the activity performed by manual intervention, and then modifies corresponding problem domain file and knowledge domain file, and updates state finally. After doing this, move to next planning step. We add a global variable called *flag*, representing whether human intervention takes place in planning process. JSHOP2 can check this variable to choose automatic plan or manual intervention. What's more, we introduce three keywords called *add*, *modify*, and *delete* to identify specific manual operations. *add* describes the fact that users add state or available resource for following planning; *modify* describes the fact that users change the value of attributes existed in system; *delete* describes the fact that users delete some state or resource existed in system. JSHOP2 saves all operators by corresponding keyword and index. When it runs, JSHOP2 determines the operator to be modified by keyword firstly. Then it identifies the specific manual operation by compared with three keywords. Finally it locates the variable to be modified by index and performs operation, such as add, modify and delete on the chosen variable. This is a complete manual intervention process. The set of updated state is used to call function which describes how JSHOP2 algorithm works named *findPlanHelper*() recursively to generate a plan list step by step. The function named *update*() visualizes the planning result. The main code is shown in Figs. 2 and 3.

```
                        manualInterventon
  Input:states,keyword
  Output:newStates

  Begin
    For(int i=0;i<states.size();i++)
    {
        index=getOperatorIndex(states.get(i));
        operator=getOperator(index);
        manualOperator=getKeyword(keyword);
        changedVar=getVar(operator);
    }
    newStates=changeState(operator, manualOperator,
                changedVar);
  End
```

Fig. 2. Code for manual intervention

```
                        taskPlanning
  Input:domain file,problem file
  Output:plan

  Begin
    tasks=JSHOP2.InternalDomain(domain file,problem file);
    if(flag)
    {
      newStates=manualInterventon(states, keyword);
      plan=findPlanHelper(newStates);
      flag=false;
    }
    else plan=findPlanHelper(states);
    update(plan);
  End
```

Fig. 3. Code for the overall task planning

5   Experiments and Results

We carry out several comparative experiments in order to demonstrate the applicability of the proposed approach to deal with automatic task planning with manual intervention. Contrast experiments are set in the same task scenario. The task set by experiment is to collect images. We need a few steps to complete this task. The main process is to set camera parameters, go to the destination, record the image, send the image, return to the departure, and transfer the image. This experiment is carried out under three different conditions:

(1) There is no manual intervention. During image recording, JSHOP2 selects the camera automatically based on current state and domain knowledge, and records images with default mode.
(2) Manually change the recording mode of camera during image recording. We try to record the most images in the same time, and guarantee the planning result is a global optimal solution.
(3) The camera selected during image recording unexpectedly failed and could not be used. It is used to simulate the occurrence of uncertainties. The initial planning result cannot be performed and needs to be manually changed based on the current state.

5.1   Planning Without Manual Intervention

In the first experiment, JSHOP2 automatically selects the camera named *camera0* according to current state and resource information under the guidance of the knowledge domain file if there is no manual intervention. At the same time, JSHOP2 uses the mode named *colour* to record images. The complete planning process and planning result are shown in Fig. 4.

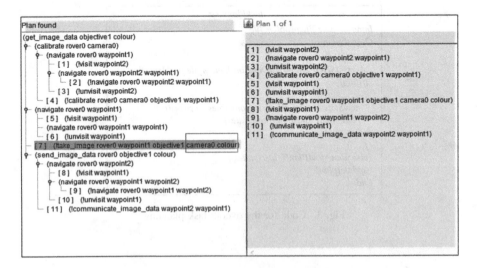

Fig. 4. Process and result for the first experiment

5.2 Planning for Optimizing Result

In the second case, we hope to store the most image information as much as possible while sacrificing the color of images. All we need is to obtain the global optimal solution of this task planning. Although JSHOP2 selects the mode named automatically in image recording step, it will be manually modified to the mode named *low_res*. JSHOP2 will complete the planning based on the result after manual intervention. The complete planning process and planning result are shown in Fig. 5.

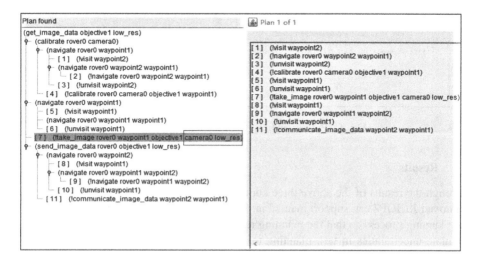

Fig. 5. Process and result for the second experiment

5.3 Planning with Uncertainties

Under the third condition, the selected camera named *camera0* is not available. Due to the existence of uncertain factors, the resources selected in the original plan may be unavailable. But JSHOP2 cannot sense the change of resource or state caused by uncertain factors during the planning process. It is assumed that unavailable resources can participate in task planning. The plan list obtained in this case is not executable. In the third experiment, JSHOP2 automatically selects camera named *camera0* in the image recording step. But it is assumed that *camera0* is accidentally damaged and users can manually replace *camera0* with *camera1*. Subsequent planning will be based on *camera1*. The complete planning process and planning result are shown in Fig. 6.

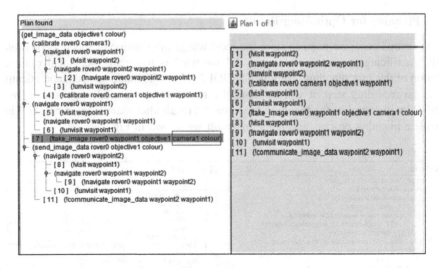

Fig. 6. Process and result for the third experiment

5.4 Results

Through the results of the above three comparative experiments, we can conclude that improved JSHOP2 can support manual intervention to modify the variables or states in the planning process so that the planning result is globally optimized. Furthermore, we simulate uncertainties in task planning to verify that the planning failure will not be returned when JSHOP2 faces sudden situation. We reach the goal of adding manual intervention to promote the JSHOP2 planner.

6 Conclusion

In this paper, we improve JSHOP2 planner with manual intervention to plan tasks. Firstly, we explain two reasons why manual intervention needs to be introduced into task planning. Then we introduce the principle of improved JSHOP2, which elaborates how JSHOP2 works with manual intervention. Finally, we verify our view through experiments that the improved JSHOP2 planner with manual intervention can effectively improve planning ability. However, under the premise that the next task has been planned, it cannot solve the problem that unexpected situation interrupts execution. So in the future, we will investigate to improve JSHOP2's ability of dynamic execution.

Acknowledgment. This research is supported in part by the National Natural Science Foundation of China under Grant No. 61571066, No. 61602054, (NSFC, 61571066, 61602054).

References

1. Sirin, E., Parsia, B., Wu, D., et al.: HTN planning for web service composition using SHOP2. J. Web Semant. **1**(4), 377–396 (2004)
2. Alami, R., et al.: Task planning for human-robot interaction. In: Proceedings of the 2005 Joint Conference on Smart Objects and Ambient Intelligence: Innovative Context-Aware Services: Usages and Technologies, Tokyo, pp. 81–85. ACM (2010)
3. Sohrabi, S., Mcilraith, S.A.: On planning with preferences in HTN. In: Computer Science, pp. 241–248 (2008)
4. Remli, M.A.B.: Automated biological pathway knowledge retrieval based on semantic web services composition and AI planning. In: International Conference on Information Retrieval and Knowledge Management, pp. 281–284. IEEE (2012)
5. Ming, G., Lei, Y., Zhang, C., et al.: A goal-driven and content-oriented planning system for knowledge-intensive service composition. In: International Conference on Information Technology and Electronic Commerce, Dalian, pp. 316–321 (2014)
6. Dvorak, F., Bartak, R., Bitmonnot, A., et al.: Planning and acting with temporal and hierarchical decomposition models. In: IEEE International Conference on Tools with Artificial Intelligence, Limassol, pp. 115–121 (2014)
7. Chen, Y.H., Cheng, M.: Enhanced HTN planning approach for COA generation. In: 2013 International Conference on Information Technology and Applications, Chengdu, pp. 272–274 (2014)
8. Georgievski, I., Nizamic, F., Lazovik, A., et al.: Cloud ready applications composed via HTN planning. In: 2017 IEEE 10th Conference on Service-Oriented Computing and Applications (SOCA), Kanazawa, pp. 81–89 (2017)
9. Ramoul, A., Pellier, D., Fiorino, H., et al.: HTN planning approach using fully instantiated problems. In: 2016 IEEE 28th International Conference on Tools with Artificial Intelligence (ICTAI), San Jose, pp. 113–120 (2016)
10. Höller, D., Bercher, P., Behnke, G., Biundo, S.: Plan and goal recognition as HTN planning. In: 2018 IEEE 30th International Conference on Tools with Artificial Intelligence (ICTAI), Volos, pp. 466–473 (2018)

Multi-task Planning with the Consideration of Task Priority

Renkang Ke[✉], Qibo Sun, Jinglin Li, Ao Zhou,
and Shangguang Wang

State Key Laboratory of Networking and Switching Technology,
Beijing University of Posts and Telecommunications, Beijing, China
kerenkangmail@163.com

Abstract. Hierarchical Task Network (HTN) is widely used for intelligent planning problems due to its simplicity and efficiency. As an intelligent planner based on HTN, JSHOP2 can complete task planning in order of precedence or randomly. In real-world tasks planning, such as automatic vehicles dispatch, has to deal with complicated auto planning problems where different tasks must be considered properly at the same time. But JSHOP2 ignores the priority of different tasks and thus fails to deal with multi-task planning problems with priorities. In this paper, we improve JSHOP2 planner by adding priorities to different task lists and task items, and adjusting the order of task execution according to priority. Furthermore, we conduct an experiment using a classic logistics problem, and get the results validate the effectiveness of our method.

Keywords: HTN planning · Multi-task · JSHOP2 · Task priority

1 Introduction

As an important field of artificial intelligence, intelligent planning has been widely studied. Hierarchical Task Network (HTN) [1] is a notable planning technique, which reveals the relationship between tasks or actions by constructing a hierarchical network and searches the network for a feasible plan. Due to its simplicity and efficiency, HTN planning is widely adopted in production line scheduling, crisis management, robotics, and network service combinations.

JSHOP2 [2] is an intelligent planning system based on HTN. JSHOP2 can solve single-task and multi-task planning problems. When solving multi-task problems, JSHOP2 supports both ordered and unordered model, which means completing tasks in an order or randomly. Due to the time, space and resource limitations, it's crucial to consider the priority of different tasks. However, vehicles have to deal with complicated auto planning problems where different tasks must be considered properly at the same time, such as the delivery order of numerous express goods.

In this paper, we extend the multi-task planning process of JSHOP2 and focus on the priority of each task list and each task item. This allows tasks with higher priority to be assigned resources and executed preferentially, while tasks with lower priority to be executed later. Therefore JSHOP2 planner can adjust the task planning order according to priorities and thus better solve the multi-task planning problems.

© Springer Nature Switzerland AG 2020
C.-H. Hsu et al. (Eds.): IOV 2019, LNCS 11894, pp. 56–63, 2020.
https://doi.org/10.1007/978-3-030-38651-1_6

The remainder of this paper is organized as follows. In Sect. 2, we make a brief introduction about the related works. Section 3 introduces the process of how JSHOP2 solve a multi-task planning problem. In Sect. 4, we propose a scheme to set priority for both task lists and task atoms, and adjust the task planning order accordingly. And then Sect. 5 evaluates the improvement of our method. Finally, we make a conclusion for the paper and discuss our future work.

2 Related Work

Georgievski et al. [3] introduce the theory and concept of HTN, and made a comparison between all HTN planners. Nau et al. [4] studied the features of SHOP2 and showed the details of developing a temporal domain and making domain optimization. Fox et al. [5] described the syntax and semantic of PDDL (Plan Domain Definition Language), and elaborated the process of plan validation. Song et al. [6] extends HTN for task planning with multiple goals. However, multi-task planning optimization is not considered. Lu et al. [7] improved JSHOP2 planner by realizing multi-task optimization in home environment, but the improvement is only available for robot. That's because the priority is set statically, and cannot be reset by the users.

We will achieve a notable solution for multi-task planning with the consideration of priority in this paper.

3 HTN and JSHOP2

The core execution logic of HTN is relatively simple. Tasks of different levels are decomposed from the upper layer to the bottom layer, and tasks of the same level are executed according to their partial orders [8]. It's our goal to decompose a complicate compound task into some simple atomic tasks so that we can get a sequence of actions as a final plan. All of our following discussions about HTN will be around JSHOP2. Notations of some core concepts in JSHOP2 planner will be given as follows:

- Task Atoms. A task atom is a basic and atomic JSHOP2 expression in the following form $([: immediate] s \ t_1 \ t_2 \ldots t_n)$, where s is a task symbol and each argument t_i is a term. A task atom with the prefix key [*:immediate*] is called an immediate task while it is an ordinary task without [*:immediate*]. If s is a symbol started with an exclamation mark, it means it's a primitive task atom, else it is a compound task atom.

- Operator. An operator is expressed in the form of $(: operator \ h \ P \ D \ A \ [c])$, where h is a primitive task atom, P is a logical precondition list, D is a delete list and A is an add list. The argument c is optional indicating the cost of an operation. The task h will be executed if P is satisfied in the current state. After h is executed, the current state of the world is modified by adding all logical atoms in D and delete all logical atoms in A.

- Method. A method is an important and most commonly use list of the following form (: *method h* [*name*₁] L_1 T_1 [*name*₂] L_2 T_2...[*name*ₙ] L_n T_n), where h is a compound ordinary task atom. Each L_i is a logical precondition list, and each T_i is a task list that contains one or more primitive tasks and compound tasks. A method indicates that the task h can be done by performing a subtask list T_i if the corresponding precondition L_i is satisfied. The subsequent decomposition will be considered only if the precondition of the current surface is not satisfied.
- Task Lists. A task list contains a task atom or a group of tasks. A group of tasks is expressed in the form ([: *unordered*] [T_1 T_2...T_n]), where T_1, T_2, ... and T_n are tasks in lists. When n is equal to zero, the task list is empty. The key word [*:unordered*] indicates the tasks do not have priorities and can be done randomly. If there is no such key word, the tasks in the list should be executed in the given order ($T_1 \rightarrow T_2 \rightarrow ... \rightarrow T_n$). In the SHOP2 planner, you can use the keyword [*:ordered*] to explicitly specify the execution order, but in JSHOP2, the keyword [*:ordered*] is discarded.

When the keyword [*:unordered*] is used, the tasks in the list can't be executed in the given order. Suppose there are two task lists $T = [t_1 \ t_2 ... t_m]$, $U = [u_1 \ u_2 ... u_m]$ and the main task list is $M = (: unordered \ T \ U)$. Then, the task items in T must be performed in the specified order ($t_1 \rightarrow t_2 \rightarrow ... \rightarrow t_m$). Similarly, the task items in U must be executed in the order ($u_1 \rightarrow u_2 \rightarrow ... \rightarrow u_n$). However, JSHOP2 allows task items among different task lists to be executed interactively. A possible execution order may be ($u_1 \rightarrow t_1 \rightarrow u_2 \rightarrow t_2 \rightarrow ... \rightarrow u_n \rightarrow tn \rightarrow ... \rightarrow tm, \ m > n$).

If some task items are marked as immediate, the planner will give priority to them each time it choose a task item to perform. In the above case, if t_1 is an immediate task, then t_1 should be executed before t_2 and u_1. The task item qualified by the key word [*:immediate*] must be executed first without any predecessor during the planning process. Therefore, only one task item can be immediate and the key word [*:immediate*] can appear only once at most. This limitation makes JSHOP2 difficult to adapt to multitasks with different priorities.

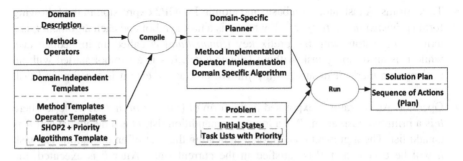

Fig. 1. The compilation process of JSHOP2

4   Multi_task with Priority Based on JSHOP2

In JSHOP2 planner, a specific domain description and the domain-independent templates are compiled to a domain-specific planner, and then it runs the planner to solve the planning problems in that domain. Figure 1 show the process after modification.

Multi-task planning with JHSOP2 can be improved by adding priority to each task list or each task item. We modify the task list expression to a new form like $([:priority] [T_1 pri_1 T_2 pri_2 \ldots T_n pri_n])$, where T_i is a task list and pri_i is the corresponding priority.

The new key word [:*priority*] is defined. Each task list is assigned a priority represented by a number. The smaller the number is, the higher priority it means. When the priority is 0, it is equivalent to immediate. JSHOP2 is a domain-independent planner, so users can set their own priority rules [9, 10]. After the grammar is improved, the tasks with higher priority are executed earlier than those with lower priority, and the tasks with equal priority are executed according to the rules in unordered mode.

It is also allowed to set priority for each task list T_i in the form $[t_{i1} pri_{i1} t_{i2} pri_{i2} \ldots t_{in} pri_{im}]$. So we can set priorities at the level of task lists and task items respectively, thus ensuring both of them are executed in order of priority. The details are as following:

1. Get the task lists of the planning problem.
2. Reorder all the task lists. For all the task lists $[T_1 pri_1 T_2 pri_2 \ldots T_n pri_n]$, rearrange them according to the ascending order of $(pri_1, pri_2, \ldots, pri_n)$, and record it as $\left[T_1' pri_1' T_2' pri_2' \ldots T_n' pri_n'\right]$.
3. Reorder the task items in each task list. For the task list T_i, assume that the given task items are placed as $[t_{i1} pri_{i1} t_{i2} pri_{i2} \ldots t_{im} pri_{im}]$. Based on the ascending order of list $(pri_{i1}, pri_{i2}, \ldots, pri_{im})$, reorder all task items of T_i, and the new task list is given as follows: $\left[t_{i1}' pri_{i1}' t_{i2}' pri_{i2}' \ldots t_{im}' pri_{im}'\right]$.
4. Initialize the executed list FT_i', and the undone list LT_i' as follows: $LT_i' = T_i'$, $FT_i' = null$.
5. Add the first task of each new task list T_i' to the candidate list, and set $candidate = \left[t_{11}' t_{21}' \ldots t_{n1}'\right]$.
6. Select a satisfied task item from the candidate list. Transverse the candidate list until we get a satisfied one. If the selected task item is t_{ij}', execute it and remove it from the candidate list.
7. Add the executed task item t_{ij}' to the completed list FT_i', and add the next task item $t_{i(j+1)}'$ from LT_i' to the candidate list.
8. If not all task lists and task items are executed, go to step 6.

5   Validation

We validate the effectiveness of our method in multi-task planning. Suppose there are two ways to transport goods between city1 and city2: air transportation or car transportation. As shown in Fig. 2, when the original city has free flights, it is preferred to use the aircraft for transportation. Otherwise, the goods are transported by car. When transporting package from city1 to city2 by air, the number of flights in city1 will be reduced by 1, and the number of flights in city2 will be increased by 1. The same is true for car transportation.

```
(:method
  ;compound task
  (deliver ?package ?from ?to)
  ;precodition1
  ((have_plane ?from ?airplane ?from_num)(call > ?from_num 0))
  ;decomposition list1
  (((!fly ?airplane ?package ?from ?to))
  ;precodition2
  ((have_truck ?from ?truck ?to_num)(call > ?from_num 0))
  ;decomposition list2
  (((!drive ?truck ?package ?from ?to))
)
```

Fig. 2. Decomposition of logistics transportation

```
(:unordered
  ((deliver package_a1 city1 city2)(deliver package_a2 city1 city2))
  ((deliver package_b1 city1 city2)(deliver package_b2 city1 city2))
  ((deliver package_c1 city1 city2)(deliver package_c2 city1 city2))
)
```

Fig. 3. Multi-task planning problems using an unordered mode

```
(:priority
  ((((deliver package_a1 city1 city2 pri 1)(deliver package_a2 city1 city2 pri 2))(pri 3))
  ((((deliver package_b1 city1 city2 pri 2)(deliver package_b2 city1 city2 pri 1))(pri 1))
  ((((deliver package_c1 city1 city2 pri 1)(deliver package_c2 city1 city2 pri 1))(pri 2))
)
```

Fig. 4. Multi-task planning with priority in planning problems

Suppose now there are three types of goods A, B, C need to be transported from city1 to city2. Each type of goods has two batches to be transported. It is our goal to successfully complete the transportation of these six batches of goods. In JSHOP2, transportation of each type of goods is defined as a task list, and transportation of each batch is defined as a task item. So there are three task lists, each list contains two task items, as shown in the Fig. 3. The JSHOP2 planner originally supports task planning in an ordered mode or an unordered mode. In an unordered mode, both tasks in tasks lists and task items are performed randomly. Therefore, there are many execution orders. One of the results is shown in Fig. 5, in which all packages are delivered in order of the statement presented in Fig. 3, *package_a1->package_a2->package_b1 ->package_b2->package_c1->package_c2*.

In actual goods transportation, different types of goods have different transportation priorities. Goods with the highest priority, like emergency letters, emergency supplies, etc., must be prioritized for transportation. Goods like fresh food must be transported in time, so their priority is second. And ordinary goods like clothes, shoes and so on have low priority. As showed in Fig. 4, we add a priority number for each task list to represent the priority of each type of goods. For the same task list, we can add a priority number for each task item. The priority number represents the priority of different batches of the same type. So the priority between every batch is *package_a1 > package_a2*, *package_b2 > package_b1*, *package_c1 > package_c2*. The planning result is shown in Fig. 6, in which the transportation order is based on priority, *package_b2-> package_b1->package_c1->package_c2->package_a1->package_a2*.

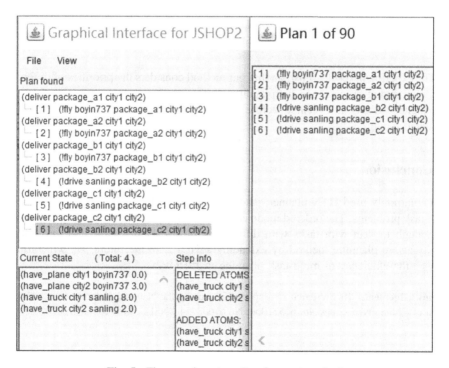

Fig. 5. The experiment results of current method

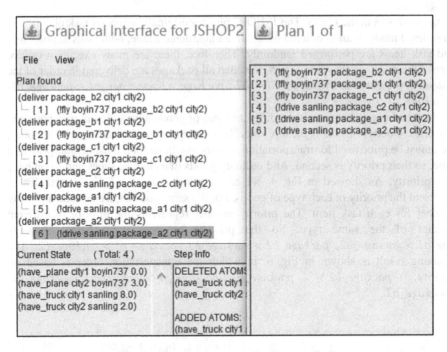

Fig. 6. The experiment result of our method

The experiment results illustrate that our method considers the priorities of different tasks in planning process, and the planning result is more reasonable because the task with higher priority is executed before that with lower priority compared with the unordered mode.

6 Conclusion

As a commonly used HTN planner, jshop2 has certain limitations in the planning of multi-task problems. The ordered mode and unordered mode of JSHOP2 are obviously not enough to deal with tasks with different priorities. In this paper, we propose a priority-aware planning method by extending JSHOP2. In the future, we will further enhance the efficiency of multi-task planning in JSHOP2.

Acknowledgement. This research is supported in part by the National Natural Science Foundation of China under Grant No. 61571066, No.61602054, (NSFC, 61571066, 61602054).

References

1. Ontanon, S., Buro, M.: Adversarial hierarchical-task network planning for complex real-time games. In: Proceedings of the 24th International Conference on Artificial Intelligence (IJCAI), pp. 1652–1658 (2015)

2. Ilghami, O.: Documentation for JSHOP2. Department of Computer Science, University of Maryland, Technical Report (2006)
3. Georgievski, I., Aiello, M.: HTN planning: overview, comparison, and beyond. Artif. Intell. **222**, 124–156 (2015)
4. Nau, D., et al.: SHOP2: an HTN planning system. J. Artif. Intell. Res. **20**, 379–404 (2003)
5. Fox, M., Long, D.: pddl2.1: an extension to pddl for expressing temporal planning domains. J. Artif. Intell. Res. **20**, 61–124 (2003)
6. Song, S., Lee, S.-W.: A goal-driven approach for adaptive service composition using planning. Math. Comput. Model. **58**(1–2), 261–273 (2013)
7. Lu, F., Tian, G., Li, Q.: An improved JSHOP2 planner oriented to service robot multi-tasks planning. In: 2016 Chinese Control and Decision Conference (CCDC) (2016)
8. Nau, D.S., Cao, Y., Lotem, A., Muñoz-Avila, H.: SHOP: simple hierarchical ordered planner. In: Proceedings of the Sixteenth International Joint Conference on Artificial Intelligence, pp. 968–973. AAAI Press (1999)
9. Liu, C., Layland, J.: Scheduling algorithms for multiprogramming in a hard real-time environment. J. ACM **20**, 46–61 (2003)
10. Biyabani, S.R., Stankovic, J.A., Ramamritham, K.: The integration of deadline and criticalness in hard real-time scheduling. In: Proceedings of the 9th IEEE Real-Time Systems Symposium, pp. 152–160 (1988)

From AI to CI: A Definition of Cooperative Intelligence in Autonomous Driving

Jun Liu$^{(\boxtimes)}$, Yang Xiao, and Jiawei Wu

Beijing University of Posts and Telecommunications, Beijing 100876, China
{liujun,zackxy,cloudsae}@bupt.edu.cn

Abstract. With the rapid development of deep learning, artificial intelligence (AI) has been widely used in many fields and gradually replaced a part of human jobs. However, the approach of improving intelligent capability of single agent is not enough to achieve complicated tasks in ever-changing environments. Cooperative intelligence (CI) is regarded as a promising way to solve this problem. In this paper, we scientifically define the three key problems of achieving cooperative intelligence, which are cooperative perception, cooperative decision and cooperative learning. We illustrate each problem with a scenario of autonomous driving as well as a brief survey of related research works. Meanwhile, we propose a system architecture and components design of cooperative intelligence system for autonomous driving.

Keywords: Artificial intelligence · Cooperative intelligence · Autonomous driving

1 Introduction

Since the beginning of history, there is a fantasy dream of releasing people from hard work by robots with machine intelligence. Lie Zi, a Chinese sage living in the Spring and Autumn Period, recorded the legend of a song and dance robot called Chang Zhe that was made by a skilled craftsman named Yan Shi in 1000 BC [1]. Another famous robot character is T-800, which is a scary killer in the film Terminator taken at the end of the twentieth century [2]. Like Chang Zhe and T-800, there are a number of robot characters in plenty of art works, which reflect people's deep emotions of yearning and fearing about **artificial intelligence (AI)**.

Whether people fear it or not, agents with artificial intelligence eventually come into our life with the development of deep learning technologies in recent years. In December 2015, Microsoft used the 152-layer Deep Residual Network to surpass human record of 5.1% for the first time with an error rate of 3.57% in the ImageNet Large Scale Visual Recognition Challenge [3]. In March 2016, Deep-Mind AlphaGo defeated the top human player in the world, Lee Sedol, in the

© Springer Nature Switzerland AG 2020
C.-H. Hsu et al. (Eds.): IOV 2019, LNCS 11894, pp. 64–75, 2020.
https://doi.org/10.1007/978-3-030-38651-1_7

game of go [4]. In October 2016, Microsoft developed a combination of convolution and LSTM deep neural network that achieves automatic speech recognition with 5.9% [5] error on the English oral language database Switchboard [6]. The performance is almost the same as human professional stenographer. This kind of technological breakthroughs have brought a new wave of "AI is coming" to the public. Even part of scientific and technical workers believe that artificial agents with strong AI are coming soon.

However, most of researchers in the field of artificial intelligence are not so optimistic. A number of researchers have pointed out that capabilities of single agent with artificial intelligence are close to the ceiling [7,8]. Although deep learning has been widely applied in many areas, such as face recognition [9], voice assistant [10] and medical assistant diagnosis [11], there is no exciting technical achievement that can be comparable to AlphaGo since 2006. It is a sign that the artificial intelligence of single agent has encountered the technical bottleneck. To solve this problem to keep going on the road to strong AI, a number of researchers are trying to find other ways, in which improving the intelligence of an agent by cooperation of a group of agents is a possible success approach.

Inspired by behavioral models of socializing insects such as bees and ants, a number of researchers have proposed novel approach to improve the capabilities of agents with simple artificial intelligence in a cooperative manner [12,13]. There are different names for this kind of emerging technology of biologically-inspired artificial intelligence, such as Distributed Artificial Intelligence [14] and Swarm Intelligence [15]. In this paper, we name it as **Cooperative Intelligence (CI)**, which is a class of technologies and methods that aim to achieve higher intelligent capabilities of agents by cooperatively working with each other and the surrounding environment. From this definition, we can see that the realization of cooperative intelligence is based on the original intelligence level of a single agent to some extent. Therefore, the development of cooperative intelligence technology are not practical in real-world owing to the limitation of the weak capability of a single agent before the emergence of deep learning technologies. As the capability of a single agent has been greatly improved by deep learning technologies, the research of cooperative intelligence is becoming a hot topic in AI related areas in recent years. Among these areas, autonomous driving is a potential industry to be greatly change by artificial intelligence. Because the huge gap between extra high safety requirements and limited intelligence of single autonomous cars, autonomous driving is one of the most important area to be improved by cooperative intelligence technologies.

In this paper, we will give the scientific problem definition of the cooperative intelligence. Then, we will describe three core concepts and tasks of the cooperative intelligence, cooperative perception, cooperative decision and cooperative learning. And we will take autonomous driving as the application scenario to illustrate the targets of these three tasks. At last, we will give the overall architecture design of cooperative intelligence enabled autonomous driving system and describe the functions and relationships of the components in the propose system.

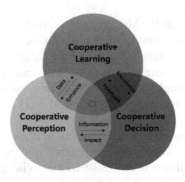

Fig. 1. Cooperation intelligence

2 Problem Definition of Cooperative Intelligence

In general, we perform our daily activities like this way: (1) Acquiring data from outside environment by our sensory organs like eyes and ears. (2) Processing and analyzing these data to plan actions for reaction by nervous system like brain. (3) Summarizing the knowledge by learning and memorizing ability to further enhancing the level of sensing and decision-making abilities. Therefore, we can generalize the intelligence capabilities of human as three key points: perception, decision and learning. Based on this concept, we propose the key modules of multi-agent cooperative intelligence as cooperative perception, cooperative decision and cooperative learning. The relationships and interactions among these three modules are shown in Fig. 1.

Cooperative perception is to acquire raw data from the outside environment, and process these data to obtain the information of outside environment. The obtained information is the input of cooperative decision. Meanwhile, the acquired data in the valuable input of cooperative learning. Cooperative decision is to choose the most effective action for achieving a kind of specific goal. The knowledge of how to choose correct action is produced by cooperative learning. The action may change the outside environment and bring impact to the subsequent cooperative perception step. The input of cooperative learning is acquired data from cooperative perception and the feedback of an action's effect from cooperative decision. Based on these input, cooperative learning continuously improve the perception model and decision-making model to enhance the intelligence capabilities of agents. Below we will scientifically define the problems of cooperative perception, cooperative decision and cooperative learning.

2.1 Cooperative Perception

Improving the perception capabilities is always a hot research topic in the field of artificial intelligence. There are a great many algorithms to enhance the perception capabilities of a single agent, such as image classification for vision capability, voice recognition for hearing capability and automatic reading comprehension for natural language understanding capability. Unlike these algorithms

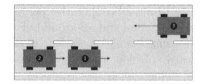

Fig. 2. Cooperation perception scenario

focusing on enhancement of single agent capabilities, the objective of cooperative perception is to obtain more comprehensive or higher quality information of outside environments by cooperatively gathering and processing data from multiple agents. We define the scientific problem of cooperative perception as below:

Cooperative Perception: Suppose there is a set of n agents, which is $A = \{a_1, a_i, ..., a_n\}$. At time t, the set of external objects perceived by a certain agent a_i is $O_t^i = \{o_1, ..., o_j, ...\}$. $o_j \in M^z$ is an object in the coordinate system. When $z = 2$, the coordinate system is two-dimensional. When $z = 3$, the coordinate system is three-dimensional. Then, we can define the cooperative perception task as:

$$P_t^i = \cup_{a_i \in A} O_t^i \tag{1}$$

In Eq. 1, P_t^i represents the set of cooperative perception results obtained by the i-th agent at time t. Note that $\cup$ is not the collection summation operator in Eq. 1. $\cup$ is a designed cooperative perception algorithms that can be performed in the cloud, terminal or edge.

In Fig. 2, we demonstrate the objective of the cooperative perception through an overtaking scenario, which is often encountered while driving. At time t, autonomous driving vehicles 1, 2, and 3, represented by a_1, a_2, and a_3 respectively, are running on a two-way two-lane road. Owing to blocked by a_1, a_2 do not know the existence of a_3 based on its optical camera, laser radar, and millimeter wave radar sensors. At this time, the object sets perceived by a_1, a_2, and a_3 are $O_t^1 = \{a_3\}$, $O_t^2 = \{a_1\}$, and $O_t^3 = \{a_1\}$. If a_2 makes decision based on such perceived result, a collision may be occurred with high possibility. In this scenario, the objective of cooperative perception is to find a suitable algorithm $\cup$ to produce $P_t^2 = \{a_1, a_3\}$ by leveraging the convergence of O_t^1, O_t^2 and O_t^3. Based on the cooperative perception, the existence of a_3 is known by a_2 and the decision of overtaking a_1 would not be made to ensure safety.

There are a number of research works that focus on cooperative perception for autonomous driving. Rauch *et al.* [16] designed and implemented a inter-vehicle object association for cooperative perception systems. The evaluated three point matching algorithms to reduce the impact of inaccurate self-localization of the communication partners for improving quality of perception data association and fusion. The simulation results show that the auction-ICP algorithm is the best one to reducing the average error between the considered object lists.

Kim *et al.* [17] proposed a multi-modal cooperative perception method that provides see-through, lifted-seat, satellite and all-around views to drivers. Based on this method, they realized a multi-vehicle cooperative driving system that can supports see-through forward collision warning, overtaking and lane-changing assistance and automated hidden obstacle avoidance. The demonstrated the capabilities and features of the proposed system through real-world experiments using four vehicles on the road. Wang *et al.* [18] studied the performance and scaling of collaborative sensing and networking for automated driving applications. They quantified the coverage gains of cooperative perception that depends on the penetration of vehicle participants. In addition, they evaluated the Vehicle-to-Vehicle (V2V) and Vehicle-to-Infrastructure (V2I) communication loads when both vehicles and RSUs are involved in the cooperative perception. The evaluation results demonstrated that the combination of vehicular/RSU cooperative perception is the most cost effective way to achieve high coverage in vehicular automated driving on high speed automated highways.

2.2   Cooperative Decision

Making the correct decision is the purpose of artificial intelligence, so decision module needs to judge the situation, plan the action and control the agent based on information of external environment obtained by perception module. Taking the autonomous driving as an example, the perception module outputs information including types, position, speed and direction of traffic involving objects like vehicles, pedestrians and bicycles, position, speed, and direction at a series of time points. Based on these information, decision module needs to predict the state of the objects in future based on physical models. Then, decision module will send out control instructions to plan the next action of the agent based on decision-making model that is abstracted from historical data and experiences. The action will change the state of the agent and outside environment. It will bring positive or negative impact on the agent. The impact can be presented by a loss function. Therefore, the objective of cooperative decision is to make decision with better loss function value by cooperation of multiple agents compared with the decision made by single agent. We define this problem as looking for a decision set D^A that minimizes the value of loss function:

$$D^A = \arg\min_{D} Loss(D) \tag{2}$$

In Eq. 2, $A = \{a_1, a_i, ..., a_n\}$ is the collection of agents. $D = \{..., D_i, ...\}$ denotes the collection of decision sets of all agents. D_i is the decision set of the i-th agent. $Loss(D)$ is the loss function under the conditions of decision set D.

In Fig. 3, we illustrate the objective of cooperative decision through an autonomous driving scenario. a_1, a_2, a_3, a_4 are four autonomous driving cars passing through a crossroad with no signal light. The objective of decision making algorithm is to allow the cars to pass through the crossroad as fast as possible while avoiding collision. Decision module of each car has to inference the possible solution based on the information gathered by the perception module within

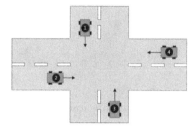

Fig. 3. Cooperation decision scenario

short intervals to avoid collision. It is very complicated and difficult if each agent can not interact and cooperate with others. If some communication and negotiation mechanisms can be established between a_1 to a_4, the decision making could be more reasonable and efficient with sufficient information from all vehicles.

Compared to traditional research works that focus on driving decision of individual vehicles, cooperative decision for autonomous driving is a relative new research topic. Yang *et al.* [19] considered analysis and synthesis problems of the cooperative control of a platoon of heterogeneous connected vehicles with directed acyclic interactions. They formulated the problem in the context of a closed-loop system and applied the internal model principle and exploited the lower-triangular structure. Based on the study, they proposed a synthesis method based on the algebraic Riccati equation sharing the dimension of single vehicle dynamics. Numerical experiments were carried out to validate the effectiveness of their method. Huang *et al.* [20] introduced a novel hybrid method consisting of the discrete cooperative maneuver switch and the continuous vehicle motion control. They implemented the method into a multi-vehicle cooperative control system with a distributed control infrastructure, leading each automated vehicle to conduct path planning and motion control separately. Simulation results in several typical traffic scenarios demonstrated the effectiveness of the proposed method.

2.3   Cooperative Learning

Perception and decision capabilities of agents both depend on effective algorithms or models. However, it is difficult for any algorithm model to directly achieve good performance in a complex environment owing to the complexity of environments. In practical, a good algorithm or model is produced based on massive training data and a number of optimization. Therefore, artificial intelligence application like autonomous driving require the agent having the learning capability of continuously improving the algorithm or model in real environment. The learning process of improving model or algorithm can be performed by individual agent or multiple agents cooperatively. In the context of deep learning method that needs diversity learning samples, it is clear that the cooperation approach is more effective to improve performance. The purpose of cooperative

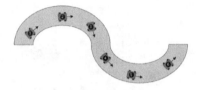

Fig. 4. Cooperation learning scenario

learning is to compute the best algorithm or model that has the minimum loss value when dealing with new samples. Therefore, we can define the problem of cooperative learning as looking for a set of model parameters w^A that minimizes the loss function value.

$$w^A = \arg \min_{w \in R^n} Loss(X, Y^w, w) \tag{3}$$

In Eq. 3, $A = \{a_1, a_i, ..., a_n\}$ is the collection of agents. R^n is the weight space of the model that has K dimensions. $w \in R^K = \{w_1, w_i, ..., w_K\}$ is one of the weight sets of the model. $X = \{x_1, x_i, ..., x_N\}$ is the collection of real samples. $Y_i^w = \{y_1, y_i, ..., y_N\}$ is the set of prediction samples in the case of model parameter w. $L_i(X, Y_i^w, w)$ is the loss function of the i-th agent in the case of model parameter w. $Loss(X, Y^w, w) \stackrel{def}{=} \frac{1}{n} \sum_{i=1}^{N} L_i(X, Y_i^w, w)$ is the loss function for all agents in the case of model parameter w, prediction set Y^w and real sample set X.

We also demonstrate the task and goal of cooperative learning through an autonomous driving scenario in Fig. 4. For autonomous driving, it is difficulty to safely control the vehicle on curved road. It is necessary to establish an effective model to achieve precise perception and decision in various scenarios. At present, the deep reinforcement learning method is proved to be an effective way owing to its excellent performance in continuous decision making. By collecting data from perception sensors during driving, deep reinforcement learning methods can continuously optimize the model using the state changes from the control action of vehicle and the rewards generated by the interaction with the environment. Based on this approach, a vehicle can continuously improve the safety and smoothness of curved road driving. Based on the data generated by cooperation of multiple vehicles, cooperative learning methods can generate better learning models by leveraging data sharing or model parameters.

In recent years, reinforcement learning has been widely adopted used to achieve intelligence in complex environment. To realize longitudinal control for any vehicle participating in dynamic collaborative driving to achieve higher-level coordination, Ng et al. [21] introduced a longitudinal vehicle model serving as the control system design platform as well as a longitudinal adaptive control system using Monte Carlo reinforcement learning. The evaluation results showed that the performance of the adaptive controller in a multi-vehicle convoy or platoon is promising and can form the basis of higher level platoon maneuvers. Matt et al. [22] created a deep Q-network (DQN) agent to perform the task of autonomous car driving from raw sensory inputs. They evaluated performance of the proposed DQN agent against several standard agents in a racing simulation environment. The evaluation results showed demonstrated the effectiveness of navigating autonomous vehicles using reinforcement learning methods. Motivated by the successful demonstrations of learning of Atari games and Go by Google DeepMind, Ahmad *et al.* [23] proposed a framework for autonomous driving using deep reinforcement learning. The proposed framework incorporated Recurrent Neural Networks (RNN) for information integration to enable the car to handle partially observable scenarios. In addition, it also integrated attention models to make vehicle focusing on relevant information. The evaluation results produced in an open source 3D car racing simulator demonstrated the feasibility of the framework. Training of deep reinforcement learning model is a computation intensive task. To reduce training time for deep reinforcement learning models for autonomous driving, Mitchell *et al.* [24] proposed a cloud computing architecture to distribute the training process across a pool of virtual machines. By parallelizing the training process, careful design of the reward function and use of techniques like transfer learning, they achieved a decrease in training time for autonomous driving task from 140 h to less than 1 h.

3   System Architecture of Cooperative Intelligence for Autonomous Driving

3.1   Overall Architecture

The implementation of cooperative intelligence system depends on two key components, cooperation module and intelligence module. In order to realize the cooperative intelligence in the autonomous driving scenario, the whole autonomous driving system including transportation facilities, networks and vehicles first needs to support the cooperation between vehicles and transportation facilities. Based on the existing autonomous driving system related technology, we design the overall system architecture of autonomous driving enabled by cooperative intelligence in Fig. 5. The system consists of four parts terminal, edge, network and cloud, connected by a V2X communication infrastructure.

Terminal: Terminal refers to the traffic participants with intelligent control capabilities. In this paper, we specifically refer to the autonomous driving vehicles with cooperation capabilities. Unlike most vehicles with primary assisted driving or autonomous driving functions, vehicles that support cooperative intelligence should be equipped with V2X communication equipments that support interchanging information with other vehicles and facilities via CAM [25] and CPM [26] messages on the V2X communication link.

Edge: Edge refers to the equipment deployed at the edge of the network, including transportation facilities, monitoring equipment and edge servers. Compared to terminal devices, edge devices have more storage capacity and powerful computing capability. Edge device can perform relatively more complicated computing tasks. In addition, owing to the deployment location, the edge device can

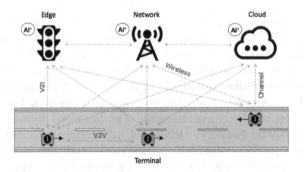

Fig. 5. Overall system architecture of autonomous driving cooperation intelligence

also perform some tasks that the terminal device can not support. For example, a traffic light with higher position can sense the motion state of the vehicles in all directions of the crossroad and broadcast to all vehicles within its coverage.

Cloud: Artificial intelligence tasks like deep learning are computation intensive, especially tasks of training deep learning model. Therefore, these kind of tasks are always performed on the cloud that has enough computing resources. Data collected by the terminal and edge devices are transmitted into cloud servers. Clusters of servers perform training task to generate and optimize models and update the models in the terminal and edge devices. In some kind of situations, part of inference tasks may also performed on the cloud.

Network: The role of the network is to connect various types of devices on the terminal, edge, and cloud to achieve better intelligence through cooperation. In the autonomous driving scenario, the two main technologies for V2X networks are short range communication (DSRC) and cellular based V2X (C-V2X). The typical technologies of DSRC and C-V2X are 802.11p [27] and 5G [28], respectively. 5G network is expected to become the main underlying network carrying cooperative intelligence for its good performance to support massive connection, broad bandwidth, low latency, high reliability and edge computing features.

3.2 Components of Cooperative Intelligence System for Autonomous Driving

Figure 6 shows the logical components and their relationships of the cooperative intelligence system for autonomous driving. Each gray block in the figure represents an agent. It should be noted that the agents include not only autonomous vehicles, but also intelligent agents with perception, decision and learning capabilities deployed on the edge and the cloud.

Autonomous driving vehicles are often equipped with a range of sensor devices including optical cameras, laser radars, millimeter wave radars, motion sensors for sensing the external environment. These sensor devices usually have a basic processing unit for pre-processing the collected raw data. At the same time, with the gradual maturity of multi-sensor data fusion technology [29], these

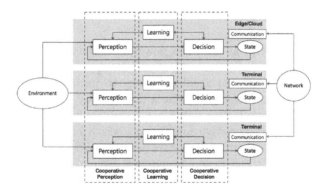

Fig. 6. Components map of cooperation intelligence for autonomous driving

sensor data will be processed in the sensor fusion computing unit. These sensor devices, basic processing units, and fusion computing units compose the perception module. The perception module converts raw data such as the external environment and vehicle state into a series of captured objects with attributes such as type, position, speed and direction of motion. Unlike the traditional single agent intelligent autonomous driving vehicle, the autonomous driving vehicle with cooperative intelligence capability will share the perception information acquired by itself with other vehicles or transportation facilities via the V2X network through the communication component. Meanwhile, the vehicle will also receive perception information from other vehicles or transportation facilities within a certain range and integrate them with the information perceived by the vehicle itself. The integrated information will be transmitted to the decision module. Autonomous driving vehicles with cooperative intelligence not only rely on their own perception information and decision strategies when making decisions, but also communicate and cooperate with other vehicles and transportation facilities through the V2X network via communication module to make control decisions. The control instruction made by decision module will change the state of the vehicle. The changed outside environment and state of the vehicle would be the input data for perception model for next round of perception and decision. Meanwhile, the data and information acquired by the perception module, the decision made by the decision module and the feedback generated from outside environment will continuously come into the learning module. The learning process can performed in a single vehicle or by the cooperation between vehicles, edge computing units and cloud computing servers through data sharing and local model parameter sharing. After learning process, the optimized model will be downloaded and updated into local computing unit of vehicles for improving intelligence capabilities.

4 Conclusion

Artificial Intelligence (AI) has shown its power of improving work efficiency and saving labor resource in many fields. However, the approach of improving intelligent capabilities of individual agent is closing to its limitation. Cooperative Intelligence (CI) has been emerged to be a hopeful way to help people achieving high level intelligence. In this paper, we scientifically defined the three key problems of achieving cooperative intelligence, which are cooperative perception, cooperative decision and cooperative learning. We have illustrated each problem in detail by a scenario of autonomous driving. For each problem, we have introduced related research works in the autonomous driving filed. At last, we proposed a system architecture and components design of cooperative intelligence system for autonomous driving. In terms of the future work, we consider two directions: (1) developing a simulation platform to evaluate the efficiency and performance of current cooperative intelligence related methods, and (2) build up a prototype of cooperative intelligence system for autonomous driving that can support three scenarios described in this paper.

References

1. Zi, L.: Liezi - Tangwen. (Annals of Spring and Autumn and Warring States Period)
2. The Terminator. https://en.wikipedia.org/wiki/The_Terminator. Accessed 2 July 2019
3. He, K., Zhang, X., Ren, S., Sun, J.: Deep residual learning for image recognition. In: IEEE Conference on Computer Vision and Pattern Recognition (CVPR) (2016)
4. Silver, D., et al.: Mastering the game of Go with deep neural networks and tree search. Nature **529**, 484–489 (2016)
5. Xiong, W., et al.: Achieving human parity in conversational speech recognition. Microsoft Research Technical Report, MSR-TR-2016-71 (2017)
6. Interview of Zhang Ba (Academician of Chinese Academy of Sciences). http://www.eeo.com.cn/2019/0524/356928.shtml. Accessed 2 July 2019
7. Waldrop, M.: What are the limits of deep learning? Proc. Natl. Acad. Sci. U.S.A. (PNAS) **116**(4), 1074–1077 (2019)
8. Sabour, S., Frosst, N., Hinton, G.E.: Dynamic routing between capsules. In: 31st Conference on Neural Information Processing Systems (NIPS), Long Beach, CA, USA (2016)
9. Wang, M., Deng, W.: Deep face recognition: a survey. https://arxiv.org/abs/1804.06655 (2019)
10. Nassif, A., Shah, I., Attili, I., et al.: Speech recognition using deep neural networks: a systematic review. IEEE Access **7**, 19143–19165 (2019)
11. Esteva, A., et al.: A guide to deep learning in healthcare. Nat. Med. **25**, 24–29 (2019)
12. Buoniu, L., Babuka, R., De Schutter, B.: Multi-agent reinforcement learning: an overview. In: Innovations in Multi-Agent Systems and Applications-1. Springer, Berlin (2010). https://doi.org/10.1007/978-3-642-14435-6_7
13. Bloembergen, D., et al.: Evolutionary dynamics of multi-agent learning. JAIR **53**, 659–697 (2015)

14. Chaib-Draa, B., Moulin, B., Mandiau, R., Millot, P.: Trends in distributed artificial intelligence. Artif. Intell. Rev. **6**(1), 35–66 (1992)
15. Bonabeau, E., Dorigo, M., Theraulaz, G.: Swarm Intelligence: From Natural to Artificial Systems. Oxford University Press, Oxford (1999)
16. Rauch, A., Maier, S., Klanner, F., et al.: Inter-vehicle object association for cooperative perception systems. In: 16th International IEEE Conference on Intelligent Transportation Systems (2013)
17. Kim, S.W., et al.: Multivehicle cooperative driving using cooperative perception: design and experimental validation. IEEE Trans. Intell. Transp. Syst. **16**(2), 663–680 (2015)
18. Wang, Y., et al.: Performance and scaling of collaborative sensing and networking for automated driving applications. In: IEEE International Conference on Communications Workshops (ICC Workshops), pp. 1–6 (2018)
19. Zheng, Y., Bian, Y., Li, S., et al.: Cooperative control of heterogeneous connected vehicles with directed acyclic interactions. IEEE Intell. Transp. Syst. Mag. **99**, 1 (2018)
20. Huang, Z., et al.: Path planning and cooperative control for automated vehicle platoon using hybrid automata. IEEE Trans. Intell. Transp. Syst. **20**(3), 1–16 (2018)
21. Ng, L., Clark, C.M., Huissoon, J.P.: Reinforcement learning of adaptive longitudinal control for dynamic collaborative driving. In: 2008 IEEE Intelligent Vehicles Symposium (July 2008)
22. Vitelli, M., Nayebi, A.: CARMA: a deep reinforcement learning approach to autonomous driving (2016). http://web.stanford.edu/anayebi/projects/CS_239_Final_Project_Writeup.pdf
23. Al Sallab, A.A., Abdou, M., Perot, E., Yogamani, S.: Deep reinforcement learning framework for autonomous driving. In: NIPS 2016 Workshop (December 2016)
24. Spryn, M., Sharma, A., Parkar, D., Shrimal, M.: Distributed deep reinforcement learning on the cloud for autonomous driving. In: Proceedings of the 1st International Workshop on Software Engineering for AI in Autonomous Systems, May 28 (2018)
25. de Cózar, V., Poncela, J., Aguilera, M., Aamir, M., Chowdhry, B.S.: Cooperative vehicle-to-vehicle awareness messages implementation. In: Shaikh, F.K., Chowdhry, B.S., Ammari, H.M., Uqaili, M.A., Shah, A. (eds.) WSN4DC 2013. CCIS, vol. 366, pp. 26–37. Springer, Heidelberg (2013). https://doi.org/10.1007/978-3-642-41054-3_3
26. Seeliger, F., et al.: Advisory warnings based on cooperative perception. In: IEEE Intelligent Vehicles Symposium Proceedings, pp. 8–11 (June 2014)
27. Jiang, D., Delgrossi, L.: IEEE 802.11p: towards an international standard for wireless access in vehicular environments. In: Vehicular Technology Conference (June 2008)
28. 3GPP Specification Set: 5G. https://www.3gpp.org/dynareport/SpecList.htm?release=Rel-15&tech=4. Accessed 2 July 2019
29. Aeberhard, M., Kaempchen, N.: High-level sensor data fusion architecture for vehicle surround environment perception. In: International Workshop on Intelligent Transportation (2011)

Utilizing Connectivity Maps to Accelerate V2I Communication in Cellular Network Dead Spots

Jon Arild Ekberg Meyer(ID), Ergys Puka(✉)(ID), and Peter Herrmann(ID)

Norwegian University of Science and Technology (NTNU), Trondheim, Norway
jon.ae.meyer@gmail.com,
{ergys.puka,herrmann}@ntnu.no
http://www.ntnu.no/iik

Abstract. On many roads in rural and mountainous areas, the cellular
network connectivity is intermittent and dead spots, i.e., zones without
any coverage, are frequent. In previous work, we developed a data dissemination protocol to accelerate the transmission of messages in dead
spots. It combines the cellular network with short-living ad-hoc networks
between vehicles. A car in a dead spot can forward messages directed
towards the environment, to the peer in its ad-hoc network that will leave
the dead spot first, effectively reducing the delay. An issue, however, is
to reliably identify the peer that is most likely the first one regaining
cellular network coverage. This problem can be solved if the borders of
the dead spot, the vehicles are in, are previously known. For that, we use
a novel technology named dead spot prediction. Here, vehicles conduct
local connectivity measurements that are aggregated to so-called connectivity maps describing the locations of dead spots on a road system.
In this article, we introduce the combination of the data dissemination
protocol with dead spot prediction. Particularly, our protocol is amended
such that connectivity maps are considered when deciding which vehicle
leaves a dead spot first. Since currently only few publicly available works
about dead spot prediction exist, we further created a prototype of such
a predictor ourselves that will be discussed as well.

Keywords: Cellular network access · Dead spots · Data dissemination
protocol · Ad-hoc network · Dead spot prediction · Connectivity map

1 Introduction

Intelligent Transport Systems (ITS) in the automotive sector rely on network
connectivity. The so-called vehicle-to-infrastructure (V2I) communication is usually carried out using cellular networks [17]. Thanks to the emerging 5G technology, even the vehicle-to-vehicle (V2V) communication, i.e., interactions between
cars, will be partially handled by cellular networks as well [13].

A problem of communication based on cellular networks, however, is the
varying network coverage. In real life, we regularly come across dead spots,

© Springer Nature Switzerland AG 2020
C.-H. Hsu et al. (Eds.): IOV 2019, LNCS 11894, pp. 76–87, 2020.
https://doi.org/10.1007/978-3-030-38651-1_8

i.e., areas without sufficient cellular network connectivity. Dead spots can be particularly found in sparsely populated areas since the cell tower infrastructure is often driven by the number of people living in an area [10]. Also mountainous terrain makes the network coverage frail as mountains and hills tend to cause echoes deteriorating the radio reception [4]. Own tests showed that the size of dead spots in very remote areas like the Australian Outback can be really large and extend hundreds of kilometers (see [14]).

To mitigate the effect of dead spots, we developed a data dissemination protocol for the transport of data from vehicles to the fixed infrastructure [14]. When vehicles have no cellular network access, they build ephemeral ad-hoc networks with other cars in their area. If one of the peers in such an ad-hoc network also has cellular network access, it can relay the messages of the other network members. If all peers are in the dead spot, the messages are forwarded to the vehicle that most likely regains cellular network connectivity first. Thus, it can send the messages earlier than its peers, and the overall transmission process is accelerated. We developed a prototypical application based on WiFi Direct [22].

A problem to be solved by the data dissemination protocol, is to find out which vehicle in an ad-hoc network has the highest probability to leave the dead spot first. In the original version, we select the car that lost cellular network access first since, assuming similar average speeds, it is supposed to be also the first one having crossed the dead spot [14]. This approach is easy to realize since we only need local connectivity measurements in the vehicles. However, it tends to be coarse since vehicles may have different speeds and can take varying routes. To overcome this weakness, we combine the data dissemination protocol with dead spot prediction. In this approach, so-called connectivity maps [20] describing dead spot areas are used. These maps inform the vehicles about the cellular network connectivity on their way. Then, they can adapt their communication accordingly (see [2,8,21]).

Since we could not find any dead spot predictors and connectivity map generators, we created our own prototype [11]. In this article, we sketch this development and discuss that one can infer from the testing results that dead spot prediction will be scalable. Moreover, we present the amendment of the data dissemination protocol such that the decision, which car in an ad-hoc vehicular network shall relay the messages, indeed incorporates aggregated dead spot prediction information.

The paper is organized as follows: In Sect. 2, we report on patents for connectivity prediction systems and some other related work. Thereafter, we sketch the prototype for dead spot prediction and discuss results of experimenting with it in Sect. 3. In Sect. 4, we introduce the data dissemination protocol. The extension of the protocol is described in Sect. 5 followed by a conclusion.

2   Related Work

Several patents provide evidence that the automotive industry has significant interest in dead spot prediction. In [8], Bosch has a distributed architecture patented in which vehicles compute dead spot elongations locally by conducting connectivity measurements. Then they transmit the local data to a central server that forwards it to other vehicles. Using the dead spot elongation data from other cars, a vehicle can decide if it needs to start a dead spot mitigation strategy. That is necessary to handle wireless applications that will not be completed when reaching the next dead spot. A similar architecture is patented by Ford [21]. The authors, however, sketch only shortly that they use a remote server but concentrate on the system layout in the vehicles. In particular, they define the structure of the dead spot prediction information that is realized by special connectivity maps [20]. In contrast, IBM does not mention a central server in its patent [2]. Instead, a mobile device takes current and historic wireless service data as well as general information about the environment (e.g., the presence of tunnels) into consideration. Using intelligent learning systems, these data are analyzed and aggregated to a predictive model anticipating dead spots.

Also dead spot mitigation strategies are protected. Bosch [16] and IBM [2] patented improvements for streaming services used in cars. Before reaching a dead spot, additional streaming data is transmitted and locally stored in the vehicle. This extra data is played while the vehicle passes the dead spot. Further, IBM has a way to ease the interruption of phone calls in dead spots patented [18]. The user is notified about the reason and the duration of the interruption, and the phone call is automatically reconnected after leaving the dead spot.

Another aspect of our work is about using hybrid systems combining cellular and vehicular networks. They are applied for various purposes (see, e.g., [12]) but, except for our own work, we only found one other approach utilizing them for dead spot mitigation. Eltahir et al. [5] use vehicles as relay stations such that a car in a dead spot may transmit messages via a number of other vehicles until reaching one that has cellular network access. In contrast to our approach [14], however, they neither allow to store data in vehicles nor to utilize their directions and positions in a dead spot. Therefore this approach can mitigate only smaller dead spots that contain sufficient traffic. For instance, in the Australian Outback where traffic is low and the dead spot size huge, this approach would not work.

3   Building Connectivity Maps

Our own prototypical dead spot predictor [11] uses an architecture close to the one patented by Bosch [8]. It extends, however, the functionality of the central server that not only forwards data received by the vehicles but also aggregates them to a connectivity map. The vehicles are provided with excerpts of this map containing dead spot predictions relevant to them. In this way, a vehicle does not need to aggregate the data from several other cars itself.

Local connectivity may change over time, for instance, due to network congestion, differing network use, or a breakdown in the cellular infrastructure (see [15]). The central server application therefore needs to constantly process incoming connectivity data. Further, newer data should be weighted higher than older one to keep the connectivity maps up-to-date.

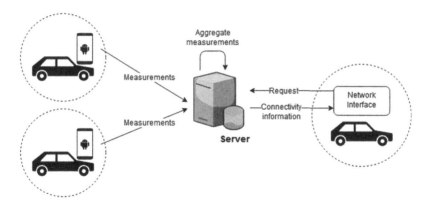

Fig. 1. The architecture of the dead spot prediction prototype.

Our prototype uses Android devices in the vehicles to collect cellular network statistics but one can also use other connectivity sensor techniques as long as the transmitted data follows the expected format. The sensed connectivity parameters include round-trip time, signal strength, jitter ratio, and packet loss. They can easily be extended in future versions if necessary. Each data point also includes the current GPS position where the measurement was taken. After receiving this information from various sources, the server continuously aggregates it into connectivity maps. The vehicles can then request information about upcoming dead spots from the server. This is shown in Fig. 1.

All client measurements taken inside a geographical area with a diameter of 50 m are conjoined. The central server aggregates the corresponding data points to a connectivity value for each geographical area. It applies special functions that reflect the particular needs of the applications for which a cellular network connection is used. For instance, the jitter ratio is more important when videos are streamed than when a text document is downloaded. Since a connectivity map is composed of the connectivity values in the geographical areas, the server produces separate maps for the different aggregation functions.

To receive a connectivity map, a vehicle provides the central server with its planned route, e.g., from the route guidance system. In our prototype, we use the format of the Google Directions API [6]. Moreover, the vehicle selects the desired aggregation function. The server then sends the connectivity map excerpt as a list of geographical area markers (including their coordinates), each referring to an area where a dead spot starts resp. ends, as well as the dead spot lengths. Two such excerpts are depicted in Fig. 2 where colored dots describe the connectivity values of the geographical areas. The greenish color of a dot refers to good connectivity in the represented area, while yellowish shows intermediate and reddish bad coverage. Missing dots indicate tunnels in which no GPS measurements can be taken. The excerpts reveal the following dead spots:

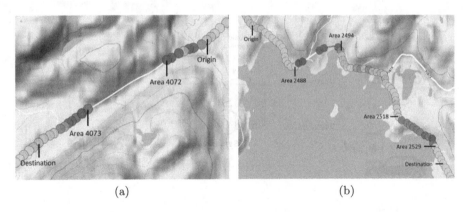

(a)   (b)

Fig. 2. Excerpts of a connectivity map from the Lofoten region in Norway.

- On the route depicted in Fig. 2a, a dead spot can be found between the geographical areas 4072 and 4073 which are 977 m apart. The tunnel in this region is probably the reason for the dead spot.
- On the route shown in Fig. 2b, there is a dead spot between areas 2488 and 2494. It's length is 661 m. Also here, tunnels seem to be the reason.
- Another dead spot on the route in Fig. 2b is between the areas 2518 and 2519. It has a length of 642 m.

In our tests, we merged all measurements for geographical areas with an extent of 50 m. Moreover, we took a sample every 250 ms such that a car running with 80 km/h produces nine data points in an area. Using this procedure, we collected more than 130,000 samples from two different locations in Norway over a couple of months. About 100,000 points were collected in the rural and highly mountainous location Lofoten, e.g., those shown in Fig. 2. The rest of the data points came from Trondheim, Norway's third largest city. We further added 3,334 data points collected in the context of earlier work about cellular network connectivity in the surroundings of Trondheim [15]. The size needed to store the data is about 30 Mb, which in the modern database world is tiny.

The 130,000 data points can be aggregated on a standard personal computer within a second. Here, the efficiency is ensured using a spatial database extender in the underlying database management system with support for geographical objects. This tool makes it possible to determine geographical proximity for thousands of locations in few milliseconds [11]. Since the application has to pair the GPS coordinates of each measurement point with an area in the database, the overall computation costs are significantly reduced.

However, only three different vehicles were used to produce this amount of data. In a real-world, large scale environment, millions of data points would be produced every day. To get a better understanding if the dead spot prediction approach is scalable, we projected our findings to the overall road traffic in Norway. The results of this analysis will be discussed in the following.

In 2018, motor vehicles in Norway ran around 46 billion kilometers [19]. We could not find information about the average speed of these cars, but detected similar data from the United Kingdom [3]. The average free flow speed of all cars there was 35 mph in 2012 which corresponds to 56.3 km/h. Since the share of motorways in Norway is only around half as large as in the UK and there are more mountainous roads, the average speed will most likely be lower. Thus, we assume an average speed value of 50 km/h: Then the motor vehicles in Norway ran 920 million hours in 2018. Using a sample rate of 250 ms, they could produce up to 13.248 trillion data points in that year. If a data center stores all these samples, e.g., to be able to consider long-term connectivity changes, and a data point is represented by 256 bytes, the overall storage size needed is around 3.4 petabytes. A larger data center should be able to handle this.

In contrast to the solution suggested by Bosch [8], we aggregate the data for geographical areas with an elongation of 50 m which will save memory. Since the road system in Norway covers 93,870 km [7], one has to keep at most 1,877,400 areas. Using a kilobyte to represent the data of one area, the overall storage size will be just around 1.9 gigabytes.

The price for this more concise way to store the data, however, is that we need to aggregate incoming data points into the connectivity values of the areas. This causes more processing effort than just storing the data. Projecting our experience, that we can aggregate 130,000 data points within a second, to the 13.248 trillion data points, that the cars in Norway could have theoretically produced in 2018, the overall computation time for aggregations will be 102 million seconds on a single PC. That is around 3.2 years such that, according to [1], the distribution of the process on 11 or 12 parallel running computers should be sufficient.

Finally, we have to look on the data transmission. To send 3.4 petabytes from the vehicles to the central server in the course of a year, affords a data transmission rate of around 820 GBit/s for the whole country. According to the fact that 5G will offer 10 GBit/s for a single connection, we consider this amount as doable. The use of compression mechanisms will alleviate the data transmission further.

Altogether, even considering the case that all cars in Norway participate in the dead spot prediction whenever they run, the approach seems scalable.

4   Data Dissemination Protocol

To reduce the waiting time for message transmissions between vehicles and their fixed infrastructure in areas where the cellular network coverage is weak, we developed a special data dissemination protocol [14]. In addition to the communication between vehicles and the infrastructure (V2I) via a cellular network, it uses short-lived ad-hoc vehicular networks (VANET) between close-by vehicles. Applying the ad-hoc network in areas in which the cellular network connectivity is low, a message can be forwarded to a vehicle which is either out of the dead spot or will likely leave it earlier than the message initiator such that the delivery of the message can be expedited.

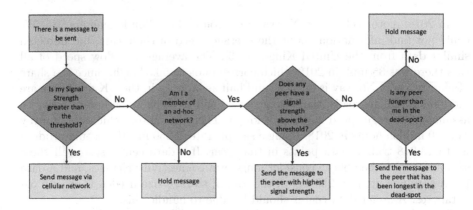

Fig. 3. Steps executed by the data dissemination protocol.

The prototype, also introduced in [14], uses Android devices in the vehicles that support WiFi Direct technology [22]. In particular, the WiFi Peer-to-Peer framework (WiFiP2P) was applied to implement WiFi Direct (see also [9]). Besides the fact that Android devices are very common, they allow us to exploit the immense capabilities of the Android OS. For instance, convenient methods to access signal strength measurements and local IP addresses are offered. As discussed below, these are features important for the realization of the protocol.

In the prototype, we use the signal strength to evaluate the cellular network coverage. That can, however, be easily extended to other forms of measurements, e.g., by applying the aggregation functions discussed in Sect. 3. If its current signal strength is below a certain threshold indicating the proximity of a dead spot, a vehicle tries to connect with other ones in its vicinity to form an ad-hoc network. If such a network can be established, the peers in it exchange their IP addresses, current signal strengths, and, if they lost cellular network coverage, the points in time, when that happened. This data is locally stored at the peers and utilized in the various steps of our protocol that are depicted in Fig. 3.

In the first protocol step, a peer veh_s which initiates the transmission of a message to the fixed environment, checks if its mobile network coverage is sufficient. If that is the case, the message is directly sent via the cellular network. Otherwise, veh_s tests if it is already part of an ad-hoc network. If it is not, it simply holds the message and the procedure is executed again when the peer either joins an ad-hoc network or leaves the dead spot.

If veh_s already belongs to an ad-hoc network while it is in a dead spot, it checks by using the locally stored signal strength information of its peers, if any of those has sufficient cellular network coverage. If this is the case, veh_s sends the message to the peer veh_b which has the best signal strength value. Then, veh_b forwards the message immediately via the cellular network.

If no peer has coverage, the message is sent to the one which presumably will leave the dead spot first in order to achieve a message delivery at the earliest opportunity. In the solution presented in [14], veh_s compares the points of time, the peers entered the dead spot, and transmits its message to vehicle veh_l that is already longest in it. As discussed in Sect. 5, we assume that all vehicles have around the same speed on the mostly small and mountainous roads where many dead spots occur. In consequence, veh_l, which entered the dead spot first, will likely be also the first one leaving it. If veh_s itself has been longer in the dead spot than all the other members of the ad-hoc network, it holds the message since it will probably be the first one regaining connectivity.

A special case is a vehicle stopping in the dead spot. In this case, it informs its peers and transfers the stored messages to other vehicles. If the stopping vehicle is not a partner in an ad-hoc network, it tries to establish a new one as long as it still stores messages in order to pass them to a peer still moving.

In [14], we also discuss the evaluation of the protocol implementation on Android devices using WiFiP2P. The most time-critical scenario for message handovers between cars is if they run in opposite directions. Since the range of WiFiDirect-based networks is around 200 m, building an ad-hoc connection, carrying out the protocol, and transmitting messages have to be completed in 6.5 seconds if both vehicles have a speed of 110 km/h. If the cars run with 80 km/h each, the data exchange has to be accomplished in nine seconds while it is 14.4 seconds for vehicles with 50 km/h. According to our test cases, the likelihood to complete the building of the ad-hoc network and the message handover in 6.5 seconds is 71%, while 97% of all trials were successfully carried out in nine seconds and all tests within 14.4 seconds. So, our example implementation seems to be reliable for cars with a speed of up to 80 km/h. But also for a speed of 110 km/h, it seems solid since, when an exchange with another vehicle fails, the sender can retry it with the next one. The likelihood that a message handover is successful in one of the first three trials is 98% when all participating vehicles have a speed of 110 km/h.

5   Updating the Data Dissemination Protocol

In our original approach [14], the decision to transmit data to the vehicle that has entered the dead spot first, rests on two assumptions: The first one is that the size of a dead spot is about the same for all vehicles. Here, we suppose that the cars use the same cellular network technology and that the network operators apply similar connectivity optimization strategies such that the extents of the dead spots are alike. The second assumption states that all vehicles have similar average speeds while passing it. This is based on the fact that many roads in rural and mountainous terrain, where dead spots are most prevalent, are minor. On this kind of roads, the speeds of the vehicles are often limited by the road quality and not their own driving characteristics. For two reasons, however, this assumption is often imprecise:

1. There can be road crossings in a dead spot. Then, we compare vehicles that possibly take different routes such that the times, they are in a dead spot, can heavily vary. For instance, the red motorcycle in Fig. 4a forwards its messages

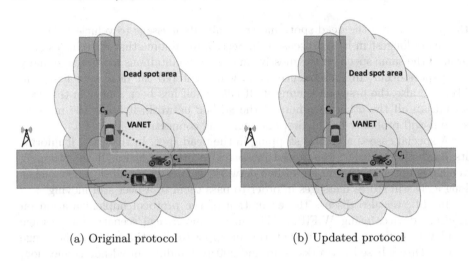

(a) Original protocol   (b) Updated protocol

Fig. 4. Behavior of the data dissemination protocol in dead spots with intersections.

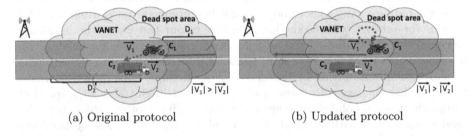

(a) Original protocol   (b) Updated protocol

Fig. 5. Behavior of the data dissemination protocol in dead spots with vehicles running at different speeds.

to the yellow car since that is already longer in the dead spot than its peers. Due to its turn, however, the yellow car has to cover a greater distance in the dead spot than the blue one which regains connectivity earlier.

2. Roads are usually used by different types of motor vehicles which may run with significant speed differences, e.g., when heavy trucks have to overcome steep climbs. This is depicted in Fig. 5a, where the motorcycle reaches the end of the dead spot earlier than the truck since the latter one is very slow. Nevertheless, since the truck is longer in the dead spot, the motorcycle falsely passes its messages to it.

Applying connectivity maps can alleviate these problems since that allows us to predict the time points, at which the vehicles reach the dead spot borders, more precisely. To get such a time estimate, we use connectivity map excerpts for computing both, the distance to the end of the dead spot and the predicted average speed.

To calculate the distance to the dead spot boundary, the current GPS location of the vehicle and the projected route are taken from the route guidance system, e.g., in the format given by the Google Directions API [6]. Further, the end point of the dead spot is retrieved from the connectivity map excerpt and the length of the way to this point is computed.

Determining the average speed is more subtle since it depends on several structural factors. One solution is to apply a pre-defined general average speed value for the vehicle class and the type of road used. While this proceeding is still relatively coarse, we can at least distinguish different types of vehicles, e.g., passenger cars, motorcycles, and trucks.

Following the ideas proposed by IBM [2], one can alternatively utilize historic information, e.g., the speeds, a vehicle used on the same road before. Moreover, one can consider general information about the route like the allowed top speeds. In free flow situations, passenger cars tend to maintain these velocities [3] such that they make good predictions for average speeds. In addition, trucks can determine their average speeds based on relevant road data like gradient angles.

A third method to establish the average speed is to extend the connectivity maps by entries describing the average speeds for different vehicle types. Here, when producing a sample, a vehicle also appends its current speed to it. From that, the central server calculates the average speeds, vehicles of a certain type use in a geographical area, and adds them to the connectivity map data. A vehicle can then utilize this information to compute its own predicted average speed for the route to the border of the dead spot.

Finding the right average speed, however, is a general problem to be solved in all dead spot mitigation strategies discussed in [2,16,18]. Thus, when applying the data dissemination protocol as an add-on to some of these techniques, we should be able to piggyback their average speed calculation methods as well.

By dividing the distance to the end of the dead spot through the average speed, we get the time, the vehicle needs until regaining cellular network connectivity. The data dissemination protocol can now be easily amended by changing the last step shown in Fig. 3. When building up an ad-hoc network, the peers now carry out the computations discussed above and report the predicted time when they will leave the dead spot instead of the time it was entered. The vehicles send their messages to the peer that signalled the earliest time point.

The two examples depicted in Figs. 4 and 5 illustrate that the new version of the data dissemination protocol is more reliable than the old one. One reason is that the new method considers the correct route of the vehicle. For instance, in Fig. 4b, the red motorcycle sends its messages to the blue car that is much closer to the dead spot boundary than the yellow one and will therefore reach it earlier. The better average speed prediction attenuates the second problem as well. As shown in Fig. 5b, the red motorcycle detects that, in spite of the longer route to the dead spot border, it will leave it earlier than the truck since its average speed is much higher. Therefore, it keeps the messages by itself.

The use of connectivity maps is also useful to decide when ad-hoc networks should be formed. They are only sensible when a vehicle is either in a dead spot or close-by. In the latter case, it can relay messages of cars that are not connected themselves. Thus, in the new version of the protocol, ad-hoc networks are only established when a vehicle is within a certain distance to a dead spot. This is more precise than the original solution, i.e., triggering the creation of ad-hoc networks after falling below a certain signal strength [14].

In our approach, we assume that all vehicles participating in an ad-hoc network have an excerpt of the connectivity map covering their current region in place. Since we suppose that these maps do rarely change dramatically in a short amount of time, their excerpts do not need to be highly up-to-date. From our tests, we assume that downloading an excerpt every 15 or 30 min and, if the connectivity is bad, also more infrequently, is sufficient.

6 Conclusion

An extension to our data dissemination protocol was introduced. The amendment incorporates dead spot prediction making the decision which peer in an ad-hoc network will leave a dead spot first, more precise. This vehicle shall receive the messages to be forwarded since it will be able to submit them earlier via the cellular network than its peers. Moreover, we reported about our prototype of a dead spot prediction system and argued that such a system will be scalable. According to our estimation, the costs to produce connectivity maps for the road networks of whole countries like Norway seem to be justifiable. Nevertheless, the effort to provide the vehicles with connectivity maps is substantial such that creating them just to improve our data dissemination protocol would be unreasonable. Therefore, the amendment presented here should be combined with other dead spot mitigation strategies like those mentioned in Sect. 2.

Next, we test the prototype with various scenarios to learn more about how the data dissemination protocol can be further improved. For instance, we conduct tests to get better predictions about the volatility of the dead spots. In [15], we discuss different road trips to a remote area in the vicinity of Trondheim. We found out that the sensed round trip time at one tour was much worse than at the other ones. To establish if that was a rare event or is a regular and often observable effect, we currently measure the cellular network connectivity at fixed places. These tests shall help us to understand better how many data points have to be created to keep the connectivity maps up-to-date. In this way, the predictor can be fine-tuned to keep the data transfer, storage, and aggregation costs discussed in Sect. 3 as low as possible.

References

1. Bræk, R., Haugen, Ø.: Engineering Real Time Systems. Prentice Hall, Upper Saddle River (1993)
2. DeLuca, L.S., Lakshmanan, G.T., Price, D.L., Smith, S.D.: Mitigating Service Disruptions using Mobile Prefetching based on Predicted Dead Spots, U.S. Patent 9 860 336, Jan 2018
3. Department for Transport: Free Flow Vehicle Speed Statistics: Great Britain 2012, June 2013

4. Driesen, P.E.: Prediction of multipath delay profiles in mountainous terrain. IEEE J. Sel. Areas Commun. **8**(3), 336–346 (2000)
5. Eltahir, A.A., Saeed, R.A., Alawi, M.A.: An enhanced hybrid wireless mesh protocol (E-HWMP) protocol for multihop vehicular communications. In: International Conference on Computing, Electrical and Electronic Engineering (ICCEEE), pp. 1–8. IEEE Computer, Khartoum (2013)
6. Google LLC: Google Maps Services, Web Services, Direction API (2019). https://developers.google.com/maps/documentation/directions/intro. Accessed 17 July 2019
7. Jaimovich, E.: Roadways, Input Sourcing, and Patterns of Specialisation. School of Economics Discussion Papers 0118, University of Surrey, UK (2018). https://EconPapers.repec.org/RePEc:sur:surrec:0118
8. Jain, V., Raghunathan, B., Kone, V.: Dead Spot Prediction Method for Wireless Vehicular Applications U.S. Patent 8 494 563, July 2013
9. Jakobsen, R.H.: Message Forwarding between Vehicles in Dead Spots. Master's thesis, Norwegian University of Science and Technology (NTNU), May 2018
10. Mecklenbräuker, C.F., et al.: Vehicular channel characterization and its implications for wireless system design and performance. Proc. IEEE **99**(7), 1189–1212 (2011)
11. Meyer, J.A.E.: Dynamic Computation of Connectivity Data. Master's thesis, Norwegian University of Science and Technology (NTNU), February 2019
12. Mukherjee, S., Baid, A., Raychaudhuri, D.: Integrating advanced mobility services into the future internet architecture. In: 7th International Conference on Communication Systems and Networks (COMSNETS), pp. 1–8 (2015)
13. Mumtaz, S., Huq, K.M.S., Rodriguez, J.: Direct mobile-to-mobile communication: paradigm for 5G. IEEE Wireless Commun. **21**(5), 14–23 (2014)
14. Puka, E., Herrmann, P.: A data dissemination protocol for vehicles with temporary cellular network inaccessibility. In: 5th IEEE International Workshop on Communication, Computing, and Networking in Cyber Physical Systems (CCNCPS). IEEE Computer, Washington, DC, June 2019. to appear
15. Puka, E., Herrmann, P., Levin, T., Skjetne, C.B.: A way to measure and analyze cellular network connectivity on the norwegian road system. In: 10th International Conference on Communication Systems & Networks (COMSNETS), pp. 595–600. IEEE Computer, Bengaluru, January 2018
16. Raghunathan, B., Jain, V.: Dead Spot Prediction Method for Wireless Vehicular Applications, U.S. Patent 8 762 482, June 2014
17. Siegel, J.E., Erb, D.C., Sarma, S.E.: A survey of the connected vehicle landscape - architectures, enabling technologies, applications, and development areas. IEEE Trans. Intell. Transp. Syst. **19**(8), 2391–2406 (2017)
18. Smith, G.J., van Leeuwen, G.W.: Mobile Communication Optimization near Wireless Dead Zone Regions, U.S. Patent 6 721 572, Apr 2004
19. Statistisk Sentralbyrå: Road Traffic Volumes (2019). https://www.ssb.no/en/transport-og-reiseliv/statistikker/klreg. Accessed 18 July 2019
20. Tseng, F.F., Filev, D.P., Makki, I.H.: Vehicular Connectivity Map, U.S. Patent 9 775 128 B2, Sept 2017
21. Tseng, F.F., Filev, D.P., Makki, I.H., Prakah-Asante, K.O., Yang, H.: Crowd Enhenced Connectivity Map for Data Transfer Intermittency Mitigation, U.S. Patent 2015/028 190, Oct 2015
22. Wi-Fi Alliance, P2P Technical Group: Wi-Fi Peer-to-Peer (P2P) Technical Specification v1.7 (2016)

Learning Route Planning from Experienced Drivers Using Generalized Value Iteration Network

Xiao Wang$^{(\boxtimes)}$, Quan Yuan, Zhihan Liu, Yushun Dong, Xiaojuan Wei, and Jinglin Li

State Key Laboratory of Networking and Switching Technology, Beijing University of Posts and Telecommunications, Beijing, China {wx_cookie,yuanquan,zhihan,dongyushun,weixjmm,jlli}@bupt.edu.cn

Abstract. Traffic congestion has long been a serious problem in cities, and route planning can improve traffic efficiency. The existing route planning approach relies on current and future traffic status. However, because traffic prediction and route planning interact with each other, the actual driving results deviate from expectations, and the performance is not satisfactory. In order to solve this problem, considering the topology of road networks, this paper proposes a route planning algorithm based on generalized value iteration network (GVIN), which uses graph convolution to extract the features of traffic flow, and then imitates human routing experience under various traffic status. Finally we evaluate the performance of the proposed network on real map and trajectory data in Beijing, China. The experimental results show that GVIN can simulate the human's routing decisions with high success rate and less commuting time.

Keywords: Route planning · Real time · Generalized value iteration network

1 Introduction

The number of vehicles has been growing rapidly, resulting severe traffic congestion problems to be solved. Choosing an appropriate route not only helps individuals reach their destinations faster, but also improves the urban traffic efficiency globally. As a consequence, many studies have been working on the route planning problem, which can be categorized into static and dynamic planning [1]. For static planning, a snapshot of traffic status is used to plan routes. For dynamic planning [2–4], both current and near future traffic flows are considered for the route planning, which can generate more efficient results.

This work was supported in part by the Natural Science Foundation of China under Grant 61876023 and Grant 61902035, and in part by the Natural Science Foundation of Beijing under Grant 4181002.

In recent years, the improvement of vehicle sensing, communication and computing capability enable vehicles to execute dynamic route planning with real-time and comprehensive traffic information [5–7]. However, the route planning of the vehicle and the evolution of the traffic status are coupled with each other, making the optimization problem difficult to solve. To overcome this problem, our previous work has leveraged value iteration network (VIN) to perform imitation learning, which learns experienced drivers' routing decisions under various traffic status [8]. However, VIN-based imitation learning can only conduct the coarse-grained grid-level routing, which is not applicable to the real road networks. As a result, the route planning does not reflect the driving law of the vehicle in the real road networks. To tackle this problem, this paper proposes a route planning algorithm based on generalized value iteration network (GVIN), which considers the topology of road networks, and then imitates human routing experience under various traffic status. The GVIN will serve as a "brain" of the vehicle, and it efficiently navigates the vehicle through the urban road networks with experience. Our contributions can be summarized as follows:

Traffic Status Characterization Based on Road Topology. A graph structure is constructed according to the topology of road networks, and the routing data of vehicles are mapped into multi-channel graph signals to present the spatial correlations of traffic status. In this way, the propagation or evolution of traffic status can be well characterized.

Structure Design of Neural Network. Considering the complexity of the decision model, GVIN as the neural network is used to learn routing from experienced drivers. By graph convolution and value iteration, GVIN can learn the mapping from traffic status to routing decisions on the graph.

Network Training and Performance Evaluation. In order to evaluate the planning ability of GVIN, this paper conducts comprehensive experiments based on the real road networks and taxi trajectories in Beijing. The results show that GVIN plan routes with high success rate and shorter traveling time.

The remainder of this paper is organized as follows: Sect. 2 introduces the related work of route planning algorithms, and we describe the problem formulation in Sect. 3. Next, the network structure and training algorithm of GVIN are introduced in Sect. 4. We design and perform a serial of experiments and the results are analyzed in Sect. 5. Finally, our work is summarized and discussed in Sect. 6.

2   Related Work

Route recommendation, which aims to improve traffic efficiency, is mainly divided into traditional and deep learning-based methods. Traditional methods are mainly based on Dijkstra and A* algorithm which neglect the evolution of traffic status. To overcome this limitation, some studies have been taking advantage of deep learning methods for route planning. Nazari et al. [9] and Zolfpour-Arokhlo et al. [10] used deep reinforcement learning to quickly provide an approximate optimal routing solution. Brahmbhatt et al. [11] proposed a convolutional neural network based algorithm for navigating in large cities using locally visible street view images. Nazari et al. [9] solved the problem of optimal routing by deep reinforcement learning, which can realize the routing of vehicles on maps with different size. Yang et al. [8] used VIN to learn the driver's routing experience and made full use of its generalization ability to yield better performance when transferred to the new environment. Li et al. [12] took further steps to consider the influence of traffic status evolution on routing behavior, and proposed a double rewarding VIN method based on traffic flow prediction.

It is demonstrated that VIN can solve the maze problem with excellent performance by dividing the state model into grids [13]. However, many routing problems cannot be simply abstracted into two-dimensional grid images, because grids cannot model the topology of road networks. The study of graph structure gave birth to GVIN [14]. Using graph convolution to simulate the value iteration algorithm, GVIN can perform better in both regular and irregular graph. GVIN solves the drawback that VIN can only find routes in the gridding scene, for the reason that the input of GVIN is no longer a grid image, but a graph structure.

3   System Model and Problem Formulation

Experienced drivers usually have deep understanding of urban traffic status, and thus their routing decisions can easily adapt to dynamic traffic status. This paper conducts route planning by learning driving decisions of experienced drivers. Firstly, we model the road networks as a weighted directed graph, then use multi-channel graph signals to characterize the traffic status based on the road topology.

3.1   Topologized Traffic Status Model

Definition 1. *Graph Map: A physical road networks can be represented by a graph $G = (\mathcal{V}, \mathbf{X}, \mathbf{E}, \mathbf{A})$, $\mathcal{V}$ is a finite set of nodes, $\mathbf{E}$ is a set of edges, $\mathbf{X}$ is a set of node coordinates, $\mathbf{A}$ is an adjacency matrix. Therefore, the actual road networks can be transformed into a graph structure, as shown in Fig. 1. Consider all road segments in the traffic network as a node set $\mathcal{V}$ of the graph, and the edge weight e_{ij} represents the traveling time required from the road segment i to the adjacent one j. The transformation between road segments and points can reflect the road topology.*

Definition 2. *Traverse Time Graph: Based on the GPS trajectory data, the average traverse time of the vehicle passing through the road segment is calculated, and the traverse times of all the road segments are combined to generate a traverse time graph (TTG).*

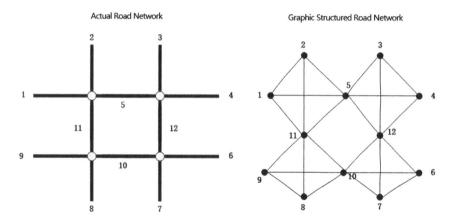

Fig. 1. The graph structure based on real road networks.

Considering that each road segment in the road networks is connected to N segments, the direction set L is constructed. Then the edge set $\mathbf{E}$ should contain $N + 1$ layers and $|L| = N + 1$, which means $\mathbf{E} = \{\mathbf{E}^{l_0}, \ldots, \mathbf{E}^{l_N}\}$ including the original segment. Specifically, the traveling time from v_i to $v_{i+d(l)}$ $(v_i, v_{i+d(l)} \in \mathcal{V})$ in the lth direction is represented as $e_i^l \in \mathbf{E}^l$, $l \in \{l_0, \ldots, l_N\}$. By merging GPS-based historical trajectories and calculating the average travel time of vehicles passing through this segment in a certain time, a TTG can be obtained. The traverse time map can reflect the speed of network traffic flow.

3.2 Building Markov Decison Process

Route planning is a process of sequential decision making and planning, so it can be modeled as a Markov decision process (MDP) [15].

Definition 3. *Driving Decision Sequence:* *Each experienced driver's trajectory is mapped into the road graph and discretize it into the driving decision sequence set* $\{a_0, a_1, \ldots, a_i, \ldots\}$, *where* $a_i \in L = \{l_{0 \sim N}\}$, *representing one choice among* $N + 1$ *actions.*

After aligning the TTG with the decision based on the timestamp, we build an MDP that contains the essence of the routing decision. MDP consists of state $S = \mathcal{V}$, $s = v \in \mathcal{V}$, the reward function of routing decision a is $R(s, a) = R(v, a) = e_v^a \in \mathbf{E}^a$, as well as transfer matrix $P(s'|s, a) = P(v'|v, a)$, $s' = v' \in \mathcal{V}$. The transfer matrix encodes the probability of entering each of the next segment in the current segment. The optimal planning of the MDP will follow the routing action sequence to the destination, which is similar to the routing of an experienced driver.

Once the MDP of the routing is determined, the planning algorithm can then be used to obtain the value function V^*, which is the value of the decision for the whole routing efficiency. The optimal policy $\pi^*(s)$ under the state s can only depend V^* for the reason that

$$\pi^*(s) = \text{argmax}_a \left[R(s,a) + \gamma \sum_{s'} P\left(s'|s,a\right) V^*\left(s'\right) \right]. \tag{1}$$

γ is the discount coefficient, $P\left(s'|s,a\right) > 0$ is a small subset of S, and only the adjacent points or itself can be reached from s.

4   Problem Solving

In order to learn navigation from taxi trajectory data, our framework consists of three modules. Figure 2 is a description of framework of navigation learning. TTG and decision sequence are obtained from trajectory data in data preprocessing module. The training module learns the mapping relationship between traffic status and action, and the route can be generated by inputting new traffic status data based on the learned experience in decision module.

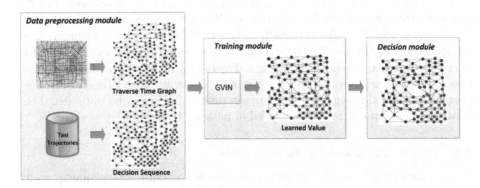

Fig. 2. A framework of navigation learning. It consists of three processes: data preprocessing, training and decision.

4.1   Learning Structure Co-Design

Value iteration (VI) algorithm is usually used to calculate V^* and π^*:

$$V_{i+1}(s) = \max_a Q_i(s,a) \quad \forall s \text{ where } Q_i(s,a) = R(s,a) + \gamma \sum_{s'} P\left(s'|s,a\right) V_i\left(s'\right). \tag{2}$$

The value function V_i in the value iteration converges to V^* when $i \to \infty$, so the optimal policy $\pi^*(s) = \text{argmax}_a Q_\infty(s,a)$ can be derived. Thus MDP and VI are applied to learn optimal routing decisions in the traffic network.

The data structure and GVIN with differentiable planning module are designed. Each iteration of VI can be regarded as previous value function V_i and reward function R through a convolution layer and max-pooling layer. Therefore by recurrently applying convolution and max-pooling k times, k iterations of value iteration are performed. When i is large enough, an approximate optimal routing decision can be obtained from the convergence value function V_i.

Based on this idea, a generalized value iteration module is proposed. We have defined the road networks model $G = (\mathcal{V}, \mathbf{X}, \mathbf{E}, \mathbf{A})$ above. The parameters of the value iteration module are defined as follows: $\mathcal{V}$ represents the road segments; $\mathbf{X}$ represents the coordinates of the road segment; $\mathbf{E}$ represents the traveling time between the road segments; $\mathbf{A}$ represents the adjacency matrix. We use $\mathbf{g} \in \{0, 1\}^{|\mathcal{V}|}$ to encode the route destination. It should be noted that $\mathbf{g}$ is a one-hot vector, which means only the row corresponding to destination is encoded as 1 and the other rows are encoded as 0.

Let $\mathbf{r}$ be the reward value signal, indicating the current road networks traffic status. The smaller the reward value is, the more congested the road segment will be. $\mathbf{q}$ indicates the Q values of the possible next routing actions. $\mathbf{v}$ is the state value, based on which a routing decision can be made.

As shown in Fig. 3, GVIN is a network structure that iteratively uses Eq. (2) to compute the state value $V^*(s)$. The input of the GVIN value iteration module is a multi-channel reward graph R of dimension $|L| \times |\mathcal{V}|$, where $|L|$ represents the number of channels, its value is $N + 1$, and $|\mathcal{V}|$ represents the total number of road segments. The reward is sent to the convolution layer containing $|L|$ layers. Each convolution channel corresponds to a specific routing decision, so convolutional channel can also be called action channel, and $Q(s, a)$ is obtained by convolution. The value for the next iteration can be generated by max-pooling layer from $|L|$ action channels. The obtained value signal is fused with the multi-channel reward value, and then the convolution and max-pooling operations are performed again. The whole process will be performed in k iterations.

The entire calculation process is as follows:

$$\mathbf{P}^{(a)} = f_P\left(G; \mathbf{w}_{\mathbf{P}^{(a)}}\right) \tag{3}$$

$$\mathbf{q}_{n+1}^{(a)} = \mathbf{P}^{(a)}\left(\mathbf{r} + \gamma\mathbf{v}_n\right) \tag{4}$$

$$\mathbf{v}_{n+1} = \max_a \mathbf{q}_{n+1}^{(a)} \tag{5}$$

In Eq. (3), $\mathbf{P}^{(a)}$ is a graph convolution kernel in the a-th channel (corresponding to routing action a), and $\mathbf{P}$ is a set of graph convolution operators obtained by training on the basis of the graph G. In Eqs. (4) and (5), the action value $\mathbf{q}^{(a)}$ in the a-th channel is obtained by convolution calculation, and updated by iteration. The value map signal $\mathbf{v}$ is obtained by the max-pooling. $\mathbf{w}_{\mathbf{P}^{(a)}}$ is a training parameter of $\mathbf{P}^{(a)}$. When the iteration is over, we can plan the path according to the rising direction of the state value v.

The core step in GVIN is to find the $\mathbf{q}$ value through the convolution operation. GVIN is based on the graph structure, and the convolution operation requires a special graph convolution kernel to better identify the traffic characteristics of the road networks.

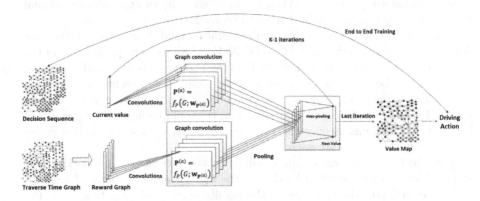

Fig. 3. Generalized value iteration network module.

4.2 Graph-Based Kernel Functions

The two-dimensional space kernel function is shift invariant. Assuming that the two-dimensional space kernel function is $K(\cdot, \cdot)$, $K(\mathbf{x}, \mathbf{y}) = K(\mathbf{x} + \mathbf{t}, \mathbf{y} + \mathbf{t})$, $\mathbf{x}, \mathbf{y}, \mathbf{t} \in \mathcal{R}^2$ is satisfied.

The shift invariance requires that the transition probability distribution is constant regardless of the origin. Based on the displacement invariance of the two-dimensional spatial kernel function and the graph adjacency matrix, the graph convolution operator $\mathbf{P} = f_P(G; \mathbf{w_P}) \in \mathcal{R}^{|\mathcal{V}| \times |\mathcal{V}|}$ can be obtained for each element $\mathbf{P}_{i,j} = \mathbf{A}_{i,j} \cdot K_{\mathbf{w_P}}(\mathbf{X}_i, \mathbf{X}_j)$. The kernel function $K_{\mathbf{w_P}}(\cdot, \cdot)$ is parameterized by $\mathbf{w_P}$ and $\mathbf{X}_i, \mathbf{X}_j \in \mathbf{X}$. $\mathbf{X}_i$ and $\mathbf{X}_j$ are the coordinate of v_i and v_j. When v_i and v_j are not connected, we define $\mathbf{A}_{i,j} = 0$ and $\mathbf{P}_{i,j} = 0$; when v_i and v_j are connected, $\mathbf{A}_{i,j} = 1$ and $K_{\mathbf{w_P}}(v_i, v_j)$ is proportional to $\mathbf{P}_{i,j}$. In Eq. (3), the graph convolution is the matrix vector product between the graph convolution operator and the graph signal $\mathbf{r} + \gamma \mathbf{v}_n$. The definition of the graph convolution kernel determines the characteristics of the traffic status that the convolution can capture. Kernel functions proposed in [14], that is, the diectional kernel, the spatial kernel and the embedding-based kernel, are shift invariant. Multi-layer neural network is used in the embedding-based kernel to directly obtain results from the graph structure and edges. Therefore, the embedding-based kernel is more flexible than the diectional and the spatial kernel, and more hidden factors can be learned.

Node embedding can be directly fed into the embedding-based kernel and allows GVIN to automatically learn the latent factors for overall planning. The (i, j) element in the graph convolution operator is

$$\mathbf{P}_{i,j} = \frac{(I_{i=j} + \mathbf{A}_{i,j})}{\sqrt{\sum_k (1 + \mathbf{A}_{k,j}) \sum_k (1 + \mathbf{A}_{i,k})}} \cdot K_{\text{emb}}(\mathbf{X}_i, \mathbf{X}_j), \tag{6}$$

where the indicator function $I_{i=j} = 1$ when $i = j$ and 0, otherwise, and the embedding-based kernel function is $K_{\text{emb}}(\mathbf{X}_i, \mathbf{X}_j) = \text{mnnet}([\mathbf{X}_i - \mathbf{X}_j])$, where mnnet $(\cdot)$ is a multi-layer neural network. The training parameters $\mathbf{w_P}$ in Eq. (3) are the weights in the neural network. In our experiments, when the graph is weighted, the adjacency matrix $\mathbf{A}_{i,j}$ of the graph is used as the input of the neural network.

4.3 Training

The complete process for training GVIN is given in Algorithm 1. For the reason that data of varying length cannot be used, our GVIN uses fixed length historical data as input. The data of each timestamp $\text{tuple}_t = (TTG_t, a_t)$ is stored in the dataset $\mathcal{D} = \{\text{tuple}_1, \ldots, \text{tuple}_t, \ldots, \text{tuple}_m\}$. Data set $\mathcal{D}$ will be randomly shuffled into many mini-batches. For the inner loop of the algorithm, the network parameters are updated using mini-batches gradient descent.

Algorithm 1. Algorithm for training GVIN

Input: Data set $\mathcal{D} = \{\text{tuple}_1, \text{tuple}_2, \ldots, \text{tuple}_m\}$, graph G and the destination $\mathbf{g}$;
Output:
1: Initialize GVIN parameters $\mathbf{w} = \left[\mathbf{w}_\mathbf{P}^{(a)}\right]$;
2: Initialize parameter gradients $\Delta \mathbf{w}$;
3: **for** each $epoch \in [1, K]$ **do**
4:     Initialize mini-batch size;
5:     $num = m/batch\_size$;
6:     **for** each $i \in [0, num]$ **do**
7:         $j = i + batch\_size$;
8:         $fd\_data = \text{tuple}_{i:j}$
9:         Perform a gradient descent step $\Delta \mathbf{w}$ on $loss = Cross\_Entropy\{fd\_data.a, V(fd\_data.TTG, fd\_data.s; \mathbf{w})\}$
10:     **end for**
11: **end for**

---

5 Experiments

5.1 Data Preprocessing

Graph Map: According to the road networks topological graph $G = (\mathcal{V}, \mathbf{X}, \mathbf{E}, \mathbf{A})$ in the northwest area of Beijing's Fourth Ring Road, road segments are transformed into nodes in G using the dual graph method, and the connections between the road segments are transformed into edges. By counting the traffic volume of each road segment, 106 main road segments carrying most of the traffic flow are selected.

Taxi Trajectories: The routes are extracted from the real taxi trajectory data, which includes more than 1,000,000 taxi data from June to September 2016. Firstly, the trajectory data located in the selected area are coarsely screened, and then the trajectory data is filtered by the latitude and longitude of each road segment, finally the time when the vehicle passes the segment is calculated. Because this paper aims to learn route planning from experienced drivers, the drivers in the non-carrying state may not have chosen the best route, so only the taxi trajectory in the carrying state is analyzed. The traffic status in the morning and evening peak periods are more complicated and congested. Therefore, according to the time of the morning and evening peaks in Beijing, the data from 7:00 to 10:00 and 17:00 to 20:00 are selected.

Traverse Time Graph: According to the selected segments, one segment is connected to up to 6 segments, so there are up to 6 driving decisions for each segment. For each segment v, the routing decision direction $l_{1\sim6}$ and a fixed period $[t, t + \Delta T]$, $\Delta T = 10\,\text{min}$, we calculate the average traverse time of all passing by taxis, and get a reward $e_v^{l,t} = -average\ time$ in TTG. If a segment has a direction that is impassable, then the $e_v^{l,t}$ is blank, so it is set to a large negative reward as the magic number, indicating that road segment v has no connected segment in direction l^{th}.

When the 6-layers TTG has been calculated, the timestamp can be removed for the reason that the routing decision a depends only on the current global traffic status regardless of time, in which way TTG of different time can be trained together. To get better results in the mini-batch gradient reduction, the TTG is mapped to $[-1, 0]$ by Min-Max normalization method.

$$\text{TTG}_{\text{norm}} = \frac{\text{TTG} - \text{TTG}_{\text{max}}}{\text{TTG}_{\text{max}} - \text{TTG}_{\text{min}}} \tag{7}$$

For the l_0 layer, which means staying layer of TTG, we manually build a reward map. Since the destination v_d of each driving decision is determined, we use $e_{v_d}^{l_0} = 1$ to denote a large reward for reaching the destination and the remaining points are set to be -1. Then $l_{1\sim6}$ and l_0 are stacked to be a 7-layers TTG, indicating the current traffic status and destination information. The 7-layers TTG is the input of the GVIN, then GVIN can get a value map by learning automatically. By gradually moving from dark node with small value (far from destination) to bright node with large value (destination), one can find routes that GVIN has learned.

5.2   Visualized Results

Route can be planned through a value map, and the values in the value map represent the reward that can be obtained by taking a decision. In order to understand the navigation capabilities of GVIN, we visualize the resulting value map and draw the planned routes. Set the road segment with high value to be bright and the road segment with a low value to be darker. The route planning procedure is a process that moves from the origin to the most bright segment. GVIN iteratively generates routing decisions starting from the origin until it reaches the destination. Figure 4 shows different cases yielded by GVIN based on the real network topology. Figure 4(a)–(c) show some successful cases, which demonstrate that the vehicle can successfully reach its destination and avoid traffic congestion. Figure 4(d) shows that although the planned route reaches the destination, but it takes longer time than real route. Figure 4(e)–(f) show failure situation, which means the planned route cannot reach the destination.

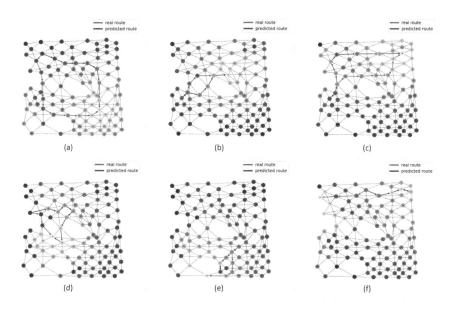

Fig. 4. Routes of GVIN and real routes

5.3   Generalizing Results

We validate GVIN performance through four metrics and compare them with Dijkstra.

Accuracy: The result of the experiment is measured by top-1 accuracy and top-2 accuracy. $top-k$ accuracy refers to the selection of k directions with the greatest probability when predicting. If there is a correct direction in them, the prediction is considered correct. Because the driver's driving decision is uncertain, Top-1 Accuracy is not high, indicating that even experienced drivers at the same location may choose different routes to the same destination. The Bayes error of the existing route planning makes it difficult to get higher top-1 accuracy. Nevertheless, higher Top-2 Accuracy indicates that our GVIN has successfully learned most of the driving decisions.

Success Rate: Given a global status TTG, a full trail from initial state is predicted by iteratively choosing the optimal next states. A trail is successful if it reaches destination via the predicted trajectory. Success rate is the ratio of the number of successful trails to that of all trails. Our high success rate demonstrates that GVIN is able to navigate in fine-grained urban model.

Saved Time Rate: By randomly selecting real taxi driving trajectories from the dataset, we create a data set $\mathbb{T} = \{(O_1, D_1, time_1), \ldots, (O_i, D_i, time_i), \ldots\}$, where O_i and D_i represent the origin and destination, and time represents the time taken from the origin to the destination. New trajectory set $\mathbb{T}' = \{(O_1, D_1, time_1'), \ldots, (O_i, D_i, time_i'), \ldots\}$ is generated by GVIN under the same time slice. Note that we only consider success trajectories. At the same time, we put forward "TTG invariant assumption", which means changing one's trajectory does not affect the global TTG, so that the TTG can be used to estimate the total time consumption of the new trajectory. More specifically, applying GVIN to a trajectory $T_i = (O_i, D_i, time_i)$ would produce a new trajectory $T_i' = (O_i, D_i, time_i')$, which saves time $\Delta time_i = time_i - time_i'$. Then saved time rate (STR) can be calculated by

$$STR = \frac{\sum_{T_i \in \mathbb{T}} \Delta time_i}{\sum_{T_i \in \mathbb{T}} time_i}. \tag{8}$$

We compare GVIN with time-based Dijkstra algorithm which is used to find the minimum traverse time path with the edge weight of traverse time. The accuracy, success rate and saved time rate are shown in Table 1.

Table 1. Performance of GVIN and Dijkstra.

Method	Top-1 accuracy	Top-2 accuracy	Success rate	Saved time rate
GVIN	58.91%	86.2%	96.5%	6.7%
Time-based Dijkstra	N/A	N/A	100%	2.1%

Increased Distance Rate: Experiments show that the GVIN driving distance is shorter than the time-based Dijkstra driving distance, and the distance-based Dijkstra driving distance is the shortest. Same as STR, applying GVIN to a trajectory $T_i = (O_i, D_i, distance_i)$ would produce a new trajectory $T_i' = (O_i, D_i, distance_i')$, and based on distance-based Dijkstra, we get shortest-distance trajectory $\mathbf{T}_i' = (O_i, D_i, \mathbf{distance}_i')$, which saves distance $\Delta distance_i = distance_i' - \mathbf{distance}_i'$, we can calculate GVIN and time-based Dijkstra increased distance rate (IDR) by Eq. (9).

$$IDR = \frac{\sum_{T_i \in \mathbb{T}} \Delta distance_i}{\sum_{T_i \in \mathbb{T}} \mathbf{distance}_i'} \tag{9}$$

The distance between the origin and the destination is divided into three levels, and the IDR of GVIN and Dijkstra is compared at each level. The results are shown in Table 2. Our result shows that the traveling distance of GVIN and time-based Dijkstra is longer than distance-based Dijkstra, but GVIN plans routes with shorter traveling distance than time-based Dijkstra in each level.

Table 2. Increased distance rate of GVIN and Dijkstra.

Distance	GVIN	Time-based Dijkstra
≤ 5 km	5.2%	5.5%
>5 km, ≤ 10 km	6.2%	6.7%
>10 km	7.7%	8.1%

6 Conclusion

This paper has discussed an end-to-end neural network for optimal route planning in urban road navigation based on global traffic status. By learning route planning from experienced drivers, GVIN can yield driving decisions imitating experienced drivers with shorter traveling distance and higher time saving rate compared to Dijkstra algorithm. Besides, GVIN conforms to the real-world vehicle driving route based on the road topology better than grid based VIN, being able to find route in a dynamically changing network. In the future, the coordination of multi-vehicle GVIN route planning will be considered on traffic balance

References

1. Montiel, O., Orozco-Rosas, U., Sepúlveda, R.: Path planning for mobile robots using Bacterial Potential Field for avoiding static and dynamic obstacles. Expert Syst. Appl. **42**(12), 5177–5191 (2015)
2. Demers, A., et al.: Experimenting with real-time ATIS: stepping forward from ADVANCE (2006)
3. Boyce, D.: A memoir of the advance project. J. Intell. Transp. Syst. **7**(2), 105–130 (2002)
4. Hu, W.-B., Nie, C., Qiu, Z.Y., Du, B., Yuan, Q.: A route guidance method based on quantum searching for real-time dynamic multi-intersections in urban traffic networks. Acta Electron. Sin. **46**(1), 104–109 (2018)
5. Wan, J., Zhang, D., Zhao, S., Yang, L.T., Lloret, J.: Context-aware vehicular cyber-physical systems with cloud support: architecture, challenges, and solutions. Commun. Mag. IEEE **52**(8), 106–113 (2014)
6. Quan, Y., Zhou, H., Li, J., Liu, Z., Shen, X.S.: Toward efficient content delivery for automated driving services: an edge computing solution. IEEE Netw. **32**(1), 80–86 (2018)
7. Luo, G., et al.: Cooperative vehicular content distribution in edge computing assisted 5G-VANET. China Commun. **15**(7), 1–17 (2018)

8. Yang, S., Li, J., Wang, J., Liu, Z., Yang, F.: Learning urban navigation via value iteration network. In: 2018 IEEE Intelligent Vehicles Symposium (IV), pp. 800–805 (2018)

9. Nazari, M., Oroojlooy, A., Snyder, L., Takac, M.: Reinforcement learning for solving the vehicle routing problem. In: Advances in Neural Information Processing Systems, vol. 31, pp. 9839–9849 (2018)

10. Yu, S., Zhou, J., Li, B., Mabu, S., Hirasawa, K.: Q value-based dynamic programming with SARSA learning for real time route guidance in large scale road networks. In: The 2012 International Joint Conference on Neural Networks (IJCNN), pp. 1–7 (2012)

11. Brahmbhatt, S., Hays, J.: DeepNav: learning to navigate large cities. In: 2017 IEEE Conference on Computer Vision and Pattern Recognition (CVPR), pp. 3087–3096 (2017)

12. Li, J., et al.: A traffic prediction enabled double rewarded value iteration network for route planning. IEEE Trans. Veh. Technol. **68**(5), 4170–4181 (2019)

13. Tamar, A., Wu, Y., Thomas, G., Levine, S., Abbeel, P.: Value iteration networks. In: Advances in Neural Information Processing Systems, vol. 29, pp. 2154–2162 (2016)

14. Niu, S., Chen, S., Guo, H., Targonski, C., Smith, M.C., Kovacevic, J.: Generalized value iteration networks: life beyond lattices. CoRR abs/1706.02416 (2017). http://arxiv.org/abs/1706.02416

15. Sutton, R., Barto, A.: Reinforcement learning: an introduction (adaptive computation and machine learning). IEEE Trans. Neural Netw. **9**(5), 1054 (1998)

Development of Low-Cost Sensors Based Multi-sensors Integration Positioning Algorithm for Land Vehicle Tracking and Monitoring Device

Chi-ho Park$^{(\boxtimes)}$ and Joong-hee Han ⓘ

DGIST, 333 Techno jungang-daero, Daegu 42988, South Korea
chpark@dgist.ac.kr

Abstract. The GNSS positioning technique are widely applied for land vehicle applications. However, the GNSS positioning technique is unable to ensure the continuity and the reliability in all land vehicle-driving environment. Therefore, to improve the accuracy of GNSS positioning technique, it is necessary to integrate additional sensors. In this study, we developed low-cost MEMS based IMU, magnetometers, and a single-frequency GNSS-RTK based positioning algorithm for the commercialization of land vehicle tracking and monitoring device. In addition, the performance of the proposed algorithm was evaluated using the data from real test-driving.

Keywords: GNSS · IMU · Magnetometer · Positioning · Land vehicle

1 Introduction

Nowadays, the positioning and navigation techniques are widely applied for land vehicle applications such automotive navigation, emergency assistance, fleet management, advanced driver assistance system (ADAS), intelligent transportation system (ITS). The representative positioning and navigation technique is the global navigation satellite system (GNSS) that can provide the position and velocity with an accuracy that is appropriate for land vehicle applications. However, the accuracy of GNSS is poor or it even fails to determine the position and velocity when the GNSS signal is blocked due to skyscrapers, tunnels, and so forth. In recent years, as multi-GNSS-based technique, the usage the global constellation of GLONASS, satellites of Galileo, and Chinese BeiDou Navigation Satellite System (BDS), was developed, the stable and accuracy of GNSS is improved. In spite of this, the standalone GNSS technique cannot guarantee an accurate and continuous position and velocity in all land vehicle-driving environment. Therefore, to overcome this problem, the GNSS should be aided by additional sensors, inertial measurement unit (IMU), vehicle motion sensors, camera, or radar [1].

Due to the complementary natures of inertial navigation system (INS) and GNSS, the GNSS/INS integrated systems were developed to improve the accuracy and reliability of navigation solutions for positioning system. The major problems of conventional INSs that used the GNSS/INS integrated systems are their considerable size

© Springer Nature Switzerland AG 2020
C.-H. Hsu et al. (Eds.): IOV 2019, LNCS 11894, pp. 101–108, 2020.
https://doi.org/10.1007/978-3-030-38651-1_10

and price that restrict land vehicle applications [2]. Recently, as a small-sized and low-cost inertial measurement unit (IMU) based on microelectromechanical system (MEMS) technology are produced, many studies have been conducted on the development of positioning technique using GNSS/MEMS based IMU [2–4]. The results of these studies indicated that the fusion of GNSS and MEMS based IMU provides the navigation solutions that partly fulfill the requirement accuracy for land vehicle applications. Therefore, this paper aim to develop and evaluate low-cost MEMS based IMU, magnetometers, and a single-frequency GNSS-RTK based positioning algorithm for the commercialization of land vehicle tracking and monitoring device. A description of the GNSS/IMU/magnetometer integration algorithm is presented in Sect. 2. A performance evaluation of the GNSS/IMU/magnetometer integration algorithm is provided in Sect. 3. The conclusions are presented in Sect. 4.

2   GNSS/IMU/Magnetometer Integration Algorithm

Figure 1 is a block diagram of the GNSS/IMU/magnetometer integration algorithm. The GNSS/IMU/magnetometer integration algorithm is implemented loosely coupled integration through EKF. When the IMU measures both angular rates and specific forces, the navigation solutions including position, velocity, and attitude are computed using the INS mechanization. For more details on INS mechanization, refer to [5]. If the magnetometer measurements are provided simultaneous with the IMU measurements, the attitude and heading reference system (AHRS) algorithm calculates the attitude information (roll, pitch, yaw), and then the AHRS update is carried out. In this paper, the AHRS algorithm is implemented through EKF. For more detailed description of the AHRS, refer to [2, 6]. In addition, if the GNSS module provides the position and velocity information, the GNSS update is conducted.

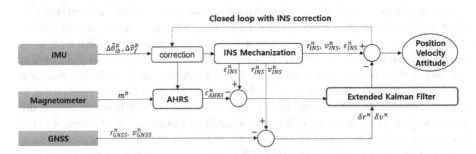

Fig. 1. Block diagram of the GNSS/IMU/magnetometer integration algorithm

In EKF-based GNSS/IMU/magnetometer integration algorithm, the state vector of the navigation error is composed of latitude error ($\delta\varphi$), longitude error ($\delta\lambda$), ellipsoidal height error (δh), north velocity error (δv_n), east velocity error (δv_e), down velocity error (δv_d), roll error ($\delta\phi$), pitch error ($\delta\theta$), and yaw error ($\delta\psi$). The state vector of the sensor error is composed of accelerometers bias ($\delta b_x, \delta b_y, \delta b_z$) and gyro bias

$(\delta d_x, \delta d_y, \delta d_z)$, modelled as first-order Gauss-Markov processes. The dynamic model is written as follows:

$$\delta \dot{x} = F \delta x + G u \qquad (1)$$

where F is the dynamic matrix, δx is the error state vector, G is the shaping matrix, u is the white noise vector. Details about the dynamic matrix, the shaping matrix, and the white noise vector can be found in [5].

The error state vector (δx) is shown in the following Eq. (2):

$$\delta x = [\delta \varphi \quad \delta \lambda \quad \delta h \quad \delta v_n \quad \delta v_e \quad \delta v_d \quad \delta \phi \quad \delta \theta \quad \delta \psi \quad \delta b_x \quad \delta b_y \quad \delta b_z \quad \delta d_x \quad \delta d_y \quad \delta d_z]^T \qquad (2)$$

The measurement model is generally expressed as follows:

$$z = H \delta x + v \qquad (3)$$

where z is the measurement vector, H is the design matrix, δx is the error state vector, v is the measurement noise vector.

In this study, the GNSS measurement vector consist of difference between the positions and the velocities estimated from INS mechanization and GNSS receiver, as shown below.

$$z_{GNSS} = \begin{bmatrix} \varphi \\ \lambda \\ h \\ v_n \\ v_e \\ v_d \end{bmatrix}_{INS} - \begin{bmatrix} \varphi_{GNSS} \\ \lambda_{GNSS} \\ h_{GNSS} \\ C_b^n \begin{bmatrix} V_{GNSS} \\ 0 \\ 0 \end{bmatrix} \end{bmatrix}_{GNSS} \qquad (4)$$

where z_{GNSS} is the GNSS measurement vector, the subscripts INS and GNSS denote the values computed by INS mechanization and the values calculated from the GNSS module, respectively, C_b^n is the direction cosine matrix from the body frame to the navigation frame, V_{GNSS} is the speed over ground provided from the GNSS module.

The design matrix for GNSS measurement model is as follows:

$$H_{GNSS} = \begin{bmatrix} I_{3\times 3} & 0_{3\times 3} & 0_{3\times 3} & 0_{3\times 6} \\ 0_{3\times 3} & -(v_{GNSS}^n \times) & 0_{3\times 3} & 0_{3\times 6} \end{bmatrix} \qquad (5)$$

where H_{GNSS} is the design matrix of GNSS, $I_{3\times 3}$ is 3×3 identity matrix, $O_{n\times m}$ is n x m zero matrix, v_{GNSS}^n is the GNSS derived velocities expressed in the navigation frame.

In addition to AHRS measurement update, the attitude computed by the AHRS algorithm is used as measurement update. The measurement vector and the design matrix for AHRS measurement model are shown in (6) and (7), respectively.

$$z_{AHRS} = \begin{bmatrix} \phi \\ \theta \\ \psi \end{bmatrix}_{INS} - \begin{bmatrix} \phi \\ \theta \\ \psi \end{bmatrix}_{AHRS} \tag{6}$$

$$H_{AHRS} = \begin{bmatrix} 0_{3\times3} & 0_{3\times3} & I_{3\times3} & 0_{3\times6} \end{bmatrix} \tag{7}$$

where z_{AHRS} is the AHRS measurement vector, the subscripts AHRS denote the attitude computed by AHRS algorithm.

3　Performance Evaluation of GNSS/IMU/Magnetometer Integration Algorithm

The test vehicle to test the proposed algorithm is shown in Fig. 2. The test device which evaluates for performing the propose algorithm, consists of motion sensor, and GNSS module. The motion sensor is InvenSense's MPU-9250 devices that combines a 3-axis gyroscope, a 3-axis accelerometer, and a 3-axis magnetometer. The total RMS (Root Mean Square) noise for gyroscopes and accelerometers are 0.1 deg/s, 8 mg, respectively. For more details on the specification of the MPU-9250, refer to [7]. The GNSS module used Ublox's NEO-M8P. The NEO-M8P supports single baseline GNSS RTK mode based on concurrent reception of GPS L1 C/A and GLONASS L1OF, or BeiDou B1 signal. The position accuracy of RTK mode is 0.025 m + 1 ppm. For more details on the specification of the NEO-M8P, refer to [8]. The GNSS antenna for GNSS module used a single-frequency GNSS antenna created by AKTGEO. In order to evaluate the performance of the proposed algorithm, Applanix's POS LV 520 was mounted on the test vehicle. The precision of horizontal position and yaw based on post-mission using the inertial, the GNSS, and DMI data obtained from POS LV 520 are 0.02 m and 0.015 deg, respectively [9].

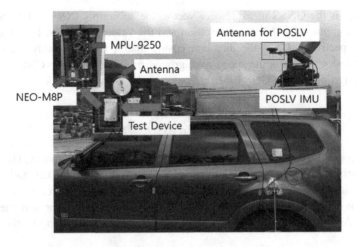

Fig. 2. Test vehicle

The data were collected on a trajectory inside DGIST (Daegu Gyeongbuk Institute of Science & Technology). The trajectory was a road, which covered speed bumps, street trees, buildings and a sloping road. The output rate of the proposed algorithm was set to 92 Hz that was equal to the output rate of the motion sensor data. The AHRS measurement update rate was set to 92 Hz. The GNSS positioning mode set to single baseline GNSS RTK based on concurrent reception of GPS and BeiDou. The GNSS measurement update was rate set to 2 Hz.

Figure 3 shows vehicle locations based on the output of the proposed algorithm (red line) with the output of POSLV 520 (blue line) for the trajectory. In addition, the position error of the proposed algorithm in the navigation frame with respect to the output of POS LV 520 is shown in in Fig. 4. The RMS of error in the north, east, and down position were 0.359 m, 0.607 m, and 0.122 m.

Fig. 3. Horizontal position (red line: proposed algorithm, blue line: POS LV 520) (Color figure online)

The velocity and the attitude error compared with POS LV 520 as reference are shown in Figs. 5 and 6, respectively. Since the position is obtained from velocity integration, the change of velocity error is similar to the position error. The RMS of error in the north, east, and down velocity were 0.245 m/s, 0.329 m/s, and 0.131 m/s, respectively. Finally, the RMS of error in attitude (roll, pitch, and yaw) are 4.0 deg, 2.5 deg, and 24.79 deg.

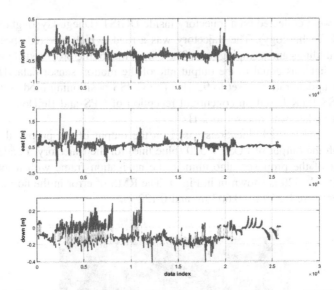

Fig. 4. The position error of the proposed algorithm with respect to POS LV 520

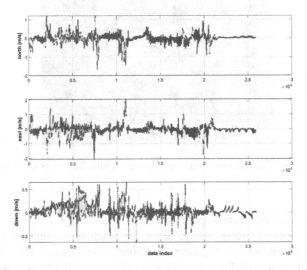

Fig. 5. The velocity error of the proposed algorithm with respect to POS LV 520

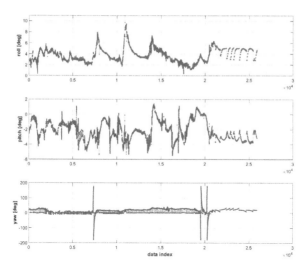

Fig. 6. The attitude error of the proposed algorithm with respect to POS LV 520

4   Conclusions

In this paper, a low cost GNSS and IMU, magnetometers integrated vehicle position algorithm was developed for the commercialization of land vehicle tracking and monitoring device. IMU data were applied for INS mechanization to compute the navigation solutions. The measurement update in the proposed algorithm consists the AHRS update and the GNSS update. In the AHRS update, the attitude computed by the AHRS algorithm is used as measurement update at every epoch. In the GNSS update, the position and speed calculated from the GNSS module is used as measurement update at an interval of 0.5 s. The proposed algorithm is implemented loosely coupled integration through EKF.

Performance was evaluated through test carried out in real road, which covered speed bumps, street trees, buildings and a sloping road. The result indicates that the proposed algorithm might provide positions within 1 meter-level accuracy. However, the error in some sections were higher than 1 m. In order to improve the proposed algorithm, we will conduct the additional performance analysis, filter tuning, and addition sensors integration.

Acknowledgements. This work was supported by the Technology development Program (S2684640) funded by the Ministry of SMEs and Startups (MSS, Korea).

References

1. Jo, K., Chu, K., Sunwoo, M.: Interacting multiple model filter-based sensor fusion of GPS with in-vehicle sensors for real-time vehicle positioning. IEEE Trans. Intell. Transp. Syst. **13**, 329–343 (2012)
2. Sasani, S., Asgari, J., Amiri-Simkooei, A.R.: Improving MEMS-IMU/GPS integrated system for land vehicle navigation application. GPS Solut. **20**, 89–100 (2016)

3. Quinchia, A.G., Falco, G., Falletti, E., Dovis, F., Ferrer, C.: A comparison between different error modeling of MEMS applied to GPS/INS integrated systems. Sensors **13**, 9549–9588 (2013)
4. Godha, S., Cannon, M.E.: GPS/MEMS INS integrated system for navigation in urban areas. GPS Solut. **11**, 193–203 (2007)
5. Shin, E.: Accuracy improvement of low cost INS/GPS for land application. University of Calgary (2001)
6. Wang, Y., Li, N., Chen, X., Liu, M.: Design and implementation of an AHRS based on MEMS sensors and complementary filtering. Adv. Mech. Eng. **214726**, 1–11 (2014)
7. Invensense. https://www.invensense.com/wp-content/uploads/2015/02/PS-MPU-9250A-01-v1.1.pdf. Accessed 26 Aug 2019
8. Ublox. https://www.u-blox.com/sites/default/files/NEO-M8P_ProductSummary_%28UBX-15015836%29.pdf. Accessed 26 Aug 2019
9. Applanix. https://www.applanix.com/downloads/products/specs/POS_LV_Datasheet.pdf. Accessed 26 Aug 2019

Multi-class Vehicle Detection Using Multi-scale Hard Negative Mining

Minsung Kang and Young-Chul Lim$^{(\boxtimes)}$

Research Division of Future Automotive Technology,
Daegu Gyeongbuk Institute of Science and Technology, Daegu, Korea
{mskang,ninolyc}@dgist.com

Abstract. The performance capabilities of object detection processes have been greatly improved due to the development of deep learning methods. As the performance of object detection methods improves, studies of problems that remained unsolved are now becoming more common. In CCTV technology, such as tracking technology, it has become easier to resolve the matching issue as the performance of object detection methods has improved. A network such as YOLOv3, a single stage multi scale based object detection method, robustly detects objects of various sizes while maintaining real-time performance. Object detection methods for multi scale structures are associated with the problem of an imbalance between a positive box and a negative box on each feature scale. In the CCTV environment, the object detection performance can be degraded due to this 'unbalance' problem because the number of objects corresponding to the positive box is relatively small. The learning time is also important because re-training is required for new environments that are constantly being added. In order to solve this problem, we propose a method that solves the unbalance problem through multi scale hard negative mining and that improves the object detection performance while also reducing the learning time.

Keywords: Object detection · Deep learning · Hard negative mining

1 Introduction

In the conventional computer vision process, the autonomous vehicle field uses optical flow [1] methods using the characteristics of the surrounding environment, and the CCTV field uses background subtraction [2] methods because the surrounding environment is fixed. Due to the development of deep learning, the boundaries between the core technologies used in each application area are disappearing. Recently, it has become possible to apply these advances to various fields, such as CCTV, autonomous vehicles, and robotics, using a single deep learning based object detection method [3]. As the boundaries between core technologies disappear, the performance capabilities of object detection methods have been greatly improved and technologies capable of detecting robust objects in various environments have been studied. There are deep learning based object detection approaches such as Region based Fully Convolutional Networks (R-FCN) [4], You Only Look Once (YOLOv2) [5] and the Single Shot Multibox Detector [6]. These two stage [3, 4] or single stage [5, 6, 8] deep learning

© Springer Nature Switzerland AG 2020
C.-H. Hsu et al. (Eds.): IOV 2019, LNCS 11894, pp. 109–116, 2020.
https://doi.org/10.1007/978-3-030-38651-1_11

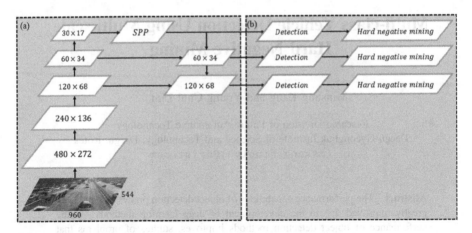

Fig. 1. The network structure of the proposed method. (a) YOLOv3 SPP, (b) detection layer and hard negative mining.

schemes show good detection performance capabilities given a considerable amount of training data for each application.

Recently, tracking, re-identification and object counting methods have been actively studied due to the improvements in object detection methods in the CCTV field [7]. A tracking method connects the same objects in successive frames using data association methods based on the object detection results. Therefore, the performance of the tracking method improves when the performance of the object detection method is improved. Hence, this tracking method can be used in various applications related to CCTV security. Detection performance is also important in the CCTV field, but short object detection times are required because a large amount of data is continuously acquired. It is also important for learning to be completed quickly because new learning environments must be re-trained.

Methods such as YOLOv3 [8], which is based on single stage multi scale features that improve the object detection performance while maintaining real-time performance, are being studied. Because this approach involves a simple structure with a single stage, it has a rapid inference speed and uses a multi scale feature map to detect objects of various sizes robustly. However, the learning speed is slow because there are many boxes to be calculated in the detection layer for each scale. In this paper, we propose a method to improve the object detection performance and improve the learning speed and efficiency through multi scale hard negative mining. The composition of this paper is as follows. In Sect. 2, we introduce several studies related to single stage multi scale features. In Sect. 3, we introduce a method for efficient learning through hard negative mining in the proposed multi scale structure. In Sect. 4, we evaluate the proposed method using the DETRAC dataset. Section 5 presents the conclusion.

Fig. 2. Data argumentation. (a) original image, (b) random distortion, (c) random scale, (d) random scale + jitter, (e) flip, (f) transformed image.

2   Related Works

Deep learning based object detection methods are available in various forms, such as the two stage [3, 4], single stage [5, 6, 8], and multi scale types [6, 8], and each method involves a tradeoff between the detection performance and the inference speed. Traditional two stage R-FCN methods focus on detection performance. They create a detection box in the first stage and perform box regression and classification in the second stage. Although the detection performance is high, the learning method for each stage is relatively difficult, and the learning time and the test time are slow. There are single stage methods such as YOLOv2 and SSD that utilize a simple network with fast learning and testing times. In the YOLO method, box regression and classification are performed on the last feature map after the backbone network. Although the detection performance is relatively low due to the simple network, these methods are widely used in applications requiring real-time performance. However, given that the YOLO method uses a single stage single feature map, it is difficult to detect all objects of various sizes.

Among single stage methods, one SSD method improves the detection performance for various object sizes due to its use of a multi scale structure. Detection is performed on feature maps of various scales, from low-level feature maps to high-level feature maps, and the final result is combined with a NMS method. However, the SSD method has a disadvantage in that there are false positives in the detection layer because the low-level feature map passes through only a few convolutional layers. To solve this

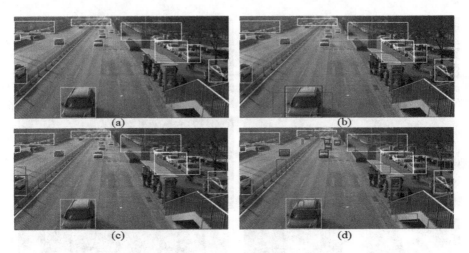

Fig. 3. Hard negative mining and ignore regions. White boxes: ignore regions, green boxes: GT, blue boxes: positive, red boxes: negative, purple boxes: negative box not updated, (a) GT image, (b) positive and negative boxes update in 30 × 17 scale, (c) 60 × 34 scale, (d) 120 × 68 scale. (Color figure online)

problem, methods such as feature pyramid networks (FPN) [9] have been proposed. These methods concatenate a low-level feature map and a high-level feature map to extract a rich feature map for use in the detection layer. In this paper, we propose a multi scale hard negative mining technique to improve the detection performance on the existing YOLOv3 SPP network.

3   Object Detection

In this paper, we propose an object detection method based on multi scale hard negative mining. The proposed method adds a SPP to the YOLOv3 network, as shown in Fig. 1. In the existing YOLOv3 method, feature maps corresponding to three scales are extracted from the network of the FPN structure and then box regression, logistic activation of the object-ness and softmax for each class are performed on each scale [8]. The existing method calculates errors and performs backpropagation on all negatives of each scale when learning. This leads to the 'unbalance' problem between the positive and negative boxes, and due to the different positives on each scale, it is learned as an error duplication of the negative type. In this paper, we propose an efficient learning method for each scale which works through a hard negative mining method.

3.1   Data Argumentation

In a fixed CCTV environment, there are not many changes of the background, implying that a data argumentation method that changes the image in order to obtain various negatives is needed. As shown in Fig. 2(c), the image size is changed by applying a random scale that resizes the image between 0.5 and 2 times. The aspect ratio of the

Fig. 4. Multi-class vehicle detection result in DETRAC validation dataset.

object is changed by applying jitter to the image, as shown in Fig. 2(d). As shown in Fig. 2(b), random distortion was applied to change the color, brightness, and other attributes. Finally, we performed a flip with a 50% probability, as shown in Fig. 2(e).

3.2   Hard Negative Mining

In order to learn positive and negative boxes effectively on the feature map of each scale, the positive-to-negative ratio was set to 1:N. As shown in Fig. 3, small boxes are detected on a scale with a large feature map, and large boxes are detected on a small scale. On each scale, the anchor box with the best match with the GT (ground truth) box was set as a positive box (blue boxes in Fig. 3(b)). After positive determination, the negatives were sorted in order of their scores, and the hard negatives with high scores were extracted N times as positive (red boxes in Fig. 3(c)).

3.3   Training Method for Ignore Regions

In the CCTV environment, "ignore regions" such as those denoted by the white square boxes in the DETRAC [10] dataset, are needed, as shown in Fig. 3(a). In a fixed camera environment, there are unnecessary areas, such as a parking lot and a guide, during attempts to detect moving objects in close proximity. In general, a deep learning based object detection method is learned as a negative, except for the box provided by the GT in the image. In general, as the GT image is needed in hundreds of thousands of images during the learning process, the unnecessary area can be designated as ignore regions to improve the efficiency of the labeling operation. In this paper, the hard negatives are not learned when overlapping ignore regions with more than a certain area (purple boxes in Fig. 3(c, d). Because there are real objects among the purple boxes in Fig. 3, but there is no GT, updating it to negative causes the object detection performance to deteriorate. Therefore, as a condition for determining the negative, a hard negative which does not overlap with the ignore regions among the high-score negatives was determined and learning was performed N times as positive.

4   Experimental Results

In this paper, the DETRAC dataset is used to evaluate the proposed method. The dataset consists of ten hours of video captured with a Canon EOS 550D camera at 24 different locations at Beijing and Tianjin in China [10]. The images were 960×540 in size and consisted in total of 83,791 labeled images. Of these, 51,721 were used for training and 32,070 were used for the evaluation. There are seven classes of GT that provide in this case Sedan, SUV, VAN, Taxi, Bus, Truck and ignore regions. We assigned positive to six objects and ignore regions to exclude negatives that overlap the region.

The proposed network generates a pre-trained model using the COCO dataset [11], learns it with the DETRAC train images, and then evaluates it with validation images. Data argumentation used the random scale, jitter, random distortion and flip processes. Based on the Darknet framework [5], we set the batch number to 64 and the subdivision number to 32 and learned with four NVIDIA TITAN XP graphics cards. The learning rate was set to 10^{-3}, gradually decreased in steps, and learning proceeded for 100 epochs. The number of default anchor boxes was set to 9, and the aspect ratio of the box was determined through clustering.

Table 1. Comparison of different results in DETRAC validataion dataset. IR: ignore regions, MSHN: multi-scale hard negative mining.

Method	IR	MSHN	mAP
Method 1	X	X	50.58%
Method 2	O	X	80.04%
Method 3 (Proposed)	O	O	93.63%

Table 1 shows the results of learning each method with DETRAC train dataset and evaluating it in validation. Method 1 is the result of not applying ignore regions (IR) and multi-scale hard negative mining (MSHN) methods in existing YOLOv3 SPP networks. As shown in Fig. 5, the performance decreases because the positive objects corresponding to the IR region are updated to negative. Method 2 did not update the IR as positive or negative as shown in Fig. 6. However, because the number of negatives is much higher than the number of positives, the precision is 0 in the recall 0.9–1.0 range as shown in Fig. 7. The proposed method 3 is the result of applying both IR and MSHN. As shown in Fig. 6, the detection performance is improved because exception handling for IR area and imbalance problem of positive and negative are solved. The proposed method detects multiclasses of various sizes and improves learning time by 20% as shown in Fig. 4.

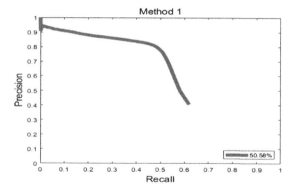

Fig. 5. Method 1 YOLOv3 SPP without IR and MSHN.

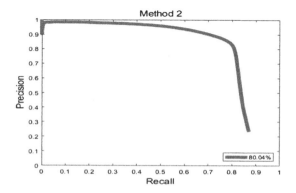

Fig. 6. Method 2, YOLOv3 SPP width IR.

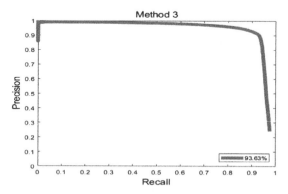

Fig. 7. Method 3, YOLOv3 SPP with IR and MSHN.

5 Conclusions

In this paper, we propose a multi-class vehicle detection using multi-scale hard negative mining. The FPN structure of the YOLOv3 SPP method is used to extract various types of features by fusing a low-level feature map and a high-level feature map. The unbalance problem of positive boxes and negative boxes was solved through hard negative mining on each scale of the feature map. GT labeling can be done effectively using ignore regions as with the DETRAC dataset. The proposed method can be trained on datasets with ignore regions without decreasing detection performance.

Acknowledgment. This work was supported by the DGIST R&D Program of the Ministry of Science, ICT. It was also funded by Daegu Metropolitan City and Daegu TechnoPark (Project name: Research institute cooperation convergence R & D project. 2019).

References

1. Horn, B.K.P., Schunck, B.G.: Determining optical flow. Artif. Intell. **17**(1–203), 185–203 (1981)
2. Elgammal, A., Harwood, D., Davis, L.: Non-parametric model for background subtraction. In: Vernon, D. (ed.) ECCV 2000. LNCS, vol. 1843, pp. 751–767. Springer, Heidelberg (2000). https://doi.org/10.1007/3-540-45053-X_48
3. He, K., et al.: Mask R-CNN. In: Proceedings of the IEEE International Conference on Computer Vision (2017)
4. Dai, J., et al.: R-FCN: Object detection via region-based fully convolutional networks. In: Advances in Neural Information Processing Systems (2016)
5. Redmon, J., Farhadi, A.: YOLO9000: better, faster, stronger. In: Proceedings of the IEEE Conference on Computer Vision and Pattern Recognition (2017)
6. Liu, W., et al.: SSD: single shot multibox detector. In: Leibe, B., Matas, J., Sebe, N., Welling, M. (eds.) ECCV 2016. LNCS, vol. 9905, pp. 21–37. Springer, Cham (2016). https://doi.org/10.1007/978-3-319-46448-0_2
7. Ristani, E., Tomasi, C.: Features for multi-target multi-camera tracking and re-identification. In: Proceedings of the IEEE Conference on Computer Vision and Pattern Recognition (2018)
8. Redmon, J., Farhadi, A.: Yolov3: an incremental improvement. arXiv preprint arXiv:1804. 02767 (2018)
9. Lin, TY., et al.: Feature pyramid networks for object detection. In: Proceedings of the IEEE Conference on Computer Vision and Pattern Recognition (2017)
10. Wen, L., et al.: UA-DETRAC: a new benchmark and protocol for multi-object detection and tracking. arXiv preprint arXiv:1511.04136 (2015)
11. Lin, T.Y. et al.: Microsoft COCO: common objects in context. In: Fleet, D., Pajdla, T., Schiele, B., Tuytelaars, T. (eds.) Computer Vision – ECCV 2014. ECCV 2014. LNCS, vol 8693, pp. 740–755. Springer, Cham (2014). https://doi.org/10.1007/978-3-319-10602-1_48

Predicting Steering for Autonomous Vehicles Based on Crowd Sensing and Deep Learning

Taiyu Liu, Jinglin Li$^{(\boxtimes)}$, and Quan Yuan

State Key Laboratory of Networking and Switching Technology,
Beijing University of Posts and Telecommunications, Beijing, China
{lty2008,jlli,yuanquan}@bupt.edu.cn

Abstract. The challenge in ensuring the reliability of autonomous vehicles is full awareness of the surrounding environment and high-precision steering control. The latest solutions to this challenge include deep learning technologies that provide end-to-end solutions to predict steering angles directly from environmental cognition information with high accuracy. Under the background of 5G technology, edge device has certain computing power, which can reduce the load of on-board computing equipment. In this paper, we present a new distributed perception-decision network model. This model allows the network's computing tasks to be offloaded to the edge computing devices to reduce the consumption of vehicle-mounted computing devices. The feasibility of the model is verified by experiments. Compared with the existing methods, the model also has a higher accuracy of steering prediction.

Keywords: Autonomous vehicles · Deep neural network · End-to-end · Crowd sensing

1 Introduction

Environmental cognition and steering control are two key issues in autonomous vehicles [1,2]. There are many solutions to the self-driving problem.End-to-end autonomous driving using artificial neural network was studied as early as 1989 [3]. With the rise of deep learning, computer vision-based approaches have been developed, and the end-to-end technology from sensor data to vehicle control has came true [4,5]. NVIDIA has trained a deep neural network to control the steering angle directly from images captured by cameras [6]. The advantages of such schemes are high accuracy and low equipment cost. At the same time, End-to-end solutions which has been proved to be effective in previous work can avoid the problem that complex road scenarios cannot be fully

This work was supported in part by the Natural Science Foundation of China under Grant 61876023 and Grant 61902035, and in part by the Natural Science Foundation of Beijing under Grant 4181002.

covered by rules [7]. The scheme is essentially an imitation of the driving data of natural drivers. The richer the training data are, the stronger the robustness of the model will be. In recent years, the development of Vehicle-to-Vehicle (V2V) technology has realized the sharing of perceptual data between vehicles, which has enhanced the vehicle's ability to perceive the global road environment [8], but also increased the computational load of onboard equipments. Mobile edge computing can realize the unloading and processing of computing tasks such as traffic situation cognition and on-board applications to edge servers, providing computing resources needed for autonomous driving service applications [9]. Therefore, we believe that a new network model is needed to offload some network computing tasks to the edge, so as to reduce the computing load of on-board equipment.

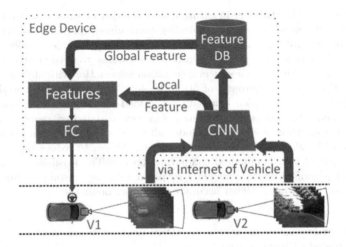

Fig. 1. The overview of our proposed model. Vehicle1 uploaded environmental information to the edge device through Vehicle-to-Everything (V2X), and the edge device extracted environmental features. Vehicle2 combines the environmental features broadcasted by edge with its own information to control steering. The prediction was made through our network (see Fig. 2 for details)

In this paper, we propose an end-to-end steering prediction model based on edge computing and deep learning (see Fig. 1). This model obtains road environment information by on-board camera, extracts road environment features by edge computing and deep neural network, and broadcasts global road environment features to autonomous vehicles in the current region. The autonomous vehicle processes the received road environment features to obtain vehicle steering control [10]. The disadvantage of the end-to-end network model is that the model is often black box, poor interpretation [11]. The network structure proposed in most researches is tightly coupled internally. We enhances the interpretability of the model structure by modularizing the model internally. The proposed model is verified on the data set of Udacity and compared with existing experiments. Our experimental results show that the distributed network model based on deep learning is feasible and has good accuracy. Our main contributions are: (1) We propose an end-to-end vehicle steering control system which adapts to edge computing scenarios; (2) We propose a loosely coupled network model that enables the computation of network models to be physically separated; (3) We verify the feasibility of the model on Udacity dataset [12].

The rest of the paper will be organized as follows: In Sect. 2, we explain the proposed approach, and provides details about the performed experiments in Sect. 3. Finally, we conclude the paper and discuss possible directions for future work in Sect. 4.

2   Proposed Approach

In essence, the goal of the problem is to construct a mapping relationship from multi-source image information to vehicle steering Angle. This problem consists of two sub-problems: one is feature extraction and fusion of multi-source image information. The second is the mapping of fusion feature to vehicle steering Angle. Formalization can be described as the following formula 1. Where E_r represents the set of current road information, R represents the vehicles in the current area, and F represents the mapping of road information features to vehicle control. Where S represents the set of steering angles.

$$F : \left\{ \sum_R E_r \right\} \to \{S\} \tag{1}$$

For feature extraction of multi-source image information, we consider using single image sequence collected by vehicle camera. The image sequence contains the road environment information of the current driving direction of the vehicle. We used Convolutional Neural Network (CNN) to extract the road feature information in the image [13]. At the edge, we collect image data of vehicles to train CNN and store the location, time and current road characteristics of each vehicle. The vehicle directly uses the CNN model trained by the edge to extract the local road features and obtain the road feature information from the edge. Figure 1 shows this process. The mapping of eigenvalue to vehicle steering angles is essentially a regression problem. Theoretically, a neural network can fit any mapping. So we fit this mapping by training Fully-Connected Networks (FCN).

In this paper, we assume that the road conditions ahead have been seen by vehicles ahead. We use edge equipment to request environmental information obtained by vehicles ahead and assist steering control. Figure 1 also illustrates our method. The proposed model is logically composed of two modules: environmental awareness module and fusion decision module. The environmental awareness module mainly uses images collected by vehicle sensors, such as monocular camera, and images collected by road edge equipment through the Internet of vehicles, such as images uploaded by other vehicles within the current network

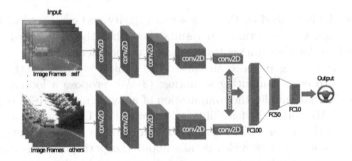

Fig. 2. CNN + FCN distributed model. Our model uses 5 convolutional layers, followed by 5 FC layers. See Table 1 for further details of our proposed architecture.

Table 1. Details of proposed architecture. The activation function that we use is Rectified Linear Unit (ReLU) and Linear function.

Layer	Type	Size	Stride	Activation
0	Input	66*200*3*2	-	-
1	Conv2D	5*5, 24Filters	(2*2)	ReLU
2	Conv2D	5*5, 36Filters	(2*2)	ReLU
3	Conv2D	5*5, 48Filters	(2*2)	ReLU
4	Conv2D	3*3, 64Filters	(1*1)	ReLU
5	Conv2D	3*3, 64Filters	(1*1)	ReLU
6	Conc	1152*2	-	-
7	FC	100	-	ReLU
8	FC	50	-	ReLU
9	FC	10	-	ReLU
10	FC	1	-	Linear

coverage, to perceive the current road environment. The fusion decision module integrates the local environmental perception information with the global perception information. The model uses convolutional neural network to extract image features and Fully-Connected Network to realize steering control.

The proposed network structure is presented as Fig. 2 shows. The network takes the images of the two cars as input, and the last layer predicts the steering angle as the network output. The details of our network are shown in the Table 1. The two images are respectively input into two CNNs (parameter sharing), and then we will process the extracted deep features, and then output the steering angle through full-connected network. Since we define the problem of steering Angle output as the problem of value regression, we use the Mean Squared Error (MSE) loss function in our network during the training.

3   Performance Evaluation

3.1   Experiment Setup

In this part, we mainly describe the data set, data preprocessing and evaluation indicators, and then introduce the experimental variable. At last, we introduce the experimental environment.

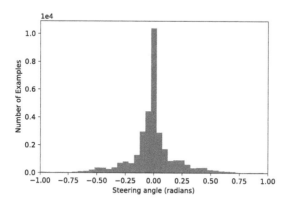

Fig. 3. The angle distribution within the training data (angle in radians), just angles between −1 and 1 radians are shown.

Dataset. We used an autonomous data set from Udacity. The data set includes images taken on both sunny and cloudy days, steering wheel angles, acceleration, braking, GPS and other datas. Furthermore, it contains image data of five different journeys, and the total collection time is 1694 s. The data are collected at a speed of nearly 20 HZ, the 480 * 640 * 3 pixels size of image. The total dataset is 3.63 GB. The distribution of steering wheel Angle on the whole dataset is shown in the Fig. 3. As shown in the figure, the dataset distribution contains a large range of steering angles, and the overall distribution is similar to the normal distribution. Since there is no data collected from the front and rear vehicles at the same time, we simulated the environment by creating a virtual vehicle ahead of another autonomous vehicle, and shared image data with the dataset.

Data Preprocessing. As there is a large overlap between continuous frames of the image data, we use image enhancement to increase the variance of the dataset in order to avoid network training overfitting. Our image enhancement technology randomly increases brightness and contrast to simulate different light intensity, and randomly adds gaussian noise to simulate signal instability and device jitter at the same time. We also tested image cropping to eliminate redundant information of sky in the image. We then trained and validated our model with 80% images and 20% images as the test set.

Evaluation Metrics. The output value of the model is the steering angle, which is a continuous variable. Mean Absolute Error (MAE) and Root Mean Square Error (RMSE) are two commonly used indicators, which are often used in literature to measure the effectiveness of control system. These two values reflect the mean error of predicted value, and as it turned out that the lower the value, the better the effect.

Experimental Variable. 5G networks can ensure highly reliable and low-latency data sharing between vehicles. This communication network can ensure the communication between the vehicle and the edge to ensure the safety and reliability of vehicle control. So we assume that the distance between the two cars is δt seconds. We take the X_t frame from the autonomous vehicle at time step T and the $X_{T+\delta t}$ frame from another vehicle at time step $(T+\delta t)$. A single input across the network contains two frames of images. In the experiment, we set different δt values to represent the influence of different distances on the decision-making of vehicles.

Implementation. We implemented it using Keras with TensorFlow back-end [14]. Finally, two GPUs (Type: NVIDIA TITAN-XP 12 GB) are used to train the model.During the experiment, we used Adam optimizer [15]. Different learning rates were tested, and the influence of setting minibatch size on the network was studied too.

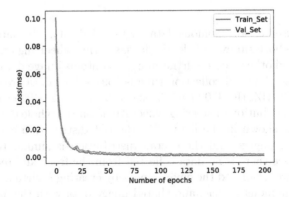

Fig. 4. Training and Validation steps with 200 epochs

3.2   Experiment Results

The training process is shown in Fig. 4. The network has a total of 200 rounds of training, and the loss function decreases rapidly at the beginning and tends

Table 2. Comparison to different δt(s) in terms of MAE

δt(s)	1	1.3	1.4	1.5	1.8	2	3
MAE($*10^{-2}$)	4.039	3.731	**3.442**	3.881	4.188	5.038	5.071

to be stable after 50 rounds of iteration. This shows that our model is feasible and can converge quickly.

The model we trained after changing the value of δt(s) is shown in the Table 2, and we can find that there is an optimal value in the model. One possible explanation is that when vehicles are too close to each other, the fusion information has redundancy, which leads to poor prediction effect; when vehicles are too far away from each other, the correlation between the fusion information is too small to assist the vehicle optimization decision. Meanwhile, we tested NVIDIA's model and got the MAE value of $4.124*10^{-2}$. Our model performed better. Our model showed good performance. We also tested the network on the test set, and the predicted results are shown in the Fig. 5. We found that the predicted value can basically correspond to the change of the actual value. However, the predicted value of the network in sharp corners is poor, because most of the training data are of small angle, and few of the data of large steering angle.

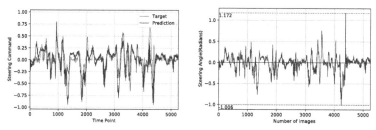

(a) Target and prediction result of steering command.

(b) The deviation between the predicted value and the actual value.

Fig. 5. The predictive performance of the model on the test dataset

4   Conclusion

In order to reduce the computational load of self-driving cars, a distributed steering angle control method based on edge computing is proposed in this paper. We proposed an End-to-End network model, which is a loosely coupled depth model using the CNN and FC layers. Experimental results show the feasibility of the network model. What's more, the experiment in this paper just relies on simulated data, and only verifies the feasibility of the model. Taking everything into consideration, more real experimental environment and data are needed in the future.

References

1. Li, J., Liu, Z., Yang, F.: Internet of vehicles: the framework and key technology. J. Beijing Univ. Posts Telecommun. **37**(6), 95–100 (2014)
2. Zhao, J., Liang, B., Chen, Q.: The key technology toward the self-driving car. Int. J. Intell. Unmanned Syst. **6**(1), 2–20 (2018)
3. Pomerleau, D.A.: ALVINN: an autonomous land vehicle in a neural network. In: Advances in Neural Information Processing Systems, pp. 305–313 (1989)
4. Thrun, S., et al.: Stanley: the robot that won the DARPA grand challenge. J. Field Robot. **23**(9), 661–692 (2006)
5. Rausch, V., Hansen, A., Solowjow, E., Liu, C., Kreuzer, E., Hedrick, J.K.: Learning a deep neural net policy for end-to-end control of autonomous vehicles. In: 2017 American Control Conference (ACC), pp. 4914–4919. IEEE (2017)
6. Bojarski, M., et al.: End to end learning for self-driving cars. arXiv preprint arXiv:1604.07316 (2016)
7. Xu, H., Gao, Y., Yu, F., Darrell, T.: End-to-end learning of driving models from large-scale video datasets. In: Proceedings of the IEEE Conference on Computer Vision and Pattern Recognition, pp. 2174–2182 (2017)
8. Wang, L., Iida, R.F., Wyglinski, A.M.: Coordinated lane changing using V2V communications. In: 2018 IEEE 88th Vehicular Technology Conference (VTC-Fall), pp. 1–5. IEEE (2018)
9. Cheng, X., Chen, C., Zhang, W., Yang, Y.: 5G-enabled cooperative intelligent vehicular (5GenCIV) framework: when Benz meets Marconi. IEEE Intell. Syst. **32**(3), 53–59 (2017)
10. Sobh, I., et al.: End-to-end multi-modal sensors fusion system for urban automated driving. In: NIPS Workshop on Machine Learning for Intelligent Transportation Systems (2018)
11. Chen, S., Zhang, S., Shang, J., Chen, B., Zheng, N.: Brain-inspired cognitive model with attention for self-driving cars. IEEE Trans. Cogn. Dev. Syst. **11**(1), 13–25 (2017)
12. Udacity. Udacity dataset (2016). https://github.com/udacity/self-driving-car/tree/master/datasets
13. LeCun, Y., et al.: Backpropagation applied to handwritten zip code recognition. Neural Comput. **1**(4), 541–551 (1989)
14. Chollet, F.: Keras (2015). http://github.com/keras-team/keras
15. Kingma, D.P., Ba, J.: Adam: a method for stochastic optimization. arXiv preprint arXiv:1412.6980 (2014)

uNVMe-TCP: A User Space Approach to Optimizing NVMe over Fabrics TCP Transport

Ziye Yang[1]([⊠]), Qun Wan[1], Gang Cao[1], and Karol Latecki[2]

[1] Intel, Shanghai, China
{ziye.yang,qun.wan,gang.cao}@intel.com
[2] Intel, Gdansk, Poland
karol.latecki@intel.com

Abstract. Recently, NVM Express® has released the new TCP transport specification for NVMe over fabrics (NVMe-oF). And there are two kinds of implementations, i.e., one in kernel space and the other in user space. The implementation in the kernel (e.g., Linux kernel) is feasible, but there are several drawbacks such as performance, flexibility, and stability. In this paper, we would like to introduce uNVMe-TCP, which follows the specification and provides the NVMe/TCP transport in user space with improved performance and usage experience. We choose the optimization in user space since it is very difficult to optimize the whole NVMe I/O stack in kernel space through different kernel modules, and the optimization may affect other applications in user space. The idea of uNVMe-TCP is to optimize the whole NVMe I/O stack on TCP transport, i.e., leveraging the lock-free user space NVMe I/O stack and configurable network I/O stack (both kernel and user space TCP stack can be supported). Currently uNVMe-TCP provides the solution on both target and initiator side, and it can be tested against Linux kernel solution with good interoperability. Besides, some experiments are conducted to demonstrate the performance of uNVMe-TCP. Compared with the kernel solution, uNVMe-TCP shows 15% to 30% latency improvement on average with FIO benchmark. And the per CPU core performance of uNVMe-TCP is promising, i.e., it is 2.2 times of the kernel on average with the increasing number of connections. Furthermore, uNVMe-TCP is also scalable in CPU aspect.

Keywords: User space NVMe over Fabrics TCP transport solution ·
User space NVMe I/O stack · Performance improvement

1 Introduction

Nowadays, NVMe [1] protocol is widely adopted, e.g., more and more PCIe SSDs driven by NVMe protocol are deployed in data centers. And there is a strong demand not only to support accessing NVMe SSDs inside the local host but

© Springer Nature Switzerland AG 2020
C.-H. Hsu et al. (Eds.): IOV 2019, LNCS 11894, pp. 125–142, 2020.
https://doi.org/10.1007/978-3-030-38651-1_13

also the remote accessing. The existing iSCSI [2] protocol cannot meet the high performance requirements while exporting the NVMe SSDs to the remote due to the protocol overhead. To mitigate this issue, NVMe over fabrics [3] protocol (aka. NVMe-oF) is invented to replace iSCSI protocol in order to explore the performance benefit brought from local PCIe SSDs to remote applications.

Currently, many different transports are defined in NVMe-oF specification in order to make NVMe protocol leverage different fabrics. And the first supported is RDMA (Remote Directly Memory Access) transport, which is available both in Linux kernel and SPDK [4,5]. The RDMA transport leverages RNIC (NIC with RDMA capablity) or InfiniBand card which can make the remote clients have similar performance experience as accessing the local NVMe SSDs in different aspects, e.g., latency, IOPS, throughput. However there are several drawbacks to promote RDMA transport, i.e., (1) The RNICs for Ethernet are very expensive, and the existing non-RDMA capable NICs cannot be reused; (2) The RDMA transport solution is limited by the physical distance, which is extremely suitable for the data exchange inside centers but not very useful to provide cloud storage service across data centers; (3) The overall network infrastructure needs to change for adapting RDMA and the existing ones could not be compatible.

To promote NVMe-oF in different usage scenarios especially for TCP based applications, NVMe standard organization (NVMe Express®) defined the TCP based transport and released the TP (technical proposal) 8000 [6] specification in Nov 2018. Before the birth of TCP transport, if users test NVMe-oF on Ethernet via non-RDMA capable NICs, they need to simulate the NIC into a virtual device with RDMA function through SoftRoCE protocol. The current implementation in Linux kernel simulates the RDMA protocol through the corresponding kernel module on top of UDP protocol. However this solution is mostly designed for test purpose only, it cannot be scaled to support real applications of high reliability requirements which can only be achieved by TCP.

Compared with the RDMA transport, the performance of TCP transport is worse since leveraging the TCP protocol brings the higher network delay. So there are lots of concerns from the very beginning of this protocol emergency. However, based on our understanding, the following reasons support the birth of NVMe/TCP transport, i.e.,

- **Backward compatibility for NICs**. If the NVMe-oF is designed to replace iSCSI protocol, it is not sufficient with only RDMA transport. We know that the iSCSI protocol can run on Ethernet with non RDMA capable NICs. Of course, if RDMA feature by the NICs can be supported, iSER protocol [7] can be used to offload data transformation. Without the NVMe/TCP transport, many existing network devices are not available to use when users transit from iSCSI to NVMe-oF protocol. Obviously, the hardware requirements of the NVMe-oF protocol on NICs have obstacles for the protocol transformation from iSCSI to NVMe-oF. For example, the data center upgrade cannot be smoothly performed if the providers do not want to add more funding for the network infrastructure. So we need the NVMe/TCP transport for the backward compatibility.
- **The emergence of NVMe virtualization**. On the premise of NVMe virtualization [8,9] implementation, the NVMe-oF target does not need to attach

a real NVMe device. Conversely, it can provide the initiator with a virtual NVMe controller. In such a scenario, high performance is not the key point and it is very suitable to use the relatively low speed TCP transport.

- **The possible TCP offloading**. Although the NVMe-oF protocol on TCP transport greatly decreases performance, offloading methodology can still be applied by Smart NIC, FPGA etc. Then the potential performance loss can be mitigated. We are looking forward to the offloading standard defined by NVMe/TCP transport in the future, then the acceptance of NVMe/TCP transport will be improved.

With the great efforts from Linux kernel community, the NVMe/TCP transport support is merged in Linux kernel main branch in January 2019. However, the performance of kernel solution is not good as expected. There are several performance degradations in the following aspects despite using TCP protocol, i.e., (1) Long NVMe I/O stack in Linux kernel; (2) I/O resource contention among different kernel threads during the NVMe command execution. And those resource contention can not be fixed due to the legacy shared resource design among CPUs in the whole I/O stack, e.g., locks in the kernel TCP/IP stack, locks in the generic block layer.

To address these issues, we provide uNVMe-TCP, which is a user space based NVMe/TCP transport target and initiator solution relied on the user space NVMe driver which can directly control the NVMe SSDs and even leverage user space TCP stack to accelerate the full data I/O stack (i.e., from network I/O stack on NICs to the NVMe I/O stack on PCIe SSDs). In summary, the following contributions are made in this paper:

- We propose a user based solution to accelerate the NVMe/TCP transport, which can be in either target or initiator side to optimize the related software. And we are the first one to provide such accelerated solution.
- We present the detailed mechanism of uNVMe-TCP and state why uNVMe-TCP can improve the performance on NVMe/TCP transport. Moreover, our uNVMe-TCP target can use restricted CPU resource to still provide expected NVMe-oF service. For example, we can leverage the CPU resource restriction API (e.g., CPU affinity setting related API in Linux to bind dedicated CPU cores) while still satisfy the I/O performance requirements. Thus, the CPU resource can be saved, which has great benefit in hyper converged infrastructure, e.g., the saved CPU resources for I/O can be used to sell more Virtual machines.
- We conduct detailed experiments and compare the performance of uNVMe-TCP with the Linux kernel based solution by various workloads and demonstrate that uNVMe-TCP is better in both IOPS and latency,e.g., 15% to 30% performance improvement on average in latency aspects, and 2.2 times of the kernel on average for per CPU core IOPS with the increasing number of connections.

The remainder of this paper is organized as follows. Section 2 presents the design of uNVMe-TCP. Section 3 describes the detailed implementation of uNVMe-TCP. Section 4 provides the performance evaluation on uNVMe-TCP and existing Linux kernel solution. Section 5 discusses some related works. Finally, we conclude this paper in Sect. 6.

2 System Design

We present the detailed design of uNVMe-TCP in this section to address the following questions: (1) Why we need the user space NVMe/TCP transport solution; (2) The architecture to design the high performance TCP transport.

2.1 Why User Space NVMe/TCP Solution

Linux kernel implements NVMe TCP transport for both target and host sides in Jan 2019. The solution provided by kernel can absolutely satisfy users' basic requirements but there are still issues such as stability, reliability, performance and etc. In this paper, we would like address the performance issue.

Generally, the data working flow for read and write in NVMe-oF target based on TCP transport can be described as, i.e., (1) NVMe read command: Data is read from the NVMe SSD through the firmware and corresponding kernel NVMe driver, then the data is loaded into the kernel buffer, after that the data is encapsulated according to NVMe/TCP PDU format and written out by network driver through NICs; (2) NVMe write command: Data comes from network and is handled by network driver and put in the kernel buffer through NVMe/TCP protocol, then it is written to the NVMe SSD through kernel NVMe driver and firmware. From the description, the whole I/O stack of NVMe/TCP request handling can be divided into network (handled by network driver) and storage I/O stack (handled by NVMe driver with general block layer). With the emergence of more and more fast NICs (e.g., from 10 to 100, 200 and even 400 Gbs) and NVMe SSDs (e.g., with continuous improved IOPS, latency and throughput), neither the network nor the NVMe storage I/O stack in kernel can fully explore the hardware capabilities. And the main reasons for the performance downgrade are:

- **Resource contention among threads (CPU cores)**. There are many different locks existing in the data I/O path, which are used to handle the resource contention (e.g., memory) among different CPU cores or threads. And the locks in the data path greatly influences the performance
- **Inefficiency of Interrupt**. Currently, the interrupt policy in kernel is not efficient for frequent small I/Os (e.g., 4 KB read/write on the NVMe SSDs). And the polled mode can be much better [10], which is proved to be really useful in DPDK [11] and SPDK [4,5].
- **I/O stack optimization challenge**. The I/O stack in kernel is designed for general purpose in order to adapt all kinds of workloads. If it is optimized for specific pattern workloads, other pattern workloads can be influenced.

2.2   Architecture of uNVMe-TCP

We design uNVMe-TCP to accelerate the NVMe/TCP transport service in user space, and the design is aimed to achieve the following purposes: (1) To avoid resource contention in handling each TCP connection based I/O qpair (queue pair), a polling group is created in each thread to handle all the connections belonging to its group. Thus there are no contentions among different threads to handle the qpair; (2) We provide encapsulated socket API, which is used to reserve the possibility to leverage user space TCP/IP stack instead of only using POSIX socket API; (3) We use polled mode instead of interrupt mode to drive the NVMe SSDs. In order to achieve this, we leverage user space NVMe driver in SPDK [4,5] to directly access the hardware through MMIO (memory mapped IO) exported by VFIO/UIO driver in the kernel.

We select the target side to illustrate the design of uNVMe-TCP since it is typical and can cover most of the design on the initiator side. As shown in Fig. 1, the target side in uNVMe-TCP has several key components, i.e., TCP transport module, thread management and user space NVMe I/O stack.

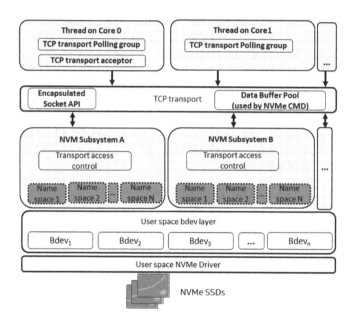

Fig. 1. Architecture of uNVMe-TCP target

TCP Transport Module. The TCP transport is mainly designed to manage the **portals** and **data buffer pool**.

– **Portal.** A portal is defined as the pair <IP address, port>. Each NVMe subsystem can listen on some several different portals and each portal can be shared by different subsystems. All portals are uniformly managed by the TCP transport through some data structures, e.g., linked list. Also, each portal has a reference count which counts how many subsystems share this portal. For example, if portal <127.0.0.1, 4420> is used by 3 subsystems, the reference count is 3. Only all the 3 subsystems are destroyed will this portal be removed from the transport.

- **Data Buffer Pool**. This pool is used to manage the data buffer used by NVMe/TCP commands on the target side. For each NVMe read/write command contained in the NVMe/TCP PDU (packet data unit) which comes from the remote, data buffer(s) will be bound to the command from the shared pool after the command is successfully parsed. The reason that we use the shared buffer pool is to control the memory footprint. Otherwise, if we manage the shared buffer pool according to the queue depth (aka. QD) of each connection, then the memory size will linearly grow as the number of connection grows. In our design, the data buffer pool is shared by the TCP polling group on each CPU core. Absolutely, the data buffer pool sharing among polling group causes the resource contention. To mitigate this issue, we adopt the following strategies, i.e., each polling group reserves several data buffers from the pool as buffer cache according to a pre-configured value when the polling group is created, and this can greatly avoid the contention among polling groups. Thus we can still use the data shared buffer methodology to control the total memory footprint and sustain the performance design purpose.
- **Encapsulated Socket API**. In uNVMe-TCP , we provide a socket API encapsulation, which can leverage both kernel TCP/IP stack API (i.e., posix) and other user space API (e.g., VPP [12] provided by fd.io project). For example, we have a prefix named "spdk_sock". For example, if we use "listen", it should be "spdk_sock_listen".

Thread Management. The uNVMe-TCP design target is forced to start up with fixed number of CPU cores configured by users. On each CPU core, there is one thread running with the affinity feature, thus we can make sure that this thread is running on the dedicated CPU core. And we leverage the thread management API in SPDK [4,5] library.

In each thread, we run a fixed function (called **reactor**) which is mainly composed of an endless loop, and the pseudo code is shown in Fig. 2. This function always runs until the application is stopped. In this loop, the reactor executes the function pointers maintained by **poller** and **event** mechanism. Each poller or event contains its own <function, args>, and the reactor execute it as E->function(E.args) or P->function(P.args) in Fig. 2.

Poller mechanism is the internal events to be executed in the thread. There are two types of Pollers provided, i.e., a timer-based Poller and a non-timer Poller, which can be maintained in two independent lists. Event mechanism is used as the communication channel among different threads. The essence of this mechanism is that each thread maintains a ring of events, which is the Multi

Producer and Single Consumer (MPSC) Model. If a thread A wants thread B to execute a event, i.e, E<function, args>, then thread A puts the event E in B's event ring. Then the reactor on each thread (such as thread B) can receive **Event** messages from any other Reactor thread (including the thread itself) for processing. For more details of reactor, poller and event, you can refer in section 2.1 of Yang's work [4].

```
While(1) {
// check the events in the ring
 For (each event E in the ring) { E->function(E.args); }

//check each non timer poller in the list
 For (each poller P in the list) { P->function(P.args); }

 //check each timer poller in the list
  For (each timer poller P in the list) {
            if (P.timer_is_out()) { P->function(p.args); }
            P.update_timer();
  }
  //break the while loop
  if (is_exit) { break; }
}
```

Fig. 2. Pseudo Code of reactor

As shown in Fig. 1, a **TCP transport acceptor** is registered as a non-timer poller in thread on core 0, it can only be registered on one thread, but can be configured on the other thread instead of the first core (e.g., core 0) shown in the diagram. The purpose of this poller is to listen on each portal (e.g., through spdk_sock_accept function) managed by the transport. When there is an incoming socket connection event, a new TCP connection with the socket info (i.e., spdk_sock in uNVMe-TCP) can be created, and such connection can be managed by the dedicated non-timer poller (i.e., **TCP transport polling group**) on each reactor thread. Currently, we use round robin algorithm to select a CPU core, and send an asynchronous message through Event call to let the dedicated thread to add the TCP connection to its polling group.

TCP Socket Group Polling. When a TCP connection is added to a TCP polling group, the socket owned by this connection is added to the socket polling group. For example, we can use the epoll related operation (e.g., epoll_ctl) in Linux to add the socket info into the socket polling group; then the socket group polling mechanism can be used. For example, we can leverage epoll_wait to check the EPOLLIN event (there is data from remote) for each connection. If such event is detected for any socket, we will begin to handle the NVMe/TCP PDU (Packet Data Unit) protocol parsing work in order to conduct the further NVMe command operation according to the NVMe-oF protocol; When the TCP disconnection event is detected by the state of the owned socket, this connection is removed from the socket polling group and will no longer be polled by the group anymore.

User Space NVMe I/O Stack. When an NVMe command is extracted by the NVMe-TCP PDU according to the NVMe-oF protocol, a user space NVMe I/O stack is used to conduct the NVMe command, which is much better than kernel's NVMe I/O stack, i.e., has lower latency and higher IOPS. And the details can be referred in section 3.2 of Yang's work [4], the performance benefit is achieved by the asynchronous polled I/O policy, lockless design, reduced I/O stack, and eliminated system call and data copy overhead. Additionally in uNVMe-TCP, zero copy mechanism is also designed in user space I/O stack.

For any NVMe write command from the initiator side, when the data for this command is read from the socket and put into the buffer allocated from the **data buffer pool**, there is no additional memory copy for writing the data into the NVMe SSD in the user space I/O stack through related NVMe subsystem, user space bdev, NVMe driver and firmware. For any read NVMe command from the initiator side, a buffer is allocated from the **data buffer pool** for this command. Thus data for this command is loaded from the NVMe SSD in the user space I/O stack through firmware, NVMe driver, user space bdev and NVMe subsystem. Before consumed by the socket, there is no data copy. Our default TCP/IP stack is kernel TCP/IP stack, so there could be memory copy for the data between user space and kernel space. However, if we leverage user space TCP/IP stack, all the data copy can be eliminated in either User space NVMe I/O stack or TCP/IP stack.

3   System Implementation

We present the implementation details of uNVMe-TCP in this section, and it supports user space NVMe/TCP transport library on both the target and host sides. Currently, our code is available in [5]. The host side code is mainly located in the file (i.e., lib/nvme/nvme_tcp.c), and the target side code is mainly located in the file (i.e., lib/nvmf/tcp.c).

3.1   Implementation Details in Target

On target side, the life cycle of the NVMe/TCP request in each TCP connection (each NVMe qpair is mapped into a TCP connection) is tracked (shown in Fig. 3) in order to make the implementation correct and reserve the further performance optimization space. Several states for NVMe/TCP request are defined the following, which are not defined in TP 8000 spec and it is a unique implementation in uNVMe-TCP.

- (1) **FREE**. The request is set in free state.
- (2) **NEW**. The request is allocated according to the PDU parsing.
- (3) **NEED_BUFFER**. The Request waits for a data buffer.

- (4) **DATA_PENDING_FOR_R2T**. The request needs to wait for the r2t slot.
- (5) **DATA_TRANSFER_FROM_HOST**. The request is handling the data from the host.
- (6) **EXECUTION_IN_NVMe_IO_STACK**. The request is sent to the user space NVMe I/O stack for execution.
- (7) **READY_TO_COMPLETE**. The request is completed from the NVMe I/O stack.
- (8) **DATA_TRANSFER_FROM_HOST**. The PDU data related with the request is sending to host.
- (9) **COMPLETED**. The Request is completed, will be set to free.

According to the queue depth (QD) negotiated with the host, each connection(a.k.a. qpair) is allocated with a fixed number of NVMe/TCP requests. If a host sends more requests while exceeding the QD of belonging qpair, it violates the NVMe-oF protocol and the NVMe command encapsulated in the CapsuleCmd (Command Capsule PDU) [6] will be rejected by the target with the NVMe response contained in CapsuleResp (Response Capsule PDU). During the life cycle of the NVMe/TCP request of each qpair, zero copy technique is used through the user space NVMe I/O stack when the data buffer is bound to the request from state (3). And this buffer is also reused by the PDUs being sent out, so there is no data copy only when we call encapsulated socket API to conduct the network write function by interacting with the kernel. Moreover, there is no lock in uNVMe-TCP user space, so the performance will be greatly improved. And the following shows the detailed information to manage the life cycle of the NVMe/TCP requests.

- Request in State (**1**): Upon receiving a NVMe/TCP PDU from the host, we can identify whether the PDU is a CapsuleCmd. If it is, a new NVMe/TCP request is allocated from the NVMe/TCP requests pool belonging to the qpair, and the state of request is changed from (**1**) to (**2**).
- Request in state (**2**): If the contained NVMe command (CMD) is valid, it goes to state (**7**); If the CMD is either a read or write CMD, the request state can be changed to state (**3**); else the request state can be changed to state (**6**).
- Request in state (**3**): If the data buffer cannot be allocated from the pool, the request remains in this state. Otherwise (a) If it is the read CMD, and the data buffer can be allocated, the request is changed to state (**6**); (b) If it is the write CMD which contained in-capsule data, then the request is changed to state (**5**); (c) If it is write CMD related PDU does not contain in-capsule data, it means that the target needs to send R2T (Ready to transfer) PDU to the host, so the request is changed to state (**4**).
- Request in state (**4**): If no more R2T PDUs can be sent, the request remains in this state. Otherwise a R2T PDU is sent out, and the target waits for the corresponding H2CData (Host to Controller Data Transfer) PDUs. And the request is changed to state (**5**).

- Request in state **(5)**: The target is to receive the data for the write CMD, and if the received data obeys the protocol (e.g., expected length, correct data with hash check), the request will be changed into state **(6)**.
- Request in state **(6)**: The CMD contained in the request is sent to the NVMe I/O stack for execution. After it is finished, the request is changed to state **(7)**.
- Request in state **(7)**: The CMD is either executed from the user space NVMe I/O stack, or the CMD is marked as the invalid CMD. So the state of the request will be changed to state **(8)**.
- Request in state **(8)**: There are two kinds of cases: (a) The completed CMD is not read command or the CMD fails executing in the NVMe I/O stack, then only the CapsuleResp (Response Capsule PDU) which contains the NVMe response (aka. RSP) info is generated and sent out to the host; (b) The CMD is read command and it is successfully executed in the NVMe I/O stack, then several C2HData (Controller to host data transfer) PDUs are generated which contains the data read from NVMe I/O stack. Furthermore, the CapsuleResp may also be generated and sent out which is according to the flag (Last_PDU) marked in the C2HDATA. And if all the PDUs is send out, the request is changed to state **(9)**.
- Request in state **(9)**: The life cycle of the request is ended, and the memory resource owned by the request (e.g., data buffer, PDU) will be freed, and the request is changed to state **(1)** and put into the request pool owned by the corresponding qpair.

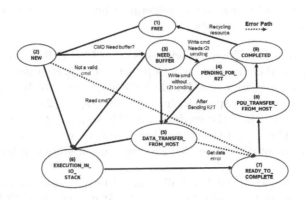

Fig. 3. NVMe/TCP request life cycle

3.2   Implementation Details in Initiator

The implementation for uNVMe-TCP on host side seems simple, since we already have the code support for PCIe and RDMA transport. Then we only need implement the relevant function APIs for the NVMe/TCP transport, and the following shows the most significant functions we need to implement:

– nvme_tcp_ctrlr_construct/destruct. The two functions are used to construct or destruct the NVMe controller for the TCP transport on the host side. For the construct function, the main idea can be divided into the following steps, i.e., (1) Allocate and initialize an NVMe controller structure (empty without the real controller information from the remote); (2) Create the admin qpair by NVMe-oF protocol via TCP connection. (3) Leveraging the admin qpair to submit the NVMe command and get the corresponding response via the TCP connection in order to fill the contents in the NVMe controller created in (1). For destruct function, it is the opposite operation, i.e., destroy all I/O qpairs and then destroy admin qpairs through TCP connection, and finally free all the resource related with the NVMe controller.

– nvme_tcp_ctrlr_create/delete/reinit_io_qpair. As described, the three functions are used to manage the life cycle of the I/O qpair. For the I/O qpair creation, we need to allocate the NVMe/TCP requests for the qpair according to the QD, then the connection connects to the target according to the TP8000 spec, which is similar to admin qpair creation.

– nvme_tcp_qpair_submit_request. This function is used to convert the local NVMe command request to the remote. The key is to construct the CapsuleCmd (Command Capsule PDU) defined in the TP 8000 spec, and then put the PDU into a list which maintains the PDU to send out. Since uNVMe-TCP provides the asynchronous polled mode mechanism, so it does not mean that the NVMe command is successfully sent to the target side, or the response is returned.

– nvme_tcp_qpair_process_completions. This function has two functionalities, i.e., (1) Call the TCP socket API (e.g., write or writev) to send out the PDU on the designated TCP connection based qpair (including both admin and I/O qpairs); (2) Receive the PDU (e.g., Response Capsule PDU), and parse the PDU to map it to the corresponding NVMe request, and execute the call back function provided by the user. Then an NVMe command can be thought as completed.

Compared with the target side, there are similar benefits on the initiator side, i.e., (1) The zero copy policy is used to reuse the data buffer provided by the up users; (2) There is no lock in the data path for doing the NVMe command operation on the TCP connection based I/O qpair. (3) There is no system call relevant with NVMe I/O stack to submit any NVMe command by nvme_tcp_qpair_submit_request. If using kernel, there is context switch overhead related with system call.

4 Experiment

In this section, we evaluate the performance of uNVMe-TCP and also compare the performance difference between the kernel solution and uNVMe-TCP in Linux environment.

The set up consists of three individual machines (One used as the target and the other two used as initiators with the same configuration). The target is equipped with Intel® Xeon® Platinum 8180 (2.50 GHz) CPU, 376 GB memory, 16 Intel® P4600TM P4600-2.0 TB NVMe SSDs and two 100GbE Mellanox ConnectX-5 NICs. Each initiator is equipped with Intel® Xeon® CPU E5-2699 v4 (2.20 GHz) CPU, 64 GB memory, one 100GbE Mellanox ConnectX-4 NIC. All the three machines are installed on Fedora 28 with kernel version 5.05. The target is connected to both initiators point-to-point directly without any switches. And each NVMe SSD equipped by the target is encapsulated as block device and exported in the individual NVMe-oF subsystem.

Five different experiments are conducted to verify the performance of uNVMe-TCP. FIO [13] is used as the performance benchmark tool, and two storage engines can be used as the FIO plugin on the host side, i.e., Linux kernel libaio engine and uNVMe-TCP FIO bdev engine. All the collected performance numbers are described for aggregated I/O per second, average latency in different usage cases. According to the following experiments, we demonstrate that uNVMe-TCP is more competitive in the I/O performance (e.g., IOPS, latency) scope and is much better in per CPU core performance aspect compared with the Linux kernel solution.

4.1 uNVMe-TCP Target I/O Scaling

The target in uNVMe-TCP was configured with 16 subsystems, and each was composed of one bdev on one Intel P4600 SSD [14]. Each of the 2 initiators was connected to 8 individual NVMe-oF subsystems which were exposed by uNVMe-TCP over 1x 100GbE NIC. And each initiator used FIO (with uNVMe-TCP bdev FIO plugin) to test the 8 individual bdevs served by uNVMe-TCP . And the core affinity of uNVMe-TCP was configured to use 1, 2, 3 and 4 cores while running following 4 KB workloads on each initiator, i.e., Random 70% read & 30% write (Randrw70%–30%) with QD from ranged in (1, 8 16, 32). For random read or random write, which has the similar trend, so we only select Randrw70%–30% as the typical workload.

The experiment results are shown in Fig. 4. For the IOPS, it is nearly scale linearly from core 1 to 2 and 2 to 3 for QD ranged from (8, 16, 32), but there is slightly drop in IOPS scaling when increasing the number of CPUs from 3 to 4. For QD = 1, the IOPS increasing does not increase when using multiple cores since all the optimization for asynchronous operation is useless since there is one active request. It was observed that the performance can hit about 0.8M IOPS in Fig. 5(d), and the RDMA transport can achieve 2.6M IOPS in the same environment [15]. Compared with the RDMA transport, the most drop is caused by the low efficiency of TCP protocol. For the latency, it also continues decreasing with the increasing of CPU cores. It is not fully linear for the IOPS and latency because the polling groups still share the data buffer, and we also use the kernel TCP stack which has some contentions on the network resource.

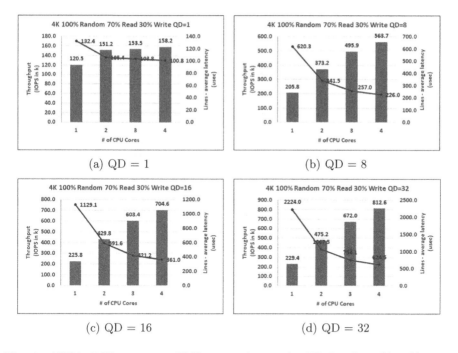

(a) QD = 1   (b) QD = 8

(c) QD = 16   (d) QD = 32

Fig. 4. uNVMe-TCP target on CPU core scaling with 4KB Randrw70%–30% workloads

4.2 uNVMe-TCP Initiator I/O Scaling

This experiment was performed in order to understand the performance of uNVMe-TCP Initiator with I/O core scaling. In this test, uNVMe-TCP target was configured similar to test case 1, but runs with 4 cores. uNVMe-TCP bdev FIO plugin was still used to target 8 individual NVMe-oF bdevs on each of the 2 initiators. FIO cpumask was configured from 1, 2, 3 and 4 cores to run following 4KB workloads from both the two initiators, and the QD is ranged from (32, 64, 128, 256). We select random read in this experiment this time since it has the similar trend for random write or random read/write.

The experiment results are shown in Fig. 5. From the diagram, we can see that IOPS scales linearly from core 1 to 2 and 2 to 3 for different QDs, and there is slight performance drop from core 3 to 4. The latency also decreases with the increasing of core numbers, and it is the expected behavior. With more CPU cores, the burden of each CPU is reduced, so the IOPS increases and the latency decreases.

4.3 uNVMe-TCP VS Linux Kernel on Latency

This experiment was designed to understand latency capabilities of uNVMe-TCP and Linux kernel in both target and initiator aspect for TCP transport. uNVMe-TCP target was configured to run on a single core with one single NVMe-oF

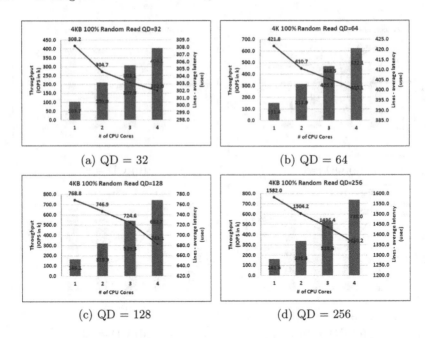

(a) QD = 32   (b) QD = 64

(c) QD = 128   (d) QD = 256

Fig. 5. uNVMe-TCP initiator on CPU core scaling with 4 KB Randread workloads

subsystem which contains a single memory based bdev (null block bdev). And for the linux target, it configures with the equivalent behavior.

The baseline of this experiment is the kernel solution, i.e., we used kernel initiator and target on both sides. In Fig. 6(a), we compare the latency between kernel target and uNVMe-TCP target through the kernel initiator. From the result, the average round trip I/O latency of uNVMe-TCP target is up to (15.7%, 20.1%, 20.9%) improvement compared with the Linux kernel target for the three kinds of workloads (randread, randwrite, randrw) with QD = 1 independently. Then we just used uNVMe-TCP target on the target side, and conducted the initiator side latency comparison shown in Fig. 6(b). The average latency of uNVMe-TCP initiator is up to (29.4%, 24.2%, 22.4%) improvement compared with the Linux kernel initiator for the three kinds of workloads (randread, randwrite, randrw) independently. Finally the end to end latency comparison between kernel and uNVMe-TCP is shown in Fig. 6(c), which directly compares the latency between kernel and uNVMe-TCP. We can see that the average latency improvement of uNVMe-TCP solution is up to (40.5%, 39.4%, 38.6%) for the three kinds of workloads (randread, randwrite, randrw) independently.

From the results, it indicates that the user space solution has benefit in latency on both target and initiator sides. Since we still leverage the kernel TCP stack, the benefit is mostly gained from the following areas, i.e., TCP group based socket polling strategy; lock-free mechanism on data I/O path.

 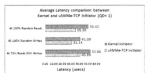 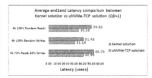

(a) Latency comparison on target side using kernel initiator

(b) Latency comparison on initiator side using uNVMe-TCP target

(c) End to end latency comparison between uNVMe-TCP and kernel

Fig. 6. Performance comparison between uNVMe-TCP and kernel solution

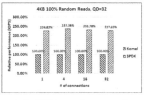 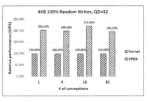 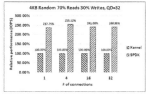

(a) 4KB random read

(b) 4KB random write

(c) 4KB random 70% read 30% write

Fig. 7. Per CPU core performance comparison between uNVMe-TCP and kernel on connection scaling case

4.4 uNVMe-TCP Performance with Increasing Number of Connections

This test case was performed in order to understand throughput/latency capabilities of uNVMe-TCP and Linux kernel target under increasing number of connections per subsystem. Number of connections (or I/O queue pairs) per NVMe-oF subsystem were varied and corresponding aggregated IOPS per CPU core were reported. Both the targets were configured with 16 NVMe-oF subsystems (1 per Intel P4600) and 2 initiators were used both running I/Os to 8 separate subsystems using Kernel NVMe-oF initiator. In this experiment, SPDK use fixed 4 CPU cores, the kernel target uses 9 to 12 CPU cores.

The test result is shown in Fig. 7, uNVMe-TCP target performs up to 2.2 times of the Linux kernel NVMe-oF target in per CPU core IOPS aspect while running three kinds of 4 KB workloads with increasing number of connections ranged from (1, 4, 16, 32) per NVMe-oF subsystem. We can conclude that uNVMe-TCP is much better than kernel solution for per CPU core performance, and it indicates that the CPU utilization is very competitive. According to our analysis, the main gain is from our lock-free user space NVMe I/O stack in data path, which avoids the CPU resource contention. Since in uNVMe-TCP , each connection is managed and handled by the TCP polling group on each CPU core, so there is no resource contentions among connections for doing the NVMe I/O.

4.5 uNVMe-TCP TCP Transport VS RDMA Transport

This experiment is used to compare the performance (e.g., IOPS and latency) between RDMA and TCP transport for NVMe-oF. The NVMe-oF target was configured with 1 subsystem which was composed of one bdev on one Intel P4600 SSD [14]. We run Fio by one job with (I/O size = 4KB, QD = 128) on the initiator side. For TCP transport, we can use kernel TCP stack(i.e., TCP (kernel) in Fig. 8) and VMA [16] (Mellanox Messaging accelerator) library (i.e., TCP (VMA) in Fig. 8). The VMA library is used to provide the compatible posix TCP programing API but leverages the hardware offloading features of the Mellanox NIC, which can both improve the latency and IOPS for the TCP workloads.

The test result is shown in Fig. 8. Without using the VMA library, the IOPS of TCP (kernel) is only about 13.7%–33.8% of the RDMA transport when testing the 3 kinds of workloads. While using VMA, the IOPS is greatly increased, i.e., the TCP (VMA) is 47.9%–91.9% of the RDMA transport. For the Latency, the TCP (kernel) is about 2.28X–7.03X of the RDMA transport by different workloads. However, when using VMA, the latency of TCP (VMA) only increased 1%–8% the RDMA transport. From this experiment, we conclude that the default kernel based TCP transport is worse than RDMA transport. However, if equipped with hardware offloading technique (e.g., via VMA in our test), the performance degradation can be reduced and close to the RDMA transport performance especially for the latency.

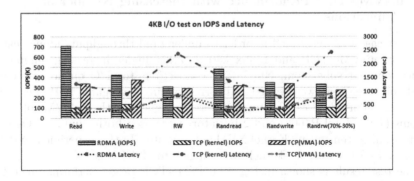

Fig. 8. Performance comparison between RDMA and TCP transport

5   Related Work

iSCSI VS NVMe-oF. Previously, iSCSI [2] is well adopted by the industry to provision block storage service by exporting the local devices (including NVMe [1] SSDs) to remote. Unfortunately, there is additional overhead while using iSCSI protocol on NVMe SSDs, i.e., NVMe → SCSI → iSCSI conversion on sender side; iSCSI → SCSI → NVMe protocol conversion on receiver side. However, if NVMe/TCP [3,6] is used, the protocol conversion can be eliminated. By the way, iSCSI has extended protocol iSER [7] to offload packet data handling on RDMA NICs, however there is no offload specification to device devices defined by NVMe/TCP transport today, hoping that there is new specification to address this issue in the future.

User Space I/O Stack Optimization for NVMe/TCP. The optimization for NVMe/TCP can be divided into two parts, i.e., TCP network packet I/O stack and NVMe I/O stack. There are lots of significant work [17–19] related to zero copy in network I/O path. Compared with those research work, we focus on how to construct a feasible zero copy I/O stack for the NVMe/TCP protocol implementation by levering those techniques. There are many works [4,10] to optimize storage I/O for NVMe SSDs in user space. For example, Yang et al. [10] proves the efficiency of applying polled mode driver into NVMe SSDs. And the main challenge is to provide a whole user I/O stack equivalent to the kernel (such as block layer, file system layer). Currently, SPDK [4] builds user space block device and simple file system (i.e., blobfs) relied on the user space polled mode NVMe driver to provide asynchronous and lock-free mechanism on data I/O path.

6   Conclusion

The design goal of NVMe over Fabrics protocol (NVMe-oF [3]) is to replace the iSCSI protocol in order to maximally explore the high performance and low latency capabilities of PCIe SSD while serving the remote hosts. Despite the nearly native performance benefit provided by NVMe-oF RDMA and FC transport, TCP transport [6] is invented to be backward compatible with the Ethernet cards without RDMA capability. Undoubtedly, the TCP performance is worse than RDMA transport. To address the performance and usability issue, we propose uNVMe-TCP, which provides a user space solution to accelerate the TCP transport relying on the whole user space NVMe I/O stack with several novel features, e.g., lock-free mechanism on data path, zero copy, polled mode and etc.

   To evaluate the performance of uNVMe-TCP, several experiments were conducted in Linux environment on standard server platforms equipped with PCIe SSDs. Compared with the Linux kernel solution, uNVMe-TCP has average 15% to 30% performance improvement in latency according to the workloads generated by FIO. Besides, uNVMe-TCP has advantage in per CPU core aspect especially deployed in the target side, i.e., it is 2.2 times of the kernel for per CPU core IOPS on average. Furthermore, we also provide some suggestions on further optimizing the TCP transport through user space TCP/IP stack or other hardware acceleration technique.

References

1. NVM Express Spec 1.3. https://nvmexpress.org/wp-content/uploads/NVM-Express-1_3d-2019.03.20-Ratified.pdf
2. IETF. Internet Small Computer Systems Interface (iSCSI). https://tools.ietf.org/html/rfc3720
3. NVM Express over Fabrics 1.0. http://nvmexpress.org/wp-content/uploads/NVMe_over_Fabrics_1_0_Gold_20160605-1.pdf
4. Yang, Z., et al.: SPDK: a development kit to build high performance storage applications. In: 2017 IEEE International Conference on Cloud Computing Technology and Science (CloudCom), pp. 154–161, December 2017
5. SPDK github. https://github.com/spdk/spdk
6. NVMe-oF - TP 8000 TCP Transport. https://nvmexpress.org/wp-content/uploads/NVM-Express-over-Fabrics-1.0-Ratified-TPs.zip
7. RDMA Consortium. iSCSI Extensions for RDMA (iSER) and Datamover Architecture for iSCSI (DA) Specifications
8. VMware Virtual NVMe support. https://kb.vmware.com/s/article/2147714
9. Yang, Z., Liu, C., Zhou, Y., Liu, X., Cao, G.: SPDK vhost-NVMe: accelerating I/Os in virtual machines on NVMe SSDs via user space vhost target. In: 2018 IEEE 8th International Symposium on Cloud and Service Computing (SC2), pp. 67–76, November 2018
10. Yang, J., Minturn, D.B., Hady, F.: When poll is better than interrupt. In: Proceedings of the 10th USENIX Conference on File and Storage Technologies (2012)
11. Data Plane Development Kit. http://dpdk.org/
12. Vector Packet Processing. https://fd.io/technology/
13. Flexible I/O Tester. https://github.com/axboe/fio
14. Intel DC series P4600 2TB SSD. https://www.intel.com/content/dam/www/public/us/en/documents/product-briefs/ssd-dc-p4600-brief.pdf
15. SPDK NVMe-oF (Target & Initiator) Performance Report Release 19.01.1. https://dqtibwqq6s6ux.cloudfront.net/download/performance-reports/SPDK_nvmeof_perf_report_19.01.1.pdf
16. Mellanox Messaging Accelerator. http://www.mellanox.com/related-docs/prod_acceleration_software/VMA_EN.pdf
17. Shivam, P., Wyckoff, P., Panda, D.: EMP: Zero-copy OS-bypass NIC-driven gigabit ethernet message passing. In: SC 2001: Proceedings of the 2001 ACM/IEEE Conference on Supercomputing, p. 49, November 2001
18. Goldenberg, D., Kagan, M., Ravid, R., Tsirkin, M.S.: Zero copy sockets direct protocol over infiniband – preliminary implementation and performance analysis. In: Proceedings of the 13th Symposium on High Performance Interconnects, HOTI 2005, pp. 128–137. IEEE Computer Society, Washington, DC (2005)
19. Li, Y.-C., Chiang, M.-L.: LyraNET: a zero-copy TCP/IP protocol stack for embedded operating systems. In: 11th IEEE International Conference on Embedded and Real-Time Computing Systems and Applications (RTCSA 2005), pp. 123–128, August 2005

An Ethereum-Based Data Synchronization Platform for Distributed Networks

Jianru Lin[1,2], Keshan Zhang[1], Sicong Zhou[1], Kangying Lin[1], Yang Yang[1], Huawei Huang[1(✉)] ⓘ, and Kun Wang[3]

[1] School of Data and Computer Science, Sun Yat-Sen University, Guangzhou 510006, People's Republic of China
huanghw28@mail.sysu.edu.cn
[2] Beijing Qizhi Ruisi Information Consulting Co., Ltd/CuriosityChina, Beijing, China
[3] Department of ECE, University of California, Los Angeles, USA

Abstract. In distributed networks, the consistent network views (e.g., network events, network topology, and device information, etc) are critical to the network operators and service providers who aim to perform the global network/service optimizations depending on the overall network views. However, to achieve the consensus over distributed networks is a challenge, because the consistent global network view requires to exchange the local network view within the distributed domain controllers. More critically, the network view in each controller is prone to be falsified by malicious attackers who intend to destroy the network consensus. To this end, we propose an Ethereum based consensus protection system that can ensure the tamper-proof network-view synchronization. In this paper, we present our design and implementation of the data-synchronization system. A prototype is developed based on the Ethereum platform. Evaluation results have demonstrated the effectiveness of our prototype.

1 Introduction

In the Internet of Things (IoT) networks shown in Fig. 1, billions of devices, such as mobile smartphones, unmanned aerial vehicles, auto-driving cars, smart factory machines, and other devices, are generating enormous amount of data. When the scale of distributed networks increases too large, to manage the overall network views will incur a super heavy burden to a centralized management entity [1]. Thus, the overall networks are usually separated into multiple domains. For example, each access network under a cell base station can be configured as an individual network domain. Under such distributed computing environment, a fundamental issue is to protect the consistent network-view over all distributed domains [2].

The network view includes (1) device information [3] such as modular parameters, connection quality, availability of storage and computation resource, (2)

© Springer Nature Switzerland AG 2020
C.-H. Hsu et al. (Eds.): IOV 2019, LNCS 11894, pp. 143–157, 2020.
https://doi.org/10.1007/978-3-030-38651-1_14

user's privacy [4] such as location data and usage of apps, and (3) other network parameters [5] such as traffic congestion and link states. In a word, the network view is critical to network operators and service providers while performing network/service optimization, such as cost-efficient workload offloading decisions, or service profit-maximization in distributed networks.

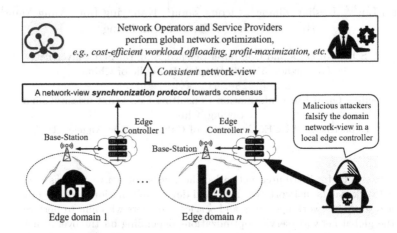

Fig. 1. The falsification attacks destroy consensus over the multi-domain distributed networks.

As implied in Fig. 1, we need a synchronization protocol dedicated for consistent network-view exchange over all distributed domains. Usually in a distributed system, to achieve a consensus would require each peer to exchange their domain views with their neighbors. The mutual data-exchange unavoidably consumes a large amount of bandwidth and computing resource in distributed networks. No matter how the consensus mechanism is implemented, to protect the consistent network-view is not easy.

To make the situation worse, the network operators face another threat that malicious attackers may falsify the network-view in the *corrupted* domain controllers, aiming to destroy the overall consensus of network view. Through a review, we find that the protection mechanism that prevents the network consensus from being falsified is missing from the existing research community. Therefore, we intend to implement a consensus protection system that enables tamper-proof mechanism for distributed networks.

In summary, our study leads to the following major contributions.

- We study the blockchain based data-synchronization problem to address the malicious *falsification attack*.
- We then implement a tamper-proof network-view protection prototype towards consensus for distributed networks, based on Ethereum platform.

The reminder of the paper is organized as follows. Section 2 reviews the related work. Section 3 introduces the design of our proposed network-view protection system, and the methodology of our implementation. Evaluation results of our prototype is shown in Sect. 4. Finally, Sect. 5 concludes this work and reveals future work.

2 Related Work

2.1 Management for Distributed IoT Networks

Recently, the trust-enhanced data management towards distributed IoT networks received a lot of attention [6–8]. For example, Qiu et al. [9] proposed a distributed flat control plane architecture, called ParaCon, which can distribute path computation load to multiple controller instances. The consistency and synchronization overhead are also considered in this design. Sharma et al. [10] proposed a distributed software-defined networking (SDN) architecture for IoT Networks, based on blockchains techniques. The proposed blockchains technique based scheme is for secure flow rule table update for IoT forwarding devices. Xiong et al. [11] studied a mobile blockchain network for edge computing, enabling IoT devices and mobile users to access resources and services from service providers. Phemius et al. [12] presented DISCO, a distributed SDN control plane that enables each domain controller to exchange the local-domain view for end-to-end network services. To handle the inter-domain traffic, Lin et al. [13] proposed a WE-Bridge mechanism, which can help SDN network operators cooperate across multiple administrative domains. Based on fog computing, SDN, and blockchain, Sharma et al. [14] proposed a distributed cloud architecture architecture to meet the design principles required to manage the raw data streams originated from IoT devices.

2.2 Consensus Protection

In the background of software-defined industrial Internet of Things, Qiu et al. [3] proposed a blockchain-based consensus protocol to cope with the collection and synchronization of network views between SDN controllers. Using this protocol, authors studied a joint optimization taking the view exchange, access control, and resource allocation into account. Zou et al. [4] proposed a consensus protocol called "Proof-of-Trust" (PoT) consensus for the crowdsourcing services. In order to address the loss of control over data, protect privacy and data sovereignty for IoT systems, Yin et al. [5] proposed HyperNet, which is a decentralized trusted networking and computing paradigm based on blockchain technique.

2.3 Unique Features of Our Work

Through the literature review, we find that the existing studies mainly include the following topics: (1) design synchronization protocol, (2) design secure data update approaches for IoT devices; and (3) propose blockchain based architecture for distributed computing.

Compared with the existing work, our major contribution is that we implement a systematic prototype for the network-view management system for distributed networks based on the Ethereum platform.

3 System Design and Implementation

In this section, we elaborate the proposed system design and implementation based on blockchain theory.

3.1 Preliminary

As a promising technique to achieve decentralized consensus, blockchain has been successfully applied into digital currency, e.g., bitcoin, for serving as a public ledger for transactions. Its secure design for supporting a distributed computing system with high fault tolerance is attracting wide attention all over the world. Blockchain will play an important role for secure decentralization in such emerging fields as Internet of Things, cyber physical systems, edge computing, social networking, crowdsourcing and next generation wireless communications, and even many other fields. In this paper, we view Blockchain as a promising technique for our tamper-proof and distributed network-view management system. By exploiting the Blockchain based technique, we intend to guarantee the strong consistency for distributed networks, and prevent from the malicious network-view falsification attacks.

We then implement our prototype using the Ethereum, which is an open source blockchain based platform.

3.2 Raw-Data Storage

As shown in Fig. 1, suppose that the raw data generated from the network devices is stored in the local database. The reason behind this data storage design is that the large-amount of raw data is generated in each local network at real time. Therefore, it is impossible and inefficient to storage the massive amount of data in each domain controller. The natural way is to store these data in a dedicated local database. The domain controller can access the database using the index of each item of raw data. That is, only the data-indices are needed to manage in the domain controllers.

3.3 Attack Model

In this paper, we propose a blockchain based network-view management system towards a particular attack model, in which the malicious attackers aim to destroy the network-wide consensus over all domain networks. We consider that the raw data located in each domain controller could be possibly falsified by the attackers *before* data-synchronization. Thus, the other peers (other domain controllers) will receive the falsified data from the domain controller under attack.

3.4   Implementation Methodology

In this part, we explain our implementation methodology. Our system mainly consists of smart contracts and a data-synchronization platform based on Ethereum.

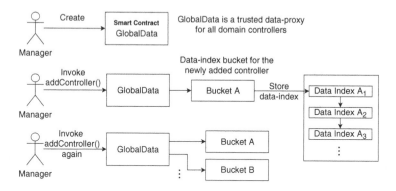

Fig. 2. The initial operations and data structure of the smart contract.

Algorithm 1. Primary smart contract **GlobalData**

1: **while** system is running **do**
2:    **constructor():**
3:       Initialize an empty listControllers
4:       Initialize an empty Bucket of each controller
5:    **addController(controller** c**):**
6:       A bucket of controller $c \leftarrow$ new Bucket()
7:    **removeController(controller** c**):**
8:       Delete c from listControllers
9:    **writeIndex(key, hash):**
10:      bkt $\leftarrow$ Bucket(operator's address)
11:      Invoke bkt.write(key, hash)
12:   **readIndex(controller** c**, key):**
13:   **Output:** hash of the key
14:      bkt $\leftarrow$ Bucket(operator's address)
15:      hash $\leftarrow$ bkt.read(key)
16: **end while**

Design of Smart Contract. We first create a smart contract named *GlobalData*, which is a trusted data-proxy for all domain controllers. Because it is designed to enable the authentication of write- and read- operations towards domain network view. From the raw-data storage strategy described in Sect. 3.2, we know that only the data-indices are necessary to be managed by each domain controller.

Foundation of Data Interaction. As shown in Fig. 2, a network *Manager* can create the aforementioned smart contract *GlobalData* at the very beginning. Then, Algorithm 1 presents the pseudo code of smart contract GlobalData. We can see that the manager can create an individual account in Ethereum for each `controller` invoking the `addController()` function. Algorithm 2, i.e., *Bucket*, is an auxiliary smart contract to the primary contract GlobalData. Bucket is in fact a data-structure used to store the data-indices for the newly created `controller` account. It is automatically generated and attached to a `controller` account. In our design, a Bucket directly connects to a list of data indices. Thus, the smart contract GlobalData can read and write the data indices through the Bucket instance it holds. In consequence, once the manager creates a new account for a new domain controller, the smart contract GlobalData will create a dedicated Bucket contract instance for the new `controller` account.

Algorithm 2. Auxiliary smart contract **Bucket**

```
1: constructor():
2:    Initialize an empty listKeyIndex
3: write(key, hash):
4:    An index item it ← ⟨key, hash⟩
5:    listKeyIndex ← it
6: read(key):
7: Output: hash of the key
8:    hash ← listKeyIndex[key].hash
```

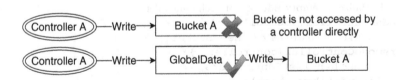

Fig. 3. The data-access proxy of each domain controller.

Data-Access Proxy. In particular, according to our design, a Bucket instance is not able to be accessed by `controller1` account directly. Because we would like GlobalData to work as a trusted third-party data access proxy for each domain controller. The details are illustrated by Fig. 3, Algorithms 1 and 2, where we see that a `controller` account indirectly manages the data-access through the medium GlobalData. For example, any controller can write the keys of their local raw data items to the smart contract GlobalData by invoking the function `writeIndex(key, hash)`. On the other hand, a controller can request to download the hash of a data index that points to an item of raw data stored in another regional controller, through the function `readIndex(controller c, key)`. However, the ⟨key, hash⟩ pairs are not directly managed by Global-Data. The auxiliary smart contract *Bucket* handles this job through its functions `write(key, hash)` and `read(key)`.

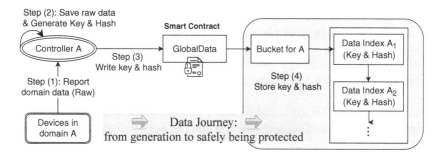

Fig. 4. The journey of the protected data from generation to being stored in a Bucket.

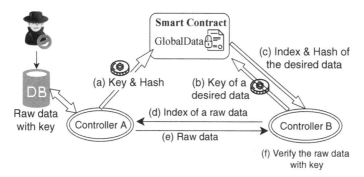

Fig. 5. `controller2` (i.e., Controller B) requires a raw data item from `controller1` (i.e., Controller A).

This design concern can not only realize the blockchain based paradigm, the management complexity in the domain controller side can be also much reduced. Thus, the domain controllers only need to protect the raw data, and send the data indices as well as their hash values to the GlobalData.

Data-Journey Under the Proposed System. From generation to being safely protected by a Bucket, the journey of the data under protection is presented as Fig. 4. The holistic procedure includes at the first step, the devices in each domain periodically report their raw data to the domain controller. In step (2), controller will save the raw data and generate the ⟨key, hash⟩ pair, which is then written to the smart contract GlobalData in Step (3). Finally, in Step (4), the data indices of each pair will be stored in a Bucket instance dedicated for each controller.

Data Synchronization. Under the proposed system, the data synchronization procedure is presented in Fig. 5. As preparation, the raw data and their keys are stored in the local database, which connects to its domain controller directly. Then, the data-synchronization can be explained by the following 5 steps.

- In step (a), the domain controller generates the Key & Hash pairs and write them to the smart contract GlobalData, by paying a certain Ethereum coins.
- In step (b) When another *controller2* intends to download the raw data in domain A via *controller1*, it needs to send the public key of the desired data to the smart contract GlobalData with paying a certain Ethereum coins.
- The smart contract will return the Hash of the desired data, in step (c). The returned Hash can be exploited to verify the raw data from domain A.
- In step (d), with the Key, *controller2* can now ask for the desired data from *controller1*.
- Finally in step (e), *controller1* find the target data from its local database, and allow the raw data to be downloaded by *controller2*.

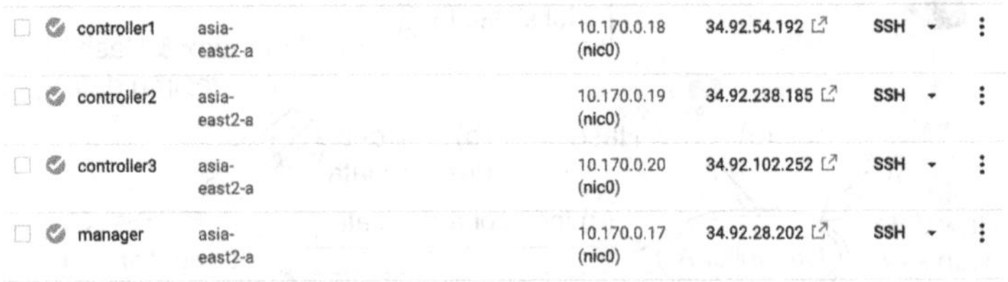

☐ ✅ controller1	asia-east2-a		10.170.0.18 (nic0)	34.92.54.192 ⬈	SSH ▾	⋮
☐ ✅ controller2	asia-east2-a		10.170.0.19 (nic0)	34.92.238.185 ⬈	SSH ▾	⋮
☐ ✅ controller3	asia-east2-a		10.170.0.20 (nic0)	34.92.102.252 ⬈	SSH ▾	⋮
☐ ✅ manager	asia-east2-a		10.170.0.17 (nic0)	34.92.28.202 ⬈	SSH ▾	⋮

Fig. 6. Launch 4 remote hosts in Google's cloud located at Hong Kong.

Fig. 7. The Genesis block of our system.

Till here, the blockchain based network-view synchronization protocol has been depicted through the elaboration of *Design of Smart contract, Foundation of Data Interaction, Data-Access Proxy, Data-Journey under the proposed System* and *Data Synchronization*. Next, we show the security of the proposed approach by theoretical analysis.

```
> personal.newAccount()
Passphrase:
Repeat passphrase:
"0x498f91d338432b60bc31e39b5ec3af5792a09f93"
```

(a) Create an account for manager

```
> personal.newAccount()
Passphrase:
Repeat passphrase:
"0xf2c682e0b66028c335b12478288399fe2a37dcf7"
```

(b) Create an account for controller1

Fig. 8. Create accounts for manager and a controller.

3.5 Security Analysis of Our System

We have the following remark that shows the security of the proposed approach.

Remark: *The proposed system is able to successfully address the attack model described in Sect. 3.3.*

As described in the specification of *Data Synchronization*, controller2 can acquire the *hash* of the desired data from the smart contract GlobalData. This hash cannot be falsified in any way, because it is stored in Ethereum. When controller1 receives a search *key* of an item of data, it will return the raw data from its local database to the destination, i.e., controller2. Suppose that this item of raw data has been falsified by an attacker before the synchronization by any other domain controllers. The verification in other controllers cannot be successful, using the acquired *hash* from smart contract GlobalData. Thus, this attack will be acknowledged. The synchronized data will be discarded accordingly. Therefore, the claim in this remark holds.

4   Performance Evaluation

4.1   Evaluation Methodology Based on a Remote Cluster

Experiment Settings. As shown in Fig. 6, we rent 4 remote google-cloud virtual machines to build a private Ethereum platform. The four machines located at Hong Kong are named manager, controller1, controller2, and controller3. Only the manager can create other mining nodes and deploy a smart contract. Each server executes the Ethereum client named *Geth* (https://www.ethereum.org/developers/). After finishing creating accounts for

the three controllers shown in Fig. 8 and generating the first block of the system
Genesis block shown in Fig. 7, all four nodes (for example, Fig. 9 shows the
node information of the manager) begin to mine blocks. Figure 10 illustrates the
money mined by all nodes. For example, manager has 4.69375e + 20 *wei* when
mining only in one hour. With the money mined, all nodes can pay the charge of
transactions, including deploying a smart contract or adding a controller by the
manager, writing data into the data-synchronization system by and a controller
and reading data from the system by other controllers.

```
> admin.nodeInfo
{
  enode: "enode://74cf38440a093889c2aaf85d8afe98727c0c4023e72eaaf5e639c47a05dcff
f5e0099dc48b44b36e9809e08b313b1adae3dd3ab5f8b5b46f6cc4d47539895f34034.92.28.202:
30303",
  enr: "0xf896b8404801fcd09e7b9df4a20813f2cc65a49f1ff950e14abea2724319bd271d5e0e
890d41541d7e7f1f4030af66e89c4ab1eecaad54cae0e35d6b141880f608608e150283636170c6c5
8365746831826964827634826970084225c1cca8973656370323536 6b31a10274cf38440a093889c2
aaf85d8afe98727c0c4023e72eaaf5e639c47a05dcfff583746370827 65f83756470827 65f",
  id: "2d0037c3dfd20865a3de107cdce2086b3eed12bd851bbe005489d1a4d948ca18",
  ip: "34.92.28.202",
  listenAddr: "[::]:30303",
  name: "Geth/v1.8.27-stable-4bcc0a37/linux-amd64/go1.10.4",
  ports: {
    discovery: 30303,
    listener: 30303
  },
  protocols: {
    eth: {
      config: {
        chainId: 8888,
        eip150Hash: "0x00000000000000000000000000000000000000000000000000000000
00000000",
        eip155Block: 0,
        eip158Block: 0,
        homesteadBlock: 0
      },
      difficulty: 131072,
      genesis: "0x5e1fc79cb4ffa4739177b5408045cd5d51c6cf766133f23f7cd72ee1f8d790
e0",
      head: "0x5e1fc79cb4ffa4739177b5408045cd5d51c6cf766133f23f7cd72ee1f8d790e0"
,
      network: 22309
    }
  }
}
```

Fig. 9. The node information of manager. Note that, the other controller nodes look
similar to this one, only the IP addresses, enode, enr, id, ip are unique to each node.

Smart Contract. After deploying smart contracts in Ethereum platform, we
first show how to create accounts for the manager and each controller. Then,
we present how to achieve the data synchronization under the protection of
blockchain technique.

There are some terminologies showing in the output panel of Ethereum software. To help understand those terminologies, we explain the important ones of
them as follows, before the demonstration of prototype.

- Status: the execution result of a transaction.
- Transaction hash: the hash of the current transaction.
- From: the party who launches this transaction.

- To: the target of this transaction.
- Gas: maximum expense that allows to invoke the smart contract.
- Transaction cost: expense of this transaction, measured by gas.
- Execution cost: expense of this execution, measured by gas.
- Hash: same with Transaction hash.
- Decoded input: input parameters transmitted from the initiator to the target of a transaction.
- Decoded output: output of a transaction.

To identify each peer in the evaluation results, we give the mapping information between each peer and its Ethereum account in Table 1.

```
> eth.getBalance('0x498f91d338432b60bc31e39b5ec3af5792a09f93')
35000000000000000000
> eth.getBalance('0xf2c682e0b66028c335b12478288399fe2a37dcf7')
40015625000000000000
> eth.getBalance('0x73d34be674b7d32f8a19b65949dae18d585b46c7')
31953125000000000000
> eth.getBalance('0x0df8843dfa5e6aa7cfd0a49c2021983a282d32da')
46937500000000000000
```

Fig. 10. The token mined by all nodes (controllers and manager).

```
→  / node read-index.js
call readIndex() method from 0x73d34be674b7d32f8a19b65949dae18d585b46c7 with arg
uments:
    controller=0xf2c682e0b66028c335b12478288399fe2a37dcf7
    key=test-key-1

return: 1
```

Fig. 11. controller2 reads the hash of a data-index from GlobalData.

Figure 7 shows the genesis block of our system. In this figure, the attribute "difficulty" is critical since it decides the difficulty of mining from genesis block. In order to accelerate the mining speed in our system, we are now using a slightly small difficulty.

Table 1. Mapping between each peer and its Ethereum account

Role	Account
manager	0x498f91d338432b60bc31e39b5ec3af5792a09f93
controller1	0xf2c682e0b66028c335b12478288399fe2a37dcf7
controller2	0x73d34be674b7d32f8a19b65949dae18d585b46c7

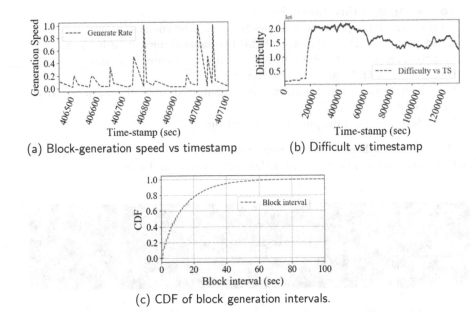

(a) Block-generation speed vs timestamp   (b) Difficult vs timestamp

(c) CDF of block generation intervals.

Fig. 12. Performance of the prototype deployed on the remote google cloud.

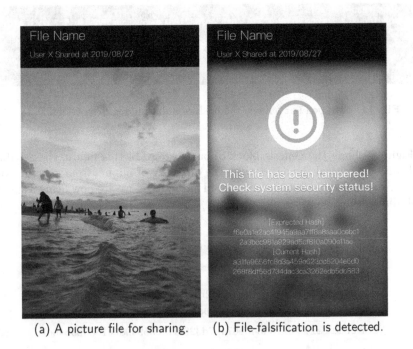

(a) A picture file for sharing.   (b) File-falsification is detected.

Fig. 13. Results of file-tamper detection.

4.2   A Case-Study of the Proposed Prototype

In the following, we will demonstrate the a case study under a prototype of the proposed system based on the aforementioned methodology. A case study is illustrated by the interactions of manager, controllers 1 and 2.

Manager with an address 0x498f91d⋯92a09f93 creates the smart contract GlobalData with a transaction address 0x3845e56⋯c40441a. This successful transaction costs 1670258 gas and with a size 6808.

Next, manager adds controller1, which owns an address 0xf2c682e0⋯a37dcf7, by invoking the addController() in smart contract GlobalData. This operation incurs smaller transaction cost and execution cost than the previous operation does.

With the first three steps, the data can be synchronized between controllers 1 and 2. The controller1 then writes an index of its local data as "test-key-1" to the smart contract GlobalData by invoking the writeIndex(key, hash) function. This index-writing operation spends 1000000 gas as the transaction cost. In particular, when the "test-key-1" is stored in GolbalData, a unit256 hash is created to form a ⟨key, hash⟩ pair in the data structure of controller1, i.e., Bucket A.

Finally, in Fig. 11, we show the results of reading the data synchronized by controller1 from controller2. First, we implement the data-read function based on a script read-index.js, to enable controller2 read the data from the smart contract GlobalData. The results return 1, which indicates that controller2 successfully has obtained the data string "test-key-1" from the GlobalData by invoking the readIndex(key) function.

From the data interaction among controllers 1, 2 and smart contract GlobalData, we can observe the tamper-proof mechanism of the proposed system. Any other more complicated application scenarios can be developed following the demonstrated sample case study.

4.3   Performance Analysis of the Proposed Prototype

Through Fig. 12, we evaluate the performance of the private-chain Ethereum-based data synchronizing system. For example, Fig. 12(a) shows the generation speed of blocks in this system. We can see that there are random perturbations when generating new blocks, if we zoom in a fine-grained time span from timestamp 406500 to 407100. Figure 12(b) illustrates the relationship between mining difficulty vs timestamp: the difficulties are dynamically tuned at each time slot. This is to make the block generation speed relatively stable within a tolerable range. Figure 12(c) displays the CDF (cumulative distribution function) of block-generation intervals of this system. It shows that 80% and 95% blocks are generated within 20 and 40 s, respectively.

We then test the file-falsification detection function of our prototype. The results are shown in Fig. 13. Note that, Fig. 13(a) is the file shared by a member, i.e., a domain controller, while Fig. 13(b) illustrates the results warned by our prototype, which detects that the original file was tampered. Thus, we can see that the proposed prototype realizes the file tamper-proof function.

5   Conclusion and Future Work

In this paper, we present the design and implementation of the proposed network-view consensus protection system. Based on the Ethereum platform, we implement a prototype. System evaluation is finally demonstrated to show the effectiveness of our prototype. More sophisticated implementation and analysis will be conducted based on our prototype.

Acknowledgement. The work described in this paper was supported by the National Natural Science Foundation of China (61902445, 61872195, 61572262), partially by the Natural Science Foundation of Guangdong (2018B030312002), partially by the Fundamental Research Funds for the Central Universities of China under Grant 19lgpy222, and partially by Natural Science Foundation of Guangdong Province of China under Grant 2019A1515011798.

References

1. Xu, C., Wang, K., Guo, M.: Intelligent resource management in blockchain-based cloud datacenters. IEEE Cloud Comput. **4**(6), 50–59 (2017)
2. Xu, C., Wang, K., Li, P., Guo, S., Luo, J., Ye, B., Guo, M.: Making big data open in edges: a resource-efficient blockchain-based approach. IEEE Trans. Parallel Distrib. Syst. **30**(4), 870–882 (2018)
3. Qiu, C., Yu, F.R., Yao, H., Jiang, C., Xu, F., Zhao, C.: Blockchain-based software-defined industrial internet of things: a dueling deep q-learning approach. IEEE IoT J. **6**(3), 4627–4639 (2019)
4. Zou, J., Ye, B., Qu, L., Wang, Y., Orgun, M.A., Li, L.: A proof-of-trust consensus protocol for enhancing accountability in crowdsourcing services. IEEE Trans. Serv. Comput. **12**(3), 429–445 (2019)
5. Yin, H., Guo, D., Wang, K., Jiang, Z., Lyu, Y., Xing, J.: Hyperconnected network: a decentralized trusted computing and networking paradigm. IEEE Netw. **32**(1), 112–117 (2018)
6. Liu, Y., Wang, K., Lin, Y., Xu, W.: Lightchain: a lightweight blockchain system for industrial internet of things. IEEE Trans. Ind. Inf. **15**, 3571–3581 (2019)
7. Li, H., Wang, K., Miyazaki, T., Xu, C., Guo, S., Sun, Y.: Trust-enhanced content delivery in blockchain-based information-centric networking. IEEE Netw. **3**, 183–189 (2019)
8. Wu, M., Wang, K., Cai, X., Guo, S., Guo, M., Rong, C.: A comprehensive survey of blockchain: from theory to IoT applications and beyond. IEEE IoT J. **6**, 8114–8151 (2019)
9. Qiu, K., Huang, S., Xu, Q., Zhao, J., Wang, X., Secci, S.: Paracon: a parallel control plane for scaling up path computation in sdn. IEEE Trans. Netw. Serv. Manag. **14**(4), 978–990 (2017)
10. Sharma, P.K., Singh, S., Jeong, Y.-S., Park, J.H.: DistBlockNet: a distributed blockchains-based secure sdn architecture for iot networks. IEEE Commun. Mag. **55**(9), 78–85 (2017)

11. Xiong, Z., Zhang, Y., Niyato, D., Wang, P., Han, Z.: When mobile blockchain meets edge computing. IEEE Commun. Mag. **56**(8), 33–39 (2018)
12. Phemius, K., Bouet, M., Leguay, J.: Disco: distributed multi-domain SDN controllers. In: IEEE Network Operations and Management Symposium (NOMS), pp. 1–8 (2014)
13. Lin, P., et al.: A west-east bridge based SDN inter-domain testbed. IEEE Commun. Mag. **53**(2), 190–197 (2015)
14. Sharma, P.K., Chen, M.-Y., Park, J.H.: A software defined fog node based distributed blockchain cloud architecture for iot. IEEE Access **6**, 115–124 (2018)

Distributed Logging Service with Distributed Hash Table for Cloud

Takayuki Kushida[✉]

School of Computer Science, Tokyo University of Technology,
Katakura, Hachouji, Tokyo 192-0914, Japan
kushida@acm.org

Abstract. The logging service on cloud is a critical component for administrators who maintain applications and solutions for end users. The service is usually a central server deployment to accept log messages from leaf computing nodes. Since several leaf computing nodes and their usages are dynamically changed for applications and solutions, the amount of generated log messages is also changed. This paper proposes the architecture and design for Distributed Logging Service (DLS) which can distribute processing powers and storage resources to leaf computing nodes with Distributed Hash Table (DHT). Those nodes generate log messages and also have DLS components locally. The evaluation results with the emulated environment show the feasibility of DLS with the scalability.

Keywords: Distributed logging · Logging service · Cloud management · Distributed Hash Table

1 Introduction

Cloud has been widely adopted in IT industry since cloud services could solve several issues of IT automation in production systems. One of cloud advantages is to acquire computing resources with user's requests as on-demand basis [18]. As the number of user's requests for cloud is changed as on-demand, the consumed computing resources are increased and decreased with those requests. In addition, the serverless computing which also dynamically manages computing resources has been emerged on cloud native environments [14].

On the other hand, the logging service on systems management is critical for production systems in enterprises, and applications in enterprises are migrated to microservice [3]. The logging service on cloud usually requires the dedicated CPU and storage resources to store log messages and search log messages. Therefore, the logging service has following challenges and issues which will be fixed for production systems in enterprises.

1. Critical backend service: Logging service is one of critical management services for production systems in enterprises. The service is always used for

© Springer Nature Switzerland AG 2020
C.-H. Hsu et al. (Eds.): IOV 2019, LNCS 11894, pp. 158–173, 2020.
https://doi.org/10.1007/978-3-030-38651-1_15

the operation and management [10]. The latest status is collected into the management system since the production system has to be always up and running without any service disruption.

2. Central Logging Service (CLS): The logging service consists of several central servers on the deployment since it is based on the central model. All log messages are forwarded to the central servers, and they are processed on them. As the single point failure for CLS can be avoided, it is high availability and has a good scalability for both incoming log messages and user's access.

3. Dynamically changing environments: In early days of IT infrastructure, resource requirements for the logging service were static since the configurations of traditional data centers were fixed. As cloud is the dynamic changed computing environment, the estimation of computing and storage resources is one of major challenges for the architecture design. In addition, the resource requirement for the logging service is also changing and it's hard to estimate the resource allocation for the logging service.

4. Dedicated CPU and storage resources: Dedicated CPU resources is required although it is the backend management service [17]. Enough CPU resources can process those log messages for CLS. In addition, dedicated disk storages to store a large amount of log messages are also required in the central servers.

A new architecture is required to fix those issues and challenges for the logging service. This paper proposes Distributed Logging Service (DLS) with the distributed model in Fig. 1. Figure 2 shows the architecture of DLS for solutions and applications on cloud. It adopts the distributed deployment model instead of the traditional central model for the logging service.

The paper consists following sections. The section of "Related Work" describes the related studies for management services which the logging service is included in. The section of "Architecture" describes the architecture and the model of the logging service on cloud. The section of "Design of Distributed Logging Service" describes the required functions and the DLS design. The section of "Evaluation" describes the evaluation and its results for DLS. The section of "Discussions" describes the issues and challenges for this study. The section of "Conclusion" describes the summary and concluding remarks.

2   Related Work

Related studies are described in this section There are two categories such as Central management systems and Distributed Hash Table.

2.1   Central Management Systems

Apache Hadoop and Spark are software stacks which can process the large amount of data [23,29], but they are also the central management systems. The well-known software product for the log management is ElasticSearch which is based on the central key-value database [10]. The architecture design is a central server which has the central database to search log messages. The central

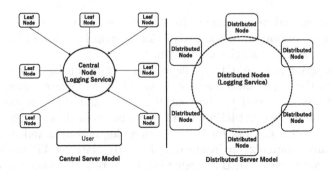

Fig. 1. Central model and distributed model

architecture model for ElasticSearch could be usually applied to usual production systems on both cloud and on-premise data center. ElasticSearch, Logstash and Kibana (ELK) are a typical log management software suite for the central architecture model [1,2]. It collects all log messages from leaf computing nodes since log agents on leaf computing nodes are forwarding to the central servers for ElasticSearch. All search and analysis processes are done in the central servers.

LogDNA is a cloud service provider for the logging service. Once the LogDNA agents are installed on leaf computing nodes, log messages on leaf computing nodes are forwarded to LogDNA service, and those log messages are stored in the central storage. Users subscribe the logging services and install LogDNA agent. The operational dashboard from LogDNA is provided to search, analyze and report those log messages [7]. It is also suitable for Kubernetes/Docker containers to see log messages for the operation and management on the environments. It is a central architecture model for logging service, but all related issues for logging service are managed by LogDNA, log management as a service.

The design of the monitoring system (PCMONS) for private cloud monitoring was proposed with the implementation. Use case scenario with the architecture and the application was described in the paper [5]. It is a centralized model for the monitoring system which receives all monitoring data on the central server.

The integrated management system for log messages from distributed sensors was proposed as well as servers and network devices [12]. It also proposes a cross-processing system for several kinds of log messages. It aims to provide a flexible method to get access to distributed log messages using log attributes and values. Although it proposes the distributed management for log messages, the prototype of the distributed processing system is implemented with the local and the central fluentd manages the log messages. Therefore, the architecture is still the central server model.

Log messages are managed on Kubernetes containers and are forwarded through stdout/stderr to outside of the container environment. The installed logging-agent-pod in Kubernetes can forward log messages to the logging services [6]. Therefore, all log messages can be processed on CLS. Since dockers on Kubernetes environment are rather small than ordinal VMs, many docker containers can be created and are generating many log messages in overall even if those containers are rather small system.

The robust and scalable technology for distributed monitoring, management and data mining have been proposed as Astrolabe [28]. It collects a large-scale system state, permitting rapid updates and providing on-the-fly attribute aggregation.

The distributed management architecture was proposed and its system performance was evaluated [13]. The basic idea is to introduce multiple cell heads in front of the management server. The management workload can be managed on those cell heads. Although the distributed management is proposed, it is still a limited distributed management.

2.2   Distributed Hash Table (DHT)

DHT has been used to support distributed contents management [19]. One of DHT implementations, Chord provides to support just one operation: given a key, it maps the key onto a node. Data location can be easily implemented on top of Chord by associating the key with each data item, and storing the key/data pair at the node to which the key maps [25]. It provides load balance, decentralized, scalability and availability. In addition, Chord has several characters for distributed operation: 1. Node Joins and Stabilizations, 2. Impact of Node Joins on Lookups, 3. Failure and Replication, 4. Voluntary Node Departures. The consistency caching to map index to data contents is used for fault tolerance [15].

The Cassandra project is one of DHS implementations [16]. It is a one hop of DHT and eventually consistent with tunable trade-offs between consistency and latency. In addition, it is more than a simple DHT because the values are not opaque, but they are structured into columns and columnFamilies, which are indexed in Cassandra.

The performance evaluation was reported on the implementation of DHash++ [8]. In this study, measurements with 425 server instances running hosts show that the latency optimizations for DHT++ can reduce the processing time by a factor of two. The time is required to locate and fetch data. In addition, the throughput optimizations result in a sustainable bulk read throughput which is related to the number of DHT hosts times the capacity of the slowest access link. Since the results of performance evaluation for DHT++ implementation can be referred to the performance aspect of DHT.

UsenetDHT is a service aiming to reduce the total storage dedicated to Usenet by storing all articles in a shared DHT [24]. The study describes the design and implementation of UsenetDHT. It allows a set of cooperating sites to keep a shared, distributed copied articles. It uses DHT that provides shared storage of those Usenet articles across the sites. This study utilizes shared storage for those articles with DHT.

Amazon Dynamo is highly available key-store database [9]. It is provided as Platform as a Service (PaaS) from Amazon Web Service. As it is characterized as a zero-hop DHT, each node maintains enough routing information locally to

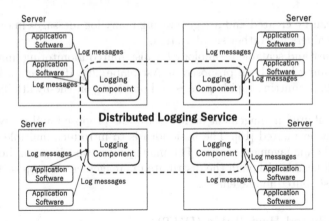

Fig. 2. Architecture of DLS

route a request to the appropriate node directly. Bigtable is a distributed storage system to manage structured data that is designed to scale to a very large size [4]. It is a central service for end users and a good evidence for the scalable DHT implementation on the local server. Although they are not focused on the distributed logging service on cloud, their studies and implementations are quite valuable for the proposed architecture and design.

3   Architecture

This section describes the architecture of the logging service for the central and distributed model.

3.1   Requirements

The architecture decision for the central and distributed model is done with the investigations.

Two major functions are required for the logging service in general. They are "Store" and "Retrieve" functions for those log messages. The "Store" function is simply to store them in the repository without a longer delay. The "Retrieve" function is to get them with the specified condition of the search. It retrieves log messages which can be used for different kinds of activities which are in development, test and operation phases.

The applications and solutions need to follow the dynamically changing computing environment. It means that the flow of log messages from leaf computing nodes has often a large amount of data for the logging service. It is accepted and processed on the logging service.

The consumption of CPU and storage resources is minimized in general. Logging service needs a lot of dedicated CPU resource to create the index and search the specific log message in the repository. In addition, an amount of storage to store log messages is required. The efficient resource management for both CPU and storage resource can be considered.

Although the logging service is the backend management service, it is critical for the production system. Because the service provides any past event with log messages. The systems management can find the failure event and the unusual message among them and understand what was happened in the past.

3.2   Central and Distributed Model

Figure 1 shows "Central Server Model" (CSM) and "Distributed Server Model" (DSM) for the logging services on the central server. The CSM accepts and processes all log messages The left side of Fig. 1 is the CSM. In the left side of Fig. 1, "Leaf Computing Nodes" send log messages to "Central Node" which is the logging service. Once Log messages are received on the logging service, they are processed to put the index and stored in the storage. User can search and retrieve the log messages through the dashboard on the logging service in the left side of Fig. 1.

The operation and management functions including the logging service usually require the central servers which collect log messages from leaf computing nodes. When a large amount of logging messages is generated and forwarded to the central servers, the large amount of CPU and storage resources are required to process and store them on time. In addition, as the peak flow of log message is supported, the idle or unused resources is reserved for the logging service on cloud. The systems management function is in general a kind of overhead function for the services even when it is mandatory required for the development, test and operation phases.

On the other hand, the DSM can be processed on those distributed nodes. The workload can be assigned to distributed nodes instead of a large central server. If there is additional overhead for DSM on the logging service, the feasibility for the logging service is investigated to support the logging service with DSM.

DSM for logging services can be considered since several drawbacks for CSM can be fixed [27]. The right side in Fig. 1 shows the DSM for the logging service. Those log messages are forwarded and stored on distributed nodes in this model instead of collecting the central server. DLS provides the processing service for log messages on those distributed nodes. It means that there is no central server to store those log messages and search the specific log message.

The management server for the logging service and the access point which supports API can be on distributed servers. They act as a part of the logging service instead of assigning to the dedicated central server which processes the transactions for the logging service.

3.3   DHT

DHT is a solid technology which can share a large amount of data with the robustness and availability on distributed nodes. Chord is one of DHT implementations [25]. It manages the hash table on the distributed nodes. Their data entries are stored into the distributed nodes with the hash table. There are several advantages for DHT: 1. There is a resilience to join and leave networks. DHT can also support the network changes. 2. Hashed data can be automatically distributed to DHT nodes. Since stored data are replicated across nodes, data loss can be avoided with the lost node. The removal of any single node doesn't have an impact at all.

On the other hand, DHT has several considered items: 1. There is no native support for events or triggers. 2. It doesn't provide absolute guarantees on data consistency and integrity. 3. It isn't efficient for group queries, range queries or other kinds of data lookups. 4. There is no authority in the setup. Therefore, any node must cooperate among them in case certain decisions need to be made. 5. The time range of lookup for data is $O(\log(n))$. It may take several seconds, depending on real location, the number of nodes and those latencies among nodes. As those considered items can be managed, DHT can be applied to the logging service.

3.4   Architecture of DLS

Figure 2 shows the architecture of DLS. Each server has the process for "Application Software" and "Logging Component". Application software on each server provides the solution services to end users. They also generate a lot of log messages which are stored in local files. The logging component on each server is deployed on the same server where the application software is running. It finds and retrieves those log messages for the request with API. In Fig. 2, those logging components are interconnected among leaf computing nodes.

In general, after the logging service is deployed on the cloud environments, service owner or user require to set up the log agent which collects and forwards log messages for their applications to the central log server.

Therefore, the central server for the logging service require enough computing resources such as CPU, memory and disk since the central server processes a lot of log messages which are forwarded by leaf computing nodes. Although the logging service on cloud is critical for the operation and management, the service is only backend operation function.

3.5   Use Case Scenarios for Retrieval and Alert Notification

Figure 4 shows the example of log messages which are generated by Web server on the operation phase. They are forbidden and error messages with date, time and IP address. Log messages with the same and similar format are stored in the logging service.

Once log messages are stored, they are searched and retrieved from the repository. If the specified server on the production system has error as the example of log messages in Fig. 4, the administrator starts investigating to know two aspects briefly: 1. One is to know the current status of the specific server. The current

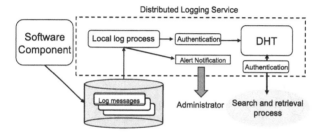

Fig. 3. Local DHT process

```
2019/05/24 22:08:22 [crit] 24841#24841: \
    *5444 SSL_do_handshake() failed \
    (SSL: error:1420918C:SSL \
    routines:tls_early_post_process_client_hello\
    :version too low) while SSL handshaking, \
    client: 192.168.1.1, server: 0.0.0.0:443
2019/05/25 12:14:40 [error] 24841#24841: \
    *5664 access forbidden by rule, client: \
    192.168.1.1, server: test, request: \
    "GET /", host: "server", referrer: \
    "https://server/documents/"
```

Fig. 4. Example of log messages

status can be investigated with the monitoring and logging service. 2. Another is to know the time when the specified server had error or was down.

In addition, if the failure is happened in the operation, log messages include the failure event. Those events are linked to generate the alert notification. Alert notifications is usually linked to failure for system/service, unusual status of the system or security incident. When the alert notification is generated with log messages, operators and administrators review the specific log message for the alert notification and execute the recovery process to solve the incident.

If the unusual failure event on the server is detected in those log messages, the alert notification is generated to notify to the administrator. The administrator fixes the issue and recover the system immediately. In addition, he/she must check those log messages and solve the root cause for the issue.

4 Design of Distributed Logging Service

This section describes the design of DLS for production usages.

4.1 Adoption of DHT and Local Process

As DHT can process log messages on distributed nodes, each node can store and retrieve them without the central server. Every node generates log messages

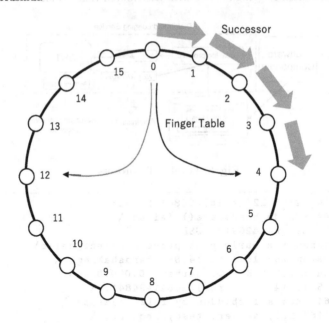

Fig. 5. DHT - Chord

which are stored into local log files at first. Those log messages are accumulated in local log files. The local agent forwards those log messages to DHT. Therefore, log messages are stored into the table in DHT.

The hash table is provided to get keys and values. Both keyes and values are defined for DHT. Keys are timestamps and type of log messages, values are the message itself. The definition can reduce the size of DHT and has the separation between the index for search and actual message contents for the retrieval.

Figure 5 shows that DHT manages logging messages for DLS. Once the query for DHT are sent to find log messages in DHT [11], it can be retrieved for the search results in DHT since DHT keeps those log messages.

Figure 3 shows the process on the local host which is one of DHT nodes. Software component in local host stores log messages to the storage. Each local host has DHT component which can accept log messages which are locally generated. They are submitted to the local part of DHT. DHT starts sharing those log messages with other DHT nodes.

DLS can also check them whether the alert notification is generated. If it's not required, the log messages are submitted to DHT. Once they are stored in DHT, search and retrieval process will get the specific log message from DHT. The administrator can search and retrieve it for the further analysis of the infrastructure issues with the operation dashboard. On the other hand, CSM for the logging service adopts to install the log agent which forwards log messages to the central server.

4.2 Lifetime for Log Messages

Log messages from leaf computing nodes are locally stored in DHT. Since they are created with various kinds of activities in those leaf computing nodes and forwarded to DHT in DLS, the storage sizes for DHT gets are growing so fast. Therefore, the expiration time for those log messages is configured so that the total size of local storage can be managed.

Old entries for log messages are simply moved to inexpensive storage from DHT once the expiration time is reached. After old ones are moved to the inexpensive repository and it takes sometime later, the oldest ones in the repository are permanently removed from DHT.

4.3 Access Control

Log messages are kept under the access control. DHT contains the hash table to store and retrieve values with keys. It is deployed to those multiple nodes. Since different users and processes get to access to DLS, local authentication for them is required to valid access to DLS.

The first item (storing) for access control is to store log messages which come from leaf computing nodes. The access control is also required to store log messages. Since local log messages are stored in the system, the process is done by the local log agent only. The second item (retrieving) for access control is to retrieve log messages for analysis on systems management. The method is based on API, and it provides access control when log messages are retrieved.

Authentication module of DLS is shown in Fig. 3. In Fig. 3, user authentication can be applied for access control. Authentication is to protect log messages from invalid access.

In other study, there is an authentication method called Hash-based Distributed Authentication Method (HDAM). It realizes a decentralized efficient mutual authentication mechanism for each pair of nodes [26]. As the authentication service on cloud can be relied on, the paper has adopted as usual authentication service.

5 Evaluation

This section describes the evaluation for the proposed architecture and design. The performance test on the emulated environment has been done to evaluate the deployment for DLS. The scalability with a reasonable performance is achieved with the proposed deployment for DLS. As the number of DHT nodes is increased, the capability to process log messages is evaluated. For example, it is examined how much the performance to retrieve log messages on DHT is changed.

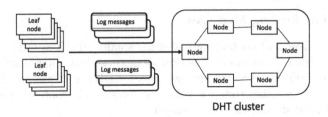

Fig. 6. Typical DLS setup on evaluations

5.1 Emulation Toolkit

The emulated environment is constructed with the DHT software emulator called OverlayWeaver [21,22]. It facilitates the implementation of routing algorithms, and runs with multiple well-known algorithms for DHT just in hundreds of lines of codes with the toolkit [20].

This toolkit also provides a common API to support higher level components which are DHT and multicast functions. It can support multiple DHT algorithms which are Chord, Kademlia, Koorde, Pastry and Tapestry. Those DHT algorithms and routing methods have been discussed and evaluated on the previous study [25].

The proposed architecture has been evaluated with Chord, DHT algorithm. It is well-know DHT algorithm and the emulated environment could be constructed with the toolkit. As it is used for DHT algorithm in the evaluation, the iterative routing is applied to DHT. It is a basic algorithm and routing method, and the evaluation has been focused on the feasibility of DLS with DHT.

5.2 Evaluation Scenarios

Figure 6 shows a typical configuration and the processing of log messages for DLS. The evaluation has adopted use-case scenarios with the typical configuration on the toolkit. In Fig. 6, those leaf computing nodes generated log messages and forward them to DHT which is a cluster of nodes. The cluster consists of several nodes on DHT. DHT cluster processes incoming log messages from leaf computing nodes. As those nodes are located at distributed locations, the processing for incoming log messages can be distributed to those nodes.

Basic functions for the logging service are "Store" and "Retrieve" for log messages. The "Store" function is to store those incoming log messages into the backend storage which is DHT in the proposed method. This process can be sequential and the submissions of log messages are different time. It can be the batch process and not related to use experience.

Thus, the "Retrieve" function is evaluated for the performance of the proposed method. It takes some time to retrieve the log message which is specified by user since many log messages are stored in DLS with DHT. The performance evaluation is to retrieve log messages from the number of stored messages.

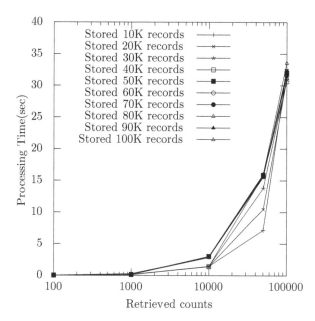

Fig. 7. Processing time for retrieved counts

The emulated environment runs on the single computer which Linux is installed. The connections among DHT nodes are the loopback network interfaces which can avoid the network overhead for the interactions among multiple computers. In this environment, the performance of DHT can be also measured with the different retrieval data set and the different number of stored messages.

5.3   Evaluation Results

Figure 7 shows the processing times for the count of retrieval records (log messages) which are stored in DLS when the number of DHT nodes is fixed at 10. The number of stored log messages in DLS is changed from 10K–100K records. The retrieved counts are changed at 100, 1000, 10000, 50000 and 100000 in Fig. 7. The processing times to retrieve log messages from those stored messages are measured with the given conditions.

Although the number of stored records which contain log messages are from 10K to 100K with increased 10K, the processing time at 100K is only a slightly different from one at 10K records. Therefore, the processing time isn't directly related to the number of stored recorded. As the number of retrieval counts is increased from 100 to 100000, the processing time is approximately 32 s at stored record 10000 in Fig. 7. The processing times are increased with the number of retrieved counts but not the linear relationship.

In Chord for DHT, each node gets routing entries for few other nodes [25]. It maintains the routing information as those nodes join and leave the system.

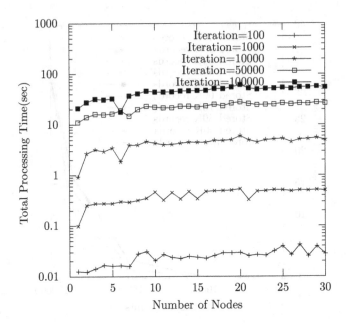

Fig. 8. Processing time for multiple nodes

As the routing table is updated, each node can resolve the hash function with information of few other nodes. As each node maintains information only about $O(\log N)$ for N, each search process can be completed in no more than $O(\log 2$ N) messages.

The overhead for the processing on DHT nodes has been evaluated.

Figure 8 shows the graph of processing time with the number of nodes which DLS consists of. The x-axis is the number of nodes from 1 to 30, and the y-axis is the processing time for the retrieval of records in DHT. When the specific record is searched, the retrievals of records (log message) are randomly selected. The number of iterations is the count to retrieve the specified log messages. Those iterations are 100, 1000, 10000, 50000 and 100000 in Fig. 8. Those processing times to retrieve log messages is directly linked to the waiting time for applications and users. In Fig. 8, although the number of DLS nodes is increased from 1 to 30, the total processing time to retrieve the specified log message is rather similar or slightly increased for the number of DLS nodes. It means that the overhead of the DLS processing time is minimum. Those iterations are the number of retrieval trials. As they are changed from 100 to 100000, the processing times to retrieve the specified log message changed as the same as those iterations. The number of iterations to retrieve the specific log messages from DLS is directly related to the processing time.

The evaluation results on the emulated environment show a scalability of DLS without any accumulated overhead.

6 Discussions

The section discusses the considerations and challenges for the proposed method.

The evaluation results exhibit to provide DLS for less overhead of DHT. The balance for the resource allocation for the logging service is considered. Less number of nodes with a large number of log messages causes some issue to process log messages in each node. When the number of leaf computing nodes which generate log messages is increased, DLS requires to increase CPU and storage resources to process them.

In addition, the search processing power is increased when the large number of log messages is stored. There is a balance between several nodes and the number of incoming log messages, and it is the search processing for the retrieved log messages. The dynamic load balance and increased computing resources can be applied to resolve it.

The CPU and storage resources for those leaf computing nodes are different in general. Some node has a large computing resource but some doesn't. The balance of resource consumption for CPU and storage is considered. For example, the node with large computing resource receives a lot of log messages but the node with less computing resource processes less log messages. DLS with hybrid approach, which consists of dedicated nodes for the log service and shared nodes with applications, can be considered in this case. In the consideration of those approaches, the DHT algorithm is updated with the resource usages instead of equally hashed allocation to store and retrieve those log messages.

7 Conclusion

The paper proposes the distributed logging service with DHT since it meets the requirements for the logging service. It could solve several issues that are faced for the current logging service with CLS. In the proposed method, the workloads to store, process and retrieve those log messages can be distributed among distributed leaf computing nodes which applications and solutions are currently deployed on. The DLS can reduce the dedicated CPU and storage resource for the systems management services and the logging service keeps the same level of service as CLS. Use cases, lifetime management and access control have been designed for DLS. The evaluation results for the retrieval counts and node overheads shows the feasibility with a scalability and a sustainable performance.

References

1. Bagnasco, S., Berzano, D., Guarise, A., Lusso, S., Masera, M., Vallero, S.: Monitoring of IaaS and scientific applications on the cloud using the elasticsearch ecosystem. J. Phys: Conf. Ser. **608**, 012016 (2015)
2. Bagnasco, S., Berzano, D., Guarise, A., Lusso, S., Masera, M., Vallero, S.: Towards monitoring-as-a-service for scientific computing cloud applications using the elasticsearch ecosystem. J. Phys: Conf. Ser. **664**, 022040 (2015)

3. Balalaie, A., Heydarnoori, A., Jamshidi, P.: Microservices architecture enables devops: migration to a cloud-native architecture. IEEE Softw. **33**(3), 42–52 (2016). https://doi.org/10.1109/MS.2016.64
4. Chang, F., et al.: Bigtable: a distributed storage system for structured data. ACM Trans. Comput. Syst. (TOCS) **26**(2), 4 (2008)
5. Chaves, S.A.D., Uriarte, R.B., Westphall, C.B.: Toward an architecture for monitoring private clouds. IEEE Commun. Mag. **49**(12), 130–137 (2011). https://doi.org/10.1109/MCOM.2011.6094017
6. Kubernetes Community: Logging architecture in kubernetes (2018). https://kubernetes.io/docs/concepts/cluster-administration/logging/
7. LogDNA Company: Logdna web site (2019). http://logdna.com
8. Dabek, F., Li, J., Sit, E., Robertson, J., Kaashoek, M.F., Morris, R.: Designing a DHT for low latency and high throughput. In: NSDI, vol. 4, pp. 85–98 (2004)
9. DeCandia, G., et al.: Dynamo: Amazon's highly available key-value store. In: Proceedings of Twenty-First ACM SIGOPS Symposium on Operating Systems Principles, SOSP 2007, pp. 205–220. ACM, New York (2007). https://doi.org/10.1145/1294261.1294281
10. Gormley, C., Tong, Z.: Elasticsearch: The Definitive Guide: A Distributed Real-Time Search and Analytics Engine. O'Reilly Media Inc., Newton (2015)
11. Harren, M., Hellerstein, J.M., Huebsch, R., Loo, B.T., Shenker, S., Stoica, I.: Complex queries in DHT-based peer-to-peer networks. In: Druschel, P., Kaashoek, F., Rowstron, A. (eds.) IPTPS 2002. LNCS, vol. 2429, pp. 242–250. Springer, Heidelberg (2002). https://doi.org/10.1007/3-540-45748-8_23
12. Ikebe, M., Yoshida, K.: An integrated distributed log management system with metadata for network operation. In: 2013 Seventh International Conference on Complex, Intelligent, and Software Intensive Systems, pp. 747–750, July 2013. https://doi.org/10.1109/CISIS.2013.134
13. Jiang, C.B., Liu, I.H., Liu, C.G., Chen, Y.C., Li, J.S.: Distributed log system in cloud digital forensics. In: 2016 International Computer Symposium (ICS), pp. 258–263, December 2016. https://doi.org/10.1109/ICS.2016.0059
14. Jonas, E., et al.: Cloud programming simplified: a Berkeley view on serverless computing. Technical report UCB/EECS-2019-3, EECS Department, University of California, Berkeley, February 2019
15. Karger, D., Lehman, E., Leighton, T., Panigrahy, R., Levine, M., Lewin, D.: Consistent hashing and random trees: distributed caching protocols for relieving hot spots on the world wide web. In: Proceedings of the Twenty-Ninth Annual ACM Symposium on Theory of Computing, STOC 1997, pp. 654–663. ACM, New York (1997). https://doi.org/10.1145/258533.258660
16. Lakshman, A., Malik, P.: Cassandra: a decentralized structured storage system. ACM SIGOPS Oper. Syst. Rev. **44**(2), 35–40 (2010)
17. Lin, X., Wang, P., Wu, B.: Log analysis in cloud computing environment with hadoop and spark. In: 2013 5th IEEE International Conference on Broadband Network Multimedia Technology, pp. 273–276, November 2013. https://doi.org/10.1109/ICBNMT.2013.6823956
18. Mell, P., Grance, T.: The NIST definition of cloud computing. NIST special publication 800(145), 7 (2011). http://csrc.nist.gov/publications/nistpubs/800-145/SP800-145.pdf
19. Rhea, S., Geels, D., Roscoe, T., Kubiatowicz, J., et al.: Handling churn in a DHT. In: Proceedings of the USENIX Annual Technical Conference, Boston, MA, USA, vol. 6, pp. 127–140 (2004)

20. Shudo, K.: Overlay weaver (2006). http://overlayweaver.sourceforge.net
21. Shudo, K., Tanaka, Y., Sekiguchi, S.: Overlay weaver: an overlay construction toolkit. In: Proceedings of Symposium on Advanced Computing Systems and Infrastructures, pp. 183–191 (2006)
22. Shudo, K., Tanaka, Y., Sekiguchi, S.: Overlay weaver: an overlay construction toolkit. Comput. Commun. **31**(2), 402–412 (2008)
23. Shvachko, K., Kuang, H., Radia, S., Chansler, R., et al.: The hadoop distributed file system. In: MSST, vol. 10, pp. 1–10 (2010)
24. Sit, E., Morris, R., Kaashoek, M.F.: UsenetDHT: a low-overhead design for Usenet. In: Proceedings of the 5th USENIX Symposium on Networked Systems Design and Implementation, NSDI 2008, pp. 133–146. USENIX Association, Berkeley (2008). http://dl.acm.org/citation.cfm?id=1387589.1387599
25. Stoica, I., et al.: Chord: a scalable peer-to-peer lookup protocol for internet applications. IEEE/ACM Trans. Netw. **11**(1), 17–32 (2003). https://doi.org/10.1109/TNET.2002.808407
26. Takeda, A., Hashimoto, K., Kitagata, G., Zabir, S.M.S., Kinoshita, T., Shiratori, N.: A new authentication method with distributed hash table for P2P network. In: 22nd International Conference on Advanced Information Networking and Applications - Workshops (AINA Workshops 2008), pp. 483–488, March 2008. https://doi.org/10.1109/WAINA.2008.203
27. Tanenbaum, A.S., Van Steen, M.: Distributed Systems: Principles and Paradigms. Prentice-Hall, Upper Saddle River (2007)
28. Van Renesse, R., Birman, K.P., Vogels, W.: Astrolabe: a robust and scalable technology for distributed system monitoring, management, and data mining. ACM Trans. Comput. Syst. **21**(2), 164–206 (2003). https://doi.org/10.1145/762483.762485
29. Zaharia, M., Chowdhury, M., Franklin, M.J., Shenker, S., Stoica, I.: Spark: cluster computing with working sets. HotCloud **10**(10–10), 95 (2010)

FLEDGE: Kubernetes Compatible Container Orchestration on Low-Resource Edge Devices

Tom Goethals[(✉)] [iD], Filip De Turck[iD], and Bruno Volckaert[iD]

imec, IDLab, Department of Information Technology, Ghent University,
Technologiepark-Zwijnaarde 15, 9052 Gent, Belgium
togoetha.goethals@UGent.be

Abstract. In recent years, containers have quickly gained popularity in the cloud, mostly thanks to their scalable, ethereal and isolated nature. Simultaneously, edge devices have become powerful enough to run containerized microservices, while remaining small and low-powered. These evolutions have triggered a wave of research into container placement strategies on clusters including edge devices, leading to concepts such as fog computing. These container placement strategies can optimize workload placement across cloud and edge clusters, but current container orchestrators are very resource intensive and are not designed to run on edge devices.

This paper presents FLEDGE as a Kubernetes compatible edge container orchestrator. A number of aspects of how to achieve low-resource container orchestration are examined, for example the choice of container runtime and how to implement container networking. Finally, a number of evaluations are performed, comparing FLEDGE to K3S and Kubernetes, to show that it is a viable alternative to existing container orchestrators.

Keywords: Edge networks · Edge computing · Container orchestration · Containers · VPN

1 Introduction

In recent years, containers have quickly gained popularity for cloud applications, thanks to their limited resource requirements and fast spin-up times compared to virtual machines [1]. The complexity of managing large amounts of containers has led to container orchestrators such as Kubernetes [2], which handles the deployment and scaling of containerized services.

Recently, edge devices have become powerful enough to be able to run containerized microservices, while remaining flexible enough in terms of size and power consumption to be deployed almost anywhere. This has lead to research aimed at deploying containers on edge devices, and shifting containerized workloads between the cloud and the edge. Most container orchestrators are designed

© Springer Nature Switzerland AG 2020
C.-H. Hsu et al. (Eds.): IOV 2019, LNCS 11894, pp. 174–189, 2020.
https://doi.org/10.1007/978-3-030-38651-1_16

to run in the cloud, and are very flexible and modular but not very mindful of resource consumption. Edge devices on the other hand, are typically low-resource devices and non-extensible, especially in terms of memory.

Additionally, container deployments in the cloud are often generic, scalable microservices, whereas those on the edge will be more suited to local computing, with less focus on scaling. This means that an edge container orchestrator should be primarily built to use minimal resources, and less for constantly moving and migrating containers.

Edge devices are often located in networks with potentially less focus on security and organization. In many cases, the device is hidden behind a router with a firewall or NAT, and IP addresses and port mappings are unpredictable.

Being designed for the cloud, most container orchestrators expect a well-organized and homogeneous infrastructure, where all network resources are predictable and controlled. Additionally, unlike intra-cloud communication, communication outside the cloud could be intercepted very easily, so all communication between the cloud and containers deployed on the edge should be secured by default. Any solution to deploy containers on edge devices should therefore not only create a heterogeneous and predictable networking environment for containers to operate in, but also secure communication with the cloud by default.

Continued development of container management tools such as Kubernetes and Docker [3] has led to the development of a number of standards, for example the Container Network Interface (CNI [4]) for container networking, and container format standards from the Open Container Initiative (OCI [5]).

Any solution for edge container deployment should be compatible with existing container standards, so it is important that they are implemented to the extent possible on edge devices. If any standards are ignored or not fully implemented, it should not affect the rest of the cluster.

The requirements for a good container orchestrator for edge devices can therefore be summarized as:

- Compatibility with modern container (orchestration) standards, or providing an adequate alternative.
- Securing communications between the edge and the cloud by default, with minimal impact on local networks.
- Low resource requirements, primarily in terms of memory but also in terms of processing power and storage.

This paper presents FLEDGE as a low-resource container orchestrator which is capable of directly connecting to Kubernetes clusters using modified Virtual Kubelets [6] and a VPN.

Section 2 presents existing research related to the topics in this introduction. Section 3 shows how FLEDGE meets the requirements put forward in this introduction, while Sect. 4 discusses alternative edge container orchestrators. In Sect. 5, an evaluation setup and methodology are presented to compare FLEDGE to alternative orchestrators. The results of the evaluations are presented and discussed in Sect. 6, with suggestions for future work in Sect. 7. Finally, Sect. 8 gives a short overview of the goals stated in this introduction, and how the results and conclusions meet them.

2   Related Work

Shifting workloads between the cloud and edge hardware has been extensively researched, with studies on edge offloading [7], cloud offloading [8], and osmotic computing [9]. Many studies exist on different container placement strategies, from simple but effective resource requests and grants [10], to using deep learning for allocation and real-time adjustments [11].

Kubernetes is capable of forming federations of Kubernetes clusters [12], but this paper aims to use a single cluster for both the cloud and the edge. There are several federation research projects that have resulted in useful frameworks, such as Fed4Fire [13], Beacon [14], FedUp! [15] and FUSE [16]. Fed4Fire requires the implementation of an API to integrate devices into a federation and works on a higher, more abstract level than container orchestration. BEACON is focused on cloud federation and security as a function of cloud federation. FedUp! is a cloud federation framework focused on improving the setup time for heterogeneous cloud federations. FUSE is designed to federate private networks in crisis situations, but it is very general and primarily aimed at quickly collectivizing resources, not for deploying specific workloads across edge clusters.

Studies exist that focus on security between the edge and the cloud, for example [17] which identifies possible threats, and [18] which proposes a Software Defined Membrane as a novel security paradigm for all aspects of microservices.

VPNs are an old and widely used technology. Recent state of the art studies appear to be non-existent, but older ones are still informative [19]. Some studies deal with the security aspects of a VPN [20], while many others focus on the throughput performance of VPNs [21,22].

A study by Pahl et al. [23] gives a general overview of how to create edge cloud clusters using containers. While FUSE [16] is capable of deploying Kubernetes worker nodes on edge devices, the resulting framework is too resource-intensive for most edge hardware. Cloud4IoT [24] is capable of moving containers between edge networks and the cloud, but it uses edge gateways which indirectly deploy containers on minimalistic edge nodes. K3S [25], which has not yet been the subject of academic studies, is based on the source code of Kubernetes. It achieves lower resource consumption by removing uncommon and legacy features, but it requires its own master nodes to run and cannot directly connect to Kubernetes clusters. KubeEdge [26] is a recent development, aiming to extend Kubernetes to edge clusters. Despite being based on Kubernetes, it is not directly compatible with Kubernetes master nodes and needs an extra cloud component to function properly.

3   FLEDGE

This section gives an overview of what a Virtual Kubelet is and how FLEDGE, written in Golang, builds on it to meet the requirements stated in the introduction.

A Virtual Kubelet is a small service which acts as a proxy for Kubernetes to any platform that can run containers, for example Amazon AWS, Microsoft Azure or edge devices. It registers itself as a node in Kubernetes and passes API calls from Kubernetes to brokers which translate those calls to the container platform they implement. These API calls include pod management, pod status, node status, logging and metrics.

The concepts of FLEDGE are shown in Fig. 1, with the Virtual Kubelet acting as a proxy to the FLEDGE broker. The FLEDGE broker is responsible for sending API calls to the edge, where they are decomposed into container networking, cgroup and namespace management, and container deployments. This collection of components will be referred to as a FLEDGE agent.

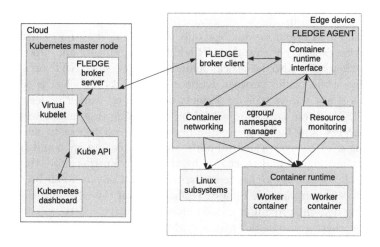

Fig. 1. Conceptual overview of FLEDGE and its use of a Virtual Kubelet.

3.1   Compatibility

One of the stated requirements for FLEDGE is compatibility with existing container standards and runtimes.

Both Docker and Containerd are popular container runtimes and both support OCI standards, and by extension Docker containers. Furthermore, since version 1.11, Docker uses Containerd as an underlying container runtime. In terms of compatibility, both runtimes are good choices, so the decision will be up to resource requirements, as discussed in Sect. 3.3.

Another aspect of compatibility is container networking. In Kubernetes, the master node makes high-level decisions on container networking, such as which IP range to assign to individual nodes. These decisions are relayed to CNI compatible plugins (eg. Flannel, Weave) on worker nodes, which translate the high-level decisions into low-level network configuration.

FLEDGE does this differently by fulfilling the role of both Kubelet and container networking plugin. The number of pods deployed on an edge node is likely to be low due to resource constraints, so the container networking handler (Fig. 1 Container networking) can be simple and naive, assigning pods the first free IP address in its range. The same handler also makes sure network namespaces are configured correctly.

By default, Kubernetes will not attempt to deploy Flannel on a FLEDGE agent. However, because the FLEDGE agent uses the IP range assigned to it by Kubernetes, the rest of the cluster will still be able to reach pods deployed on it. This means that this approach is sufficient, despite not implementing CNI.

3.2 Security and Stability

Edge devices, especially consumer grade, often operate in networks with little to no security and organization. Not only may the devices find themselves in unexpected topologies with random IP address assignments and unknown port mappings, they may also be stuck behind a router with NAT or a firewall. Additionally, while traffic between Kubernetes and its Kubelets is secured by default, this is not always true for services deployed on worker nodes.

In FLEDGE, these issues are solved by connecting edge nodes to the cloud using OpenVPN and building a container network on top of it, as shown in Fig. 2. Using a VPN ensures that all ports are available and open and IP address assignments are logical and reachable by the cloud. Furthermore, the physical network of the device no longer matters, the virtual network can be organized according to any parameters. Finally, traffic between the edge and the cloud is encrypted by default, providing a basic layer of security.

However, there are some downsides to this approach. Using OpenVPN, especially with encryption, is a drain on system and network resources, likely reducing the scalability of the cluster. Moreover, VPN overhead may have a significant impact on edge devices, which have limited computational power. Anyone with physical access to the device can still gain access to the system, and possibly even cloud resources through the VPN. This problem is exacerbated because like Kubernetes and K3S, the FLEDGE agent requires root access to run properly, so hardware security and OS-level security are required to prevent these problems.

Figure 3 gives an overview of the different networks involved in a setup with FLEDGE nodes. Green arrows indicate traffic flows allowed by FLEDGE, while red ones indicate traffic flows forbidden by default. This shows that all devices in the VPN or the Kubernetes pod network can reach each other, but other devices can only be reached by being in the same physical network.

Container images may contain software or data that needs to be protected from unauthorized access. Both the FLEDGE agent and container runtimes

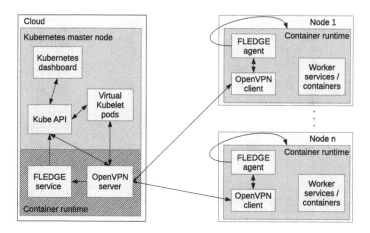

Fig. 2. High-level overview of network traffic flow of FLEDGE, using OpenVPN to connect edge nodes to the cloud.

could potentially be abused to access container images, but some steps can be taken to mitigate this.

Containers and pods are assigned different file system namespaces by container runtimes. While the root user can still access these namespaces, root login can be disabled and the file systems can be protected from other users. To minimize chances of container images being copied, and to avoid clutter, they can be removed when no longer running. However, this will increase the time required for redeployment of containers, thereby affecting performance. Finally, FLEDGE cleans up all containers, images and network infrastructure on shutdown.

3.3   Low Resource Use

An important choice for low resource use is the container runtime. As Sect. 3.1 showed, both Docker and Containerd are good choices in terms of compatibility. However, as Docker actually relies on Containerd since version 1.11, Containerd is likely the more resource-friendly option. This choice will be further evaluated in Sect. 6.

The choice for a custom container networking solution in FLEDGE is optimal in terms of resource requirements. While normal CNI plugins for Kubernetes are run as containers, a flexible and durable approach, they also require more resources than simply embedding container networking into the orchestrator process.

Both namespace and cgroup handling have been implemented in FLEDGE. While FLEDGE relies on the container runtime to set up the namespaces and cgroups setup for the first container of a pod, it reuses those namespaces for all other containers in the same pod. This approach is compatible with both Docker and Containerd, and has the added benefits of being very simple.

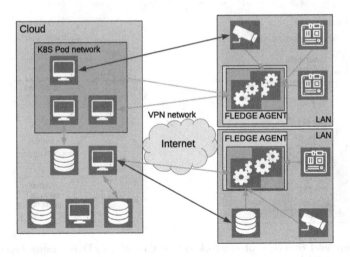

Fig. 3. Overview of network traffic flows in a cluster using FLEDGE nodes. Green arrows indicate possible traffic flows. (Color figure online)

4   Alternatives

This section discusses some alternative container orchestrators, giving a short history and possible advantages and disadvantages for each, which will then be compared to FLEDGE in terms of resource requirements.

4.1   Kubernetes

Kubernetes [2] is a widely used container orchestrator originally inspired by Google Borg [27]. Due to its popularity and extensive development, it has contributed to several container standards. Because it is made to run in the cloud, it is very flexible. However, as Sect. 6 shows it also uses a lot of resources, making it hard to use on edge devices.

An important difference between FLEDGE and Kubernetes is that the latter requires all swapping to be disabled in order to run, which can cause serious problems on devices with limited memory. FLEDGE has no such requirement, allowing all memory subsystems to perform as intended.

4.2   K3S

K3S [25] is a novel container orchestrator based on Kubernetes, modified specifically for edge devices. Version 0.1.0 was released in February 2019, while the version used for the evaluation is v0.3.0 from March 2019. K3S has its own master nodes, unlike FLEDGE which connects to Kubernetes master nodes.

Unlike FLEDGE, which starts from scratch and builds around Kubernetes compatibility, K3S starts with the full Kubernetes source code and eliminates deprecated or little-used functionality. Like FLEDGE, it prefers to hard wire certain types of functionality. For example, it uses Flannel for container networking and forces the use of Containerd.

While being built from the full Kubernetes source means K3S has excellent support for standards, this may also be a disadvantage in terms of resource requirements. It also has its own join mechanism and is, for the moment, incompatible with Kubernetes master nodes, so it cannot directly connect to existing Kubernetes clusters.

4.3   KubeEdge

KubeEdge [28] is an early stage Edge Computing Framework built on Kubernetes and Docker. Its first release was in December 2018, with version 0.3.0 being released as of May 2019. It consists of a cloud part and an edge part [29], with the cloud part interfacing with the cloud Kubernetes API and taking care of node management. The edge part is deployed on each individual device and takes care of pod and low-level facility management.

While its functions include deploying Kubernetes pods on edge networks, it aims to be an entire ecosystem for edge computing, including storage and event-based communication based on MQTT [30]. Because it is hard to isolate the container orchestration part, KubeEdge will not be evaluated in this paper. However, since it uses Docker, it is unlikely to be resource efficient, a point which will be proven in Sect. 6.

5   Evaluation Setup

With the most important concepts of FLEDGE explained and alternative orchestrators discussed, an evaluation environment can be set up and a number of evaluations can be performed. These are intended to validate the choice of container runtime and compare FLEDGE to K3S v0.3.0 and Kubernetes v1.14 in terms of resource requirements. The source code of FLEDGE is made available on Github[1].

5.1   Methodology

Figure 4 shows the hardware setup used for the evaluations, which is run on the imec Virtual Wall [31].

The VWall master node fulfills the role of K3S/Kubernetes master node. Because FLEDGE is aimed at worker nodes, the specifications and performance of this node are not important.

The VWall server (x64) is used to determine the resource requirements of each orchestrator on an x64 worker node. This device runs Ubuntu 18.04 and has an AMD Opteron 2212 processor at 2 GHz and 4 GiB RAM.

---

[1] https://github.com/togoetha/fledge.

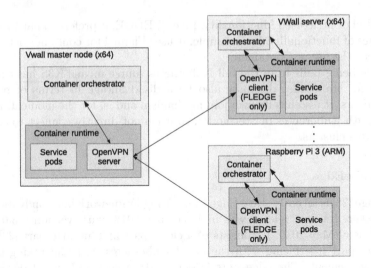

Fig. 4. Overview of the hardware setup used for the evaluation. Note that the Open-VPN containers are only used by FLEDGE, other orchestrators connect directly to the master node via LAN.

The Raspberry Pi 3 is used to evaluate each orchestrator on an ARM device, specifically armhf. This device runs Raspbian with kernel version 4.14.98-v7+ on the default hardware configuration, specifically 1 GiB RAM and a quad-core 1.2 GHz CPU. All devices are in the same geographical location and are connected by Gigabit LAN (100 Mbps max for Raspberry Pi 3). The OpenVPN server and clients are only used when FLEDGE is deployed on the worker nodes. Kubernetes and K3S connect to the master node directly via LAN. All evaluations will be run on both armhf and x64.

For Kubernetes, Docker is used, while Containerd is required by K3S. The container runtime used by FLEDGE is specified in each evaluation.

Storage requirements are measured using the df command [32], both before and after orchestrator setup. This approach takes not only the orchestrator into account, but all dependencies and libraries as well. To ensure proper measurements, the devices are wiped after each run.

Determining memory use is more complex than measuring storage requirements. Unlike the myriad files involved in a container orchestrator, the process running it are more easily identified, allowing for precise and detailed measurements. During orchestrator setup some processes will require memory, used to launch containers or initialize facilities, which is later released. This means that memory use must be monitored for a significant amount of time.

Processes can have private and shared memory. Measuring both memory sets is easy, but a fair method is needed to calculate the exact amount of memory used by each process.

Taking the above into account, each evaluation measures the memory use of a set of processes every 30 s, over a period of 15 min. The pmap [33] command is used to determine the Proportional Set Size (PSS) [34] of each process, which is calculated according to:

$$M_{total} = P + \sum^i S_i/N_i$$

where P is private memory, S_i are various sets of shared memory, and N_i is the number of processes using any piece of shared memory.

5.2 Container Runtime

This evaluation aims to show that the choice of container runtime can have a large impact on the resource requirements of a container orchestrator. To verify this and determine the best choice, FLEDGE is set up using both Docker and Containerd.

To avoid interference from other containers, no pods or containers are deployed other than the FLEDGE agent and a VPN container. To determine the overhead of containerizing FLEDGE, a third case is evaluated in which the FLEDGE agent runs as a host service instead of being deployed as a container.

The processes monitored for this evaluation are the container runtime, the FLEDGE agent, the VPN client container and container shims [35].

5.3 Orchestrator Comparison

In order to verify that FLEDGE is a low-resource solution for edge container orchestration, this evaluation compares it against Kubernetes and K3S. In the Kubernetes comparison, Flannel is used as a CNI plugin and the master node is allowed to deploy kube-proxy [36] on the edge node. Since FLEDGE has its own container networking, Flannel will not be deployed on the FLEDGE edge node. In the K3S comparison, no kube-proxy will be deployed on FLEDGE.

In this evaluation, FLEDGE is run as a host service and uses Containerd as a container runtime. The monitored processes are the container orchestrator, container runtime, shims and any deployed containers.

6 Results

This section presents the results of the evaluations described in Sect. 5. While the results for storage requirements are simple bar charts representing the median case, the results for memory consumption are more dynamic, including whiskers for the median absolute deviation.

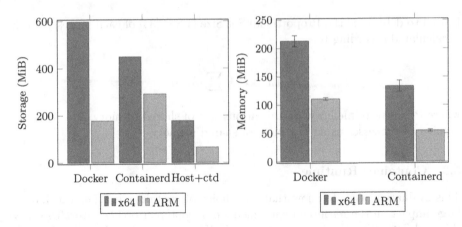

Fig. 5. Storage and memory requirements of FLEDGE using different container runtimes. The Host+ctd category shows the results for FLEDGE running as a host service.

6.1 Container Runtime

Figure 5 shows the storage requirements for FLEDGE deployments with Docker and Containerd.

An important observation is that in all cases, FLEDGE requires significantly less storage on ARM than it does on x64, though the exact amount varies. The combination of FLEDGE and Docker, for example, requires 3 times as much storage on x64 as it does on ARM. While the results suggest that Containerd is much less efficient on ARM than Docker, these numbers conflict with the fact that Docker uses Containerd to run containers. The reason for this is rooted in how Containerd and Docker handle container filesystems and mounts. In order for a containerized FLEDGE agent to be able to deploy containers on Containerd itself, many directories and files need to be mounted into the FLEDGE agent container. It turns out that Containerd mounts have a lot of overhead, resulting in the large container filesystem shown in Fig. 5. To validate this theory, another evaluation was done by deploying a FLEDGE agent as a host service, shown as "Host+ctd". The Containerd installation for this evaluation was also optimized, resulting in a 73 MiB size reduction on x64, and a 14 MiB reduction on ARM. The result is very resource efficient, at the cost of not having the FLEDGE agent isolated in a container. Note that this same approach does not affect Docker much, indicating that while it may use Containerd as a runtime, it has a more efficient method of handling file system layers.

Figure 5 also shows the memory consumption of FLEDGE deployments with Docker and Containerd. The ARM versions are again much more efficient, using up to 50% less memory than x64 in the case of Docker and 65% in the case of Containerd. The results show that Containerd is by far the best container runtime to use with FLEDGE. When running FLEDGE as a host service, the

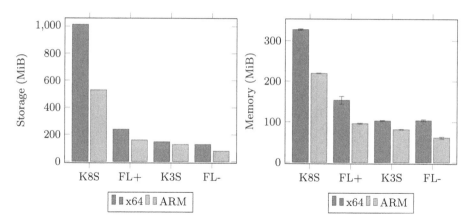

Fig. 6. Storage and memory requirements of evaluated container orchestrators. FL+ and FL- indicate FLEDGE running with and without kube-proxy, respectively.

total resource requirements are only 80 MiB storage and 50 MiB memory on ARM, including a VPN client container.

6.2   Orchestrator Comparison

Figure 6 shows the storage requirements for all container orchestrators. Note that FLEDGE is included twice in this chart; with a kube-proxy ("FL+") and without a kube-proxy ("FL-"). Considering functionality, it is best to compare Kubernetes to FLEDGE with a kube-proxy, and K3S to FLEDGE without a kube-proxy.

Compared to Kubernetes, FLEDGE ("FL+") only needs around 25% as much storage on x64 and 40% on ARM. This large difference can be attributed to many factors, including the choice of Containerd over Docker and the integration of several plugins instead of running them as containers.

When comparing FLEDGE ("FL-") to K3S, the difference is smaller than with Kubernetes, but still significant. FLEDGE requires about 10% less storage on x64, and around 30% less on ARM.

The results for memory consumption are shown in Fig. 6, using the same notation for FLEDGE with and without kube-proxy. These results are less spread out than those of the storage requirements.

For starters, FLEDGE only requires about half as much memory as Kubernetes on both x64 and ARM. Note that simply eliminating Flannel and implementing a custom container networking solution already saves 36 MiB of memory on x64 and 24 MiB on ARM, or around 10% of Kubernetes' memory consumption.

Compared to K3S, FLEDGE has similar memory consumption on x64, but around 25% less on ARM. Considering that most IoT/edge devices are ARM based, this is a significant improvement.

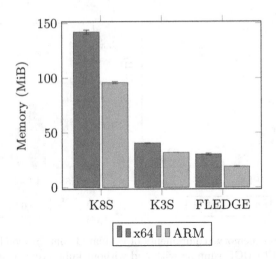

Fig. 7. Memory consumption of the main process of each container orchestrator. For Kubernetes, Flannel was included in the measurement because other orchestrators provide a container network by default.

Finally, Fig. 7 compares the memory consumption of the container orchestrator processes alone, without any other processes. In the case of Kubernetes, Flannel has been included because K3S and FLEDGE provide container networking by default. These results show that in its current state, FLEDGE uses only about 25% as much memory as Kubernetes, and 50% to 60% as much as K3S.

These results show that compared to both Kubernetes and K3S, FLEDGE uses significantly less resources, especially when comparing orchestrator processes directly.

7   Future Work

This paper presents a fully operational container orchestrator for edge devices, but there are still some aspects of FLEDGE that can be improved.

For starters, placing the Virtual Kubelets in the cloud may not be ideal. When running in the cloud, they can buffer commands in case a FLEDGE agent becomes unavailable, but they also require a small amount of storage and memory. Additionally, since all Virtual Kubelets are run in their own pod, the amount of master nodes in the cloud will have to scale with the maximum number of pods per node, instead of using one master node to manage all edge nodes. For these reasons it may be more efficient to integrate the Virtual Kubelet into the FLEDGE agent.

Many other container runtimes than the ones used in FLEDGE exist, including rkt [37] and CRI-O [38]. Docker and Containerd were chosen because of their popularity and support for container standards, but it is possible that other container runtimes use less resources.

Because K3S is based on Kubernetes, it may be possible to modify FLEDGE so that it can also connect to K3S clusters. Considering the original use of Virtual Kubelets, it could also pass Kubernetes deployments to K3S.

FLEDGE uses OpenVPN to build a network environment, but many other VPN solutions exist, which may prove to be faster or more reliable for use with FLEDGE.

8 Conclusion

The introduction puts forward three requirements for an effective container orchestrator on edge devices.

FLEDGE is presented as a solution that meets these requirements. A VPN is used to homogenize edge networks and to provide a basic layer of security for communication between the edge and the cloud. Compatibility with container standards is achieved by using OCI API's to communicate with container runtimes. CNI can be safely ignored using a custom implementation without affecting the rest of the cluster. Low resource requirements are achieved by choosing the optimal container runtime and through the custom implementation of select functionality, such as container networking.

To validate the low resource requirements of FLEDGE, a number of evaluations are performed. The resource requirements for FLEDGE using both Docker and Containerd are examined, showing that Containerd only needs about half the resources Docker does, and confirming that it is the optimal container runtime for FLEDGE.

K3S and Kubernetes are discussed as alternatives to FLEDGE, and evaluated to determine their resource requirements. The results shows that FLEDGE only requires 50–60% less resources than a Kubernetes worker node, and around 25–30% less resources than K3S on ARM devices. On x64, FLEDGE resource requirements are similar to those of K3S.

In conclusion, FLEDGE can deploy Kubernetes pods on edge devices while using significantly less resources than either Kubernetes or K3S. Despite this, it is highly experimental and many topics for future work on improving FLEDGE are discussed.

Acknowledgment. The research in this paper has been funded by Vlaio by means of the FLEXNET research project.

References

1. Felter, W., Ferreira, A., Rajamony, R., Rubio, J.: An updated performance comparison of virtual machines and Linux containers. In: 2015 IEEE International Symposium on Performance Analysis of Systems and Software (ISPASS) (2015). https://doi.org/10.1109/ISPASS.2015.7095802

2. What is Kubernetes? https://kubernetes.io/docs/concepts/overview/what-is-kubernetes/
3. Why Docker? https://www.docker.com/why-docker
4. CNM vs CNI. https://www.nuagenetworks.net/blog/container-networking-standards/
5. About OCI. https://www.opencontainers.org/about
6. Virtual kubelet. https://github.com/virtual-kubelet/virtual-kubelet
7. Mach, P., Becvar, Z.: Mobile edge computing: a survey on architecture and computation offloading. IEEE Commun. Surv. Tutor. **19**(3), 1628–1656 (2017). https://doi.org/10.1109/COMST.2017.2682318
8. Kumar, K., Lu, Y.-H.: Cloud computing for mobile users: can offloading computation save energy? Computer **43**, 51–56 (2010). https://doi.org/10.1109/MC.2010.98
9. Villari, M., Fazio, M., Dustdar, S., Rana, O., Ranjan, R.: Osmotic computing: a new paradigm for edge/cloud integration. IEEE Cloud Comput. **3**(6) (2016). https://doi.org/10.1109/MCC.2016.124
10. Santoro, D., Zozin, D., Pizzolli, D., De Pellegrini, F., Cretti, S.: Foggy: a platform for workload orchestration in a Fog Computing environment. In: 2017 IEEE International Conference on Cloud Computing Technology and Science (CloudCom) (2017). https://doi.org/10.1109/CloudCom.2017.62
11. Morshed, A., et al.: Deep osmosis: holistic distributed deep learning in osmotic computing. IEEE Cloud Comput. **4**(6) (2017). https://doi.org/10.1109/MCC.2018.1081070
12. Kubernetes federation. https://kubernetes.io/docs/concepts/cluster-administration/federation/
13. Wauters, T., et al.: Federation of internet experimentation facilities: architecture and implementation. In: Proceedings of the European Conference on Networks and Communications, pp. 1–5 (2014)
14. Moreno-Vozmediano, R., et al.: BEACON: a cloud network federation framework. In: Celesti, A., Leitner, P. (eds.) ESOCC Workshops 2015. CCIS, vol. 567, pp. 325–337. Springer, Cham (2016). https://doi.org/10.1007/978-3-319-33313-7_25
15. Bottoni, P., Gabrielli, E., Gualandi, G., Mancini, L.V., Stolfi, F.: FedUp! Cloud federation as a service. In: Aiello, M., Johnsen, E.B., Dustdar, S., Georgievski, I. (eds.) ESOCC 2016. LNCS, vol. 9846, pp. 168–182. Springer, Cham (2016). https://doi.org/10.1007/978-3-319-44482-6_11
16. Goethals, T., Kerkhove, D., Van Hoye, L., Sebrechts, M., De Turck, F., Volckaert, B.: FUSE: a microservice approach to cross-domain federation using docker containers. In: CLOSER 2019, the 9th International Conference on Cloud Computing and Services Science, pp. 90–99 (2019)
17. Puthal, D., Nepal, S., Ranjan, R., Chen, J.: Threats to networking cloud and edge datacenters in the internet of things. IEEE Cloud Comput. **3**(3) (2016). https://doi.org/10.1109/MCC.2016.63
18. Villari, M., Fazio, M., Dustdar, S., Rana, O., Chen, L., Ranjan, R.: Software defined membrane: policy-driven edge and internet of things security. IEEE Cloud Comput. **4**(4) (2017). https://doi.org/10.1109/MCC.2017.3791014
19. Chowdhury, N.M.M.K., Boutaba, R.: Network virtualization: state of the art and research challenges. IEEE Commun. Mag. **47**(7) (2009). https://doi.org/10.1109/MCOM.2009.5183468
20. Hamed, H., Al-Shaer, E., Marrero, W.: Modeling and verification of IPSec and VPN security policies. In: 13th IEEE International Conference on Network Protocols (ICNP 2005) (2005). https://doi.org/10.1109/ICNP.2005.25

21. Pohl, F., Schotten, H.D.: Secure and scalable remote access tunnels for the IIoT: an assessment of openVPN and IPsec performance. In: De Paoli, F., Schulte, S., Broch Johnsen, E. (eds.) ESOCC 2017. LNCS, vol. 10465, pp. 83–90. Springer, Cham (2017). https://doi.org/10.1007/978-3-319-67262-5_7

22. Kotuliak, I., Rybár, P., Trúchly, P.: Performance comparison of IPsec and TLS based VPN technologies. In: 2011 9th International Conference on Emerging eLearning Technologies and Applications (ICETA) (2011). https://doi.org/10.1109/ICETA.2011.6112567

23. Pahl, C., Lee, B.: Containers and clusters for edge cloud architectures - a technology review. In: 2015 3rd International Conference on Future Internet of Things and Cloud (2015). https://doi.org/10.1109/FiCloud.2015.35

24. Dupont, C., Giaffreda, R., Capra, L.: Edge computing in IoT context: horizontal and vertical Linux container migration. In: 2017 Global Internet of Things Summit (GIoTS) (2017). https://doi.org/10.1109/GIOTS.2017.8016218

25. Rancher Labs - K3S Lightweight Kubernetes. https://k3s.io/

26. Xiong, Y., Sun, Y., Xing, L., Huang, Y.: Extend cloud to edge with KubeEdge. In: 2018 IEEE/ACM Symposium on Edge Computing (SEC) (2018). https://doi.org/10.1109/SEC.2018.00048

27. Verma, A., Pedrosa, L., Korupolu, M., Oppenheime, D., Tune, E., Wilkes, J.: Large-scale cluster management at Google with Borg. In: EuroSys 2015 Proceedings of the Tenth European Conference on Computer Systems, Article No. 18 (2015)

28. KubeEdge: A Kubernetes Native Edge Computing Framework. https://kubeedge.io/en/

29. What is KubeEdge: Architecture. https://docs.kubeedge.io/en/latest/modules/kubeedge.html#architecture

30. Light, R.A.: Mosquitto: server and client implementation of the MQTT protocol. J. Open Source Softw. https://doi.org/10.21105/joss.00265

31. imec Virtual Wall. https://www.ugent.be/ea/idlab/en/research/research-infrastructure/virtual-wall.htm

32. The DF command. https://www.linuxjournal.com/article/2747

33. pmap - report memory map of a process. https://linux.die.net/man/1/pmap

34. Propertional Set Size (PSS). http://lkml.iu.edu/hypermail/linux/kernel/0708.1/3930.html

35. Docker components explained. http://alexander.holbreich.org/docker-components-explained/

36. kube-proxy. https://kubernetes.io/docs/reference/command-line-tools-reference/kube-proxy/

37. Getting started with rkt. https://coreos.com/rkt/docs/latest/getting-started-guide.html

38. CRI-O, lightweight container runtime for Kubernetes. https://cri-o.io/

Accelerated Promethee Algorithm Based on Dimensionality Reduction

Tarek Menouer[1]([✉]), Christophe Cérin[2], and Patrice Darmon[1]

[1] UMANIS, 7 Rue Paul Vaillant Couturier, 92300 Levallois-Perret, France
{tmenouer,pdarmon}@umanis.com
[2] University of Paris 13, LIPN/CNRS UMR 7030, 93430 Villetaneuse, France
christophe.cerin@lipn.univ-paris13.fr

Abstract. This paper presents an accelerated Promethee (*Preference Ranking Organization METHod for Enrichment Evaluations*) multi-criteria algorithm based on dimensionality reduction in large scale environments. In our context, the Promethee algorithm is used to select from a large set of objects, one or a small set of objects with a good compromise between several qualitative and quantitative criteria. The exact solution can be used by applying the exact multi-criteria Promethee algorithm. However, the drawback, with this type of exact algorithm, is the long execution time due to the combinatorial aspect of the problem. The exact Promethee computing time is linked both to the dimension of the problem (number of qualitative and quantitative criteria) and the size of the problem (number of objects). To address the previous drawback, we propose to accelerate the Promethee algorithm in combining the exact Promethee algorithm with an algorithm inherited from the Machine Learning (ML) field. The experiments demonstrate the potential of our approach under different scenarios to accelerate the respond time.

Keywords: Performance optimization · Machine learning algorithms (K-Means) · Multi-criteria algorithm

1 Introduction

In the literature, several multi-criteria algorithms have been proposed in the past [8,9,14]. These algorithms have been used with success to solve many problems [2], as scheduling problems [11] or profiles recommendation [10].

Among the different multi-criteria algorithms, we would like to mention the Promethee (*Preference Ranking Organization METHod for Enrichment Evaluations*) algorithm which is a multi-criteria decision aid system [14]. The benefit of the Promethee algorithm is that it allows to select, from a large set of objects, one object or a small set of objects with a 'good' compromise between several qualitative and/or quantitative criteria. However, the main drawback of the Promethee is the long execution time to solve a problem with a big size (number

© Springer Nature Switzerland AG 2020
C.-H. Hsu et al. (Eds.): IOV 2019, LNCS 11894, pp. 190–203, 2020.
https://doi.org/10.1007/978-3-030-38651-1_17

of objects) and a large dimension (number of qualitative and quantitative criteria). The exact Promethee computing time is linked to the problem dimension, problem size and the uses of a sorting step in the overall process.

To improve the computing time for the solution, we propose, in this paper, a new accelerated Promethee algorithm, based on Machine Learning method. The solution of the initial problem is now an approximation compared to the exact algorithm. One challenge is to estimate the quality of the solution, we mean the gap between the exact and the approximated solution.

The accelerated Promethee algorithm is based on dimensionality reduction. For instance, the principle consists to reduce the number of candidate objects by applying algorithm inherited from the Machine Learning field. For instance, in our approach the K-means algorithm is used to reduce the size of the problem. Then, in the second step, we apply the exact Promethee algorithm on a reduced number of objects to get a solution in a reasonable computing time and with a certain quality.

The organization of the paper is as follows. Section 2 presents some related works. Section 3 is divided into Subsect. 3.1 which describes the exact Promethee multi-criteria algorithm, and Subsect. 3.2 which describes the k-means clustering algorithm. Section 4 describes our accelerated Promethee algorithm based on a combination between the exact Promethee and K-means algorithms. Section 5 introduces exhaustive experiments that allow the validation of our accelerated Promethee algorithm. Finally, a conclusion and some future works are given in Sect. 6.

2   Related Work

In this section, we start by presenting, briefly, some multi-criteria algorithms. Then, we present a short overview of multi-criteria related problems and an example of a large scale multi-criteria study. Finally, we conclude this section by a positioning.

2.1   Short Overview of Multi-criteria Algorithms

In the following subsection we present two multi-criteria algorithms (i) TOPSIS [9]; and (ii) Kung [8].

TOPSIS (Technique for Order Preference by Similarity to an Ideal Solution) is a multi-criteria algorithm which allows to choose from a big set of objects the solution with the shortest distance from the best solution and the furthest distance from the worst solution [12]. However, the use of the TOPSIS algorithm requires, for each criterion, a weight and information related to the minimization or maximization of the criterion. To find a solution, the TOPSIS algorithm goes through the following 7 steps:

- Fill a Decision Matrix (DM) of n lines (number of objects) and c columns (number of criteria). Each value f_{ij} in DM represents the value of the object o_i in $criterion_j$.

- Calculate the Normalized Decision Matrix (NDM). The normalized value $r_{ij} = f_{ij}/\sqrt{\sum_{i=1}^{n} f_{ij}^2}$, for $i = 1, ..., n$ and $j = 1, \cdots, c$.
- Calculate the Weighted Normalized Decision Matrix ($WNDM$). The weighted normalized value $v_{ij} = r_{ij} \times w_j$, for $i = 1, ..., n$ and $j = 1, \cdots, c$. With w_j is the weight of the jth criterion, and the $\sum_{j=1}^{c} w_j = 1$.
- Determine the best (A^+) and the worst (A^-) solutions.

$$
\begin{aligned}
A^+ &= \{v_1^+, ..., v_c^+\} & A^- &= \{v_1^-, ..., v_c^-\} \\
&= \{(max(v_{ij}|i=1,...,n)|j \in I'), & &= \{(min(v_{ij}|i=1,...,n)|j \in I'), \\
&\quad (min(v_{ij}|i=1,...,n)|j \in I'')\} & &\quad (max(v_{ij}|i=1,...,n)|j \in I'')\}
\end{aligned}
$$

I' is associated to the criteria having the positive impact, and I" is associated to the criteria having a negative impact.
- Calculate the Separation Measures (SM), using the n-dimensional Euclidean distance. The separation of each object from the best solution is given by the following SM_i^+ formula:
$SM_i^+ = \sqrt{\sum_{j=1}^{c}(v_{ij} - v_j^+)^2}$, for $i = 1, \cdots, n$.
The separation of each object from the worst solution is given by the following SM_i^- formula:
$SM_i^- = \sqrt{\sum_{j=1}^{c}(v_{ij} - v_{ij}^-)^2}$, for $i = 1, \cdots, n$
- Calculate the Relative Closeness (RC) to the best solution. For each object o_i, the RC_i is defined by the following RC_i formula:
$RC_i = SM_i^-/(SM_i^+ + SM_i^-)$, $i = 1, \cdots, n$.
- Score objects according to their RC value.

Kung algorithm [8] is also an other algorithm used in the multi-criteria decision context [5]. As presented in [5], Kung algorithm firstly sorts objects in descending order according to the first criterion. Thereafter, the set of objects are recursively halved as Top half (T) and Bottom half (B) sub set of objects. As T is better than B in the first criterion, so we check the B for domination with T. The solutions of B which are not dominated by solutions of T are merged with members of T to form merged set of objects M. This means, in the case of a minimization function, that a solution x_1 is better than other solution x_2, if the value of x_1 is smaller than the value of x_2. The algorithm, called Front(P), can be summarized in two steps:

- Sort objects according to the order of importance in the first criterion and rename the population of objects as P of size N.
- Front(P): if $|P| = 1$, return P as the output of Front(P). Otherwise, T = Front($P^1 - P^{|P/2|}$) and B = Front($P^{|P/2|+1} - P^P$). IF i^{th} non-dominated solution B is not dominated by any non-dominated solution of T, create a merged set M = {T U i}. Finally, return M as output of Front(P).

2.2   Short Overview of Multi-criteria Related Studies

In this subsection, we present some multi-criteria related studies [10,11].

In [11], a new scheduling strategy based on multi-criteria decision algorithm is proposed. The principle of this strategy consists to choose, from a set of nodes, able to execute a new submitted container, the node which has a good compromise between several criteria. According to the results presented in [11], the new scheduling strategy based on the multi-criteria algorithm allows to improve the performance comparing to others scheduling strategies.

In [10], also a multi-criteria algorithm is used to recommend profiles. The goal of the work presented in [10] consist to score a set of profiles configured according to multi-criteria and saved in a database according to their similarity compared to a new profile. In this study, the multi-criteria algorithm is used to compute the distance score between each profile saved in a database and the new profile.

2.3 Large Scale Multi-criteria Algorithm

In [4], two practical Large Scale Multi-Objectives Scheduling (LSMOS) strategies are proposed. The goal of the work proposed in [4], consists to show how we can improve the computing time obtained by using a Kung multi-criteria algorithm.

2.4 Positioning

The novelty of this paper is to propose a new accelerated Promethee multi-criteria algorithm adapted for large scale environments with thousand of objects. The benefit of our approach is that it allows to get a solution faster than with an exact Promethee method. The difference between this study and the study presented in [4], is that our study is based on Promethee multi-criteria algorithm. However, the study proposed in [4] is based on Kung multi-criteria algorithm.

3 Key Algorithms Used by the Accelerated Promethee Algorithm

In this section, we present the exact Promethee and K-means algorithms which will be used as key building blocks of our approach depicted in Sect. 4.

3.1 Exact Promethee Algorithm

The exact Promethee (*Preference Ranking Organization METHod for Enrichment Evaluations*) algorithm presents a multi-criteria decision aid system [14]. It gives a good compromise between several qualitative and quantitative criteria. The Promethee algorithm allows to compare objects between them pair by pair, along different criteria for each object. All criteria of objects are evaluated according to two functions: (i) Minimization; and (ii) Maximization. That means, each criterion can be minimized or maximized. However, the use of the Promethee algorithm requires two informations for each criterion: a weight and a preference function. In our context, we suppose that the weight of all criteria are the same and equal to 1. However, the preference function characterizes the difference for a criterion between the evaluations obtained by two possible objects into a preference degree ranging from 0 to 1. In [7], six basic preference functions have been proposed. In this work we use the usual preference functions describe in following. To summarize, the Promethee algorithm is composed of four steps [15]:

1. It computes for each pair of possible objects ($Object_a$ and $Object_b$) and for each criterion, the value of the preference degree. Let $g_j(Object_a)$ be the value of a criterion j for $Object_a$. We note $d_j(Object_a, Object_b)$ $(d_j(Object_a, Object_b) = g_j(Object_a) - g_j(Object_b))$, the difference of value of a criterion j for $Object_a$ and $Object_b$. $P_j(Object_a, Object_b)$ is the value of the preference degree of a criterion j for $Object_a$ and $Object_b$. The preference function used to compute these preference degrees is defined such as:

$$P_j(d_j) = \begin{cases} 0 \ d_j \leq 0 \\ 1 \ d_j > 0 \end{cases}$$

2. It computes for each pair of possible objects, a global preference index. Let C be the set of considered criteria (qualitative and/or quantitative) and w_j the weight associated to the criterion j. The global preference index for a pair of possible $Object_a$ and $Object_b$ is calculated as follows:

$$\pi(Object_a, Object_b) = \sum_{j \in C} W_j \times P_j(Object_a, Object_b)$$

3. It computes for each possible object the positive outranking flow $\phi^+(Object_a)$ and the negative outranking flow $\phi^-(Object_a)$. Let A be the set of objects with size of n. The positive and negative outranking flow of objects are calculated by the following formula:

$$\phi^+(Object_a) = \frac{1}{n-1} \sum_{x \in A} \pi(Object_a, x)$$

and

$$\phi^-(Object_a) = \frac{1}{n-1} \sum_{x \in A} \pi(x, Object_a)$$

4. It uses the outranking flows to establish a complete ranking between the objects. The ranking is based on the net outranking flows $\phi(Object_a)$ which is calculated as follows: $\phi(Object_a) = \phi^+(Object_a) - \phi^-(Object_a)$. In our work, the first objects returned by Promethee algorithm are objects with the highest net outranking values.

Example of How the Exact Promethee Algorithm Works. Assume that at time t_0, three objects exist ($Object_a$, $Object_b$, $Object_c$) with different criteria as it is presented in Table 1. In our context, the Promethee algorithm will be used to select form the set of objects, the object which has a good compromise between several criteria. As explained before, the exact Promethee algorithm starts by computing for each pair of possible objects a difference value in each criterion $(d_x(Object_i, Object_j))$ and the preference degree $(P_x(Object_i, Object_j))$. Then, the system calculates the global preference index $\phi(Object_i)$. In Table 2 with the first pair objects $(Object_a, Object_b)$, the difference value for the criterion 1 is $d(Object_a, Object_b) = 3 - 1 = 2$. However, as this difference value is positive, using an usual preference function, the preference degree equals to 1 (as presented in Table 3).

As in our work we suppose that the weight of all criteria equal to 1, the global preference index of the first pair of objects $(Object_a, Object_b) = 2 \times 1 + 1 \times 1 = 3$ (as it is presented in Table 3). Finally, to get the rank of objects and select the object which has a maximum rank, the system calculates the positive and negative outranking flow and the net outranking flow parameters. Table 4, shows how the system calculates these different parameters. For example, for $Object_a$, the positive outranking flow (ϕ^+) is $\frac{1}{2}(3 + 2) = 2.5$. The negative outranking flow (ϕ^-) is $\frac{1}{2}(0 + 0) = 0$. The net outranking flow $(\phi = \phi^+ - \phi^-)$ is 2.5 $(2.5 - 0)$.

Table 1. Objects with different criteria configurations

Objects	Criterion 1	Criterion 2
$Object_a$	3	2
$Object_b$	1	1
$Object_c$	2	1

Table 2. Computing of the difference value of criteria

Pair of objects	Difference value of criteria	
	Criterion 1	Criterion 2
$d(Object_a, Object_b)$	2	1
$d(Object_a, Object_c)$	1	1
$d(Object_b, Object_a)$	-2	-1
$d(Object_b, Object_c)$	-1	0
$d(Object_c, Object_a)$	-1	-1
$d(Object_c, Object_b)$	1	0

Using Promethee algorithm, the $Object_a$ is the first selected object because it has the maximum net outranking flow. This result confirms our expectation. As it is presented in Table 1, the $Object_a$ is the object with the high value in each criterion.

Table 3. Computing of the preference degree and the global preference index

Pair of objects	Preference degree		Global preference index
	Criterion 1	Criterion 2	
d($Object_a$, $Object_b$)	1	1	3
d($Object_a$, $Object_c$)	1	1	2
d($Object_b$, $Object_a$)	0	0	0
d($Object_b$, $Object_c$)	0	0	0
d($Object_c$, $Object_a$)	0	0	0
d($Object_c$, $Object_b$)	1	0	1

Table 4. Computing of the net outranking flow and a rank of each object

Objects	ϕ^+	ϕ^-	ϕ	Rank
$Object_a$	2.5	0	2.5	1
$Object_b$	0	2	−2	3
$Object_c$	0.5	1	−0.5	2

3.2   K-means Clustering Algorithm

K-means clustering algorithm is a type of unsupervised learning algorithm [13]. The goal of this algorithm is to build clusters of data, with the number of clusters is represented by the variable K [13]. The algorithm works iteratively to assign each data point to one of K clusters. Data points are clustered based on feature similarity. The principle of the K-means algorithm is described as follows:

1. Randomly choose k objects as center objects;
2. Calculate the distance between each object and each center object. Then, assign each object to the cluster which has the nearest center object;
3. Recalculate the new center object of each cluster;
4. Repeat step 2 and 3 until you achieve a cluster stability.

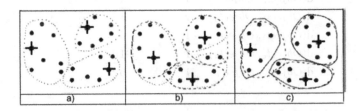

Fig. 1. Partitioning based on K-means [13]

Example of How the K-means Algorithm Works. Let us consider a set of objects as depicted in Fig. 1 presented in [13]. Let us also suppose that the number of clusters we want to have equal to 3 (k = 3). According to Fig. 1, we arbitrarily choose three objects, each object represent an initial cluster center. In Fig. 1(a), each initial center is marked by symbol (+). Then, each object from the set of objects is assigned to a cluster based on the cluster center to which it is the nearest. Next, the cluster centers are updated. That means, each cluster recalculates its center based on the current objects in the cluster. Using the new cluster centers, objects are redistributed to the clusters based on which cluster center is the nearest (Fig. 1(b)). The process of iteratively reassigning objects to clusters to improve the partitioning is referred to as iterative relocation (Fig. 1(c)). Eventually, no reassignment of the objects in any cluster occurs and so the process terminates. The resulting clusters are returned by the clustering process.

4   Accelerated Promethee Algorithm Based on K-means

The novelty of this paper is in the introduction of a new accelerated Promethee algorithm to reduce the exact Promethee computing time. The goal is to combine the exact Promethee with the K-means algorithm to find, quickly from a large set of objects, one object or a small set of objects which has a good compromise between multi-criteria.

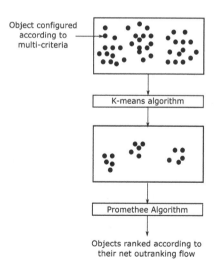

Fig. 2. Accelerated Promethee algorithm based on K-means

As shown in Fig. 2 and Algorithm 1, the principle of the proposed accelerated Promethee algorithm consists to start by applying the K-means algorithm on all

Algorithm 1. Accelerated Promethee algorithm based on K-means and exact Promethee algorithms

---

Input: I, set of all objects with size equal to n.

Input: K, empiric value used by the K-means algorithm (for instance, choose $K = 2 \times \log_2(n)$).

Output: R, set of objects with size equal to n' ($n' < n$).

V = center objects of all clusters returned by K-mean algorithm apply on input I.
for i $\Leftarrow$ 1 to K **do**
    E[i] = Add randomly α objects around V[i].
end for
R = set of objects returned by the exact Promethee algorithm on objects saved in E.

---

set of objects to form K clusters with the same characteristics. K can be chosen to be equal to $2 \times \log_2(n)$, with n being the size of the problem, i.e. the number of objects. This step reduces the state space of the problem. Then we choose a set of objects in each cluster, for instance randomly, but it is possible to choose objects at a certain distance of the centroid or by applying the best known K-Nearest Neighbors (KNN) algorithm [3]. The set of resulting objects is called E. The objective is to have more information to improve the accuracy of the result. Finally, apply the exact Promethee algorithm on set E in order to obtain a result set of objects R. The objects returned by our accelerate Promethee algorithm are ranked according to their net outranking score.

5   Experimental Evaluation

In this section, we present some experimental evaluation to demonstrate the potential of our work. The following experimentations are done on Intel Xeon machine. The used machine is booked from Grid5000 platform [6], an experimental large-scale testbed for distributed computing in France. Our approach is implemented in Go programming language. Go is an open source programming language that makes it easy to build simple, reliable, and efficient software.

In this experimental evaluation, we propose to validate our approach according to 6, 8, 10 and 12 criteria. Each criterion has a random value varying between 0 and 100. The goal of our experiments is not to focus only on the computation time of our algorithm but rather to exemplify the quality of the approximated solution of our approach.

The focus of our paper is in providing with a methodology aiming to combine an exact method for the decision, a clustering method and a dimensionality reduction method. The problem of finding a realistic workload in a context of many criteria and many objects is an issue. In following, the k-means algorithm is used with $k = 2 \times \log_2(n)$ (n number of the input objects). The number of objects returned by k-means is equal to $\frac{n}{2}$.

5.1 Comparison Between the Exact and the Accelerated Promethee Algorithms

Figure 3 (respectively Figs. 4, 5 and 6) shows a comparison between the computing time obtained using the exact and the accelerated Promethee algorithms using 6 (respectively 8, 10 and 12) criteria. As a result, we note, from Figs. 3, 4, 5 and 6, that the computing time obtained with the accelerated Promethee is very small compared to the computing time obtained with the exact Promethee algorithm. Table 5 shows the speedup obtained using the accelerated Promethee algorithm compared to the exact Promethee algorithm. We notice that the speedup increases with the problem size. When the problem size becomes larger, the speedup is more important. This is a nice property of our implementation.

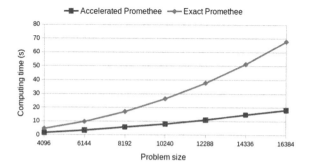

Fig. 3. Comparison between the exact and the accelerated Promethee algorithms configured with 6 criteria

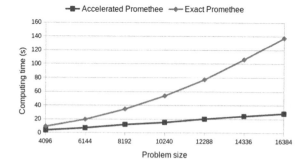

Fig. 4. Comparison between the exact and the accelerated Promethee algorithms configured with 8 criteria

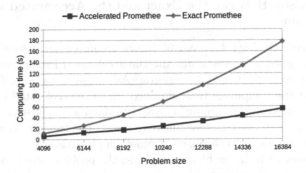

Fig. 5. Comparison between the exact and the accelerated Promethee algorithms configured with 10 criteria

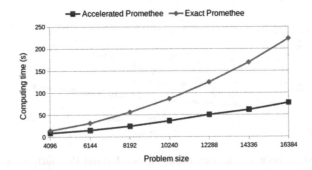

Fig. 6. Comparison between the exact and the accelerated Promethee algorithms configured with 12 criteria

Table 5. Speedup between the exact and the accelerated Promethee algorithms configured with 6, 8, 10 and 12 criteria

Problem size	Speedup			
	6 criteria	8 criteria	10 criteria	12 criteria
4096	2.85	2.39	1.93	1.64
6144	2.91	2.79	2.03	2.07
8192	2.97	2.9	2.55	2.3
10240	3.32	3.57	2.74	2.37
12288	3.46	3.82	2.96	2.47
14336	3.48	4.37	3.08	2.76
16384	3.73	4.86	3.18	2.89

5.2   Metrics of Performance

We now propose to compare the exact value returned by the Promethee algorithm and the approximated value returned by our accelerated Promethee algorithm. To do this comparison, we propose to use the Sorensen-Dice index [1]. Note that the comparison is done between the first 50 and 100 objects returned by the accelerated and the exact Promethee algorithms. Note also that each time the Promethee algorithm is used it returns objects ranked according to their net outranking flow. Sorensen-Dice index [1] is a statistic index used for comparing the similarity of sample sets. It is defined as

$$DSC(A, B) = \frac{2 \times |A \cap B|}{|A| + |B|}.$$

With $A = (a_1, a_2, \ldots, a_n)$ and $B = (b_1, b_2, \ldots, b_n)$ are two vectors composed from a set of objects.

Table 6. Sorensen-Dice index for the first 50 objects returned by the accelerated and the exact Promethee algorithms

Problem size	Sorensen-Dice index			
	6 criteria	8 criteria	10 criteria	12 criteria
4096	0.55	0.56	0.47	0.5
6144	0.5	0.48	0.47	0.55
8192	0.47	0.5	0.58	0.46
10240	0.54	0.55	0.57	0.53
12288	0.54	0.5	0.56	0.52
14336	0.56	0.52	0.56	0.53
16384	0.61	0.58	0.48	0.63

Table 6 (resp. Table 7) represents the Sorensen-Dice indexes obtained by comparing the exact and the accelerated Promethee algorithm based on 6, 8, 10 and 12 criteria between the first 50 objects (resp. 100 objects) returned by the accelerated and the exact Promethee algorithms. We notice that the Sorensen-Dice index values in Tables 6 and 7 are varying between 0.46 and 0.61. These results confirm the potential of our approach method to predict the exact Promethee result.

5.3   General Discussion

In our approach, each criterion may have a weight depending on the user need. In this series of experiments, we do not investigate the impact of the weights on criteria regarding the performance and quality of the result. The originality of Promethee is in mixing qualitative and quantitative criteria. In this paper, we

Table 7. Sorensen-Dice index for the first 100 objects returned by the accelerated and the exact Promethee algorithms

Problem size	Sorensen-Dice index			
	6 criteria	8 criteria	10 criteria	12 criteria
4096	0.55	0.51	0.49	0.51
6144	0.5	0.49	0.51	0.57
8192	0.5	0.52	0.55	0.46
10240	0.52	0.52	0.54	0.52
14336	0.5	0.54	0.56	0.53
16384	0.55	0.57	0.49	0.56

do prefer to focus on the originality of our work which is in a coupling between methods inherited both from the field of combinatorial optimization and from the field of machine learning. The context is to find a solution, with a good respond time, when we have a problem with a big size (number of objects) and a large dimension (number of criteria).

6   Conclusion

We presented in this paper an accelerated Promethee algorithm adapted for large scale environment to reduce the exact Promethee computing time. The proposed accelerated Promethee algorithm is based on the dimensionality reduction to choose an object or a small set of objects with a good compromise in a multi-criteria context. The principle consists to use the K-means algorithm to reduce the number of candidate objects, then to apply the exact Promethee on a reduced number of objects. We discussed in this paper the conditions to get a quick answer versus a precise answer. A balance between the normal law to use (i.e. the shape of the data) and the expected precision should be identified. In practical cases, to satisfy the final user, we have shown the impact of such considerations on the obtained results. As a perspective, we plan to investigate more in deep the quality metrics, to be able to observe the solution according to different point of view regarding the data.

Acknowledgments. We thank the Grid5000 team for their help to use the testbed. Grid'5000 is supported by a scientific interest group (GIS) hosted by Inria and including CNRS, RENATER and several universities as well as other organizations.

References

1. Jackson, D.A., Somers, K., Harvey, H.H.: Similarity coefficients: measures of co-occurrence and association or simply measures of occurrence? Am. Nat. **133**(03), 436–453 (1989)

2. Behzadian, M., Kazemzadeh, R., Albadvi, A., Aghdasi, M.: Promethee: a comprehensive literature review on methodologies and applications. Eur. J. Oper. Res. **200**(1), 198–215 (2010)
3. Cover, T., Hart, P.: Nearest neighbor pattern classification. IEEE Trans. Inf. Theory **13**(1), 21–27 (1967)
4. Cérin, C., Menouer, T., Lebbah, M.: Accelerating the computation of multi-objectives scheduling solutions for cloud computing. In: 2018 IEEE 8th International Symposium on Cloud and Service Computing (SC2), pp. 49–56, November 2018
5. Ding, L., Zeng, S., Kang, L.: A fast algorithm on finding the non-dominated set in multi-objective optimization. In: The 2003 Congress on Evolutionary Computation 2003, CEC 2003, vol. 4, pp. 2565–2571, December 2003
6. Grid5000: https://www.grid5000.fr/
7. Brans, J.P., Mareschal, B.: Promethee Methods. In: Figueira, J., Greco, S., Ehrogott, M. (eds.) Multiple Criteria Decision Analysis: State of the Art Surveys. International Series in Operations Research & Management Science, vol. 78, pp. 163–186. Springer, New York (2005). https://doi.org/10.1007/0-387-23081-5_5
8. Kung, H.T., Luccio, F., Preparata, F.P.: On finding the maxima of a set of vectors. J. ACM **22**(4), 469–476 (1975)
9. Lai, Y.-J., Liu, T.-Y., Hwang, C.-L.: Topsis for MODM. Eur. J. Oper. Res. **76**(3), 486–500 (1994). Facility Location Models for Distribution Planning
10. Menouer, T., Darmon, P.: New profile recommendation approach based on multi-criteria algorithm. In: 2018 IEEE International Conference on Big Data (Big Data), pp. 4961–4966, December 2018
11. Menouer, T., Darmon, P.: New scheduling strategy based on multi-criteria decision algorithm. In: 2019 27th Euromicro International Conference on Parallel, Distributed and Network-Based Processing (PDP), pp. 101–107, February 2019
12. Opricovic, S., Tzeng, G.-H.: Compromise solution by MCDM methods: a comparative analysis of VIKOR and TOPSIS. Eur. J. Oper. Res. **156**(2), 445–455 (2004)
13. Han, J., Pei, J., Kamber, M.: Data Mining: Concepts and Techniques, 3rd edn. Elsevier, Amsterdam (2011)
14. Deshmukh, S.C.: Preference ranking organization method of enrichment evaluation (promethee). Int. J. Eng. Sci. Invent. **2**, 28–34 (2013)
15. Taillandier, P., Stinckwich, S.: Using the Promethee multi-criteria decision making method to define new exploration strategies for rescue robots. In: International Symposium on Safety, Security, and Rescue Robotics (2011)

Implementing a Business/Technology Architecture Alignment-Oriented Process Applied to the Social-Sanitary Sector

Fernanda Lugmaña-Hidalgo[1]([⊠]) 🆔 and José Luis Garrido[2] 🆔

[1] Research Center on Information and Communication Technologies (CITIC), University of Granada, c/Pdta. Gómez Montero, 2, 18014 Granada, Spain
flugmana@ugr.es
[2] Software Engineering Department, University of Granada E.T.S.I. Informática y Telecomunicación, c/Pdta. Saucedo Aranda s/n, 18014 Granada, Spain
jgarrido@ugr.es

Abstract. Nowadays, enterprises are increasingly looking for business and technological strategies which offer huge market opportunities and numerous competitive advantages. Such strategies cause that the enterprises undergo continuous changes, especially regarding their Business Processes (BPs) and integration between them and Information and Communication Technologies (ICT). The integration between new business models and technological changes require to address the complexity of aligning the Enterprise Architecture (EA). The reason being that if any EA component is not prepared to reach such changes, or it is missing, then EA anomalies arise and consequently, leading to misalignment. In this sense, this paper introduces a new EA alignment-oriented process, in which the EA anomalies are identified through symptoms, causes and location; a solution to fix and prevent them is formulated through diagnosis and therapy; and the Business Process (BP) is (re-) modeled and the EA is (re-) designed as a consequence to easier find the EA components where the therapy should be applied, independently of the EA level where the anomalies are found, thus contributing to the EA alignment. The proposal is illustrated by using a case study of a dependents admission BP in an organization belonging to the social-sanitary sector. We assume that the support to that BP could be the result of the coexistence of different technologies such as Legacy Systems and Microservices.

Keywords: Architecture alignment · Business Processes · Microservices

1 Introduction

Nowadays, with the aim of remaining competitive, enterprises are increasingly looking for business and technological strategies which offer huge market opportunities and numerous competitive advantages. Such strategies cause that the enterprises undergo continuous changes, especially regarding their Business Processes (BPs) [1] and integration between them and Information and Communication Technologies (ICT). The integration between new business models and technological changes require to

© Springer Nature Switzerland AG 2020
C.-H. Hsu et al. (Eds.): IOV 2019, LNCS 11894, pp. 204–219, 2020.
https://doi.org/10.1007/978-3-030-38651-1_18

address the complexity of aligning the Enterprise Architecture (EA). EA is defined as *"a coherent whole of principles, methods, and models that are used in the design and realization of an enterprise's organizational structure, BPs, software architecture, information systems, and infrastructure"* [2].

The main reason to address EA alignment, defined as *"the problem of designing architectures at the infrastructure, application, and business levels such that each fits optimally with the other architectures"* [3] is because if any EA component is not prepared to reach to that strategic changes, or it is missing, then EA anomalies arise, i.e. evidence of something is working wrong (e.g. lack of integration between BPs and ICT, system warnings or errors, etc.) and consequently, leading to misalignment. For instance, the EA in social-sanitary organizations usually defines and implements protocols (e.g. action, adaptation, hygiene) that are the core of its operation [4]. Those protocols can be represented as a Business Process Model (BPM) [1] (e.g. by using the Business Process Model Notation (BPMN) [5]) in the EA. At the same time, these processes are performed by stakeholders and supported by certain technological EA components such as software applications and services, legacy systems, communication networks, etc. These components should be correctly aligned with each other. In this way, the EA components, independently of the EA level where they are placed, should contribute to the achievement of the same business goals [6], e.g., stakeholders' expectations, economic benefits, best response times, etc.

This paper introduces an EA alignment-oriented process in which firstly, the EA anomalies are identified through the symptom detection, the causes that origin these symptoms, and the BPs where they are found. Secondly, a solution to fix and prevent such anomalies is formulated through a diagnosis and a therapy. Thirdly, the Business Process (BP) is (re-) modeled and the EA is (re-) designed as a consequence to easier find the EA components (organized as a layered Service-Oriented Architecture (SOA) where the therapy should be applied, independently of the EA level where the anomalies are found. The focus is on managing the anomalies that can be found from the business/ICT perspective (i.e. at the BP, application and technology EA levels).

The proposal is illustrated by using a case study of a dependents admission BP in a social-sanitary organization. The case study comes from a specific real BP in that sector, where interviews were conducted with social-sanitary professionals (they mentioned some anomalies detected in that BP). For the purposes of this case study, we assume that the support to that BP could be the result of the coexistence of Legacy Systems and Microservices. On the one hand, the existence of legacy systems (i.e. systems implemented with technologies now outdated) because they are still fulfilling their purpose and therefore are kept in this type of organizations [7]. On the other hand, the existence of Microservices, defined as *"an evolution of services-oriented architecture style where a service is divided into other smallest services"* [8] because one of the features that they provide is the polyglotism, thus contributing to the integration between systems.

This paper describes related work in Sect. 2. Section 3 briefly describes the SOA design model used for the EA. Section 4 introduces the EA alignment-oriented process. Section 5 describes the case study in the social-sanitary sector. Section 6 summarizes conclusions and future work.

2 Related Work

This section describes related work on the topic of EA alignment. In [9] some results of a deep analysis of literature review about IT alignment are provided by addressing questions such as: What have we learned? What is disputed? Who are contributors to the debate? The answers to these questions also help for a better understanding of IT alignment, and their relevant concepts. In [10] a Business and Information Systems Misalignment model (BISMAM) is described, in which EA misalignment is handled as human body disease because in both cases the system is not working correctly. BISMAM aims to understand, classify and manage these misalignments by establishing a misalignment classification scheme. It links EA views, misalignment symptoms and causes, and defines techniques to detect, correct and prevent misalignments. The nomenclature and conceptualization of BISMAM (symptoms, causes, diagnosis and therapy) is very useful specially to detect and fix anomalies through various dimensions (etiology, symptom classification, etc.). However, it does not address BP (re-) modeling and EA (re-) designing as part of a solution to these anomalies.

Another research work proposed in [11] provides a suitable support to manage the alignment between BP and software systems by suggesting evolution actions when misalignment is detected. It proposes an approach including modeling (in UML) and providing a set of metrics for evaluating the alignment level. However, it does not serve as a means to easier find the EA components where the therapy should be applied to the BPM and EA design.

In [12] is proposed a problem-aware framework for establishing requirements traceability, in the context of goal-oriented requirements engineering. This framework helps to ensure that requirements specifications are aligned to stakeholders' needs. It is done by considering why these needs arise, which problems are detected by stakeholders, and which systems can be used to fix these problems. It uses ontological concepts, a NFR framework (goal-oriented model to represent functional and not functional requirements), and Problem Interdependency Graphs (PIG) (to represent problems) organized by layers. This work also aims to align EA, but only at a higher EA level, where aspects such as enterprise goals and mission, organizational structure, and human resources are considered.

3 A SOA Design Model for EA

The EA design can result in a complex task since it implies to having a deep acknowledgement and full vision of all the enterprise components. For this reason, an EA layered model is adopted (see Fig. 1). This model is based on the standard language ArchiMate [13] which serves to design EA as service-oriented model [2]. In this model, the service concept transcends through the following EA layers: (1) the **Business Layer** offers services to external customers, the services are realized in the organization by BP; (2) the **Application Layer** supports the business layer with application services which are realized by software applications and services; and (3) the **Technology Layer** offers infrastructure services. This design is flexible and well-structured, by somewhat facilitating the adoption of strategic changes [2].

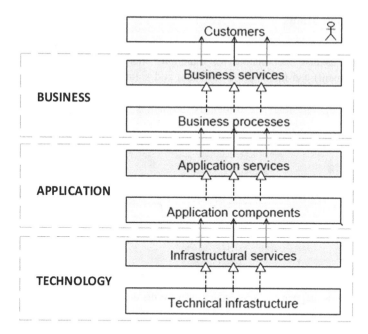

Fig. 1. EA layered view. (adapted from source: [2], p. 209)

As shown in Fig. 1, each EA layer is in turn composed by two sublayers [2]. The first one represents the service interfaces sublayer (although the components could not be really services), and the second one represents the realization layer, which includes: internal behavior, object, and resources. Actually, the realization layer embraces any type of component (e.g. database access components, store procedures, web services, batch process, among others) at the business, application and technology layers, but externally, they are all exposed as services thanks to the service sublayer.

4   An Enterprise Architecture Alignment-Oriented Process

This section introduces an EA alignment-oriented process, which is motivated by the enterprise need of integrate their business models and technological changes and thus remaining competitive. This process focuses especially on the detection and solution of anomalies that usually occurs in EA. To this end, the approach should successfully align EA components at different levels, from the BPs to technological solutions that provide support to them, i.e., the focus is on the business, application and technology layers. Other more abstract levels include aspects such as enterprise goals and mission, organizational structure, and human resources. These are key aspects with high impact on the BP definition and ICT design decisions, where this research work is focused on.

4.1   Conceptual Model

One of the main objectives of the EA alignment-oriented process is that the enterprise architect (who is also responsible for managing this knowledge to ensure IT and business alignment) can manage the detection and solution of anomalies. We define a conceptual model (Fig. 2) in order to represent the concepts (and the relationships between them) that are relevant to identify anomalies and formulate a solution.

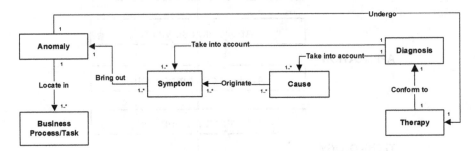

Fig. 2. UML class diagram for conceptual model for the detection and solution of anomalies.

According to this conceptual model, an anomaly is something that deviates from what is standard, normal, or expected in an enterprise. In order to fix it, this anomaly undergoes therapy that is a set of actions whose purpose is to fix an anomaly. This therapy is conforming to a diagnosis that describes an analysis in precise terms of the anomaly, taking into account causes and symptoms. Causes are the underlying factors that cause the anomaly [10] and originate symptoms. Symptoms are defined as subjective evidence of an anomaly [10] which bring out its existence. An anomaly is located at one or more BPs, and more specifically, in certain tasks of the BPs. A *Business Process* is defined as "*a unit of internal behavior or collection of causally-related units of internal behavior intended to produce a defined set of products and services*" [1].

4.2   Process Phases

The EA alignment-oriented process is applied by the enterprise architect or other actors with similar responsibilities in the enterprise. This process comprises four phases that are carried out iteratively (Fig. 3), in each phase is possible to go back to previous ones as many times as required for achievement the EA alignment. The Phases 1 and 2 are part of the detection and solution of anomalies. Each detected anomaly produces an instance of the conceptual model (Fig. 2). The phases are described in detail as follows.

Identify EA Anomalies. The first phase identifies EA anomalies in three steps shown in Fig. 4: Detect symptoms, find out causes, and locate BPs/Tasks.

Detect Symptoms. The symptoms detection is usually an interaction between the stakeholders and the enterprise architect, with the help of the enterprise document collection where they alert about an anomaly. For example, the enterprise document

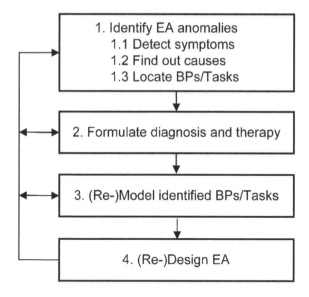

Fig. 3. Process phases.

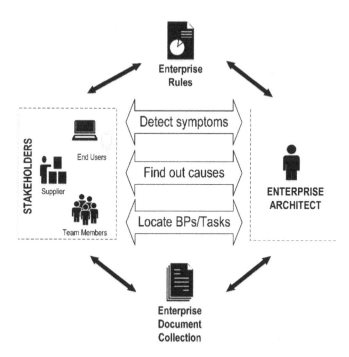

Fig. 4. Flow diagram of the identification of anomalies.

collection can include periodic anomaly reports that are generated when the number from stakeholders' complaints exceed a maximum limit established in the enterprise rules.

This step detects symptoms. They can be classified depending on the EA level from where **they were detected**:

- **Business Level.** Signals that worry to stakeholders or their needs. This type of anomalies could be detected through: (1) short meetings where each department head exposes deficiencies in several enterprise aspects (procedures, arrangements, processes, mechanisms, among others); and (2) system for complaints where the customers or suppliers can expose the problems that they evidence.
- **Application Level.** Warnings or errors that systems show. This type of anomalies is easily detectable through the system logs, screen messages and alerts, or system crashes.
- **Technological Level.** System and hardware faults, where the technicians report the anomalies (e.g. disconnections, server unavailability, etc.).

Find Out Causes. This step is tackled from two perspectives. On the one hand, as interaction between the stakeholders and the enterprise architect in order to find out why the anomalies happen (i.e. the causes which originate the symptoms). This interaction is important, because the enterprise architect requires to have the knowledge from other specialists (e.g. software architects/engineers, infrastructure architects/engineers, developers, among others) in the area regarding to the anomaly. On the other hand, this step takes inputs from enterprise document collection and enterprises rules (e.g. when submitting a report). They could be accessed by using several mechanisms (dashboards, KPIs, forecast, etc.) that facilitate the enterprise government. All of them provide useful information about finding out the real cause of the anomaly.

Locate BPs/Tasks. The BP location is also seen as an interaction between the stakeholders and the enterprise architect. Usually, the experience and walkthroughs of the stakeholders can provide enough valuable information to identify what are the BPs where the anomaly is. However, thanks to documents such as periodic anomaly reports even the specific tasks of that BPs can be located.

Formulate Diagnosis and Therapy. Once anomalies have been identified, the enterprise architect should formulate a diagnosis by taking into account the symptoms detected by stakeholders and the analyzed causes. This diagnosis must be the as accurate and clear as possible in order to formulate the appropriate therapy. After, the therapy should be conforming to the diagnosis, thus fixing the detected anomalies without imposing an additional cost, excessive time, incurring in higher security risks or the creation of other anomalies.

(Re-) Model Identified BP. As a result of the Phase 1, there will be BPs (and even of the specific tasks in them) where the anomaly was found. In this phase, if needed, the identified BP must be (re-) modeled, i.e. when the therapy actions must be carried out in those terms. For example, if the therapy regards a new implementation that automates a manual task, then, the BP will be (re-) modeled by using another type of task different to the manual one.

(Re-) Design EA. This phase consists of (re-) designing the service-oriented EA by applying techniques such as traceability. Traceability is defined as: "*A technique for tracking, analyzing, and managing the impact an architectural artifact has on a solution architecture design*" [14]. By using traceability, we ensure that all involved component in the anomaly are found and taken into account to apply the therapy. For instance, if a component must be changed at certain level, by traceability we could follow which are the other components that will be affected at other levels. In this sense, the knowledge about all the components involved in an anomaly, independently of the EA level, contributes to the suitably ICT and BP integration.

5   Case Study

The proposal for EA alignment is applied to a case study in the social-sanitary sector. This case study is built as a result from interviews conducted with social-sanitary professionals who explain how this type of organization works and is organized. Additionally, these professionals mentioned several significant problems which are faced by them. Whereupon, the studied BP is the dependents admission one. The support of this BP is based on the coexistence of Legacy Systems and Microservices.

5.1   General Description

In a BP for dependents admission, there is a protocol to be carried out at the reception of dependents [4]. In this context, the idea about the protocol formalization, with an appropriate representation language, with clear and well-defined semantics, would enable the systematic verification of guidelines and protocols [15]. According to [15], the term protocol is in general used for a specialized version of a guideline, and in [16] a guideline is identified as a process. Hence, we can model this protocol as a BP.

The protocol in this case study is depicted in the Fig. 5 and described in detail as follows. The administrative staff records new dependents' histories in two different systems: (1) the own system where they store all the necessary data for the day-to-day work; and (2) the system whose internal structure is unknown for the organization, but stores the data in the National Health System for autonomy and care for dependents. From now on, this system will be considered as a Legacy System, because no matter how, it still serves in order to insert data into the National System database. Once, the dependent histories are recorded in both systems, the social-sanitary staff is notified about the new admission. The social-sanitary staff welcomes new dependents on the admission day and shows the assigned room to them through verbal and non-verbal communication by considering physical or cognitive limitations of dependents. Finally, the social-sanitary staff inventories clothing and personal items of dependents.

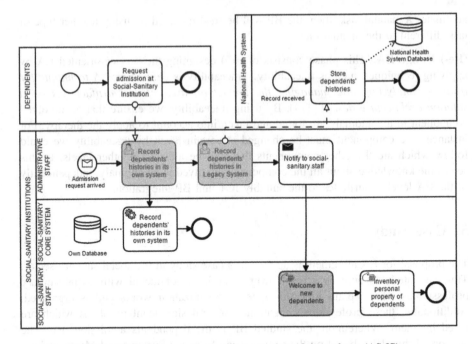

Fig. 5. BPM action protocol at the reception of dependents (AS-IS).

5.2   Application of the EA Alignment-Oriented Process

According to periodic anomaly report, the administrative staff detects several anomalies, for example, increase of dependents' complaints related to loss of dependents' personal property, **accomplishment of repetitive tasks, and communication problems between the social-sanitary staff and some new dependents with physical or cognitive limitations**. We will apply the process to these two last anomalies (in bold) in the action protocol at the reception of dependents.

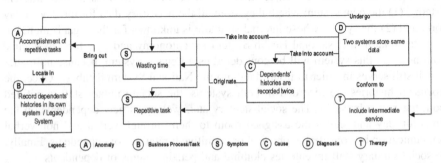

Fig. 6. Instance of conceptual model for detection and solution of anomalies – anomaly 1.

Identify EA Anomalies. It is done for each one of the two selected anomalies as follows.

- **First anomaly:** *Accomplishment of repetitive tasks* (which is represented in the instantiation of the conceptual model in Fig. 6).

Detect Symptoms. At business level, through system for complaints, the administrative staff complains about the complexity and loss of time when they record new dependents' histories (Symptom: Wasting time), as the dependents' histories must be recorded in two different systems (Symptom: Repetitive task).

Find Out Causes. The social-sanitary organization stores the dependents' histories in two different systems (own and the legacy system). Both systems require information about this organization. On the one hand, the stakeholders use the own system to manage and plan business resources. On the other hand, official external entities impose the storage of this information in their systems, more specifically the National Health System requires the dependent histories. Therefore, none could be omitted (Cause: Dependents' histories are recorded twice).

Locate BP/Tasks. According to the anomalies report, the location of them is in the protocol at the reception of dependents (BPs/Tasks: Record dependents' histories in its own system and Record dependents' histories in Legacy System).

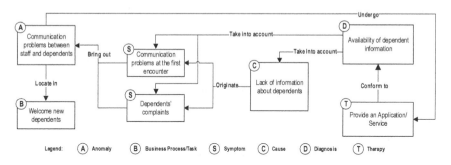

Fig. 7. Instance of conceptual model for detection and solution of anomalies – Anomaly 2.

- **Second anomaly:** *Communication problems between the social-sanitary staff and new dependents with physical or cognitive limitations* (which is represented in the instantiation of the conceptual model in Fig. 7).

Detect Symptoms. At business level, through the system for complaints, the new dependents with physical or cognitive limitations expose the communication problems between them and the social-sanitary staff at the first encounter (Symptoms: Communication problems at the first encounter and Dependents' complaints).

Find Out Causes. At the time of welcoming or in the accompaniment, there are many communication problems between the social-sanitary staff and some new dependents with physical or cognitive limitations. It is due to that the social-sanitary staff do not know about the physical or cognitive limitations of the new dependents at the first encounter (Cause: Lack of information about dependents).

Locate BP/Tasks. According the anomalies report, the location of them is in the protocol at the reception of dependents (BP/Task: Welcome new dependents).

Formulate Diagnosis and Therapy. In this phase, a diagnosis and therapy is formulated for each anomaly on basis of the previous phase:

- In the first anomaly, the users lose a lot of time inserting the same data in two different systems (i.e., by each new dependent, its information must be recorded in the two systems) (Diagnosis: Two systems store same data). Therefore, it should be implemented an intermediate service (Therapy: Include intermediate service) which consumes the services of the own system in order to insert data in the Legacy System.
- In the second anomaly, there is the possibility of slowing down the normal flow of a process due to the lack of information in the correct moment (Diagnosis: Availability of dependent information). The technology can contribute to avoid these anomalies. Therefore, a possible solution could be based on the implementation of a new application (e.g. it could be a mobile application) for accomplishing with the following requirement: provision of the dependent's information to the social-sanitary staff immediately after its record, as well as an interactive guide of how they should communicate with the new dependents (Therapy: Provide an Application/Service).

(Re-) Model Identified BP. Once one therapy for each anomaly is formulated, this phase must be accomplished and the action protocol at the reception of dependents must be (re-) modeled according to such therapy.

Figure 8 shows the new BPM (TO-BE model) which includes the changes made according to the proposed therapy with new implementation by taking into account the services-oriented approach of this process. There are some changes in comparison to the previous BPM (AS-IS model). Firstly, the solution of the first anomaly is modeled (in orange color). Now, the Record dependents' histories in its own system user task is enough to record also the dependent histories in legacy system. Consequently, the business resources are optimized since the user must record the dependents' histories only once now. As indicated by the therapy, it should be implemented an intermediate service which consumes the services of the own system in order to insert the same data in the Legacy System. Consequently, the Record dependents' histories in Legacy System service task is created and connected to the Record dependents' histories in its own system service task (responsible of storing data in Own Database). Also, the intermediate service is now the one that connects to the Legacy System. The solution of the second anomaly is modeled in red color. The Assign interactive guide of communication and Send notifications service tasks, and the Receive notification with

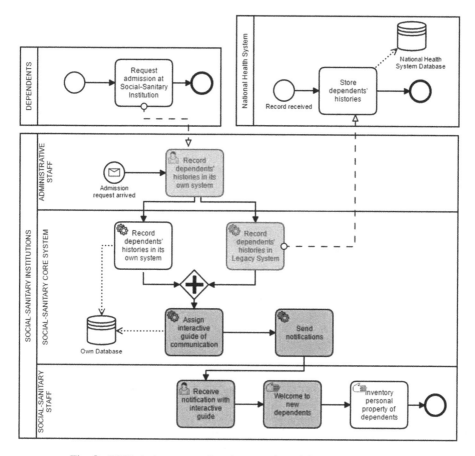

Fig. 8. BPM Action protocol at the reception of dependents (TO-BE).

`interactive guide` user task are created in order to automate the `Welcome the new dependents` manual task.

(Re-) Design EA. This phase consists of (re-) designing the service-oriented EA. For better identification of the modifications to be made in the EA design, the Fig. 9 shows the existing EA design (AS-IS) before applying the therapy.

As mentioned previously, we assumed that part of the technology that support the BPs is implemented as Microservices. Then, to design this type of architecture, we follow the Microservices-oriented architecture "Spring Cloud Netflix" according to [17], where there are three common elements (represented as application components): (1) **Edge Service**, which centralizes requests from the application services; (2) **Load Balancer**, which performs load balancing; and (3) **Registry**, where the Microservices are deployed.

On the other hand, the EA depicted in the Fig. 9 helps us to illustrate the EA layered model adopted in this work (see Sect. 3). The services transcends through the three EA layers: (1) at Business Layer the `Dependent record` service is offered to

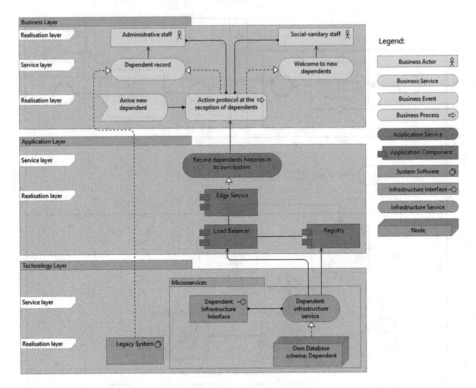

Fig. 9. EA design of case study in the social-sanitary sector (AS-IS).

the dependents and is realized in the organization by Action protocol at the reception of dependents BP; (2) at Application Layer the Record dependents' histories in its own system service supports the business layer which is realized by the Microservices components (Edge Service, Load Balancer and Registry); and (3) at Technology Layer the Record dependent infrastructure service support the higher layer.

Figure 10 depicts the new EA design (TO-BE) that includes the changes made (at the design level) according to the proposed therapy. For instance, in relation to the first anomaly, the therapy recommends the creation of an intermediate service. In design there is a solution that can be used for the creation of this service. By applying the pattern in [18], the intermediate service consumes the services of the own system in order to insert the same data in the Legacy System. This new service (called usually as Intermediate Service) is included in the EA design, which will be responsible of inserting the data in the Legacy System. That service consumes the Record dependents' histories in its own system application service, and, in turn, consumes the Microservices placed at the technology layer in order to access to own database.

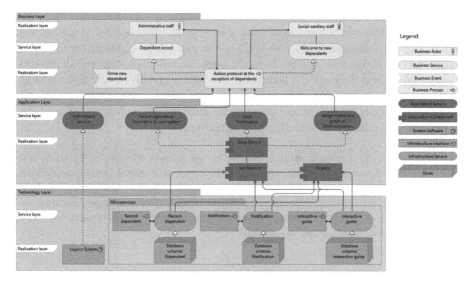

Fig. 10. EA design of case study in the social-sanitary sector (TO-BE).

6 Conclusions and Future Work

This work proposes an EA alignment-oriented process that consists of: (1) the EA anomalies identification; (2) the formulation of a solution for fixing them; and (3) a BPs (re-) model and EA (re-) design based on the solution of the anomalies. In order to accomplish the one and two previous points, this process is based on the definition of a model that helps to understand and conceptualize the problem of detection and solution of anomalies. In order to accomplish the previous third point, it proposes a phase to represent and model semi-formally the BPs and their respective tasks by using BPMN, as well as to design EA. The last two phases will help us for decision-making at business, application and technological EA levels, by showing all EA components involved when an anomaly exists, thus contributing to the business and technology alignment and their integration. Currently, the enterprise architect is who applies this process and leads meetings with the suitable stakeholders in order to receive anomaly reports, find out the causes of them and locate BPs/Tasks where is the anomaly. However, in the case of this role does not explicitly exist in the enterprise, it can be adopted in different way and performed by somebody else.

We illustrate this process by using a case study from the social-sanitary sector. However, the scope of the proposed process is broad because it can be applied to current and common components present in the EA of any the organization (bank, health, education, government, among others). After applying this process to the case study, we can conclude that it helps us to identify anomalies through the instantiation of a conceptual model, and visualize the EA components involved in an anomaly solution through the BP and EA design models.

Later, we are planning that this process forms the basis of a formal EA alignment-oriented method, then we are taking into account the follow points: (1) we have not found a formal guide, model, or tool to formulate the therapy and diagnosis. In future work, we will define in a more systematic way how to formulate the diagnosis and therapy, thereby formalizing this phase; (2) in the case study, a pattern for the intermediate service design was applied. In future work, we will exploit the use of patterns as a relevant support to design EA and model BPs; and (3) finally, we are also planning on incorporating several metrics to evaluate the performance through the use of different cases of study where we will compare the time results, with and without using the method, and consequently verifying its effectiveness.

Acknowledgment. This research work is funded by the Spanish Ministry of Economy and Competitiveness -Agencia Estatal Investigación- with European Regional Development Funds (AEI/FEDER, UE) through the project ref. TIN2016-79484-R.

We wish to extend our sincere thanks to Ms María Dolores González, social-sanitary technician from "Oasis" Cáritas Diocesana Institution, who helped and collaborated with their valuable information, feedback and suggestions.

References

1. Dumas, M., La Rosa, M., Mendling, J., Reijers, H.A: Fundamentals of Business Process Management. vol. 1, p. 2. Springer, Heidelberg (2013). https://doi.org/10.1007/978-3-662-56509-4
2. Lankhorst, M.: Enterprise Architecture at Work: Modelling, Communication and Analysis. Springer (2009). https://doi.org/10.1007/978-3-642-29651-2
3. Hinkelmann, K., Gerber, A., Karagiannis, D., Thoenssen, B., Van der Merwe, A., Woitsch, R.: A new paradigm for the continuous alignment of business and IT: combining enterprise architecture modelling and enterprise ontology. Comput. Indu. **79**, 77–86 (2016)
4. Madrid.org, Protocolos Asistenciales en residencias de Mayores, Consejería de Familia y Asuntos Sociales, Servicio Regional de Bienestar Social. http://www.madrid.org/cs/Satellite?blobcol=urldata&blobheader=application%2Fpdf&blobheadername1=Content-Disposition&blobheadervalue1=filename%3DBVCM007151.pdf&blobkey=id&blobtable=MungoBlobs&blobwhere=1352857974016&ssbinary=true. Accessed 08 June 2018. (In Spanish)
5. Muehlen, M., Recker, J.: How much language is enough? Theoretical and practical use of the business process modeling notation. In: Bubenko, J., Krogstie, J., Pastor, O., Pernici, B., Rolland, C., Sølvberg, A. (eds.) Seminal Contributions to Information Systems Engineering, pp. 429–443. Springer, Heidelberg (2013). https://doi.org/10.1007/978-3-642-36926-1_35
6. Escofet, E., Rodríguez-Fórtiz, M.J., Garrido, J.L., Chung, L.: Strategic e-business/IT alignment for SME competitiveness. In: Computer Engineering: Concepts, Methodologies, Tools and Applications, pp. 1427–1445. IGI Global (2012)
7. Bennett, K.: Legacy systems: coping with success. IEEE Softw. **12**(1), 19–23 (1995)
8. Fowler, M., Lewis, J.: Microservices (2014). http://martinfowler.com/articles/microservices.html. Accessed 26 Nov 2018
9. Chan, Y.E., Reich, B.H.: IT alignment: what have we learned? J. Inf. Technol. **22**(4), 297–315 (2007)
10. Carvalho, R., Sousa, P.: Business and Information Systems MisAlignment Model (BISMAM): an holistic model leveraged on misalignment and medical sciences approaches. Proc. BUSITAL **8**, 105 (2008)

11. Aversano, L., Grasso, C., Tortorella, M.: Managing the alignment between business processes and software systems. Inf. Softw. Technol. **72**, 171–188 (2016)
12. Park, G., Chung, L., Hong, J.E., Garrido, J.L., Noguera, M.: Problem-aware traceability in goal-oriented requirements engineering. In: SEKE, pp. 569–574 (2016)
13. The Open Group: The ArchiMate® Modeling Language, an Open Group Standard. http://www.opengroup.org/archimate/. Accessed 14 Feb 2019
14. Zhang, L.J., Chee, Y.M., Abdel-Hamid, T., Zhou, N.: U.S. Patent No. 9,342,279. Washington, DC: U.S. Patent and Trademark Office (2016)
15. Ten Teije, A., et al.: Improving medical protocols by formal methods. Artif. Intell. Med. **36** (3), 193–209 (2006)
16. Lenz, R., Reichert, M.: IT support for healthcare processes–premises, challenges, perspectives. Data Knowl. Eng. **61**(1), 39–58 (2007)
17. Cloud.spring.io: Spring Cloud Netflix. https://cloud.spring.io/spring-cloud-netflix/single/spring-cloud-netflix.html. Accessed 24 Feb 2019
18. Gamma, E., Helm, R., Johnson, R., Vlissides, J.M.: Design Patterns: Elements of Reusable Object-Oriented Software. Addison-Wesley Professional Computing Series (1995)

A Lightweight Time Series Main-Memory Database for IoT Real-Time Services

Lina Lan[✉], Ruisheng Shi, Bai Wang, Lei Zhang, and Jinqiao Shi

Beijing University of Posts and Telecommunications, Beijing 100876, China
{lanlina, shiruisheng, wangbai, zlei,
shijinqiao}@bupt.edu.cn

Abstract. With the rapid development of Internet of things (IoT), a large number of IoT sensing devices produces amounts of sensing data in every second. These data should be processed in real-time to support IoT real-time services. The growth of IoT real-time services has been hampered due to the barriers of data storage efficiency and data processing performance with the traditional database system architecture. This paper proposes a lightweight time series main-memory database (TSMMDB) system for IoT real-time services. Firstly, we propose a tree structure of IoT sensing data model based on the IoT real-time monitoring business. The leaves of the tree are three-dimension tables. The data can be retrieved according to time, resource and measure. Based on the data model, we propose a customized virtual heap and virtual heap memory allocator. The applications can access the whole data in the database in their own processes based on shared memory without transferring data, and can achieve data persistence automatically based on memory mapping. The flexible data locality memory allocation makes the adjacent time series data storing in the continuous memory space which improves the data clustered analysis performance. The data access algorithm of TSMMDB has ideal time complexity, and experimental results show that TSMMDB has better performance significantly than the traditional main-memory database and disk-based relational database.

Keywords: Main-memory database · Internet of things · Real-time service · Time series data · Virtual heap memory allocator

1 Introduction

With the rapid development of Internet of things (IoT), the network applications have become extremely rich, and the data generated by all kinds of services has exploded. The era of big data has come. In particular, a large number of sensors, RFID tags, cameras and other devices widely deployed in IoT generate a large amount of sensing data all the time. These original sensing data have the characteristics of time series.

This work is supported by Key Research and Development Program for Guangdong Province under grant No. 2019B010137003, the Fundamental Research Funds for the Central Universities (Grant no. 24820192019RC56).

The original version of this chapter was revised: The Grant no. should be "24820192019RC56", not "2018RC56". This has now been corrected. The correction to this chapter is available at https://doi.org/10.1007/978-3-030-38651-1_33

C.-H. Hsu et al. (Eds.): IOV 2019, LNCS 11894, pp. 220–236, 2020.
https://doi.org/10.1007/978-3-030-38651-1_19

They are generated periodically, and only appended but not updated after being written into database. These characteristics are different from the data characteristics of traditional information systems. Therefore, new and higher requirements are put forward for the storage, access and processing of original time series sensing data. Traditional database system architecture are difficult to meet these requirements.

As the speed of memory is 5 orders of magnitude faster than disk, with the rapid growth of memory capacity and the continuous decline of price, memory has become an important resource of data processing system [1–4]. Storing the entire dataset in memory and conduct in-memory computing and data analytics can greatly improve the speed of data access and data processing. The in-memory database is becoming more and more important in in-memory computing. An in-memory database is essentially storing the "working version" of the database in memory.

In the process of data analysis, a large amount of data need to be exchanged between the application program and the database system. If the data transfer speed between processes is not fast enough, it is difficult to exert the performance of in-memory computing [2]. The inter-process communication mode provided by modern operating systems including pipe, socket and shared memory, cannot meet the requirements of in-memory computing performance well. The pipe and socket modes need to transfer data and the speed is not far enough. Shared memory mode does not need to transfer data, but the application is responsible for the synchronization mechanism of shared memory, which is difficult to develop and maintain. There are limitations of efficiency data sharing between traditional in-memory databases and applications. It is difficult to provide the efficiency performance of parallelism and concurrency control capacity in main-memory database system [5–7].

In recent years, the development trend of main-memory database is to design high performance memory database system for different application requirements. Stonebraker et al. [8] proposes VoltDB, which is suitable for high frequency concurrent access requests with a large number of small single transactions. Xie et al. [9] proposes Hekaton adopts the lock-free concurrency model to improve concurrency processing performance to support high-concurrency OLTP application scenarios. SAP HANA proposes methods to optimize in-memory data access, and optimize data writing [11, 12, 14, 16]. Pelkonen et al. [17] proposes Gorilla, a time series in-memory database, to provide efficient data storage and access for monitoring the Internet distributed service for Facebook. Meng et al. [18] proposes memory instant snapshot sharing mechanism to improve the speed of data sharing between database and applications.

These works have achieved outstanding results and greatly promoted the development of main-memory database technology. However, there are still some deficiencies in the efficient data storage and access of time series data in IoT. The massive time series sensing data in IoT brings new challenges to the main-memory database: (1) How to store time series data for applications conducting efficient analysis. (2) How to support applications to read and write data much faster. The previous studies cannot solve the problems well.

Focus on the challenges, we propose a lightweight main-memory database system TSMMDB (Time Series Main-Memory DataBase). Firstly, the data model and data storage strategy of IoT time series data are proposed. Based on the data model, a customized virtual heap and virtual heap memory allocator is proposed, and the physical memory pages are shared between processes, so that application can access the data in the whole database in the application's own process space. It is no longer limited by the traditional inter-process communication mode, which greatly improves the efficiency of data access for applications.

The main contributions of this paper are as follows:

- It proposes the data model and data storage strategy of time series data. The data model adopts tree structure, and the leaf node is three-dimension table based on time, resource and measure.
- It proposes a customized virtual heap and virtual heap memory allocator. The data objects in virtual heap created by applications can be persisted automatically based on memory mapping. A flexible data locality in memory allocation is obtained.
- The performance evaluation is carried out. Experimental results show that the performance of TSMMDB is obviously better than both traditional in-memory database and disk-based relational database.

The remainder of this paper is organized as follows: In Sect. 2, we present the related work. In Sect. 3, we present the data model of IoT time series sensing data. In Sect. 4, we present the data storage strategy of TSMMDB. In Sect. 5, we describe the overall structure and detail design of TSMMDB. In Sect. 6, we introduce the performance evaluation of TSMMDB. Finally, we conclude the paper in Sect. 7.

2 Related Work

At present, there are some in-memory database systems integrated with data analysis and data mining tools to achieve high efficiency of data analysis and processing. For example, SAP HANA combines the database server with the application server to reduce the cost of data movement [10, 13, 15]. However, excessive coupling between DBMS and data analysis programs will bring new problems and increase the cost of software development and maintenance.

Both Hyper [20] and SAP HANA [10, 13] use fork to create child processes to realize data sharing between DBMS and data analysis programs. When DBMS receives an analysis request, the main process calls fork to produce a child process to handle the request. Since the child process and the main process can share all the physical memory, the child process can immediately get a memory snapshot of the main process, which can be used to read and write data. The isolation between the main process and child process is ensured by the write-replication provided by the operating system.

The parent and child processes can avoid the data movement by the fork sharing memory mode, but this method has some deficiencies as follows: (1) The data analysis program should be embedded into DBMS using dynamic link library, thus increasing the coupling of data analysis program and DBMS, which makes the development of data analysis program becoming too complicated. (2) Since a child process cannot have more than one parent process, the child process in fork mode cannot get memory snapshot from multiple processes at the same time. That is to say, this mode does not support data analysis program to take memory snapshot in multiple processes as data source, which seriously restricts the application scope of data analysis program.

Therefore, to achieve efficient data sharing and reduce the coupling between the application and the database remain the unsolved technical issues which are main-memory database system currently addressing.

3   IoT Sensing Data Model

3.1   Data Model

The sensing data generated by IoT sensing devices such as sensors, cameras, RFID tags, etc., are collected periodically. The collection period can be different.

The IoT sensing data management business involves several entities: Network, LogicNE (logical device), NEInstance (physical device), Group (counter group) and Counter. Each device can set different collection intervals. Each network contains multiple logical devices. Each logical device consists of multiple physical devices. Each physical device consists of multiple groups. Each group consists of multiple counters. The counters collect the sensing data exactly.

According to the analysis of the business, the IoT sensing data model can be organized in a tree structure shown in Fig. 1.

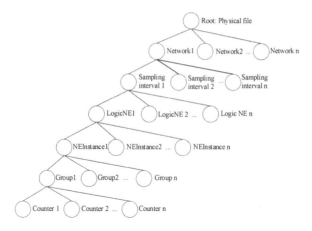

Fig. 1.   The data model of IoT sensing data.

In Fig. 1, the root of the tree is the physical file that stores all the data. Physical File contains multiple Networks. Network refers to IoT services. The different Networks refer to different IoT services, such as temperature monitoring service, humidity monitoring service, video monitoring service, etc. The sensing data in each IoT service is composed of data of multiple collection periods (Sampling Intervals). Each Sample Interval contains data from multiple logical devices (LogicNEs). LogicNEs refer to virtual IoT devices, which are resource objects accessible by IoT services and consist of multiple physical devices (NEInstances). For example, the temperature monitoring equipment of a room in a certain building is a logical equipment, which actually consists of multiple physical equipment of temperature sensors deployed in the room. Physical devices under logical devices are actually deployed sensing devices, such as temperature sensors, humidity sensors, light sensors, cameras, RFID tags, etc. A physical device (NEInstance) can contain 1 or more than one Group. Each Group contains 1 or more than one Counter, which actually collects sensing data periodically. The data types in each Group are consistent, such as numeric, graphical, etc.

The data collected each time is represented by a three-dimension table, where the row represents each specific device (Resource Instance), and the column represents multiple data collected by the device (Counter) at one time. The third dimension is the timestamp. The three dimensions determine the position in the table. All kinds of data collected are stored in the table, such as temperature value, humidity value, image taken by the camera, video image taken by the camera during a period of time, etc. The three-dimension table of IoT sensing data is shown in Fig. 2.

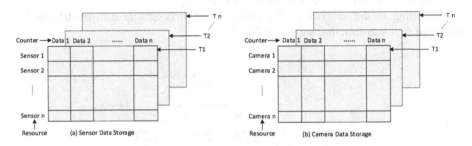

Fig. 2. Three-dimension table of IoT sensing data.

In Fig. 2, Table[r][c][t] represents the c data of the r sensing device at time t. T_1, T_2 ... T_n represents the collection time. r, c and t, respectively, which can locate the access position of the value of a data of a certain device at a certain time. Figure 2(a) represents the three-dimension table storage of sensor sensing data, and the data type is numeric. Figure 2(b) shows the three-dimension table storage of camera sensing data, and the data type is image type.

3.2   Structure of Persistent Objects

According to the data model of IoT sensing data in Figs. 1 and 2, the design of persistent objects is carried out, as shown in Fig. 3.

The retrieval chain of sensing data access is persNetwork→persPeriod→ persLNE→persNEInstance→persGroup→Table[r][c][t].

Without loss of generality, this model can be applied to general time series data model.

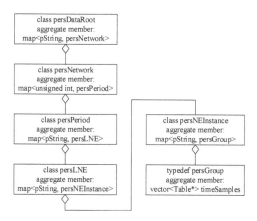

Fig. 3. The structure of persistent objects of IoT sensing data.

4 Data Storage Strategy

The TSMMDB database is made up of a set of data files. Considering the time series characteristics of data flow, physical files are divided according to time granularity T_f. T_f represents how many days of data are stored in a physical file, for example, $T_f = 1$ represents one day of data stored in a file. The application can set T_f value based on business requirements. When $T_f = 1$, if data is collected every 15 min, the number of RC (Resource-Counter) tables in each Group in one day will be $4*24 = 96$. All of these tables will be stored in one file. In TSMMDB System, the default configuration is $T_f = 1$.

Multiple physical files form a database in time series. For the old obsolete data, it can be backed up to historical data devices and then moved out of the database by data storage strategy. The number of the most recent files saved in the in-memory database is N_f. $N_f = 30$ indicates that the most recent 30 files are saved in the in-memory database. If each file holds one day's data, that's the most recent 30 days data. The data storage strategy is shown in Fig. 4. In Fig. 4, $T_f = 1$ and $N_f = 30$ are set in the storage strategy.

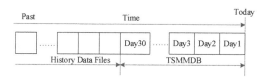

Fig. 4. The data storage strategy of TSMMDB.

For IoT service scenario, the historical data usage probability is much lower than the latest data. Application services can formulate data management policies and configure parameters T_f and N_f according to specific requirements. There is a parameter

MaxN$_f$ referring to the upper limit of the number of files in TSMMDB. So N$_f$ ≤ MaxN$_f$ should be meet.

The database physical file contains data and the corresponding index information.

5   TSMMDB System

5.1   System Overview

TSMMDB is a lightweight embedded memory database. The TSMMDB program is embedded in the application and runs as a module of the application, working with other modules of the application to complete the application functions. Since TSMMDB is part of the application, the application process can access to data throughout TSMMDB in the application's own process space. The data in TSMMDB can be accessed simultaneously by different applications.

The overall structure of TSMMDB system is shown in Fig. 5. TSMMDB system includes TSMMDB database, Reader module, Writer module and Manager module. Among them, Reader and Writer are the interface modules that provide application access, and Manager is the configuration function module.

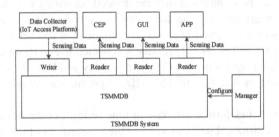

Fig. 5. System architecture of TSMMDB.

TSMMDB stores sensing data. TSMMDB provides the write function in Writer module, the read function in Reader module. Applications implements their write and read function to TSMMDB through Writer and Reader module.

In the application of IoT sensing data management, Data Collector, such as IoT Access Platform, implements real-time writing of sensing data collected to TSMMDB through Writer interface. Various data analysis applications, such as CEP (Complex Event Processing), GUI, etc., read sensing data from TSMMDB in real-time through Reader interface for data analysis or display.

The Manager module implements the configuration of TSMMDB, such as database size, memory address space planning, etc. T$_f$, N$_f$, MaxN$_f$ and other parameters can be configured according to the data storage policy of the application.

TSMMDB supports multiple readers and writers working simultaneously. Multiple applications of TSMMDB share the data in TSMMDB. In Fig. 5, IoT Access Platform, CEP and other applications (Apps) share data in TSMMDB. The application can access the data in the whole database in its own process through shared memory, which changes the communication mode between the traditional application and the database process. It greatly improves the efficiency of data access, and improves the data real-time processing performance. TSMMDB provides the reader and writer API for application, which reduce the coupling and complex of application development and maintenance.

In order to achieve efficient memory allocation and memory read and write operations, TSMMDB Reader and Writer are implemented in C++. The applications can be implemented in other languages, such as C++, Java, etc.

5.2   System Overview

The structure of the process's memory address space is shown in Fig. 6. In Fig. 6, stack space grows down, heap space grows up, and they're so far apart that they don't usually meet.

The memory where an application allocate is in the heap generally, as shown in Fig. 6. Virtual heap refers to the space created outside the heap for the application to allocate memory, and the location of virtual heap is shown in Fig. 6. Applications can create multiple unrelated virtual heaps and use them simultaneously. Unused virtual heaps can be recycled by the operating system.

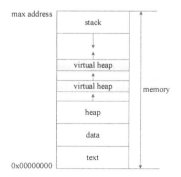

Fig. 6. Virtual heap in the memory address space of a process.

Each virtual heap corresponds to a database physical file on disk, which corresponds to a memory map. The memory mapping to physical file is shown in Fig. 7. Objects created in the virtual heap are called Persistent Objects, and Persistent Objects in the virtual heap are saved to database files by memory mapping automatically as shown in Fig. 7.

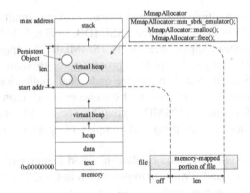

Fig. 7. Virtual heap object persistence based on memory mapping.

The virtual heap is managed by a customized memory allocator defined as class MmapAllocator, which is similar to the malloc allocator. The MmapAllocator calls mmap() of operation system to simulate the malloc's sbrk function to obtain memory space from the virtual heap. Thus implement the persistence of objects in virtual heap.

Algorithm 1: virtual heap memory allocator, is defined as follows:

Algorithm 1: definition of virtual heap memory allocator.

1: class MmapAllocator{
   //Dedicate memory of virtual heap.
2: void_t* MmapAllocator::mm_sbrk_emulator(ptrdiff_t increment); //Use mmap() to get memory and return the memory pointer to the virtual heap. Resize the virtual heap size by increasing the virtual heap's sbrk pointer by "increment" value. If the call is successful, the old value of the sbrk pointer is returned, otherwise -1 is returned.
   //Malloc the virtual heap memory for a resource instance.
3: void* MmapAllocator::malloc(size_t size); //Returns long word aligned block memory of at least "size" bytes in the mmap()ed region owned by this instance.
   //Free the memory of a resource instance.
4: void MmapAllocator::free(void* ptr); //Puts the block of memory referenced by "ptr" on a free list.
5: }

The design and implementation of Algorithm 1 refer to the algorithm and source code of Professor Douglas Lea of State University of New York [19]. This algorithm achieves a good balance among many factors, such as speed, space utilization, portability, and adjustability.

The relationship between MmapAllocator and the virtual heap is shown in Fig. 7.

5.3   Persistence of Database Objects

Persistence Based on Memory Mapping. Memory database uses memory mapping principle to achieve the persistence of objects. An in-memory database is essentially storing a "working version" of the database in memory. Virtual heap memory allocator uses mmap() system call to map database physical files from disk to the memory address space of the process. Through mmap() mapping, the application can access to ordinary files efficiently. Processes can operate on ordinary files like reading and writing memory, without having to call file operations like read(),write(), etc. It greatly improves the speed of data reading and writing. With mmap() system call, the applications reading/writing data cost far less time than normal way.

The working principle of virtual heap object persistence based on memory mapping is shown in Fig. 7. A chunk of data of "len" length in the disk file is mapped to a virtual heap of memory of "len" length starting from the "start addr" address. The objects created in the virtual heap are persistent objects, which can be persisted to file automatically based on memory mapping mechanism. By using memory mapping, data persistence is actually done by the operating system itself.

By updating the memory data in the mapping segment, writing to the mapping file can be completed. When data is written to memory, the file is not immediately updated. The file is updated when the file system refresh daemon finds that the memory page has been modified and pushes the page to the file system using putpage routine of the file system [15].

Once the data is written to memory, it can be immediately visible to the query process. Since the data is used in memory, disk I/O does not affect data access performance.

Definition of Persistent Objects. Applications directly link to shared function libraries of TSMMDB to create and use the persistent objects. Objects allocated in the virtual heap are persistent objects. The application needs to plan out a contiguous range address space for the virtual heap to use to avoid address space conflicts.

Algorithm 2 describes the definition of persistent string objects, persistent vector containers and persistent map containers.

Algorithm 2: definition of persistent objects.

//Define persistent string object as pString.
1: typedef basic_string<char, char_traits<char>, MmapAllocator<char>> pString;
   //Define the persistent pString object by the following 2 steps.
   //1) Define the memory allocator of pString object.
2: typedef MmapAllocator<pString> pStringAllocator;
   //2) Define a persistent vector container for storing pString objects.
3: typedef vector<pString, pStringAllocator> pStringVector;
   //Define the persistent persObject object by the following 2 steps.
   //1) Define the memory allocator of persObject object.
4: typedef MmapAllocator<persObject> persObjectAlloc;
   //2) Define persistent vector container for storing persObject object.
5: Typedef vector<persObject, persObjectAlloc> persObjectVector;
   //Define the persistent pKey2pObject object by the following 2 steps.
   //1) Define the memory allocator of pKey2pObject object.
6: typedef MmapAllocator<pair<persKey, persObject>> pKey2pObjectAlloc;
   //2) Define persistent map container for storing pKey2pObject object.
7: typedef map<persKey, persObject, less<pString>, pKey2pObjectAlloc>
   pKey2pMappedMap;

There are two points should to note about the definition of the persistent objects:

(1) If objects need to be created in the heap, use the default memory allocator. Objects that are not in the virtual heap are not persistent objects, and are not automatically stored in database files.
(2) If objects need to be created in the virtual heap, MmapAllocator based memory mapping is required. First, define the memory allocator for the persistent object, and then define the persistent container for such persistent objects. Objects in the virtual heap are persistent objects, and their data is saved into the database file automatically.

Creation and Use of Persistent Objects. Algorithm 3: creation and use of persistent objects.

Algorithm 3: creation and use of persistent objects(eg. class counter).
// Construct objects at memory addresses in the virtual heap.
1: counter* pc = new(MmapAllocator::allocate(sizeof(counter))) counter ();
   //Object persistence in the vector container, using the memory-mapped allocator
   class MmapAllocator to replace the default standard library's Allocator.
2: vector< counter, MmapAllocator< counter > >;

The database persistent objects created by MmapAllocator are used in the same way as regular objects. It is very easy for applications to use persistent objects.

5.4   Memory Allocation for Data Locality

The accessed data can be stored in a continuous address space, which can significantly improve the reading efficiency. Therefore, considering the characteristics of business applications, the data locality mechanism is designed.

For the application scenarios of time series data flow, the processing of original data is mostly based on the data of several adjacent sample periods. For example, the maximum temperature, the minimum temperature and the average temperature in one hour; the cumulative traffic on a port in one hour. Similarly, there are statistics of the last day, statistics of the last week, statistics of the last month, etc. If the data accessed by each calculation is concentrated in a few memory pages, rather than scattered over a large number of memory pages, the performance of the system will undoubtedly be significantly improved. This is the advantage of data locality.

Based on this idea, the database system should allocate a batch of time-adjacent persistent objects to the adjacent memory according to the request of the application. Algorithm 4 defines the ClusteredFactory template class to provide a memory pool for implementing data locality.

Algorithm 4: definition of memory pool.

```
1: template <class typeToCluster> class ClusteredFactory {
2:   private:
3:     union ClusteredInstance {
        //Member to manage free instance in a singly linked list.
4:       ClusteredInstance* freeLink;
        //The storage to use for the actual clustered instances.
5:       char payLoad[sizeof(typeToCluster)];
6:     }
      //Track the current size to use in our allocation algorithm.
7:     unsigned int currentSize;
      //Actual clustered instance storage and free list.
      //Implemented as a vector<> of pointers to arrays of instances so the memory does
        not move around as the number of chunks grows.
8:     typedef vector<ClusteredInstance*,MmapAllocator<ClusteredInstance*>>
        pClusterPtrVec;
9:     pClusterPtrVec chunkStorage;
10:    ClusteredInstance* freeList;
11: }
```

The ClusteredFactory object gets the memory space of the object to be created from the memory pool. By using memory pool, the Table objects are clustered by assigning all Table objects memory of a Resource in a virtual heap at one time as shown in Fig. 9 (b).

The memory pool allocation strategy is as follows: When the last memory pool space is used up, a whole block of continuous memory is allocated as the memory pool according to the memory size required for half of the current number of instances. So the next batch of instances that need to allocate memory will allocate adjacent memory and will be clustered together.

For each Group, there is a set of RC (Resource-Counter) tables (pRCtable class) named timeSamples. To allocate the set of tables to adjacent Memory Chunks, timeSamples should be defined as:

typedef vector<ClusteredFactory<pRCtable>, MmapAllocator<ClusteredFactory<pRCtable>>> timeSamples;

But not be defined as:

typedef vector<pRCtable, MmapAllocator<pRCtable>>> timeSamples;

Thus, when allocating memory, pRCtable instance defined in ClusteredFactory class will allocate adjacent memory from the memory pool, as shown in Fig. 9(b). Figure 9(a) shows the memory allocation and data writing without data locality mechanism. Table is not allocated in consecutive memory pages, and data of adjacent time cannot be written in consecutive memory pages, such as *10:00 write data, 10:15 write data,* and *10:30 write data* are not in contiguous memory space. With the data locality mechanism used for Fig. 9(b), Table is defined as a pointer type to the address where actual instance is stored. Instances are allocated in contiguous memory and they are clustered together as shown in Clustered Tables. The data of adjacent time is written in consecutive memory pages, such as *10:00 write data, 10:15 write data* and *10:30*

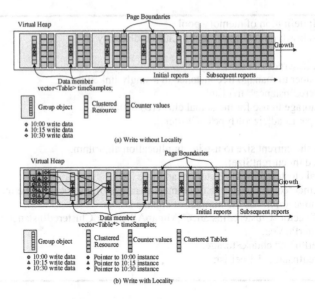

Fig. 8. Data locality in memory.

write data. Pointers in Group point to these consecutive memory addresses where the actual data is stored.

The data locality mechanism enables the data accessed per computation to be concentrated in a few consecutive memory pages rather than scattered in a large number of memory pages, which can significantly improve the performance of the system.

5.5   Time Complexity of Data Access Algorithm

The in-memory database data model is constructed using map. Each map is indexed by a RB (Red Black) tree. The database data model is a multi-level tree structure, as shown in Fig. 1. The index of the database is a multi-level RB tree. The RB tree is a balanced binary search tree, which guarantees that, in the worst case, the time complexity of the basic dynamic set operation is $O(\lg M)$ where M is the element number of the set.

Assuming data is average distributed, the map size of each layer is the same, and the size of each Table is the same. N is the total number of counters in a collection period. There are n layers in the tree. N_i is the size of the map of the i-th layer, i = 1, 2 … , n.

$N = N_1 * N_2 * N_3 * \ldots * N_n$, where:

N_1: size of map in layer 1;

N_2: size of map in layer 2;

…

N_{n-1}: size of map in layer n − 1;

N_n: the size of a Tuple, which is actually the size of an array of integers that stores the value of the Counter.

The query condition in the data model is the keyword of RB tree of each layer. As the worst case query complexity of RB tree of layer i is $O(lg(N_i))$, the query complexity of this multi-layer RB tree is:

$$T(N) = O(lgN_1 + lgN_2 + \ldots + lgN_{n-1} + lgN_n) = O(lg(N_1 * N_2 * N_3 * \ldots * N_n))$$
$$= O(lgN)$$

In the worst case, the time complexity of the database access is $O(lgN)$, which achieves the ideal time complexity.

6 Experimental Evaluation

6.1 Performance Comparison Between TSMMDB and Traditional DBMSs

Experiment 1: performance comparison of different DBMSs.

The performance of TSMMDB is compared with the traditional main-memory database Redis and the relational database MySQL.

The experiment process is: when the application receives the collected sensing data packet, it is stored in the database, and the application records the processing time. The three DBMSs are used separately, and the processing time are recorded in each DBMS running.

Experimental environment: Intel Xeon(R) Gold 5115 CPU 2.40 GHz*40, 62.4 GB RAM, 609.3 GB Hard Disk, OS: CentOS Linux 7 with 64-bit. DBMS software: Redis 4.0.2 64 bit. MySQL 5.5.59 Community Server.

The number of packets that can be processed per second by the three DBMSs are shown in Fig. 9(a). The processing time of each packet are shown in Fig. 9(b).

In Fig. 9(a), the average number of packets handled by TSMMDB is 2.25×10^4 packets/second, Redis handles 1.17×10^4 packets/second and MySQL handles 0.82×10^4 packets/second. The throughput of TSMMDB is about 92% more than Redis, and about 174% more than MySQL. The throughput of Redis is about 43% more than MySQL.

In Fig. 9(b), the average processing time of each packet is 0.046 ms for TSMMDB, 0.09 ms for Redis and 0.124 ms for MySQL. The access speed of TSMMDB is about 48% faster than Redis, and about 63% faster than MySQL. The access speed of Redis is about 27% faster than MySQL.

It can be seen that the access efficiency of TSMMDB is higher than that of Redis and MySQL, while Redis is higher than MySQL.

The experimental results show that: (1) Both the two memory databases, TSMMDB and Redis, are faster than disk database MySQL. (2) Between the two memory databases, TSMMDB is faster than Redis. TSMMDB provides the application accessing the database through shared memory, while Redis need transfer data from Redis server process to the application process by inter-process communication. Thus TSMMDB achieve efficient data sharing between in-memory database and the application which has significant advantages over traditional inter-process communication.

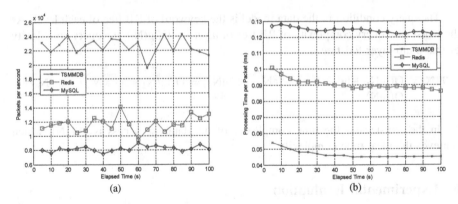

Fig. 9. Performance comparison between different DBMSs. (a) Number of packets per second. (b) Processing time per packet.

6.2   System Resource Usage of TSMMDB

Experiment 2: system resource usage of TSMMDB.

Experiment data: data of 4 networks were collected every 15 min, 2M sensor counters were collected at each interval of each network, and 4 bytes of data were stored in each counter. The data stores for 30 days. The data collected and stored in main-memory of one day is $96 \times 4 \times 2M \times 4 = 3.072$ GB. The TSMMDB data of 30 days reaches $3.072 \times 30 = 92.16$ GB which stores in the 30 files.

The CPU usage is shown in Fig. 10(a). The Memory usage is shown in Fig. 10(b). The horizontal coordinate is the number of collected networks, ranging from 1 to 4, and the vertical coordinate is respectively the CPU usage in Fig. 10(a) and Memory usage in Fig. 10(b). When the number of networks is 1, consisting of 2M number of sensors, the CPU usage is 43.6%, and Memory usage is 15.1 GB. When the number of networks is 4, consisting of 8M number of sensors, the CPU usage is 51%, and Memory usage is 18.2 GB.

In Fig. 10, the curve basically rises in a straight line, that is, with the increase of network load, the CPU usage and memory usage both increase linearly. Linear growth is an ideal curve, much better than exponential growth.

The experiment shows that the CPU and memory consumption of TSMMDB meet the requirements of IoT sensing data management. With the expansion of the network scale, the growth of CPU usage and memory usage show an ideal linear growth. The performance of TSMMDB can meet the requirements of IoT sensing data management operation index.

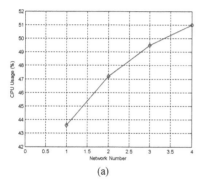
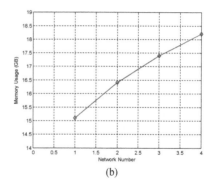

(a)   (b)

Fig. 10. TSMMDB system resource usage. (a) CPU usage. (b) Memory usage.

7 Conclusions

This paper proposes a lightweight embedded main-memory database system TSMMDB to meet the IoT real-time data processing requirements of large amount of data storing, high performance processing and low overhead. The data model is the tree structure and the leaf node adopts the three-dimension table based on time, resource and measure. The data in TSMMDB is in the customized virtual heap memory allocated by virtual heap memory allocator. The application can access the whole database in its own process without transferring data. The data object persistence is automatically based on memory mapping. An optimization of memory allocation based on data locality is adopted to store time-adjacent data in continuous memory space to improve clustered data analysis efficiency. The performance comparison experiment shows that the performance of TSMMDB is obviously better than traditional in-memory database and disk-based relational database.

In the future, we will apply TSMMDB to more IoT application scenarios, such as real-time monitoring, real-time data analysis, etc. At the same time, we will further evaluate the performance of concurrent processing of TSMMDB.

References

1. Kunkle, D., Cooperman, G.: Solving Rubik's cube: disk is the new RAM. Commun. ACM **51**(4), 31–33 (2008)
2. Zhang, H., et al.: In-memory big data management and processing: a survey. IEEE Trans. Knowl. Data Eng. **27**(7), 1920–1948 (2015)
3. Larson, P.Å., Levandoski, J.: Modern main-memory database systems. Proc. VLDB Endow. **9**(13), 1609–1610 (2016)
4. Ailamaki, A.: The next 700 transaction processing engines. In: Proceedings of the 2017 ACM International Conference on Management of Data, pp. 1–2. ACM (2017)
5. Lahiri, T., et al.: Oracle database in-memory: a dual format in-memory database. In: 2015 IEEE 31st International Conference on Data Engineering (ICDE), pp. 1253–1258. IEEE (2015)

6. Kim, J., Salem, K., Daudjee, K.: Write amplification: an analysis of in-memory database durability techniques. In: Proceedings of the 3rd VLDB Workshop on In-Memory Data Management and Analytics. ACM (2015). Article No. 1
7. Plattner, H.: A common database approach for OLTP and OLAP using an in-memory column database. In: Proceedings of the 2009 ACM SIGMOD International Conference on Management of data, pp. 1–2. ACM (2009)
8. Stonebraker, M., Weisberg, A.: The VoltDB main memory DBMS. IEEE Data Eng. Bull. **36**(2), 21–27 (2013)
9. Xie, X., Chai, E., Zhang, X.: Hekaton: efficient and practical large-scale MIMO. In: Proceedings of the 21st Annual International Conference on Mobile Computing and Networking, pp. 304–316. ACM (2015)
10. Färber, F., Cha, S.K., Primsch, J., Bornhövd, C., Sigg, S., Lehner, W.: SAP HANA database: data management for modern business applications. ACM SIGMOD Rec. **40**(4), 45–51 (2011)
11. Färber, F., et al.: The SAP HANA database-an architecture overview. IEEE Data Eng. Bull. **35**(1), 28–33 (2012)
12. Sikka, V., et al.: Efficient transaction processing in SAP HANA database: the end of a column store myth. In: Proceedings of the 2012 ACM SIGMOD International Conference on Management of Data, pp. 731–742. ACM (2012)
13. Sikka, V., Färber, F., Goel, A., Lehner, W.: SAP HANA: the evolution from a modern main-memory data platform to an enterprise application platform. Proc. VLDB Endow. **6**(11), 1184–1185 (2013)
14. Nica, A., Sherkat, R., Andrei, M., et al.: Statisticum: data statistics management in SAP HANA. Proc. VLDB Endow. **10**(12), 1658–1669 (2017)
15. Lee, J., Moon, S.H., Kim, K.H., et al.: Parallel replication across formats in SAP HANA for scaling out mixed OLTP/OLAP workloads. Proc. VLDB Endow. **10**(12), 1598–1609 (2017)
16. Andrei, M., Lemke, C., Radestock, G., et al.: SAP HANA adoption of non-volatile memory. Proc. VLDB Endow. **10**(12), 1754–1765 (2017)
17. Pelkonen, T., et al.: Gorilla: a fast, scalable, in-memory time series database. Proc. VLDB Endow. **8**(12), 1816–1827 (2015)
18. Meng, Q., Zhou, X., Wang, S.: Memory instant snapshot sharing mechanism and its application in database. Chin. J. Comput. **41**(28), 1912–1927 (2018)
19. Lea, D.: http://g.oswego.edu/dl/html/malloc.html. Source code: ftp://g.oswego.edu/pub/misc/malloc.c
20. Kemper, A., Neumann, T.: HyPer: a hybrid OLTP&OLAP main memory database system based on virtual memory snapshots. In: Proceedings of the 2011 IEEE 27th International Conference on Data Engineering, Hannover, Germany, pp. 195–206 (2011)

A Review on Blockchain-Based Systems and Applications

Jingyu Zhang[1,3], Siqi Zhong[1,3], Jin Wang[1,2,3(✉)], Lei Wang[2,3],
Yaqiong Yang[1,3], Boyang Wei[1,3], and Guoyao Zhou[1,3]

[1] School of Computer and Communication Engineering,
Changsha University of Science and Technology, Changsha 410004, China
{zhangzhang, jinwang}@csust.edu.cn,
zhongsiqi@stu.csust.edu.cn, yangyaqiong729@163.com,
455258872@qq.com, moska9417@163.com
[2] School of Information Science and Engineering,
Fujian University of Technology, Fujian 350118, China
[3] School of Civil Engineering, Changsha University of Science and Technology,
Changsha 410004, China
leiwang@csust.edu.cn

Abstract. Blockchain technology is a combination of distributed data storage, peer-to-peer network, consensus mechanism, timestamp technology, encryption algorithm and other computer technologies. It provides a new solution for the secure distributed cloud data storage system. Blockchain can provide a decentralized secure storage architecture that does not require the accumulation of trust, and it can provides new solutions for cloud storage security and can be applied in time-sensitive areas. This paper summarizes the existing blockchain-based systems and applications, and we mainly review the applications of blockchain traceability technology in various fields, the blockchain decentralized applications, and other blockchain applications in data security protection, respectively. This work may bring new opportunities and challenges for the development of various industries in the future.

Keywords: Blockchain technology · Distributed storage · Cloud storage security

1 Introduction

The blockchain is essentially a distributed database over peer-to-peer networks [1]. It stores all transactions on a peer-to-peer network in a secure, verifiable, and transparent manner [2]. A complete blockchain system includes many technologies (e.g., the consensus algorithms, proof-of-work mechanisms, digital signature, timestamp technology [3]). The blockchain system has the following characteristics: (1) Decentralization; (2) Reliable database; (3) Collective maintenance; (4) Security and credibility; (5) Anonymity; (6) Open source programmable. It provides a new solution for the secure distributed cloud data storage system.

© Springer Nature Switzerland AG 2020
C.-H. Hsu et al. (Eds.): IOV 2019, LNCS 11894, pp. 237–249, 2020.
https://doi.org/10.1007/978-3-030-38651-1_20

Generally, the development process of blockchain is divided into three stages, which are called blockchain 1.0, blockchain 2.0 and blockchain 3.0 respectively. Table 1 compares three different stages of blockchain. In the blockchain 1.0 stage, the main focus is on peer-to-peer transactions, and Bitcoin is the most famous application. In the blockchain 2.0 stage, The traceability of blockchain technology and the tamper-resistance of data provide a decentralized and trusted environment for intelligent contracts. In December 2013, Vitalik Buterin [4] developed a public blockchain platform with intelligent contract function – Ethereum application platform, Blockchain 2.0 stage is also known as the Ethereum blockchain stage. The blockchain 3.0 focuses on the integration of blockchain technologies and other fields (e.g., financial industry, Internet of Things (IoT)). Enterprise-level blockchain platform becomes the focus of research.

Table 1. Comparison of each blockchain development stage.

	Bitcoin blockchain	Ethereum blockchain	Hyperledger fabric
Issues to improve	The financial crisis, traditional centralized financial institutions	The limited application scenarios of Bitcoin	Slow transaction speed of public blockchain, unguaranteed transactions
Consensus mechanism	Proof of Work (PoW)	PoW, Proof of Stake (PoS)	Practical Byzantine Fault Tolerance (PBFT)
Network layer protocol	TCP-based p2p	TCP-based p2p	HTTP/2-based p2p
Programming language	Bitcoin script, Ivy	Solidity, Serpent, Mutan, LLL	Go, Java, JavaScript
Data model	Transaction-based UTXO model	The account-based model (includes contract accounts and external accounts)	The account-based model
Application scenarios	Bitcoin trading, asset delivery	Decentralized applications, ether trading, smart contracts	Supply chain management, property registration, asset management, etc.

In the remaining of this paper, Sect. 2 introduces the combination of blockchain, and traceability technology, and the applications in the field of property rights and asset delivery. In Sect. 3, the decentralized applications in blockchain systems are introduced. Section 4 introduces the blockchain applications in data security and data privacy protection. Section 5 summarizes the work of this paper.

2 The Applications of Blockchain Traceability Technology

Traditional traceability technology adopts centralized data storage to manage product information. This centralized management lacks the trust of consumers to conduct reliable data tracking. Blockchain technology has the characteristics of decentralization and distribution, which can solve the problem of lacking trust in centralized systems. Meanwhile, the introduction of timestamp technology in blockchain can add a time dimension to blockchain-based internet. That makes data easier to trace back, and the timestamp can be used as an important basis for proof of existence.

2.1 Blockchain Applications for Supply Chain Traceability Systems

The traditional supply chain management system is insufficient to meet the requirements of consumers for product quality. And many companies and governments are looking for a safer and more efficient way to track products. Through blockchain, a shared distributed ledger, we can make product information transparent. The information stored in the blockchain will not be tampered with, and the commodity's locations in the supply chain can be tracked in real time, providing extraordinary transparency and security. Therefore, the combination of blockchain traceability technology and supply chain management has attracted the attention of researchers. The traceability application model of the product blockchain platform developed with the e-commerce is shown in Fig. 1.

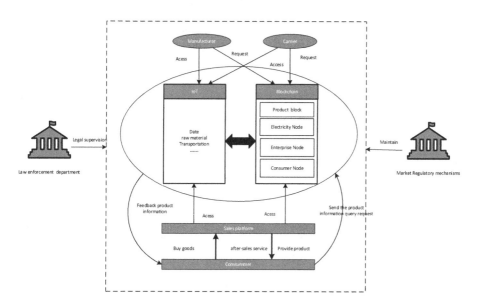

Fig. 1. Traceability application model of the product blockchain platform.

In the supply chain management process, it is urgent to introduce new technologies to improve the security, transparency and integrity of supply chain data. Therefore, it is very important to study the specific operational mechanism and application value of applying the blockchain to the supply chain traceability management. Fu et al. [5] proposed a blockchain technology solution, which uses blockchain technology to track inter-organizational business processes in an enterprise. In order to implement blockchain technology correctly in the supply chain, Perboli et al. [6] analyzed the needs and goals of different participants and combined with blockchain technology to create a business model that can highlight and simultaneously solve problems in economy and customer satisfaction. In terms of solving the fraud problems of enterprise entities and market supervision problems, Lin et al. [7] proposed a blockchain-based food safety traceable system service, and a new blockchain data management architecture. In order to avoid fraud, Figorilli et al. [8] adopted a synergistic method of RFID technology and blockchain to realize a wood chain electronic tracking online information system based on RFID sensor and open source technology within a blockchain architecture.

2.2   Blockchain Applications of Intellectual Property Protection

The existing research proves that the applications of blockchain technology to copyright management can effectively improve the problem of intellectual property rights. It mainly utilizes the openness, traceability, tamper-resistance, decentralization, anonymity and autonomy of the blockchain to solve issues (e.g., the rights attribution certificate, the copyright circulation traceability, the intelligent tracking situation, intellectual property protection and deposit certificates).

The intellectual property protection in the multimedia field is very weak, and the characteristics of blockchain technology (e.g., credibility, transparency, decentralization) make it compatible with the basic principles of copyright to deal with the above problem [9]. [10] proposed a decentralized data management framework, which uses a new blockchain data protocol to control user data. A new secure data protection method based on data hiding and blockchain technology provides basic security services for digital video network transmission [11]. In this paper, the improvement of digital copyright protection system based on digital watermark mainly focuses on the algorithm which ignores the generation and storage of watermark information. Meng et al. [12] proposed a blockchain copyright management system design scheme based on digital watermark information. In order to effectively improve anti-counterfeiting issues in the supply chain, Toyoda et al. [13] proposed a product ownership management system based on radio frequency identification technology for product anti-counterfeiting. This work further realized a proof-of-concept experimental system based on a blockchain decentralization application platform.

2.3   Blockchain Applications for Asset Delivery

Currently, asset delivery usually relies on third-party trust institutions to supervise and prove the transaction process. Such centralized trust institutions have trust problems such as missing transaction information and information being tampered with. The blockchain solution provides proof for the asset delivery transactions traded between the two individual parties. The interactive relationship of each role in the asset delivery management system based on blockchain is shown in Fig. 2.

At present, some researchers have used blockchain technology to improve the asset delivery certification system. Hasan H.R et al. [14] proposed a decentralized proof of delivery (PoD) solution for PoD of digital assets. [15] presented a blockchain based POD solution of shipped physical items that uses smart contracts of Ethereum blockchain network, and the solution incentivizes each participating entity including the seller, transporter, and buyer to act honestly, and it totally eliminates the need for a third party as escrow. [16] presented a solution and a new general framework using the popular permissionless Ethereum blockchain to create a trusted, decentralized proof of delivery system that ensures accountability, auditability, and integrity. The proposed solution uses Ethereum smart contracts to prove the delivery of a shipped item between a seller and a buyer irrespective of the number which intermediate transporters needed. Utz et al. [17] addressed the energy production, consumption structure changes, and the coordination of assets, equipment, and stakeholders in the energy market by introducing a blockchain-based smart contract ecosystem. Based on existing research, the work in [18] introduces a built-in mechanism to reduce the transaction risks caused by the irreversibility of transactions in blockchain systems. This mechanism can replace a trust-based, centralized, bureaucratic registration with a tamper-proof and autonomous transactional database system that includes secure registration and transaction process. Furthermore, the authors proposed a novel approach to mitigate adverse selection effects in lemon markets by providing a reliable, transparent, and complete record of each marketable asset history information.

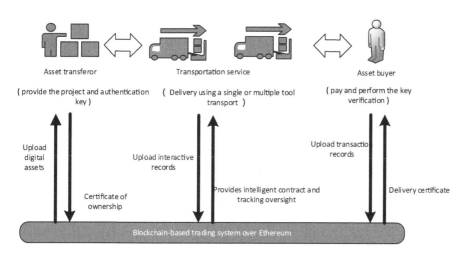

Fig. 2. Delivery management system based on blockchain

3   Decentralized Applications Based on Blockchain

Blockchain has the characteristics of distributed data storage, so it is suitable for the field of decentralized applications such as decentralized voting. Applying the blockchain to the electoral field can mainly eliminate the possibility of potential intended manipulation, and ensure the safety and fairness in addition. It will also improve the convenience of the electoral process. Because voters do not have to pay more time and energy, the participation rate will inevitably increase. Therefore, voting with the blockchain technology can also reflect the main public opinion as much as possible. The decentralized voting application model is shown in Fig. 3. Utilizing the decentralized distributed nature of the blockchain, users can vote for specific candidates in an untrusted distributed environment, and each vote is recorded on the blockchain.

There are many methods for electronic voting, but most of them lack transparency and auditability. Currently, many papers have proposed solutions for this problem by using blockchain technology. Pawlak et al. [19] introduced an auditable blockchain voting system (ABVS), which described the electronic voting process and components of a supervised network voting system with audit and verification functions. On this basis, [20] studies the applications of multi-agent systems and intelligent agent in ABVS. In order to solve the problems of voting fraud and hacking in election and administrative management, [21] proposed a new voting model to solve these problems, which provides a fast, safe and high-throughput voting system. To prevent tampering, Shukla et al. [22] designed a private blockchain by creating a peer-to-peer network, which maintain a shared distributed ledger with voting transactions. This method also designed an application that hides the complexity of the underlying architecture from users to improve security. To facilitate decision-making in a decentralized and secure manner, Zhang et al. [23] proposed a local blockchain voting protocol, which allows peers to vote on the existing blockchain network. [24] introduced a new electronic voting system based on blockchain, which improves the security and reduces the cost of holding national elections. Fusco et al. [25] proposed a new electronic voting system based on blockchain technology. The system is called password voting system, aiming to improve the traceability of voting operations and audit methods. [26] applied blockchain technology's resistance to double spending to prevent double voting on electronic voting systems, and this work proposed a new electronic voting system to ensure credible sources to realize end-to-end verifiable electronic voting scheme. [27] took an in-depth evaluation of the end-to-end verifiable electronic voting scheme, and proved the effectiveness of the proposed method in realizing the end-to-end verifiable electronic voting scheme.

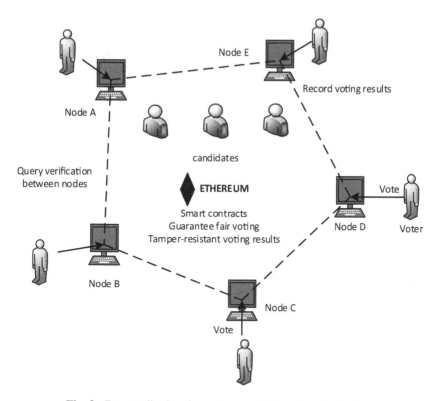

Fig. 3. Decentralized voting system model based on blockchain

4 Decentralized Applications in the Field of Data Security

The rise of cloud storage has led to the explosive growth of data scale in all walks of life. However, trust has become the biggest problem of big data, which will hinder the safe data transmission. Blockchain technology provides a new solution to the problem of data security and privacy protection, which combines the features of tamper-resistance and traceability with smart contracts that automatically execute default instructions [28] to ensure the safe storage and transmissions of data resources. This section reviews the research in finance, Internet of Things and healthcare, and summarizes relevant technologies and development prospects.

4.1 Data Protection in the Financial Industry

Due to various advantages of blockchain, its applications in the financial industry has been widely used. Compared with traditional payment, blockchain payment can directly realize end-to-end payment for both sides of the transaction without involving intermediary institutions, and it can greatly improve the speed.

In the study of how to apply blockchain technology to auctions to maximize social welfare, researchers made the following work. [29] proposed an optimal auction method of marginal resource allocation based on deep learning in the blockchain network. Based on the typical auction security requirements, Blass et al. [30] proposed a new auction protocol running on top of blockchains and guaranteeing bid confidentiality against malicious parties. The inherent transparency and the resulting lack of privacy pose a huge challenge to many financial applications. To solve the above problems, [31] proposed a sealed bidding auction smart contract that can be verified on Ethereum blockchain. To solve the traditional payment problems, a lot of work has been done based on the combination with blockchain. The paper [32] proposed a blockchain-based digital payment scheme that can deliver reliable services on top of unreliable networks in remote regions. Real-time gross settlement system is the cornerstone of inter-bank payment business, and Wang et al. [33] introduced an end-to-end inter-bank payment system prototype based on Hyperledger Fabric enterprise blockchain platform. The prototype supports gross settlement, gridlock resolution, and reconciliation for inter-bank payment business. In the existing online payment systems, information such as reputation could be manipulated by the malicious. For this problem, [34] proposed Reptor, a model for calculation of trust and reputation with the values stored on a blockchain-based payment system's ledger. Zhao et al. [35] studied data security and privacy problem for reliable cyber physical system, and proposed a new secure pub-sub system that uses fairness payment with reputation based on blockchain.

4.2   Internet of Things Data Access Management

IoT equipment installation and deployment in the family in each industrial fields, including transportation, oil, natural gas, energy and manufacturing [36]. The deployment of the IoT equipment range is very wide, and people already know that they are vulnerable to various attacks. As the growth of the importance of privacy, people begin to pay close attention to reliable Internet equipment safety management and access control problem [37]. Blockchain technology has been leading to the birth of many new solutions since 2018. Numerous reports and articles have pointed out that blockchain may be the next key development, and by 2019, nearly 20% of all IoT deployments may have basic blockchain services.

IoT devices can be registered using blockchain to efficiently and reliably organize, store and share data streams. In terms of data security management, Chao et al. [38] proposed a design of blockchain connection gateway, which can adaptively and safely maintain the user privacy preference of IoT devices in the blockchain network. To solve the security and reliability of IoT cloud storage, [39] studied the typical security and privacy issues in the IoT, and developed a new framework to integrate the blockchain with the Internet of Things. The proposed method can provide great guarantee for the data and various functions in the Internet of Things with the ideal scalability, which support authentication, decentralized payment, etc. [40] proposed an out-of-band two-factor authentication scheme for IoT devices based on Blockchain infrastructure. they implemented the IoT and Blockchain integrated system with Eris Blockchain and equivalent computing devices to emulate IoT devices. Alblooshi et al. [41] presents a general framework and solution to manage and trace back the true origin of ownership for an medical IoT devices (MIoT). Alblooshi et al. [42] proposed a new threshold Internet of things service system based on blockchain: Beekeeper. It is still challenging to apply blockchain to IoTs due to resource constraint characteristics of embedded devices and significant delays in processing and validating transactions.

4.3   Healthcare Data in Blockchain Systems

At present, there are mainly two ways to protect the privacy of medical data [45]. One way is to store medical data in a local database and set up a database access control strategy, other way is to encrypt medical data with the patient's key and share the key when needed. However, both of the above ways have defects. Blockchain is a highly secure distributed data storage platform, which is changing the way how healthcare information is stored and shared [43]. It makes the work more convenient and reduces the maintenance cost while paying attention to the security and accuracy of data. In the healthcare field, blockchain technology has obvious advantages over other existing technologies, and will play a greater role for the applications of blockchain technology in the healthcare field in the future.

In order to ensure the integrity and traceability of medical data, the paper [46] proposed a secure electronic health record system based on cloud computing by using blockchain technology. Another work [47] proposed a blockchain-based secure and privacy-preserving personal health information sharing scheme for diagnosis improvements in e-Health systems. As IoT devices and other remote patient monitoring systems increase in popularity, security concerns about the transfer and logging of data transactions arise. In order to handle the protected health information generated by these devices, [48] utilized blockchain-based smart contracts to facilitate secure analysis and management of medical sensors. There is also a challenge to guarantee the security and the privacy of locations recorded in a blockchain system. Healthcare systems based on blockchain have advantages in terms of decentralization and openness to deal with the above issue. The paper [49] introduced a blockchain-based multi-level privacy-preserving location sharing scheme for telecare medical information systems. Li et al. [50] proposed a blockchain-based medical data preservation system, and they leveraged the blockchain framework to provide a reliable storage solution and ensure the primitiveness, verifiability of stored data while preserving privacy for users.

Table 2 summarizes the situation of the combination with blockchain in the fields of finance, IoT and healthcare. In general, the application of blockchain technology in various fields in the future has a broad prospect, and it is also full of challenges.

Table 2. The combination summary for blockchain and various applied fields

	Blockchain and finance	Blockchain and IoT	Blockchain and Healthcare
Traditional disadvantages	Lack of trust, slow cross-border payment speed, low data security	Lack of privacy, vulnerability to attacks	Data tampering, separated data storage, incomplete patient information
Advantages of combination	Decentralized, improved transaction speed, improved data security	Privacy protection, data storage security, access control protection	High data security, complete patient information
Current development situation	Early development, deployed in most blockchain projects	Begins from 2015, for the management and security of IoT devices	Late start, less applications
Application scenarios	Bitcoin trading, hyperledger, justice and charity, etc.	Smart city, Internet of Vehicles, etc.	Electronic health record, DNA wallet, protein folding, etc.
Blockchain stage	Blockchain1.0, 2.0, 3.0	Blockchain3.0	Blockchain3.0
Reference index	[29–35]	[36–42]	[43–50]

5 Conclusion

As an untampered, time-sequentially verifiable chain-like storage architecture, block-chain can provide a new solution for the secure distributed cloud data storage system, and it is becoming one of the current hottest research fields. This paper summarizes the relevant applications and research of existing blockchain technology. We mainly review the applications of blockchain traceability technology in various fields, the blockchain decentralized applications, and other blockchain applications in data security protection, respectively. As investigated by the above studies, blockchain will contribute to improving the solutions in multiple fields such as the Internet of Things, smart city and supply chain. It will also bring new opportunities and challenges for the development of various industries in the future.

References

1. Zou, J., et al.: Blockchain Technology Guide. China Machine Press, Beijing (2018)
2. Al-Jaroodi, J., Mohamed, N.: Blockchain in industries: a survey. IEEE Access **7**, 36500–36515 (2019)
3. Chen, W., Zheng, Z., Cheuk-Han Ngai, E., Zheng, P., Zhou, Y.: Exploiting blockchain data to detect smart ponzi schemes on ethereum. IEEE Access **7**, 37575–37586 (2019)

 4. Lin, F., Qiang, M.: The challenges of existence, status, and value for improving blockchain. IEEE Access **7**, 7747–7758 (2019)
 5. Yonggui, F., Zhu, J.: Big production enterprise supply chain endogenous risk management based on blockchain. IEEE Access **7**, 15310–15319 (2019)
 6. Perboli, G., Musso, S., Rosano, M.: Blockchain in logistics and supply chain: a lean approach for designing real-world use cases. IEEE Access **6**, 62018–66202 (2018)
 7. Lin, Q., Wang, H., Pei, X., Wang, J.: Food safety traceability system based on blockchain and EPCIS. IEEE Access **7**, 20698–20707 (2019)
 8. Figorilli, S., et al.: A blockchain implementation prototype for the electronic open source traceability of wood along the whole supply chain. Sensors **18**, 3133–3146 (2018)
 9. Bodó, B., Gervais, D., Quintais, J.P.: Blockchain and smart contracts: the missing link in copyright licensing? I J Law and Inf. Technol. **26**(4), 311–336 (2018)
10. Vishwa, A., Hussain, F.K.: A Blockchain based approach for multimedia privacy protection and provenance. In: 2018 IEEE Symposium Series on Computational Intelligence, pp. 1941–1945. IEEE, Bangalore (2018)
11. Zeng, J., Zuo, C., Zhang, F., Li, C., Zheng, L.: A solution to digital image copyright registration based on consortium blockchain. In: Wang, Y., Jiang, Z., Peng, Y. (eds.) IGTA 2018. CCIS, vol. 875, pp. 228–237. Springer, Singapore (2018). https://doi.org/10.1007/978-981-13-1702-6_23
12. Meng, Z., Morizumi, T., Miyata, S., Kinoshita, H.: Design scheme of copyright management system based on digital watermarking and blockchain. In: 2018 IEEE 42nd Annual Computer Software and Applications Conference, pp. 359–364. IEEE, Tokyo (2018)
13. Toyoda, K., Mathiopoulos, P.T., Sasase, I., Ohtsuki, T.: A novel blockchain-based product ownership management system (POMS) for anti-counterfeits in the post supply chain. IEEE Access **5**, 17465–17477 (2017)
14. Hasan, H.R., Salah, K.: Proof of delivery of digital assets using blockchain and smart contracts. IEEE Access **6**, 65439–65448 (2018)
15. Hasan, H.R., Salah, K.: Blockchain-based solution for proof of delivery of physical assets. In: Chen, S., Wang, H., Zhang, L.-J. (eds.) ICBC 2018. LNCS, vol. 10974, pp. 139–152. Springer, Cham (2018). https://doi.org/10.1007/978-3-319-94478-4_10
16. Hasan, H.R., Salah, K.: Blockchain-based proof of delivery of physical assets with single and multiple transporters. IEEE Access **6**, 46781–46793 (2018)
17. Utz, M., Albrecht, S., Zoerner, T., Strüker, J.: Blockchain-based management of shared energy assets using a smart contract ecosystem. In: Abramowicz, W., Paschke, A. (eds.) BIS 2018. LNBIP, vol. 339, pp. 217–222. Springer, Cham (2019). https://doi.org/10.1007/978-3-030-04849-5_19
18. Notheisen, B., Cholewa, J.B., Shanmugam, A.P.: Trading real-world assets on blockchain, an application of trust-free transaction systems in the market for lemons. Bus. Inf. Syst. Eng. **59**, 425–440 (2017)
19. Pawlak, M., Guziur, J., Poniszewska-Marańda, A.: Voting process with blockchain technology: auditable blockchain voting system. In: Xhafa, F., Barolli, L., Greguš, M. (eds.) INCoS 2018. LNDECT, vol. 23, pp. 233–244. Springer, Cham (2019). https://doi.org/10.1007/978-3-319-98557-2_21
20. Pawlak, M., Poniszewska-Marańda, A., Guziur, J.: Intelligent agents in a blockchain-based electronic voting system. In: Yin, H., Camacho, D., Novais, P., Tallón-Ballesteros, Antonio J. (eds.) IDEAL 2018. LNCS, vol. 11314, pp. 586–593. Springer, Cham (2018). https://doi.org/10.1007/978-3-030-03493-1_61
21. Srivastava, G., Dwivedi, A.D., Singh, R.: Crypto-democracy: a decentralized voting scheme using blockchain technology. In: Proceedings of the 15th International Joint Conference on e-Business and Telecommunications, pp. 674–679. SciTePress, Porto (2018)

22. Shukla, S., Thasmiya, A.N., Shashank, D.O., Mamatha, H.R.: Online voting application using ethereum blockchain. In: ICACCI 2018, pp. 873–880. IEEE, Bangalore (2018)
23. Zhang, W., et al.: A privacy-preserving voting protocol on blockchain. In: IEEE CLOUD 2018, pp. 401–408. IEEE, San Francisco (2018)
24. Hjalmarsson, F.P., Hreioarsson, G.K., Hamdaqa, M., Hjalmtysson, G.: Blokchain-based e-voting system. In: IEEE CLOUD 2018, San Francisco, USA, pp. 983–986 (2018)
25. Fusco, F., Lunesu, M.I., Pani, A.P.: Crypto-voting, a blockchain based e-voting system. In: KMIS, pp. 221–225 (2018)
26. Kshetri, N., Voas, J.M.: Blockchain-enabled E-voting. IEEE Softw. **35**, 95–99 (2018)
27. Khan, K.M., Arshad, J., Khan, M.M.: Secure digital voting system based on blockchain technology. IJEGR **14**(1), 53–62 (2018)
28. Li, Y., Huang, J., Qin, S., Wang, R.: Big data model of security sharing based on blockchain. In: BigCom 2017, pp. 117–121. IEEE, Chengdu (2017)
29. Luong, N.C., Xiong, Z., Wang, P., Niyato, D.: Optimal Auction for Edge Computing Resource Management in Mobile Blockchain Networks, A Deep Learning Approach. In: 2018 IEEE International Conference on Communications, pp. 1–6. IEEE, Kansas City, USA (2018)
30. Blass, E.-O., Kerschbaum, F.: Strain: a secure auction for blockchains. In: Lopez, J., Zhou, J., Soriano, M. (eds.) ESORICS 2018. LNCS, vol. 11098, pp. 87–110. Springer, Cham (2018). https://doi.org/10.1007/978-3-319-99073-6_5
31. Galal, H.S., Youssef, A.M.: Verifiable sealed-bid auction on the ethereum blockchain. FC 2018, pp. 265–278. IEEE, Nieuwpoort (2018)
32. Yining, H., et al.: A delay-tolerant payment scheme based on the ethereum blockchain. IEEE Access **7**, 33159–33172 (2019)
33. Wang, X., Xu, X., Feagan, L., Huang, S., Jiao, L., Zhao, W.: Inter-bank payment system on enterprise blockchain platform. In: IEEE CLOUD 2018, pp. 614–621. IEEE, San Francisco (2018)
34. Ahn, J., Park, M., Paek, J.: Reporter: a model for deriving trust and reputation on blockchain-based electronic payment system. In: 2018 International Conference on Information and Communication Technology Convergence, pp. 1431–1436. IEEE, Jeju (2018)
35. Zhao, Y., Li, Y., Qilin, M., Yang, B., Yong, Yu., Pub-Sub, S.: Blockchain-based fair payment with reputation for reliable cyber physical systems. IEEE Access **6**, 12295–12303 (2018)
36. Dorri, A., Kanhere, S.S., Jurdak, R.: MOF-BC: a memory optimized and flexible blockchain for large scale networks. Futur. Gener. Comput. Syst. **92**, 357–373 (2019)
37. Yekini, T.A., Jaafar, F., Zavarsky, P.: Study of trust at device level of the internet of things architecture. In: 2019 IEEE 19th International Symposium on High Assurance Systems Engineering, pp. 150–155. IEEE, Hangzhou (2019)
38. Chao, S.-C., Chen, J.-F., Chunhua, S., Yeh, K.-H.: A Blockchain connected gateway for BLE-based devices in the internet of things. IEEE Access **6**, 24639–24649 (2018)
39. Novo, O.: Blockchain meets IoT: an architecture for scalable access management in IoT. IEEE Internet Things J. **5**, 1184–1195 (2018)
40. Wu, L., Du, X., Wang, W., Lin, B.: An out-of-band authentication scheme for internet of things using blockchain technology. In: ICNC 2018, pp. 769–773. IEEE, Maui (2018)
41. Alblooshi, M., Salah, K., Alhammadi, Y.: Blockchain-based ownership management for medical IoT (MIoT) devices. In: 2018 International Conference on Innovations in Information Technology (IIT). pp. 151–156. IEEE, Al Ain (2018)
42. Zhou, L., Wang, L., Sun, Y., Lv, P.: BeeKeeper: a blockchain-based IoT system with secure storage and homomorphic computation. IEEE Access **6**, 43472–43488 (2018)

43. Kaur, H., Alam, M.A., Jameel, R., Mourya, A.K., Chang, V.: A proposed solution and future direction for blockchain-based heterogeneous medicare data in cloud environment. J. Med. Syst. **42**(8), 156:1–156:11 (2018)
44. Chen, Y., Ding, S., Xu, Z., Zheng, H., Yang, S.: Blockchain-based medical records secure storage and medical service framework. J. Med. Syst. **43**(1), 5:1–5:9 (2019)
45. Tian, H., He, J., Ding, Y.: Medical data management on blockchain with privacy. J. Med. Syst. **43**(2), 26:1–26:6 (2019)
46. Wang, H., Song, Y.: Secure cloud-based EHR system using attribute-based cryptosystem and blockchain. J. Med. Syst. **42**(8), 152:1–152:9 (2018)
47. Zhang, A., Lin, X.: Towards secure and privacy-preserving data sharing in e-health systems via consortium blockchain. J. Med. Syst. **42**(8), 140:1–140:18 (2018)
48. Griggs, K.N., Ossipova, O., Kohlios, C.P., Baccarini, A.N., Howson, E.A., Hayajneh, T.: Healthcare blockchain system using smart contracts for secure automated remote patient monitoring. J. Med. Syst. **42**(7), 130:1–130:7 (2018)
49. Ji, Y., Zhang, J., Ma, J., Yang, C., Yao, X.: BMPLS: blockchain-based multi-level privacy-preserving location sharing scheme for telecare medical information systems. J. Med. Syst. **42**(8), 147:1–147:13 (2018)
50. Li, H., Zhu, L., Shen, M., Gao, F., Tao, X., Liu, S.: Blockchain-based data preservation system for medical data. J. Med. Syst. **42**(8), 141:1–141:13 (2018)

Tuning Runtimes in Open Source FaaS

David Balla[1]($\boxtimes$), Markosz Maliosz[1], Csaba Simon[1], and Daniel Gehberger[2]

[1] Department of Telecommunication and Media Informatics, High Speed Networks
Laboratory, Budapest University of Technology and Economics, Budapest, Hungary
{balla,maliosz,simon}@tmit.bme.hu
[2] Ericsson, Montreal, Canada
daniel.gehberger@ericsson.com

Abstract. A dynamically expanding area of cloud computing is Function as a Service (FaaS). FaaS allows customers to develop, run, and manage application functionalities on cloud infrastructure without the burden of building and managing a virtual infrastructure. The vast majority of FaaS services used in production are provided by public cloud operators, but a growing number of open source FaaS frameworks offer an alternative deploying on-premises FaaS services. FaaS frameworks support different programming language runtimes. The performance of such systems is dependent on these language runtimes. Our goal is to show and analyze this dependency, and provide insights to the important aspect when performance is essential. This paper provides a measurement based evaluation of the capabilities of different language runtimes in FaaS frameworks. We evaluate three different workloads (echo, compute intensive, and data intensive) on the selected runtimes.

Keywords: Function as a Service · Language runtimes · Latency measurements

1 Introduction

According to the latest trends, virtualization technologies are getting more and more granular. Hefty virtual machines (VM) had been replaced by lightweight container based technologies such as Docker or LXC or micro VMs, e.g. Firecracker, that enable to run micro-services over cloud environments more easily. In the last years, Function as a Service (FaaS) has started to emerge. In case of FaaS, instead of providing the complete runtime environment, the user only registers functions and declares when these functions should be triggered. The pricing of FaaS in public clouds is more granular, as users are only billed for the compute resources used during the execution time of their functions [26]. Functions running in an FaaS system can be lightweight building blocks of a higher level service, they benefit from using container based virtualization or micro VMs. Function instances are created dynamically upon function invocation, and they are available for some period of time, defined by the cloud service provider. After that time, they are getting evicted and the associated resources

© Springer Nature Switzerland AG 2020
C.-H. Hsu et al. (Eds.): IOV 2019, LNCS 11894, pp. 250–266, 2020.
https://doi.org/10.1007/978-3-030-38651-1_21

freed till the next invocation. FaaS is an emerging technology; several cloud service providers e.g. Amazon Web Services, Google Cloud, and Microsoft Azure, have FaaS solutions. On the other hand, FaaS had been embraced by the open-source community; numerous FaaS environments are available in GitHub, such as OpenFaaS, Kubeless, Nuclio or Fission [11–14]. According to the GitHub statistics, the most frequently maintained open-source FaaS initiative is OpenFaaS [10]. In this paper, we investigate the behaviour of selected function runtime environments. We selected and examined runtimes, that are common in open source and also in public FaaS providers, such as Amazon Web Services (AWS), Microsoft Azure, and Google Cloud. Thus, in our work, we investigated Python(v2.7), Node.js, and Go based runtimes [27–29].

We focus our investigations on the runtimes because these are the executions environments in each of the FaaS platforms, as when a function is called, at the end of the chain it is the runtime that executes the function code. Therefore, the runtime performance is crucial to the overall FaaS performance.

The scope of this paper is to show the limitations, and the mechanisms that influence the performance and scalability of each runtime, and not the comparison of the performance of the different runtimes. We implemented three kinds of functions for each of the selected runtimes. The three functionalities are: a function that implements an echo service, a compute intensive, and a data intensive function. The first two do not use external services, while in the data intensive function, the function code interacts with an external database. These kinds of functions are found in modern web applications generally running in cloud environments [24,25].

Our work almost exclusively relies on the codebase of the OpenFaaS function runtimes, with only subtle modifications. OpenFaaS is a framework developed in Go for building serverless functions with Docker and Kubernetes. We based our work on OpenFaaS because it is a very popular platform according to the GitHub stars [10]. The architecture of OpenFaaS is relatively simple, and in many aspects, it is similar to the other open source FaaS platforms, e.g., it had been written in Go, and as most of the solutions, it uses Docker containers on top of Kubernetes.

This work is well-aligned with the principles of Knative [22]. Knative is an open source platform originally developed by Google and currently supported by various other companies. It is envisioned as a general solution for serverless workloads, with tight Kubernetes integration, scaling to zero and Istio based networking. Knative only specifies that user functions must be provided as containers and they must be able to serve HTTP requests. Some FaaS projects, such as OpenWhisk have already announced that they possibly move over to Knative execution [23]. While we do not use Knative in our experiments, our findings regarding FaaS runtimes are directly applicable.

2   FaaS Architecture

FaaS environments are implemented on top of a distributed architecture. Services running in these architectures are mostly using lightweight virtualized environments such as containers or micro VMs.

Open-source FaaS systems are almost exclusively implemented on top of Kubernetes. Kubernetes implements an orchestration layer to be able to manage Docker containers in a unified way. Function instances are running in Kubernetes pods, encapsulated into Docker containers. For reliable operations Kubernetes can be set us as High Availability cluster.

Accessing the functions requires a common interface, which in case of open source FaaS solutions is mostly implemented by an HTTP server, which converts the requests to be processable by the functions and maintains health-checking tasks. In case of open-source systems, the user-functions are inserted into a wrapper function supported by the FaaS system. Accessing the functions is implemented over HTTP, thus the function-wrappers implement a lightweight webserver, that forwards the queries to the user-function. Therefore the webserver plays a very important role in the function execution chain. Thus we focus our evaluation on the webserver implementations of different language runtimes in the followings.

Besides the function instances, the other fundamental building block of an FaaS infrastructure is the Gateway, which ensures an access point to the system and proxies user queries to the function instances. The gateway is usually implemented as a front proxy, which routes the requests to the appropriate functions. The communication between the gateway and the functions is implemented through a Kubernetes service instance which hides the function pods behind a common IP address and load balances the request between the function instance replicas, as it is depicted in Fig. 1.

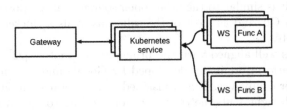

Fig. 1. General FaaS architecture

2.1   Function Runtime Implementation in OpenFaaS

By default, function runtimes in OpenFaaS are implemented with a tiny Go based webserver, the function watchdog. The watchdog parses and forwards the inbound requests to the function via standard IO as it can be seen in Fig. 2.

On the other hand, OpenFaaS has a new HTTP based function implementation, that only proxies the requests to the function via HTTP. In the latter case, the function is encapsulated into a Flask based HTTP server. According to our measurements, using the new watchdog implementation results in better response times (see Fig. 3). However, the solution using the new watchdog is currently not part of the main OpenFaaS code-base, and only available from the Incubator repository of OpenFaaS.

Fig. 2. OpenFaaS function runtime

Fig. 3. Latency comparison of OpenFaaS watchdog implementations in case of Python runtime, with echo functionality

3   Language Runtimes Overview

3.1   Python

In case of Python, one of the most frequently used webserver implementations is Flask. Flask is built upon the Werkzeug webserver [32], which is implemented on top of BaseHTTPServer and SocketServer [33]. Originally Flask implements a single threaded webserver, however, the SocketServer layer enables it to be instantiated by using the Threading or the Multiprocessing library of Python. The listed implementations provide different performance characteristics, as we will show it later.

The single threaded implementation of Flask shows a simple queuing behaviour in case of concurrently arriving requests. When Flask is used with the Threading library, threads are using the same Python interpreter, which can lead to serious race conditions. The Global Interpreter Lock (GIL) is shared between all the threads and ensures that only one thread uses the interpreter at the same time. Python threads are real system threads, managed by the scheduler of the host operating system. In the case of IO bound tasks, cooperative multitasking is implemented. On the other hand, when it is about CPU bound tasks, preemptive multitasking is applied, which is implemented by periodic checks. Periodic checks are triggered after 100 interpreter ticks. However, according to [7] interpreter ticks show varying behaviour. Flask, using the Threading library, starts a new thread for each of the inbound requests. Therefore serious race-conditions can occur in case of a bursty traffic pattern. The Multiprocessing based implementation avoids the race condition of threads caused by waiting on the GIL. In this case, instead of sharing the interpreter, the main thread initializes an interpreter for each of the threads. When using the Multiprocessing library with Flask, the number of serving threads should be assigned in advance. Thus, it results in multiple single threaded webservers working together on serving the incoming load.

3.2   Node.js

Originally Node.js supports the implementation of single threaded webservers. Single threaded Node.js webserver implementations show similar queuing behaviour to the single threaded Python Flask. On the other hand, the platform supports running worker threads since version v10.5.0, enabling that each incoming request to be served by a dedicated worker [8]. However, in case of using the new worker thread based implementation, we could observe similar behaviour to the threading based implementation of Python Flask. The initialization of each worker thread requires to open a file in which the task is implemented, furthermore a new event-loop, a JavaScript engine and a Node.js instance is started for the new thread [31]. The platform also supports creating child processes by using the cluster library [37]. In this case, each of the children has an individual interpreter, thus no race condition can occur.

3.3   Similarities Between Python and Node.js

There are similarities between Python and Node.js. Both of these two languages are interpreted, therefore we can see similar behaviour patterns. The threading library in Python can be corresponded to the new worker threads in Node.js; on the other hand, the multiprocessing implementation of Flask is similar to the cluster based solution in Node.js.

3.4   Golang

The Go language is designed to support massively parallel applications. Each of the application level threads is implemented by Goroutines. Goroutines are the concurrency units of Go and are scheduled by the Go framework. Each Goroutine is a coroutine, therefore Goroutines are scheduled in a cooperative way. The Go runtime implements a two-level scheduling mechanism [35]. The Go runtime manages several threads preemptively scheduled by the operating system. Goroutines are assigned to threads initiated by the runtime [30]. The number of runtime threads can be configured by the user. In the case of compute intensive functions, the parallel operation can be achieved by increasing the number of runtime threads. According to our measurements, in case of using the Go application with a single runtime thread, a bursty load can cause heavy queuing behaviour. In the case of IO bound operations, the effects of cooperative scheduling can be observed. As Goroutines drop the computing resources after the initiation of an IO operation, other Goroutines can be transitioned to running state.

4   Test Environment

4.1   Underlay Infrastructure

For our measurements, we used an environment supported by CloudLab. Our physical environment consisted of four xl170 computers, equipped with Ten-core Intel E5-2640v4 CPUs with Hyper-Threading capabilities, 64 GBs of RAM and Mellanox ConnectX-4 25 GB NICs [9]. We ran the Kubernetes cluster with one master and four worker nodes. For cluster networking, we used the Weave Net implemented by Weaveworks [34].

4.2   Function Runtime Implementation

Focusing on the function runtimes, we had separated the function environments from the FaaS environment and ran them on top of Kubernetes, without having managed them by an upper FaaS layer. Therefore we removed the gateway and monitoring facilities of the FaaS system and stressed the functions via the Kubernetes service instance. We relied on the codebase of OpenFaaS function runtimes, which uses the new watchdog based solution. However, we removed the watchdog component from the function runtime pods. We believe that in this case, the function watchdog is a redundant component of the architecture since all of its tasks can be handled by the webserver in which the user function is encapsulated. By eliminating the FaaS related components from the function runtime pods, we could examine the raw performance of a function running on top of Kubernetes and could eliminate the overhead given by the FaaS environment.

4.3   Test Functions

Our test functions were running in Kubernetes pods, without any resource limitations and scaling rules being configured. We redesigned the function runtimes of OpenFaaS and implemented the function runtime environments to be able to work in both sequential and parallel way. Therefore, we could test the performance of the examined function runtimes under highly concurrent loads as well.

As we did not use the FaaS framework, we removed the parts of the function wrappers that are responsible for monitoring and health-checking tasks.

In case of Python, we extended the Flask implementation to be able to operate in a single threaded way, but also be able to use the threading and the multiprocessing based implementations to be able to process queries in a parallel way since the original implementation is only able to use the threading based implementation of Flask.

In case of Node.js the original OpenFaaS implementation uses the Express.js. However, we did not measure performance differences between Express.js and Node.js, therefore to keep our code simple, we used Node.js. OpenFaaS Node.js solution only supports sequential processing of requests. Therefore we extended this solution to be able to use the new Worker-Thread based implementations including threadpools as well, and it can also make use of the cluster library which leverages the gains of starting a predefined number of Node.js servers and load balancing requests between them.

In case of Go, we used the OpenFaaS Golang HTTP implementation [1] which uses the default HTTP solution implemented by the HTTP library of Go. As Go supports writing highly parallel applications, and parallelism is implemented in the framework of Go, we did not make any extensions that support parallel processing.

In each of the cases, we examined the configuration when several individual function instances reside in the system in a distributed way. In case of Python and Node.js, we compared the parallel processing solutions with the case when several single threaded function instances served the requests in a distributed way. See Fig. 4(a). In case of database communication, implemented in Go, we tried to find the best number of runtime threads. After that, we examined the effects of running Go function instances in a distributed way, that are using the previously calculated number of runtime threads. In case of the echo and compute intensive functions, we compared the performance of single threaded Go functions running in a distributed way to the case when multiple runtime threads had been assigned to the functions.

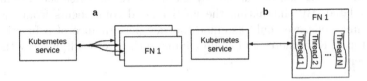

Fig. 4. Single threaded functions, that are only capable of sequential processing of requests (a) vs single function instance that can process requests in a parallel way(b)

As the majority of functions in a web based environment do some computing, load in or retrieve data from a database or return some data, we implemented these kinds of functions. The first is an echo function; the second is a function that implements a compute intensive task by calculating the value of π in 50.000

steps. The third type of workload deals with database operations. Functions in an FaaS system are expected to be stateless, and therefore, external state storage solutions are used. The performance of these, typically NoSQL database accesses, is crucial for the overall system. Therefore we implemented three functions that perform read modify write operations with different database implementations, to show that both the database implementation and the FaaS runtime variants affect the performance.

For the functions implementing database communication, we selected three modern databases to cover real-life scenarios used in the industry: Redis, MongoDB, and Cassandra. Redis is an in-memory key-value store, mostly used to fulfill caching tasks or to implement message broker functionalities. Redis is implemented in C [2], and as it stores data in memory, we expected fast response times. MongoDB is a document store, which is used to store unstructured data, stored in collections, organized into JSON structures [3–5]. MongoDB is implemented in C++, however, document stores having more complex mechanisms than key-value stores we expected response times from MongoDB higher than the ones produced by Redis. In our setup, MongoDB was configured to use the WiredTiger as an underlying key-value store. Cassandra also implements a NoSQL database, however, it is implemented in Java. In contrast with MongoDB, Cassandra stores structured data and operates on tables [6]. As Cassandra is implemented in Java in contrast with the previous two solutions, we expected the poorest performance for this case.

The data sent to and read from the databases consisted of a unique UUID generated by the function at the invocation phase, and a string with the value of "Hello".

4.4 Load Generator

For the measurements, we used the Hey tool, which is an HTTP load generator written in Go [36]. Hey sends a given number of requests in a given concurrency level and prints the statistics of the responses. It is able to simulate highly concurrent user requests by starting several worker threads defined by the concurrency level. The operation of each worker thread is sequential, i.e., it only sends the next request after the response for the previous request has been received.

For each of the measurements, we applied a load which had a concurrency level of 100, and we recorded 10.000 measurement points. In all of the cases, Hey had been used to send HTTP GET requests.

5 Evaluation

In this section we show and evaluate the results of our measurements. We used cumulative distribution functions to visualize the latency series resulted by the measurements. As the latency values resulted by the measurements cover a wide range, we used logarithmic scale in case of the horizontal axis.

5.1 Python

As we have discussed, we used Flask to implement our Python function runtimes. We investigated the behaviour of the runtime in case of using the underlying Flask webserver implementation in a way that the processing of requests was done either in a sequential or in a parallel way. We will show, that in case of Python, using the threading library can be beneficial in case of IO bound functions. However, it can result in serious performance decreases for compute intensive CPU bound operations. We will show two alternatives that can be used instead of the threading implementation. We show that using the multiprocessing library outperforms the threading based implementations. On the other hand, starting several function instances that are capable of serving requests sequentially can be an alternative to the multiprocessing based implementation in a Kubernetes environment.

Echo. In case of the echo operation, the function immediately returns a short static HTML response. In this case, the operation is so short in time that starting an interpreter for the function can dominate the whole completion time of the operation as it can be seen in Fig. 5. However, running the function instances in a distributed way, it performs at least an order of magnitude better than the other solutions.

Fig. 5. Python echo

Compute Intensive. In case of Flask using the threading library, CPU bound functions keep the GIL and compute resources busy, and other threads have to compete for them. In this case, the Python scheduler preempts the currently running thread and takes the GIL from it, therefore giving a chance to the other threads to run. However, in this case, race conditions can occur, since as we mentioned, Python threads are managed by the scheduler of the OS, while the Python scheduler is not in cooperation with the OS scheduler. In Fig. 6 we show that single threaded implementation of a function can perform an order of magnitude better than the threading based implementation. We also showed that by using the multiprocessing library, we can reach further increase in performance. Nevertheless, when using separate single threaded function pod instances instead of the multiprocessing implementation, we could reach one order of magnitude performance gain in case of the median latency values.

Fig. 6. Python compute

Data Intensive. In the case of data intensive IO bound functions, using the threaded implementation of Flask, better performance can be reached on average. Since, in this case, threads are giving up the CPU after an IO operation, in contrast to CPU bound functions, therefore, let other threads to run. In opposite to the single threaded operation, there is no need to wait for each function call to finish. However, using the multiprocess based implementation of Flask can result in further performance gains. As it has been introduced, the multiprocessing library assigns an individual interpreter to each thread, preventing race conditions. Starting individual interpreters nevertheless adds extra overhead to the runtime of serving a function call, however, this additional overhead is negligible to the whole function runtime latency. Furthermore, when using the multiprocessing based Flask implementation, the maximum number of processes should be set; thus, no more function invocations can be served than the number assigned to it. In our measurements, we set the maximum number of processes equal to the number of available CPU cores in one of the computers. We constructed a new configuration to eliminate the extra overhead of starting an interpreter each time a function is invoked, by creating as many single thread based function containers as many processes we had in the multiprocessing case, and ran them in a distributed way on top of our Kubernetes architecture. According to Fig. 7, the threading based implementation shows better performance than the single threaded one; however, multiprocessing based implementation can further improve the latency. It also can be seen that the distributed solution could still reduce the median latency of serving the function calls, although it resulted in higher tail latency values.

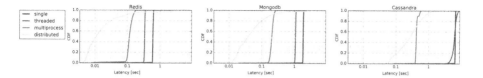

Fig. 7. Python database

We showed that IO bound functions using separate single threaded pods in a distributed way can reach significantly better average performance than all the other solutions, however, in this case, the tail of the latency values showed spectacularly large outliers. To mitigate these latency values, we combined the performance gain of the threaded implementation with the multiple function pod based solution. As a result, we could reduce the tail latency values as it can be seen in Fig. 8.

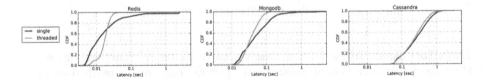

Fig. 8. Mitigation of longtail latency values by using python threads

5.2 Node.js

According to our measurements, Node.js showed the poorest performance with the new worker threads. It can be seen that using a pool of workers starting a limited number of worker threads can improve the tail latency, but on the other hand it gives an extra overhead to the median latency values. The single threaded implementation gives at least an order of magnitude performance increase. However, in case of Node.js, there is no significant difference between the latency results of the cluster based solution where several child processes are initialized and the one where multiple single threaded function pods are running in a distributed way over Kubernetes.

Echo. In case of the echo operation, the single threaded implementation performs better than the worker thread based implementation by two orders of magnitude. However, both the cluster based and the distributed solutions outperform the single threaded solution, on the other hand, the performance of these latter two is nearly identical (Fig. 9).

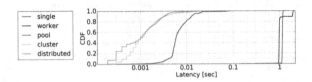

Fig. 9. Node echo

Compute Intensive. Compute intensive Node.js functions showed similar performance characteristics to the ones resulted from the echo functionality. As it is shown in Fig. 10, the single threaded and the new worker thread based implementations have a very low standard deviation. The single threaded implementation also outperforms the new worker thread based solution. On the other hand, the Cluster based and distributed solution outperforms all the other cases, though in this case, we can see the queuing behaviour of requests that is caused by the limited number of processing instances.

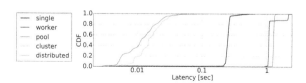

Fig. 10. Node compute

Data Intensive. Data intensive Node.js functions showed the same latency characteristics than the preceding two cases. However, in the results, it is shown that several single threaded function instances show better performance both in case of the median and the tail latency values compared to the cluster based implementation. In this case, according to the significant latency gap between the single threaded and worker-thread based implementations, we have not combined the proposed distributed solution with the worker-thread based implementations (Fig. 11).

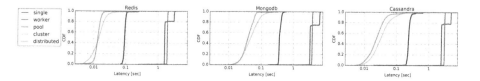

Fig. 11. Node database

5.3   Golang

Our Go function runtime implementation uses the default HTTP server built on Go's HTTP library, which initiates a Goroutine for each of the function calls. Goroutines are running on top of threads started by the Go runtime, and these threads are scheduled and managed by the OS. However, the number of these threads can be defined before starting the Go program.

Echo. The echo functionality implemented in Go performs almost identically when running the single threaded solution in a distributed way or when several runtime threads were assigned to the function instances (Fig. 12).

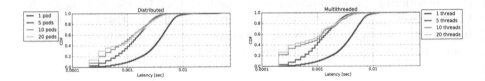

Fig. 12. Go echo

Compute Intensive. Goroutines that implement a compute intensive job are not preempted by the Go scheduler, as the Go runtime implements cooperative multitasking of the Goroutines, thus in the case of highly parallel loads, requests may get queued. According to this behaviour, in case of CPU bound operation, there is no significant difference in the latency results if the application is using multiple runtime threads or separated into several single threaded Go applications in a distributed way over Kubernetes. This is shown in Fig. 13. According to our measurements, the latter setup shows slightly better results, which can be explained by the fact that in case of a webserver based application, using multiple runtime threads makes the completed requests wait for transmit operations until the thread, responsible for sending out the results, is scheduled again. While with multiple single threaded applications, the requests are balanced between the servers, therefore, fewer requests are queued at the transmit phase.

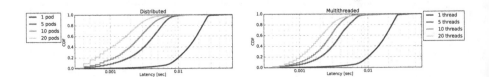

Fig. 13. Go compute

Data Intensive. As we discussed, Goroutines implement cooperative multitasking, thus, in case of IO bound operations, they yield compute resources and let another Goroutine run. According to our measurements, when IO bound functions are in use, the median latency values are converging to a threshold regardless of the number of threads started by the Go runtime. Table 1 shows this converging tendency according to the number of runtime threads, in case of a function which communicates with the databases. We assigned three runtime threads for the Go function runtime in case of Redis and MongoDB communication, as according to Table 1 we got the best performance values. In case of operations on the Cassandra database, according to Table 1, we configured our Go function runtime to use 7 runtime threads, and we deployed these applications into Kubernetes pods. We observed that increasing the number of function instances can reduce the latency until the number of 6 instances. After 6 function instances, the results indicate performance degradation. This behaviour can be seen in Fig. 14.

Table 1. Median latency values produced by data intensive Go functions according to the no. of runtime threads

Threads	Redis	Mongo	Cassandra
1	0.261	0.646	0.944
2	0.021	0.083	0.173
3	0.008	0.043	0.096
4	0.008	0.052	0.069
5	0.007	0.06	0.055
7	0.008	0.045	0.044
10	0.008	0.044	0.042
20	0.008	0.057	0.042

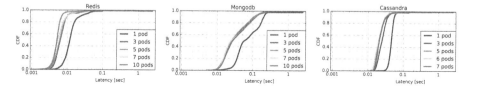

Fig. 14. Go Database

The performance decrease over 6 function instances can be explained by the number of available CPU cores in our Kubernetes cluster. This can be derived back to a packing problem, as each of the function pods uses 7 Go runtime threads, since a compute node had 20 physical cores. Therefore only 6 function instances could be instantiated in our cluster without having any race conditions between the threads and the CPUs assigned to them.

Compute and echo functions showed similar characteristics as both of them can be taken as a CPU bound operation, though the latter one only uses a single operation which has a very short execution time and it is unlikely to get scheduled out by the OS scheduler.

6   Related Work

Baldini et al. posed several open questions related to FaaS in [15]; they showed challenges from multiple points of view. FaaS poses system level challenges, e.g., scaling, cold starts, resource limitations, and also security issues can come up, while it is also challenging from the operations' side.

Lee et al. [18] provided a comparison on the performance of the main public FaaS services, also arguing that concurrent invocation is important; they also considered timer based runtime overhead measurements.

Open-source FaaS platforms are also emerging, in [10] Mohanty et al. compares open-source FaaS platforms from several aspects.

One of the hottest topics in FaaS is autoscaling. A PID controller based solution to control containers, where performance reports (observed response time) from the application within the container are proposed by Abranches et al. [19,20]. An alternative approach used an ARIMA based user activity prediction to govern the Kubernetes scaling process [21].

The other most challenging topics of FaaS is related to cold starts. Therefore a lot of research papers had been published in this topic. Manner et al. in [16] posed several hypotheses that can influence cold starts, Manco et al. in [17] showed that unikernels can provide lower startup times than containers.

The findings in the related work show that many factors correspond to the latency of the functions. In our investigations we showed, that in addition, the configuration of parallel processing capabilities of the language runtimes and the database implementation plays also a significant role in the latency, in some cases not in the obvious way, as we highlighted in our measurements and analysis.

7   Conclusion

In this paper, we provided a brief insight into open-source serverless architectures. The function runtimes are located at the end of the call-chain and are responsible for running the user-defined functions. As these call-chains in opensource FaaS systems are implemented over HTTP, the runtimes implement an HTTP server. We investigated the performance characteristics of these runtimes in case of an echo, compute intensive and data intensive functionality, using Python, Node.js, and Go HTTP server options.

In open source FaaS platforms the runtime parameters, e.g. concurrency levels, thread handling, etc. can be tuned for performance, therefore we investigated these opportunities. Our results show that Go functions outperformed all the variants in case of the median latency values. Python showed the poorest performance in case of compute intensive and echo functions. Albeit Go functions showed the best median latency values, though the longtail latency values of Go based data intensive functions showed spectacularly high outliers. On the other hand, according to the measurements performed with Node.js data intensive functions showed fewer outliers than the ones related Go or Python. According to the measurements, the Python runtime can be further optimized, however, even the optimized Python runtime cannot outperform the other two runtimes.

Acknowledgment. The research has been supported by the European Union, co-financed by the European Social Fund (EFOP-3.6.2-16-2017-00013, Thematic Fundamental Research Collaborations Grounding Innovation in Informatics and Infocommunications.

References

1. OpenFaaS: of-watchdog. https://github.com/openfaas-incubator/golang-http-template
2. Redis: Introduction to Redis. https://redis.io/topics/introduction
3. Agrawal, S., et al.: Survey on Mongodb: an open-source document database. Int. J. Adv. Res. Eng. Technol. (IJARET) **1**, 4 (2015)
4. Mongodb: Document Databases. https://www.mongodb.com/document-databases
5. Sullivan, D., Sullivan, J.: NoSQL key-value database simplicity vs. document database flexibility. InformIT blog, 16 Sepetmber 2015. http://www.informit.com/articles/article.aspx?p=2429466
6. DataStax: What is Apache Cassandra^{TM}?. https://academy.datastax.com/planet-cassandra/what-is-apache-cassandra
7. Beazley, D.: Understanding the Python GIL. PyCON 2010, 20 February 2010. http://www.dabeaz.com/GIL/
8. Node.js: Node.js v10.16.0 Documentation. https://nodejs.org/dist/latest-v10.x/docs/api/worker_threads.html
9. Cloudlab: The Cloudlab Manual (2019). https://docs.cloudlab.us/hardware.html
10. Mohanty, S.K., et al.: An evaluation of open source serverless computing frameworks. CloudCom (2018)
11. Fission. https://github.com/fission/fission
12. Kubeless. https://kubeless.io/
13. OpenFaaS. https://kubeless.io/
14. Nuclio. https://nuclio.io/
15. Baldini, I., et al.: Serverless computing: current trends and open problems. In: 2017 IEEE 37th International Conference on Distributed Computing Systems Workshops (ICDCSW) (2017)
16. Manner, J., et al.: Cold start influencing factors in function as a service. In: Fourth International Workshop on Serverless Computing (WoSC) 2018 (2018)
17. Manco, F., et al.: My VM is lighter (and safer) than your container. In: 26th Symposium on Operating Systems Principles, October 2017
18. Lee, H., et al.: Evaluation of production serverless computing environments. In: 2018 IEEE 11th International Conference on Cloud Computing (CLOUD) (2018)
19. de Abranches, M.C. Solis, P.: An algorithm based on response time and traffic demands to scale containers on a Cloud Computing system. In: IEEE 15th International Symposium on Network Computing and Applications (NCA), pp. 343–350, October 2016
20. de Abranches, M.C., Solis, P., Alchieri, E.: PAS-CA: a cloud computing auto-scalability method for high-demand web systems. In: IEEE 16th International Symposium on Network Computing and Applications (NCA), pp. 1–4 (2017)
21. Jin-Gang, Y., Ya-Rong, Z., Bo, Y., Shu, L.: Research and application of auto-scaling unified communication server based on docker. In: 10th International Conference on Intelligent Computation Technology and Automation (ICICTA), pp. 152–156 (2017)

22. Knative. https://cloud.google.com/knative/
23. McGee, J.: IBM Cloud teams with Google and open community to help build Knative and expand the power of serverless, IBM Blog. https://www.ibm.com/blogs/cloud-computing/2018/07/24/ibm-cloud-google-knative-serverless/
24. Wasson, M., Buck, A., Roberts, J., Wilson, M.: N-tier architecture style. Microsoft Azure (2018). https://docs.microsoft.com/en-us/azure/architecture/guide/architecture-styles/n-tier
25. Microsoft: Enterprise solution patterns using Microsoft.NET. Microsoft (2014). https://docs.microsoft.com/en-us/previous-versions/msp-n-p/ff647095(v=pandp.10)
26. Hellerstein, J.M., et al.: Serverless computing: one step forward, two steps back, December 2018
27. AWS: AWS lambda developer guide (2019). https://docs.aws.amazon.com/lambda/latest/dg/welcome.html
28. Google Cloud: Cloud functions documentation (2019). https://cloud.google.com/functions/docs/
29. Microsoft Azure: Azure functions documentation. https://docs.microsoft.com/en-us/azure/azure-functions/
30. Kennedy, W.: Scheduling In Go. Adranlabs blog (2018). https://www.ardanlabs.com/blog/2018/08/scheduling-in-go-part2.html
31. Henningsen, A.: Node.js: the road to workers. In: Node.js Italian Conference (2018). https://addaleax.net/workers-nodefest/
32. Flask. https://github.com/pallets/flask
33. Werkzeug. https://github.com/pallets/werkzeug
34. Weaveworks: Introducing weave net. https://www.weave.works/docs/net/latest/overview/
35. Tu, L., et al.: Understanding real-world concurrency bugs in go. In: ASPLOS 19, April 2019
36. Hey. https://github.com/rakyll/hey
37. Node.js: Node.js v8.16.0 documentation. https://nodejs.org/docs/latest-v8.x/api/

Achieving Dynamic Resource Allocation in the Hadoop Cloud System

Tsozen Yeh[(✉)] and Shengchieh Yu

Department of Computer Science and Information Engineering,
Fu Jen Catholic University, New Taipei City, Taiwan
`yeh@csie.fju.edu.tw`, `yushengchieh@gmail.com`

Abstract. Cloud computing has been extensively adopted to handle the enormous amount of data from Internet of Things, Big Date, and many other cutting-edge research areas in recent years. As cloud systems serve more and more jobs, it will be getting more difficult for time-critical or urgent jobs with high priority in a busy cloud environment to complete their execution as soon as users would like to have. To facilitate the prompt execution of those jobs, it is imperative for cloud systems to provide schemes expediting their execution. The Apache Hadoop is one of the most popular cloud platforms in cloud computing. Unfortunately, it is not equipped with flexible mechanisms to hasten the course of prioritized jobs. There had been various approaches proposed to accelerate the execution of prioritized jobs from different aspects. However, those approaches not only target at just certain existing Hadoop job schedulers but also require modifications made to those job schedulers. Thus, they cannot be directly applied to other job schedulers without major porting efforts, much less to new job schedulers developed in the future. We designed and implemented a new scheme enabling dynamic resource allocation to jobs selected by job schedulers. As a result, without making changes to job schedulers, our scheme could help some current and future Hadoop job schedulers speed up the execution of jobs with high priority. Experimental results demonstrate that jobs executed with high priority can reduce their execution time by up to 68.28%.

Keywords: Cloud computing · Hadoop · HDFS · Scheduling

1 Introduction

The cloud computing has shown its promising future in many areas. As the cloud infrastructure keeps expanding, large cloud systems could easily host a vast number of programs running at the same time. Consequently, in a busy cloud system, the executing progress of urgent or time-critical jobs could be significantly delayed, which potentially could lead to unfavorable results or even job failures. It will be desirable if the cloud system can let users decide which jobs can be run with high priority so the course of their execution can be accomplished more promptly.

© Springer Nature Switzerland AG 2020
C.-H. Hsu et al. (Eds.): IOV 2019, LNCS 11894, pp. 267–283, 2020.
https://doi.org/10.1007/978-3-030-38651-1_22

Among the cloud computing platforms, the Apache Hadoop is considered one of the most widely used across different cloud computing communities [1,11,12,24,27,28]. Nevertheless, the design of Hadoop architecture makes it difficult to provide prioritized execution for time-critical jobs. In Hadoop, the job scheduling is done by job schedulers. Currently, Hadoop supports three job schedulers including Capacity Scheduler (CS), Fair Scheduler (FS), and First In First Out (FIFO) scheduler. CS maintains predefined portions of resources to different job queues. Jobs in each job queue will be executed in a first-come-first-serve order, which means there is at most one running job in each queue. FS also keeps multiple queues like CS does except for the concurrent execution of all jobs in each queue. Unlike FS and CS, FIFO scheduler retains only one job queue and all jobs in the queue get executed according to their submission order. Both CS and FS are commonly used across various environments because of their flexibility in resource arrangement while the nature of FIFO largely limits its usage in practice. To support prioritized execution, it is necessary for prioritized jobs to obtain more system resources during their execution. The default setting of CS does not support prioritized execution. With extra efforts, the system administrator could change the setting to run prioritized jobs prior to the execution of regular jobs. Nonetheless, in CS, each queue still can have only one job in execution even if there are other pending prioritized jobs in the queue. This means that a pending prioritized job in a queue still needs to wait for the completion of the currently running job before it can launch its execution. For FS, there is no way to conduct prioritized execution. Similarly, FIFO does not support prioritized execution due to its essence.

As job schedulers are the ones deciding which job could start its execution and when it gets scheduled to receive system resources, it is reasonable to make changes to job schedulers to speed up the execution of prioritized jobs. Not surprisingly, previous studies had taken this approach to fulfill prioritized execution in Hadoop [23,29]. The main issue with this type of approaches is their portability. It could take great efforts to carry their design and implementation to other existing job schedulers, much less to new job schedulers created in the future. Ideally, it will be great if a given mechanism of prioritized execution could be easily ported to current and future job schedulers with little or even no cost to them. As stated, CS already has supported prioritized execution to some degree and it is unlikely to be ameliorated without modifying CS. Therefore, we designed and implemented a new scheme to realize prioritized execution by dynamically allocating resources in FS without altering FS itself. As our approach works on resource allocation instead of FS, it is easy to carry our scheme to the next generation of FS as well as to future job schedulers under the current Hadoop architecture. With our dynamic resource allocation, users can flexibly adjust the percentage of resources that regular jobs should give away to prioritized jobs. By gaining extra resources, prioritized jobs could complete their execution sooner. We evaluated our design and implementation by executing the same set of programs with and without high priority under various configurations. Experimental results show that jobs can shorten their execution time by up to 68.28% if they are executed with high priority. The remainder of this paper is organized as follows. Section 2 reviews previous works related to Hadoop scheduling and the Hadoop Distributed File System. Section 3 describes the design and implementation of our model. Section 4 presents experimental results. Section 5 concludes this paper, and the future work is discussed in Sect. 6.

2   Related Work

Scheduling algorithms can largely affect the course of job execution. To make prioritized jobs run faster, most studies focused on launching their execution promptly [23,29]. Some works applied the idea of bidding to allow users to utilize their allotted budgets in exchange for job priority for their prioritized jobs [23]. Like all other software, Hadoop must reply on the underlying operating system to function appropriately. Because jobs in Hadoop often require a large amount of disk operations, previous efforts also aimed to quickly deliver disk I/O generated from jobs with high priority to shorten their execution time [7,30]. The slow disk speed has been viewed as a bottleneck affecting the overall system performance. To lessen the negative impact of slow disk operation, some models used memory-based computing to lower the cost of using disk in Hadoop [6,17]. Researchers had proposed ways to better Hadoop scheduling algorithms from various aspects. Some focused on meeting job deadlines [15,26] and some strived for reducing mean completion time of jobs in dynamic heterogeneous Hadoop environments [20]. In a large cluster, mixing centralized and distributed scheduling could also help improve the overall system performance [14]. In addition, the awareness of network bandwidth or resources consumed could also be a consideration when designing scheduling algorithms in Hadoop [16,19,25].

The Yet Another Resource Negotiator (YARN) is the infrastructure managing resources in Hadoop. The computing resource in the Hadoop cluster is measured and distributed in a unit of "container", which is a logical resource bundle consisting of memory and CPU. Not surprisingly, there have been studies on containers to improve the system performance [10,21,22]. The default file system in Hadoop is called Hadoop Distributed File System (HDFS). It is a distributed file system consisting of a NameNode and multiple DataNodes. The NameNode maintains and manages the entire HDFS namespace. DataNodes provide computing resources and store cloud data [12,24]. The failure of the NameNode will bring down the entire HDFS [2,8,13]. HDFS employs redundant NameNodes to supersede the active NameNode in the case of NameNode failure. The failover time of initiating a redundant NameNode to be the new active NameNode could cause problems, which is addressed by the AvatarNode in Facebook, the Standby NameNode in Cloudera, and other research works [3,4,8,18]. The reliability of Hadoop data is also an important topic. Both file duplication and system recovery help assist data reliability [5,9].

3   Dynamic Resource Allocation in YARN

The time required to complete a job involves two parts. The first relates to the timing that a job gets selected by the job scheduler. The second concerns the amount of resources a job receives each time it is chosen. To quicken the progress of prioritized jobs, both parts could help achieve the goal. Unfortunately, under the current Hadoop architecture, the first part is totally done by the job scheduler. It means any attempt made in the first part to expedite the execution of prioritized jobs will inevitably cause modifications to the job scheduler, which results in the aforementioned portability issue. Hence, we focus on the second part through allocating more resources to prioritized jobs to speed up their execution.

3.1   Job Submission and Resource Adjustment

During a job submission, users only need to decide if that job can give away its allocated resources when prioritized jobs are running. Take the well known program "wordcount" for example. In the original YARN, a typical launch is like "hadoop jar wordcount.jar wordcount wordcount-input-file wordcount-output-file". In our version of YARN, users just need to type "hadoop jar wordcount.jar wordcount wordcount-input-file wordcount-output-file **-D yield=1**" to indicate this job could relinquish its resources. Otherwise, users will set "**-D yield=0**" to point out that the job will not give away its sources. In a way jobs with the setting of "-D yield=1" are considered as regular jobs while jobs with the setting of "-D yield=0" are viewed as prioritized jobs as they could have extra resources deducted from regular jobs. Consequently, during the submission of a job, users can set the value of the "yield" flag to zero to direct our system to execute that job with high priority. For convenience, we set the default value of "yield" to one if users do not use it in job submission as practically most jobs are regular jobs. Once a job starts its execution, its resource allocation is totally controlled by the YARN. Currently, there are many YARN commands that users can utilize to manage running jobs in Hadoop. For example, "yarn -list" can show all application and their corresponding information such as their application IDs. To make our scheme more flexible, we add a new command, "yarn applicationID -D yield=1 (or -D yield=0)", to let users reset the priority of the job with the specified application ID during its execution. They also can decide the maximum percentage, namely deduction ratio, of resources can be deducted from regular jobs when there are prioritized jobs in execution. The deduction ratio is a system-wide parameter. Those deducted resources will be allocated to prioritized jobs to accelerate their execution. To decrease the execution time of prioritized jobs as much as possible, by default we manage to have all regular jobs temporarily stop getting new resources when prioritized jobs are in execution, which means the default deduction ratio is 100%. Users can use the command, "yarn -D ratio=x%", to dynamically adjust the deduction ratio at any time and our system will act accordingly. To make it easier for users, they can directly reset the deduction ratio at x% during any job submission by setting

"-D ratio=x%". For instance, "hadoop jar wordcount.jar wordcount wordcount-input-file wordcount-output-file -D ratio=20%" means all regular jobs now will be assigned at most 80% (1–20%) of their originally allocated resources during the execution of prioritized jobs.

3.2 Scheduling Process

YARN is the infrastructure managing system resource and job scheduling in Hadoop. It mainly consists of Resource Manager (RM), Node Manager (NM), and Application Master (AM). Figure 1 illustrates their relation with regard to job execution. The clients represent users submitting jobs. The RM oversees the entire system resources (CPU time and/or memory) and makes appropriate resource allocation. Each computing node in Hadoop has an instance of NM running on it, which constantly monitors useable resources on that computing node and reports on the real-time information to the RM. The relationship between the RM and the NM is like that of the master and the slave. Each job has a corresponding AM to direct the execution of the job during its entire life cycle. Under the Hadoop MapReduce model, each job is divided into multiple smaller tasks. Each task can be separately executed in a unit of resources called "container". The AM of each job constantly reports to RM the number of containers that job still needs to complete its execution. Meanwhile, for a running job, its AM also keeps track of allocated containers and tasks executed therein to manage the executing progress of the job. Job scheduling is completely governed by the job scheduler, which is a component in RM. When there are free resources available, the job scheduler will select a job to accept system resources. As discussed, Hadoop offers FS, CS, and FIFO job schedulers. Both FS and CS allow the system administrator to configure multiple job queues with various shares of system resources. The FIFO, as its name shows, has only one job queue, which has very limited usage. The process of selecting a job to utilize resources contains two stages. The first stage selects a job queue and the second stage picks a job from that selected job queue. Once a job is selected by the job scheduler, RM will try to assign the chosen job certain number of containers, which could exist on any computing node. Often a job is composed of many tasks and each task needs a container to complete its work. As a result, individual jobs usually will go through many cycles of the job selection before their completion.

3.3 Priority Design on the Resource Manager

Our goal is to make certain that prioritized jobs will employ extra resources to reduce their execution time under the condition of not modifying job schedulers. There are two points that RM must address to achieve the goal. The first is to discriminate prioritized jobs from regular jobs. The second is to ensure prioritized jobs could obtain more resources during the resource allocation. The first point is about how to pass the priority of a job and the deduction ratio (if set) to RM. Under the current YARN, the values of "yield" and "ratio" together with the user's submission will be submitted to RM. We then can get the job priority

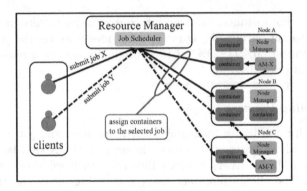

Fig. 1. Scheduling components in YARN

and deduction ratio on the RM site. When a job is submitted, there will be
an object namely RMApp created in RM to represent that job. For a given
job, we insert the priority of that job into its corresponding RMApp in YARN
to register its job priority. As to the deduction ratio, our approach maintains
a global deduction ratio for all regular jobs in the entire system so we keep
its latest value in RM. The second point is not as straight as the first one.
As explained, the system resources are managed and distributed in a unit of
"container". This indicates that prioritized jobs need to gain more containers
each time they get selected. However, the overall system resources is fixed for a
given Hadoop cluster, which implies that we need to make regular jobs "yield"
some of their allocated containers when they are scheduled to collect containers.
By doing so, those "yielded" containers could be given to prioritized jobs to
fasten their execution.

How to reserve containers from regular jobs is an important work. In the
YARN architecture, each job has a corresponding RMApp object as well as
an AM managing its executing progress as seen in Fig. 1. Each AM constantly
monitors its containers in use and notifies RM how many more containers it
needs to complete the entire job. In other words, RM knows the number of
containers still needed for every running job in the system. For a given AM,
when RM learns the number of containers that AM requires, the number will be
passed into the job scheduler to decide how many containers will be allocated
to the corresponding job next time it is scheduled to have containers. In our
original design, the number of containers requested from an AM of a regular job
will be temporarily reduced to zero to save containers for prioritized jobs if they
exist in the same job queue where that regular job resides in. As a consequence,
no containers will be given to that regular job under the circumstances. In the
case of a deduction ratio is set, the number passed into the job scheduler will
be decreased in accordance with the deduction ratio. When all prioritized jobs
complete, the allocation of containers will back to the normal way like original
YARN does, which means no containers will be deducted from regular jobs any
more. To appropriately adjust the number of containers (requested by an AM)

passed into the job scheduler, we need to know the priority of the job that AM represents. The AM itself does not keep the priority of its corresponding job. Every job in the system has a unique job ID to designate its identity. For any job, both its corresponding RMApp object and its AM object record its job ID. We use the job ID of an AM object to locate the corresponding RMApp object in RM. Once the corresponding RMApp is found, we can learn the priority of the job recorded in that RMApp.

As explained, the process of scheduling a job to use resources includes two stages under the current YARN architecture. For CS, this two-stage process could potentially cause a problem if we just directly reserve containers from regular jobs when prioritized jobs exist in the same queue where those regular jobs stay in. For FS, the two-stage process will not cause any problems in our original model. We will use Fig. 2 as an example to illustrate this potential impact on CS and explain how we revise our model to address it. Figure 2 shows a simple scenario with three queues, namely queue A, queue B, and queue C. There are five jobs submitted, in the order of $a1$ to $a5$, in queue A and three jobs submitted in queue B with the submission order of $b1$ to $b3$. The queue C has four jobs with the first submission of $c1$ and the last submission of $c4$. The jobs with shadow ($a1$, $a3$, $b2$) represent prioritized jobs and others mean regular jobs. The first stage, selecting a job queue, does not have problems. It is the second stage, picking a job from the selected queue, could cause the risk. In FS, during the second stage, every job in the same queue will be picked in turn to receive resources. Take the queue A for example, FS picks $a1$ to $a5$ in rotational order in the second stage. In other words, $a1$ to $a5$ execute concurrently. Jobs in queue B and queue C get picked in the same way. In our original model, whenever $a2$, $a4$, or $a5$ is chosen, by default our system withholds all its allocated containers. In CS, in the selected queue, always the one with the earliest submission time will be picked, which means only one job can be executed at any moment in a queue. In this example, $a2$ cannot start its execution until $a1$ completes. Similarly, $b2$ will start its execution after $b1$ totally finishes its work, and $c2$ will behave in the same way. With our original model, $b1$ will obtain either no (by default) or fewer (if the deduction ratio is set) containers than it should have each time. In the default case, $b1$ cannot acquire new containers to finish its work, which means $b2$ will not start its execution under such circumstances. Jobs in queue C will not face the same problem because there is no prioritized jobs in it. Even our main goal is FS, we need to make sure that our model does not impact CS in an unexpected way. Fortunately, this problem can be solved with a slight change in our original design. We revised our model in the following way. For a regular job, instead of always taking its containers away when there exist prioritized jobs in its job queue, we now do that only when any one of those prioritized jobs has already started its execution. Otherwise, our model will not deduct containers from regular jobs. As a result, in the above scenario, $b1$ will acquire containers as usual in that $b2$ is not running during the execution of $b1$. Thus, our model will not alter the container allocation in any way when CS is the scheduler used in Hadoop environments.

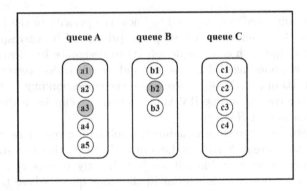

Fig. 2. A potential impact on CS

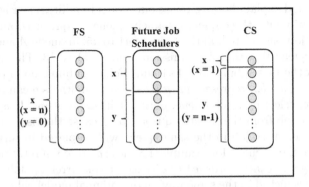

Fig. 3. Contents of a queue in FS, CS, and future job schedulers

3.4 Portability for Future Job Schedulers

Portability is a very important issue in real-world environments. Ideally, we hope our model can be directly applied to future job schedulers developed under the current YARN architecture. The current two-stage job scheduling in the YARN architecture is actually a very flexible design. The system administrator can set a configuration of multiple queues with different shares of system resources to meet various requirements. The future job schedulers may schedule jobs to accept containers in a way different from FS and CS. Nevertheless, for a given queue, any job in that queue must either have started or have not yet started its execution. For those have started their execution, they are known as active jobs in YARN. Those have not started are referred to as pending jobs. Suppose there are totally n jobs in a given queue with x active jobs and y pending jobs. We will have $n = x + y$ at any time even values of n, x, and y for each queue may be different. Figure 3 demonstrates the situation for what a given queue would like in FS, CS, and future job schedulers. The leftmost represents a queue in FS and the rightmost depicts a queue in CS. The middle one illustrates the contents of a queue in future job schedulers. For the case of FS, it will launch all jobs in any given queue as soon as possible. This means, under the vast majority of time, its x is equal to n and its y is equal to zero in every queue. For the case of CS, its x is equal to one and its y is equal to $n-1$ in all queues. For future job schedulers, its x should be within the range of one and n. In our model, for an active regular job, we will deduct containers from it if there are active prioritized jobs in its job queue. If we further examine FS and CS, we can realize that both set their numbers of active jobs at two extremes. FS sets the value of x to n and CS keeps the value of x to one. For a given queue in future job schedulers, as long as it has more than one active job, its active prioritized jobs could employ extra containers deducted from its active regular jobs. Consequently, our model can help future job schedulers fasten their active prioritized jobs.

4 Performance Evaluation

We built a Hadoop cluster to evaluate the performance of our design and implementation. The Hadoop version installed was 3.1.0. The Hadoop cluster had one NameNode and three DataNodes connected in a LAN environment through a 1Gbps switch. All four computers were equipped with identical hardware and software including an Intel i5-4590 3.3 GHz CPU, 8 GB of DDR3 memory, and a 1TB Seagate 7200rpm disk. The host operation system was Ubuntu 16.04 LTS. We conducted experiments of the same jobs under various conditions in the Hadoop environment with original YARN and our YARN supporting prioritized execution. The job scheduler used is FS as it is our main target to realize prioritized execution. For brevity, we will refer to the original Hadoop environment with original YARN as "regular YARN" while our environment as "prioritized YARN" respectively.

4.1 Experimental Design

We conducted four groups of experiments to evaluate the performance of job execution with and without high priority under different cases. The system is configured with three job queues equally sharing the system resources. Practically, it is very common to equally allocate resources to job queues. The default behavior of FS can reallocate resources of a queue with no job in it to other job queues hosting jobs. The first group of experiments focuses on the situation where the deduction ratio is 100%, which means our system will temporarily prevent regular jobs from using new resources. This is the case where users want to accomplish prioritized jobs as fast as possible. The second group explores the situation with the deduction ratio 50%. This represents the circumstances where users would like to hasten the execution of prioritized jobs with a moderate effect on regular jobs. The third and the four groups resemble the first two groups respectively. The difference is that there are more jobs competing for resources in the latter two groups than in the former two groups. We want to investigate if our system could help prioritized jobs further when more jobs compete for system resources. All test cases were repeated for three times to get their average values in our experiments. To avoid the caching effect, the Linux cache was cleared out between test cases. Each test case included sixteen jobs executing concurrently. Eight of them were MapReduce programs, which means they require system resources allocated by YARN during their execution. The rest of eight jobs were non-MapReduce programs including four doing file reading and four doing file writing. Even their execution directly communicated with HDFS and did not involve services from YARN, they still consumed and contended for system resources. Each of the sixteen jobs processed a different file with the size of 10 GB. The reason to mingle MapReduce jobs with non-MapReduce jobs is to correspond with regular Hadoop environments hosting both types of jobs at the same time. The MapReduce jobs contained WordCount, Grep, WordMean, WordMedian, TeraSort, and RandomWriter. Both WordCount and Grep had two instances. The rest of four had one instance each. Totally, there were eight MapReduce jobs in experiments. The WordCount is a widely known program calculating the counts of individual words in files. The Grep, as its name suggests, searches for a given string in files. The WordMean computes the average length of words in files and the WordMedian finds the median length of words in files. The TeraSort simply does sorting on files and the RandomWriter inserts random data into the HDFS.

4.2   One Prioritized Job: Equal Resource Allocation and 100% Deduction Ratio

Figure 4 shows the assignment of the eight MapReduce jobs into three queues in the first group of experiments. The queue one hosted three jobs including the first instance of WordCount (denoted as WordCount-1), RandomWrite, and WordMedian. Both instances of Grep (denoted as Grep-1 and Grep-2) were in the second queue, and the third queue had the rest of three MapReduce jobs. For original YARN, all eight MapReduce jobs were executed as usual. For prioritized YARN, WordCount-1 was executed with high priority and other jobs were run as regular jobs. Table 1 lists the results for this group. The rows marked with "job" show the names of the sixteen jobs in a set of four. The rows begin with "orig. YARN" list the time (in seconds) required to complete the corresponding jobs under original YARN as described above. The "prio. YARN" rows report the corresponding time (in seconds) under our prioritized YARN. The improvement percentages manifest the improvement of prioritized YARN over original YARN. The WordCount-1 took 2720.72 s to finish its execution in original YARN while the time was decreased to 863.00 s in our prioritized YARN, generating an improvement of 68.28% ((2720.72−863.00)/2720.72). This clearly demonstrates that the job executed with high priority could speed up its execution in prioritized YARN when the deduction ratio was set at 100%. It is expectable that other regular MapReduce jobs could be affected due to the deduction of containers from their resource allocation during the execution of WordCount-1. As a reminder, once WordCount-1 completed its execution, the container allocation to regular jobs immediately backed to their normal way. Interestingly, some regular jobs, such as Grep-1 and WordCount-2, also performed better in prioritized YARN. We do not know the cause for certain. We infer that as the WordCount-1 completed less than one-third of its original time $((863.00/2720.72) = 31.72\%)$, the resource contention among regular jobs could promptly be less competitive, which may reduce the execution time of some jobs. Altogether, some regular jobs in prioritized YARN performed better than their counterparts in original YARN and some did worse.

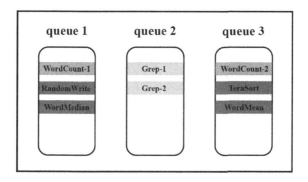

Fig. 4. The assignment of MapReduce jobs in three queues

4.3 One Prioritized Job: Equal Resource Allocation and 50% Deduction Ratio

The second group of experiments was conducted to examine the performance improvement of a prioritized job when the deduction ratio is set at 50%. We carried out experiments the same way as we did in the first group except for the setting of the deduction ratio. Table 2 details the results. The WordCount-1 took 1621.88 s to complete its execution in prioritized YARN. Its performance improvement was 40.39%, which is smaller than its improvement, 68.28%, in the first group. This is reasonable as regular jobs only gave up at most 50%, instead of 100% of their allocated containers during the execution of WordCount-1.

4.4 Two Prioritized Jobs: Equal Resource Allocation and 100% Deduction Ratio

In the third group, we explored the situation where resource contention is more competitive than the case in the first group. The MapReduce jobs in Fig. 4 was rearranged as shown in Fig. 5. Both WordCount-1 and Grep-1 were executed with high priority. The other four jobs in queue one as well as jobs in queue two and three were run as regular jobs. The deduction ratio was set at 100%. As more jobs stayed in the queue one, it became more competitive to gain resources. We were interested in finding how our model functions under such circumstances. Table 3 details the outcome of the third group. Both prioritized

Table 1. One prioritized job: three queues with equal resource allocation and 100% deduction ratio

job	WordCount-1	Grep-1	WordMean	WordMedian
orig. YARN	**2720.72**	1599.30	1709.36	1828.11
prio. YARN	**863.00**	1457.96	1784.65	2298.25
improvement	**68.28%**	8.84%	−4.40%	−25.72%
job	WordCount-2	Grep-2	TeraSort	RandomWriter
orig. YARN	1836.57	1604.85	3141.83	1283.41
prio. YARN	1705.29	1411.39	3001.39	1562.25
improvement	7.15%	12.05%	4.47%	−21.73%
job	Write-1	Write-2	Write-3	Write-4
orig. YARN	5891.88	6566.33	5802.02	6745.02
prio. YARN	6000.90	6889.53	6098.10	6370.46
improvement	−1.85%	−4.92%	−5.10%	5.55%
job	Read-1	Read-2	Read-3	Read-4
orig. YARN	5696.83	4612.95	5842.80	5433.72
prio. YARN	5001.27	5070.87	5156.18	5693.25
improvement	12.21%	−9.93%	11.75%	−4.78%

jobs executed faster in prioritized YARN. The WordCount-1 and Grep-1 gained an improvement of 56.66% and 53.10% respectively. For the WordCount-1, its improvement was smaller than its counterpart, 68.28%, in the first group. In fact, it ran faster than what we expected under the condition that the execution time of Grep-1 was reduced by 53.10%. In all, compared with the case of group one, it is good that both prioritized jobs could noticeably shorten their execution time with the cost of moderately less performance improvement of one prioritized job. The rest of four jobs in queue one spent more time to complete their jobs in prioritized YARN since they stopped receiving containers during the execution of WordCount-1 and Grep-1.

4.5 Two Prioritized Jobs: Equal Resource Allocation and 50% Deduction Ratio

The experiments in the fourth group were conducted in the way as those in the third group except that the deduction ratio was set at 50% instead of 100%. Table 4 presents the numbers. The performance improvements in this group were lower than those in the third group as the deduction ratio was set at 50%. The WordCount-1 had an improvement rate of 29.00% and the Grep-1 did 23.31% better in prioritized YARN. Both numbers were smaller than their counterparts in the third group. If we examine the values of the deduction ratio and the performance improvement in both groups, there roughly exists a positive correlation in between. The 50% deduction ratio in the fourth group is one-half of the 100% in the third group. Interestingly, the 29.00% for WordCount-1 in the fourth group is close to one-half of the 56.66% for WordCount-1 in the third group ($29/56.66 = 51.18\%$). The Grep-1 also has a similar situation. For the rest of four MapReduce jobs, they performed better in the fourth group than in the third group for the reason that they only yielded at most 50% of their allocated containers during the execution of WordCount-1 and Grep-1.

Table 2. One prioritized job: three queues with equal resource allocation and 50% deduction ratio

job	**WordCount-1**	Grep-1	WordMean	WordMedian
orig. YARN	**2720.72**	1599.30	1709.36	1828.11
prio. YARN	**1621.88**	1731.58	1837.57	2111.23
improvement	**40.39%**	−8.27%	−7.50%	−15.49%
job	WordCount-2	Grep-2	TeraSort	RandomWriter
orig. YARN	1836.57	1604.85	3141.83	1283.41
prio. YARN	2035.90	1715.06	3124.89	1526.53
improvement	−10.85%	−6.87%	0.54%	−18.94%
job	Write-1	Write-2	Write-3	Write-4
orig. YARN	5891.88	6566.33	5802.02	6745.02
prio. YARN	6497.31	6075.01	6109.72	6473.58
improvement	−10.28%	7.48%	−5.30%	4.02%
job	Read-1	Read-2	Read-3	Read-4
orig. YARN	5696.83	4612.95	5842.80	5433.72
prio. YARN	5452.39	4149.91	6012.66	5293.93
improvement	4.29%	10.04%	−2.91%	2.57%

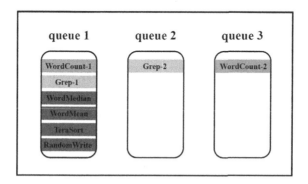

Fig. 5. The assignment of MapReduce jobs in three queues - a more competitive situation

Table 3. Two prioritized jobs: three queues with equal resource allocation and 100% deduction ratio

job	WordCount-1	Grep-1	WordMean	WordMedian
orig. YARN	**2340.84**	**1606.38**	1720.52	1808.71
prio. YARN	**1014.45**	**753.32**	2156.10	2420.65
improvement	**56.66%**	**53.10%**	−25.32%	−33.83%
job	WordCount-2	Grep-2	TeraSort	RandomWriter
orig. YARN	2118.76	1602.35	3117.11	1281.94
prio. YARN	2055.56	1603.52	4038.63	1610.09
improvement	2.98%	−0.07%	−29.56%	−25.60%
job	Write-1	Write-2	Write-3	Write-4
orig. YARN	7553.57	6903.24	7598.16	7386.96
prio. YARN	7536.11	7374.49	7348.72	7499.80
improvement	0.23%	−6.83%	3.28%	−1.53%
job	Read-1	Read-2	Read-3	Read-4
orig. YARN	5411.63	5884.46	6196.49	5116.98
prio. YARN	4802.30	5421.20	5648.42	6004.88
improvement	11.26%	7.87%	8.84%	−17.35%

Table 4. Two prioritized jobs: three queues with equal resource allocation and 50% deduction ratio

job	WordCount-1	Grep-1	WordMean	WordMedian
orig. YARN	**2340.84**	**1606.38**	1720.52	1808.71
prio. YARN	**1662.01**	**1231.96**	1928.46	2083.20
improvement	**29.00%**	**23.31%**	−12.09%	−15.18%
job	WordCount-2	Grep-2	TeraSort	RandomWriter
orig. YARN	2118.76	1602.35	3117.11	1281.94
prio. YARN	2238.51	1557.71	3706.96	1502.07
improvement	−5.65%	2.79%	−18.92%	−17.17%
job	Write-1	Write-2	Write-3	Write-4
orig. YARN	7553.57	6903.24	7598.16	7386.96
prio. YARN	7517.94	7391.63	7354.78	7510.52
improvement	0.47%	−7.07%	3.20%	−1.67%
job	Read-1	Read-2	Read-3	Read-4
orig. YARN	5411.63	5884.46	6196.49	5116.98
prio. YARN	6241.21	5406.35	5613.42	4978.12
improvement	−15.33%	8.12%	9.41%	2.71%

5 Conclusions

As users rely more and more on cloud computing to accomplish their works, it will be better if they can make decisions on the priority of individual jobs and cloud system could expedite the execution of jobs with high priority as expected. Hadoop is one of the most widely used cloud platforms in the community of cloud computing. Unfortunately, it only supports prioritized execution in a very limited way. Researchers had proposed various methods to modify job schedulers to conduct prioritized execution. Nevertheless, any modification to job schedulers will unavoidably lead to the issue of portability, which makes it difficult for future distribution. We proposed and implemented a new approach to dynamically allocate more containers to prioritized jobs to accelerate their execution. Our design also allows users to choose the percentage of resources regular jobs should yield to prioritized jobs. Our approach does not make any changes to job schedulers. As a result, the distribution of our approach to future job schedulers developed under the current YARN architecture is very easy. Theoretically, our design could help nearly all future job schedulers to support prioritized execution to some degree. The experimental results under various situations validate our design and implementation. Jobs executed with high priority could lessen their execution time by up to 68.28%.

6 Future Work

Currently, our implementation provides one level of priority, which means jobs could only be executed with regular or high priority. The one-level priority could further be extended to multi-level priority to make our design more flexible. In the meanwhile, we do not put a limit on the number prioritized jobs allowed in the system at this time. If all jobs are executed with high priority, they will have the same priority in reality. We may limit the number or percentage of prioritized jobs to promise the acceleration of their execution.

References

1. http://en.wikipedia.org/wiki/apache_hadoop
2. http://hadoop.apache.org/docs/current/hadoop-project-dist/hadoop-hdfs/federation.html
3. https://www.facebook.com/notes/facebook-engineering/under-the-hood-hadoop-distributed-filesystem-reliability-with-namenode-and-avata/10150888759153920
4. http://www.cloudera.com/content/cloudera-content/cloudera-docs/cdh4/4.2.0/cdh4-high-availability-guide/cdh4hag_topic_2_1.html
5. Agarwal, S., Borthakur, D., Stoica, I.: Snapshots in Hadoop distributed file system. Technical report, EECS Department, University of California, Berkeley, November 2010 (2011)
6. Armbrust, M., et al.: Spark SQL: relational data processing in spark. In: Proceedings of the 2015 ACM SIGMOD International Conference on Management of Data, pp. 1383–1394. ACM (2015)

7. Blagojevic, F., Guyot, C., Wang, Q., Tsai, T., Mateescu, R., Bandic, Z.: Priority IO scheduling in the cloud. In: Proceedings of USENIX Conference on Hot Topics Cloud Computing, pp. 1–6 (2013)

8. Borthakur, D., et al.: Apache Hadoop goes realtime at Facebook. In: Proceedings of the 2011 ACM SIGMOD International Conference on Management of Data, SIGMOD 2011, pp. 1071–1080. ACM, New York (2011). https://doi.org/10.1145/1989323.1989438

9. Bui, D.M., Hussain, S., Huh, E.N., Lee, S.: Adaptive replication management in hdfs based on supervised learning. IEEE Trans. Knowl. Data Eng. **28**(6), 1369–1382 (2016)

10. Burns, B., Oppenheimer, D.: Design patterns for container-based distributed systems. In: 8th {USENIX} Workshop on Hot Topics in Cloud Computing, HotCloud 2016 (2016)

11. Buyya, R., Broberg, J., Goscinski, A.M.: Cloud Computing: Principles and Paradigms, vol. 87. Wiley, Hoboken (2010)

12. Ghemawat, S., Gobioff, H., Leung, S.T.: The Google file system. In: ACM SIGOPS Operating Systems Review, vol. 37, pp. 29–43. ACM (2003)

13. Hunt, P., Konar, M., Junqueira, F.P., Reed, B.: ZooKeeper: wait-free coordination for internet-scale systems. In: Proceedings of the 2010 USENIX Conference on USENIX Annual Technical Conference, vol. 8, pp. 11–11 (2010)

14. Karanasos, K., et al.: Mercury: hybrid centralized and distributed scheduling in large shared clusters. In: 2015 {USENIX} Annual Technical Conference, {USENIX}{ATC} 2015, pp. 485–497 (2015)

15. Kc, K., Anyanwu, K.: Scheduling Hadoop jobs to meet deadlines. In: 2010 IEEE Second International Conference on Cloud Computing Technology and Science (CloudCom), pp. 388–392. IEEE (2010)

16. Kondikoppa, P., Chiu, C.H., Cui, C., Xue, L., Park, S.J.: Network-aware scheduling of MapReduce framework on distributed clusters over high speed networks. In: Proceedings of the 2012 Workshop on Cloud Services, Federation, and the 8th Open Cirrus Summit, pp. 39–44. ACM (2012)

17. Li, H., Ghodsi, A., Zaharia, M., Shenker, S., Stoica, I.: Tachyon: reliable, memory speed storage for cluster computing frameworks. In: Proceedings of the ACM Symposium on Cloud Computing, pp. 1–15. ACM (2014)

18. Oriani, A., Garcia, I.C.: From backup to hot standby: high availability for HDFS. In: 2012 IEEE 31st Symposium on Reliable Distributed Systems (SRDS), pp. 131–140. IEEE (2012)

19. Qin, P., Dai, B., Huang, B., Xu, G.: Bandwidth-aware scheduling with SDN in Hadoop: a new trend for big data. IEEE Syst. J. **11**, 2337–2344 (2015)

20. Rasooli, A., Down, D.G.: An adaptive scheduling algorithm for dynamic heterogeneous Hadoop systems. In: Proceedings of the 2011 Conference of the Center for Advanced Studies on Collaborative Research, pp. 30–44. IBM Corporation (2011)

21. Renner, T., Thamsen, L., Kao, O.: CoLoc: distributed data and container colocation for data-intensive applications. In: 2016 IEEE International Conference on Big Data (Big Data), pp. 3008–3015. IEEE (2016)

22. Rista, C., Griebler, D., Maron, C.A., Fernandes, L.G.: Improving the network performance of a container-based cloud environment for Hadoop systems. In: 2017 International Conference on High Performance Computing & Simulation (HPCS), pp. 619–626. IEEE (2017)

23. Sandholm, T., Lai, K.: Dynamic proportional share scheduling in Hadoop. In: Frachtenberg, E., Schwiegelshohn, U. (eds.) JSSPP 2010. LNCS, vol. 6253, pp. 110–131. Springer, Heidelberg (2010). https://doi.org/10.1007/978-3-642-16505-4_7

24. Shvachko, K., Kuang, H., Radia, S., Chansler, R.: The Hadoop distributed file system. In: 2010 IEEE 26th Symposium on Mass Storage Systems and Technologies (MSST), pp. 1–10. IEEE (2010)

25. Tan, J., Meng, X., Zhang, L.: Coupling task progress for MapReduce resource-aware scheduling. In: 2013 Proceedings IEEE INFOCOM, pp. 1618–1626. IEEE (2013)

26. Varga, M., Petrescu-Nita, A., Pop, F.: Deadline scheduling algorithm for sustainable computing in Hadoop environment. Comput. Secur. **76**, 354–366 (2018)

27. Vavilapalli, V.K., et al.: Apache Hadoop yarn: yet another resource negotiator. In: Proceedings of the 4th Annual Symposium on Cloud Computing, p. 5. ACM (2013)

28. White, T.: Hadoop: The Definitive Guide, 3rd edn. O'Reilly, Newton (2012)

29. Yeh, T., Huang, H.: Realizing prioritized scheduling service in the Hadoop system. In: 2018 IEEE 6th International Conference on Future Internet of Things and Cloud (FiCloud), pp. 47–54. IEEE (2018)

30. Yeh, T., Sun, Y.: Enabling prioritized cloud I/O service in Hadoop distributed file system. In: The 16th IEEE International Conference on High Performance Computing and Communications, pp. 256–259. IEEE (2014)

qCUDA-ARM: Virtualization for Embedded GPU Architectures

Bo-Yu Huang and Che-Rung Lee[✉]

Department of Computer Science,
National Tsing Hua University,
HsinChu, Taiwan
cherung@cs.nthu.edu.tw

Abstract. The emergence of Internet of Things (IOT) is changing the ways of computing resources acquisition, from centralized cloud data centers to distributed pervasive edge nodes. To cope the small amount of diversity problem for IOT devices and applications, two research trends are investigated for the system design of edge nodes: heterogeneity and virtualization. In this paper, we consider the integration of those two important trends and present a virtualization system for embedded GPU architectures, called qCUDA-ARM. The design of qCUDA-ARM is based on the framework of qCUDA, a virtualization system for x86 servers. Because of the architectural differences between x86 servers and ARM based embedded systems, many subsystems of qCUDA-ARM, such as memory management, need to be redesigned. We evaluated the performance of qCUDA-ARM with three CUDA benchmarks and two real world applications. For computational intensive jobs, qCUDA-ARM can reach similar performance of the native system; and for memory bound programs, qCUDA-ARM can also have up to 90% performance of that of the native one.

Keywords: GPU · CUDA · Virtualization · Embedded system · ARM

1 Introduction

The deluge of Internet-of-Thing (IoT) [10] has changed the landscape of how services are provisioned and managed. Traditional cloud computing platforms that centralize all resources in data centers, although enhance the utilization and availability, cannot provide a satisfactory response time for real-time applications and the desired network bandwidth for massive number of interconnected IOT devices. New computing paradigm, called fog computing or edge computing [5], was proposed to solve those issues brought by IOT. It decentralizes the computing resources by widely deploying edge servers, which need not be as powerful as those used in data centers, to support the IOT demands of computation, networks, and storage.

However, the design of edge server architectures remains an open problem [11, 16, 24] owing to the diversity of IOT applications and the deployment methods

© Springer Nature Switzerland AG 2020
C.-H. Hsu et al. (Eds.): IOV 2019, LNCS 11894, pp. 284–302, 2020.
https://doi.org/10.1007/978-3-030-38651-1_23

of edge nodes. On the one hand, those edge nodes should be low power and inexpensive so that they can be widely distributed in various environments. On the other hand, they should be powerful enough for different types of programs to extend its usability. Although many IOT applications request only a modest computing resource, some of them have higher demands for computation power, network capacity, or storage space. One of the examples is Artificial Intelligent (AI) IOT, or named AIOT, applications whose model sizes are usually large and the computation complexity is high, even just for inference. Moreover, many AI applications are time sensitive, such as self-driving car or disaster forecasting systems. For them, a high performance edge server is required.

To take on the challenge, two major trends of system design are currently investigated: heterogeneity and virtualization. A heterogeneous system contains more than one types of processors so that different applications can find the proper resources to use. One example is ARM's big.LITTLE architecture [21], which combines slow but battery-saving LITTLE cores with fast but more energy-intensive big cores. Another example is the embedded GPU (Graphics Processing Unit) architecture, such as Nvidia's Jetson [4] or MediaTek's Helio [2], which couples CPU for sequential control with GPU for parallel computation. The second trend is virtualization, which adds another dimension of flexibility to ease the architectural design of edge nodes. It can customize a specific hardware resource and create an isolated environment for each application.

One of the most popular virtualization techniques used in edge nodes is containerization [6], which supports application level isolation and shares OS and hardware level resources. Although it has many merits, such as fast and light-weighted, containerization has many intrinsic problems. First, applications must be built for the same or similar OS environments which limits its flexibility of usage. Some legacy programs that designed for specific OS or libraries cannot be run on containers. Second, the isolation provided by containers is not strong enough to defense many malicious attack. The security remains a big concern for container based virtualization. As the result, the server virtualization techniques are still important for IOT applications. Although it has higher performance degradation than containerization, many researches have studied how to reduce its overhead and make it more efficient [13,17].

In this paper, we investigate the integration of those two important trends: heterogeneity and virtualization. We consider the server virtualization techniques for embedded GPU architectures. Although the GPGPU virtualization techniques has been studied for a decade, none of them are designed for embedded GPU architecture, to the best of our knowledge. One of the reason is that an embedded GPU architecture is usually built upon system on chip (SoC), which integrates CPU, GPU and numerous sensors on one single board. With the power constrains and limit computation capability, its virtualization is difficult implement.

The system we designed is called qCUDA-ARM, because it is based on the qCUDA GPGPU virtualization framework and designed for ARM based embedded GPU architecture. The basic virtualization method used in qCUDA is the

API remoting method, which submits Nvidia CUDA APIs from a VM to the host machine, executes the API on the host GPU, and retrieves the results from GPU back to VM's CUDA programs. Because the memory design and used APIs of embedded GPU architecture are different from those in ordinary servers, a simple system porting does not work. We redesigned the memory mapping mechanism, which optimizes the performance of memory access, and implemented the new front-end and back-end functions for memory related APIs for qCUDA-ARM.

We evaluated the performance of qCUDA-ARM on an Nvidia TX2 development board using three different benchmarks and two applications, and compared the results with native CUDA. The results show that for computation intensive applications, qCUDA-ARM can have a similar performance as the native one; and for memory bound benchmarks, the performance can also reach up to 90% of the native CUDA.

The rest of this paper is organized as follows. Section 2 introduces backgrounds of server virtualization and related works for GPGPU virtualization. Section 3 presents the design and system architecture of qCUDA-ARM. Section 4 shows experimental results, and the conclusion and future work are given in the last section.

2   Background

2.1   Virtualization

Virtualization is one of the key technologies to enable the modern cloud computing architectures. It does not only increase the hardware utilization of servers by consolidation, but also adds a great flexibility for provisioning, load balance, auto scaling, and fault tolerance with the live migration ability.

The basic software unit in virtualization is a "virtual machine" (VM), which is an standalone and isolated system with an operating system and applications inside. Behind multiple VMs, a thin layer of software, called a hypervisor or a virtual machine monitor (VMM), manages the execution of VMs on a physical machine, and dynamically allocates computing resources to them. Those VMs on a hypervisor are called guest machines, and the physical machine is called the host machine.

For different computing resources, the virtualization of IO devices is more complex than CPU virtualization and memory virtualization owing to the diversity of devices. In a full-virtualization environment, where guest OS cannot be modified, an IO device can only be virtualized by emulation and hardware assisted virtualization. However, they have different drawbacks. The emulation of each type of devices is inefficient in terms of performance and implementation, and the hardware assisted virtualization is usually expensive and only available for high-end devices.

Alternatively, the para-virtualization techniques, which need to modify the guest OS or targeted applications, are more often used for IO virtualization. A common para-virtualization framework for IO devices is virtio [19], which provides a standardized interface for VMs to access simplified virtual devices.

An IO device virtualized by virtio consists of two parts: the front-end and the back-end. The front-end subsystem acts as a device driver inside the guest OS, and the back-end subsystem emulates the operations of devices in the hypervisor. Their communication is defined by the virtio framework.

2.2   GPGPU Virtualization

Graphics Processing Unit (GPU) is a specialized processor originally designed for faster computer graphics calculation. The major differences between CPU and GPU are their architectures and operation methods. A CPU usually consists of few cores which are optimized for sequential processing. A GPU may contain thousands of smaller cores to execute multiple simple tasks simultaneously. Because of their superior performance, GPUs are also used to accelerate many applications other than computer graphics, such as scientific computing, video coding, and machine learning. Such usage of GPUs is also called General-purpose computing on graphics processing units (GPGPU).

One of the most successful GPGPU architectures is CUDA (Compute Unified Device Architecture) [3], which is a parallel computing platform with related application programming interfaces (APIs). The CUDA platform provides new syntax of high level languages for software developers to access to the computation elements of GPU. CUDA contains two kinds of APIs: run-time API and driver API, which manages CUDA kernel functions and CUDA context respectively.

As more and more GPGPU applications deployed in the cloud platforms, GPU virtualization gains increasing attentions. Four commonly used Virtualization techniques for GPGPU are direct-passthrough, mediated passthrough, API remoting and full virtualization, which are introduced below.

Direct-Passthrough. Direct-passthrough is a hardware assisted virtualization technique designed specifically for PCI or PCIe devices. It allows direct access from the guest OS to the physical PCI or PCIe hardware devices. Each VM is assigned one or more GPUs as PCI devices. Since the guest OS bypasses the virtualization layer to access the GPUs, the overhead of passthrough mode is low so its performance can be maintained as that in the bare-metal mode. Moreover, since each VM uses its own GPU APIs, no reengineering and modification of GPU APIs is required. However, GPUs cannot be shared among VMs, or even the host when it is used.

Mediated Passthrough. Mediated passthrough is also a hardware assisted virtualization, by which a virtual GPU (vGPU) with full GPU features is presented to each VM. VMs can directly access performance-critical resources, without intervention from the hypervisor in most cases, while privileged operations from guest are trap-and-emulated to provide secure isolation among VMs. The vGPU context is switched per quantum, to share the physical GPU among multiple VMs without user notice.

gVirt [15] is one of example for mediated passthrough. It allows each VM to access the two buffers directly (pass-through) without intervention from the hypervisor. For this purpose, the graphics memory resource is partitioned by the gVirt Mediator so each VM can have its own frame and command buffers in the partitioned memory. At the same time, privileged GPU instructions are trapped and emulated by the gVirt Mediator in the driver domain of Xen. This enables secure isolation among multiple VMs without significant performance loss.

Full Virtualization. Full-virtualization allows native driver be run on the guest without modification of libraries and drivers. The major difficulties are that GPUs have very complex architecture and most GPU vendors do not open source their drivers. GPUvm [22,23] is one of full-virtualization implementation, which is for Nvidia GPU on Xen hypervisor. It utilizes an open-source GPU driver Nouveau, the works of reversed engineering by envytools, and Gdev [14], a CUDA driver runtime library for Nouveau, to emulate virtual GPU device model and uses an aggregator for isolating and scheduling among virtual machines.

G-KVM [12] is another full GPGPU virtualization solution based on KVM. It leverages on the memory mapping between guest address space and hypervisor address space to improve MMIO related performance.

API Remoting. API remoting is a virtualization method that enables GPU sharing among multiple VMs through a programming API interface. User-space applications running on guest operating systems can leverage the GPU through its programming API (e.g., OpenCL, OpenGL and CUDA) with no changes to the source code, and without the need for the hypervisor to provide a virtual GPU abstraction.

Each API call passes through the three layers of the API Remoting framework: front-end, transport and back-end. The front-end, installed in the guest OS, implements the API stubs that forward the calls using the transport layer. The back-end running on the host handles the call requests received over the transport and executes them on the GPU hardware using the actual API library. The transport layer is designed to minimize the communication overhead between back-end and front-end, and relies on a zero-copy memory sharing mechanism. Alternative implementations can exploit network sockets to enable GPU sharing among different physical server nodes.

In API-remoting, the GPU related libraries and drivers in the guest need to be modified to intercept the API calls from user programs and to take care the responses from the host. Recently, many API remoting methods for GPGPU virtualization have been proposed, such as gVirtuS, LoGV, vCUDA, rCUDA, mrCUDA and virtio-CL [7–9,18,20].

3   Design and Implementation

This section presents the system architecture of qCUDA-ARM. Since it is based on the framework of qCUDA, we will first introduce the components of qCUDA.

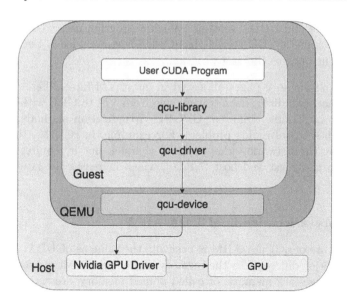

Fig. 1. qCUDA system architecture

Then their major difference, the memory management system, will be compared and contrasted. Last, other implementation details of qCUDA-ARM are illustrated.

3.1   QCUDA System Architecture

qCUDA utilizes the API remoting method on QEMU-KVM hypervisor to virtualize the CUDA architecture. The communication between VM and host machine replies on the virtio framework [19]. The system architecture of qCUDA is shown in Fig. 1. It consists of three components: qcu-library, qcu-driver and qcu-device. The functions of each component are illustrated as follows.

- The qcu-library provides the native CUDA interface to guest CUDA program, and handles the passing parameters. Users can use Nvidia CUDA Compiler NVCC to compile their programs, and link qcu-library with users' program. The job of qcu-library is to transfer a CUDA run-time APIs to driver APIs, so that they can be run in host. NVCC adds those CUDA functions in the compiled GPU binary, and wraps them into ARM ELF format.
- The qcu-driver is the communication channel between the VM and the host, which copy parameters of CUDA runtime APIs from the guest user-space to the guest kernel-space. A value parameter will be copied directly; but a pointer parameter requires additional conversion. Since the original pointer is in the guest virtual address (GVA), its value must be converted to a guest physical address (GPA).
- The main job of qcu-device is to receive CUDA commands from qcu-driver and execute related operations in the host. It also needs to store variables for

CUDA events and CUDA streams. When a program uses CUDA event in a virtual machine, a CUDA event in qCUDA virtio device is created and its index is sent back to the user program.

Because the memory pages allocated in guest VM have different addresses in the host machine, direct data transferring from VM to GPU without address translation is impossible. Different GPGPU virtualization methods utilize various approaches to solve this problem. For example, in rCUDA, the data are transferred by the network socket or RPC channel, but it requires extra data copy between the guest and host [7,8,20], which increases the latency of data movement.

3.2   Memory Allocation in qCUDA-ARM

The architecture of qCUDA-ARM is basically the same as qCUDA, as shown in Fig. 1. The major difference is the memory management. More specifically, the allocation of page-lock memory, or called pinned memory, are entirely different.

Normally, the memory allocated by `malloc()` is pageable, Which means the allocated memory region can be paged in/paged out by the OS. To improve the memory access performance, a programmer can allocate data with pinned memory using `cudaHostAlloc()` or `cudaHostRegister()` provided by CUDA runtime APIs. The difference between them is that `cudaHostAlloc()` first allocates a memory region and then page-lock this region, while `cudaHostRegister()` takes an already allocated memory region as input and page-lock it.

The function `cudaHostAlloc()` function cannot be directly used by qCUDA since the pinned memory should be seen in the host. Hence, qCUDA implements the function `cudaHostRegister()` by modifying `malloc()`. If a memory region will be registered as a pinned memory, qCUDA calls `cudaHostAlloc()` inside `malloc()`. After all, `cudaHostAlloc()` is conceptually equal to `malloc()` plus `cudaHostRegister()`.

Figure 2 shows the flow of allocating the pinned memory in qCUDA using `cudaHostAlloc()`. It has four steps.

1. When a CDUA program allocates pinned memory with `cudaHostAlloc()` in VM, the qcu-library executes the hooked `malloc()` to allocate a continuous memory region in Guest Virtual Address(GVA).
2. Since the hooked `malloc()` is a wrapper of `mmap()` system call, it will synchronously trigger the `mmap()` file operation in qcu-driver and allocate several memory chunks. Each of these memory chunk is physically contiguous in Guest Physical Address (GPA) and they are encapsulated as a group, as described in Sect. 3.1.
3. The qcu-device creates a device file under/dev directory and maps each memory chunk onto this file iteratively, so any operation toward this file on the host is equal to access the memory allocated in the guest. At this moment, the guest allocated memory can be accessed from the host but still can be page-out by the OS.
4. Each memory chunk are page-locked on host by calling `cudaHostRegister()`.

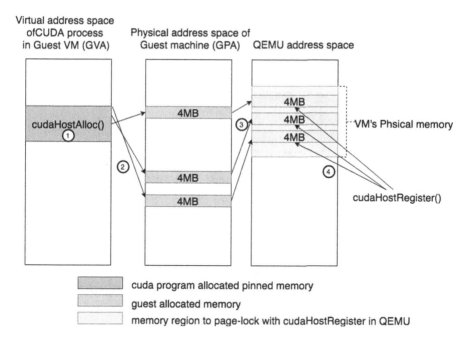

Fig. 2. The pinned memory allocation by `cudaHostAlloc()` in qCUDA

However, `cudaHostRegister()` is supported only on I/O coherent devices
[1] which do not include ARM architecture because the caching attribute of an
existing allocation cannot be changed on the fly. As the result, qCUDA-ARM
needs to implement `cudaHostAlloc()` in a different way. The idea is allocating
another pinned memory region and maps this region back to the memory region
allocated by guest CUDA program.

Figure 3 shows the flow of memory allocation for pinned memory in qCUDA-
ARM. It has five steps. Step 1 to step 3 are identical to the flow in qCUDA,
which allocate guest memory regions, but the allocated memory regions are not
pinned. We call these memory region as guest memory region on host (GMR).
The guest pinned memory that can be accessed from the host via the device
node under /dev directory, is called GMR_fd.

The step 4 and step 5 are described as follows

4. qcu-device calls the `cudaHostAlloc()` function to allocate another page-lock
   memory region on the host, called host pinned memory (HPM), which has
   the same size as GMR.
5. qcu-device calls `mmap()` system call with MAP_SHARED flag to map GMR_fd
   into HPM.

Since MAP_SHARED flag is specified, any updates on GMR_fd are visible to
HPM and vise versa. This operation make the data content identical on both
region and can be transparently transferred from guest to host GPU or vise
versa.

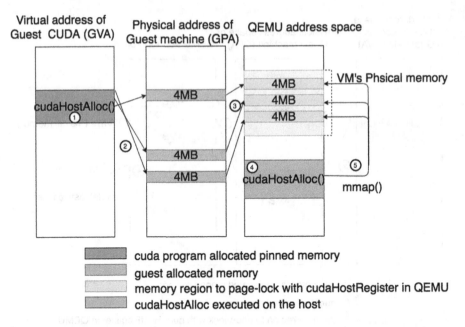

Fig. 3. The pinned memory allocation by `cudaHostAlloc()` in qCUDA-ARM.

Although the memory mapping method of qCUDA-ARM needs additional memory region, which is inefficient, it can be used to accelerate the performance of `cudaMemcpy()` and `cudaMemcpyAsync()`. The function `cudaMemcpy` and `cudaMemcpyAsync()` are used to copy data between host memory and GPU memory. Their difference is that `cudaMemcpyAsync()` is an asynchronous operation with respect to the host, so the call may return before the copy is complete. For convenience, we use only `cudaMemcpy()` to illustrate the idea.

The memory region allocated by `cudaHostAlloc()` of qCUDA is a set of memory chunks. Since these memory chunks are separately distributed in the host virtual address space, when the guest CUDA program needs to copy this memory region to/from the GPU memory, qcu-device requires multiple function calls of `cudaMemcpy()`, which delegates the bandwidth performance.

In qCUDA-ARM, the HPM region is contiguous and it's content is identical to GMR, so we can leverage on this region to reduce the number of memory copy into one in qcu-device. Figure 4 shows the memory copy process of qCUDA-ARM. When the guest CUDA program calls `cudaMemcpy()`, it provides `src`, the starting address of memory region to be transferred. This address needs to be converted from the memory space of GMR (Guest Memory Region on Host) to HPM (Host Pinned Memory). Let the starting address of GMR and HPM are `GMR_ptr` and `HPM_ptr` respectively. The offset between `src` and `GMR_ptr` can be calculated by `src-GMR_ptr`. So the starting address of the region to be transferred in HPM, named `src'`, is

$$HPM\_ptr + (src - GMR\_ptr). \tag{1}$$

By replace `src` to `src'` in qcu-device, the data can be transferred with only one `cudaMemcpy()` invocation.

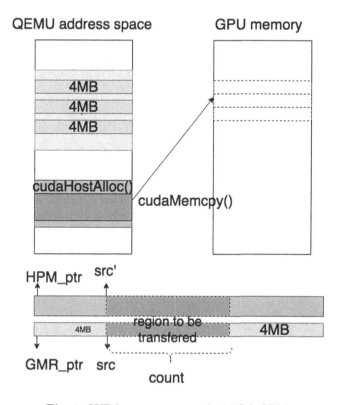

Fig. 4. CUDA memory copy of qCUDA-ARM

4   Experiments

We have three sets of experiments. The first set of experiments evaluate the performance of qCUDA-ARM using three benchmark programs: BandwidthTest, MatrixMultiply, and VectorAdd. The second set of experiments evaluate the scalability of qCUDA-ARM, in which more than one VMs are executed simultaneously to show the performance changes. The last set of experiments run two real world applications, Edge Detection and Cryptocurrency Miner, to show more realistic performance data. Each result is the average from 20 experiments.

All the experiments are compared qCUDA-ARM's performance with native GPU system. These experiments are conducted on Nvidia TX2 development board, which has four ARM-A57 cores, two Denver 64-bit CPUs, 8 GB L128 bit DDR4 Memory, 2 GB eMMC 5.1 Flash for storage and Nvidia Pascal GPU. The

GPU is of compute capability 6.2 and equipped with two streaming multiprocessors (SM), each of which provides 128 1.3-GHz cores that share a 512-KB L2 cache.

The TX2 runs Ubuntu 16.04 LTS with our modified Linux Tegra-Ubuntu 4.4.38 kernel and with CUDA toolkit version 8.0 installed, which includes NVCC compiler, runtime libraries, device driver and CUDA sample codes. Each virtual machine has 4 cores, 4 GB of RAM, 16 GB QCOW2 format disk image and running Ubuntu 14.04.5 LTS with Tegra-Ubuntu 4.2.0-19-generic kernel and with CUDA toolkit version 8.0 installed.

4.1   Benchmarks

Memory Bandwidth. This experiment measures the bandwidth between host memory and device memory by Nvidia's bandwidthTest benchmark to estimate the data transferring rates from host to device (H2D) and from device to host (D2H). The data size is from 1 KB to 1 GB, doubled the data size at each step.

We compared the performance of bandwidthTest for two kinds of memory allocation methods: pinned and pageable. For most memory intensive applications, pinned memory will be used. We can see their performance differences in the experiments.

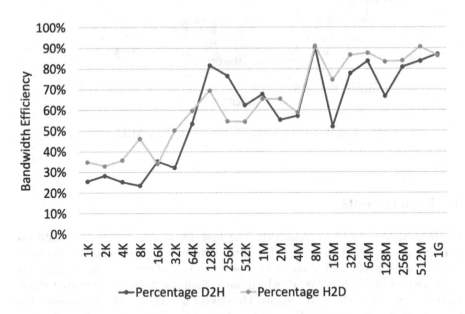

Fig. 5. qCUDA-ARM bandwidth efficiency (pinned memory)

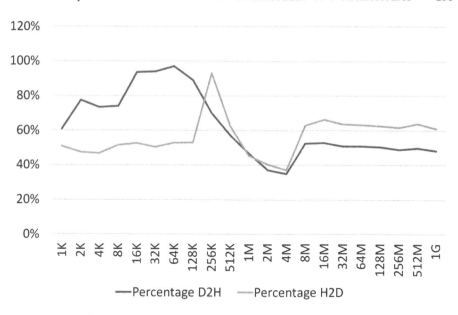

Fig. 6. qCUDA-ARM bandwidth efficiency (pageable memory)

Figure 5 shows the bandwidth efficiency of pinned memory for qCUDA-ARM comparing to the native CUDA. The X-axis is data size in byte and Y-axis is the bandwidth efficiency, which is defined as

$$\frac{\text{bandwidth of qCUDA-ARM}}{\text{bandwidth of native}} \times 100\% \tag{2}$$

As can be seen, for both H2D and D2H, qCUDA-ARM can achieve up to 90% of the native CUDA, and the averages are around 80%. The curves show the trend of performance. The larger data to transfer, the better bandwidth efficiency is. It is because no matter how large the data size is, the overhead of virtualization, mainly for address conversion, is almost fixed. So the efficiency can approach the native. However, there are still fluctuations, which should be caused by the allocation process to find large enough free space.

The second experiment evaluates the bandwidth efficiency of pageable memory by using the modified bandwidthTest benchmark. Figure 6 shows the result, in which the definition of bandwidth efficiency is the same as (2). Although for D2H or H2D, qCUDA-ARM can achieve more than 80% of the native CUDA performance in some cases, the average is around 60%, much lower than that of the pinned memory.

Moreover, as the data size grows, the efficiency decreases. The reason is that qCUDA-ARM uses the same mechanism as qCUDA for allocating pageable memory, which is chunk by chunk. So the larger data, the more virtualization overhead. However, it can be also seen that the curves are much smoother than those in the first experiments. The reason should be the allocation of small continuous memory chunks are much easier than allocating a large continuous memory space.

Matrix Multiplication. Matrix matrix multiplication $C = AB + C$ is a compute-bound benchmark with time complexity of $O(n^3)$ for an $n \times n$ matrix A and B.

Figure 7 shows the total elapsed time of this benchmark on both qCUDA-ARM and native CUDA. The X-axis is the matrix dimension, which is ranged from 32 to 4096, and the Y-axis shows two types of data. The first is the execution time, in milliseconds, on physical machine (PM) and on virtual machine (VM). The second type is the performance ratio, compared to the native CUDA, whose definition is

$$\frac{\text{Execution time on VM}}{\text{Execution time on PM}} \times 100\% \qquad (3)$$

As can be seen, the performance gap of qCUDA-ARM and native CUDA is shrunken as the dimension n grows. This is because the most time in matrix matrix multiplication is spent on computation, which does not influenced by the API remoting method.

Vector Addition. The benchmark vectorAdd computes $C = A + B$, where A, B and C are all vectors of dimension n. It is an I/O-bound problem (H2D/D2H), as can be seen in the program profile later.

Figure 8 shows the total execution time of this benchmark at both qCUDA-ARM and native machine. The X-axis is vector length, from 10^6 to 256×10^6, and Y-axis shows to types of data. The first of execution time (in milliseconds) of physical machine (PM) and of virtual machine (VM). The second is the performance ratio, as defined in (3). As can be seen, for smaller vector size, the performance of qCUDA-ARM is similar to that to native. However, as the vector size grows, the performance degradation of qCUDA-ARM increases. For $n = 128M$, qCUDA-ARM can achieve only 65% performance of native CUDA.

4.2   Scalability

We evaluated the scalability of qCUDA-ARM on TX2 using multiple qCUDA-ARM, which can share single GPU to multiple VMs at the same time.

Memory Bandwidth. For memory bandwidth, we run the benchmark on one, two, three, and four virtual machines simultaneously. For native CUDA, we also run one to four benchmarks at the same time. The data size if fixed to 256 MB.

Figure 9 show the bandwidth efficiency of pinned memory for qCUDA-ARM and native CUDA. The X-axis is the number of VM, and the y-axis shows the averaged bandwidth efficiency, defined in (2), from multiple VMs. The results for H2D and D2H are similar. Although bandwidth ratio decreases at the number of

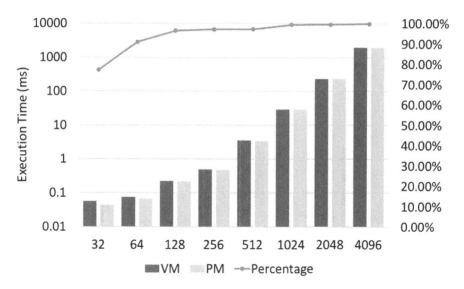

Fig. 7. Matrix multiplication performance.

VM increases, the performance degradation is slow. The pageable memory has similar result, except its degradation is larger.

The performance ratio, as defined in (3), of matrix-matrix multiplication is almost a constant for one VM, two VMs, three VMs and four VMs, which are nearly 100%, when the matrix size is larger than 512×512.

4.3   Real Applications

In this section we used two real world applications to evaluate the performance of qCUDA-ARM. One is edge detection, which is usually used in the pre-processing of object detection, image segmentation, and many other computer vision applications. Another one is the cryptocurrency miner, which is a popular application hungry for any computing resources.

Sobel Edge Detection. This benchmark is a GPGPU implementation of Sobel Operator, which aims to identify the edges of the objects in an image. The Sobel operator uses a pair of 3×3 convolution masks: one estimating the gradient in the x-direction and the other estimating the gradient in the y–direction.

Figure 10 shows the performance results on both native and qCUDA-ARM. The X-axis is the resolution, which are $1920 \times 1080(6$ MB$)$, $4928 \times 3624(47$ MB$)$ and $12000 \times 6000(130$ MB$)$, and the Y-axis shows two types of data. The first one is the Frame Per Second (FPS) on physical machine (PM) and on virtual machine (VM). The second type of data is the performance degradation, calculated by

$$\frac{\text{FPS of VM}}{\text{FPS of PM}} \times 100\%. \tag{4}$$

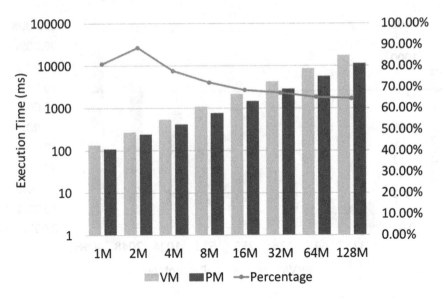

Fig. 8. Execution time of vectorAdd of qCUDA-ARM and CUDA native and their performance ratio.

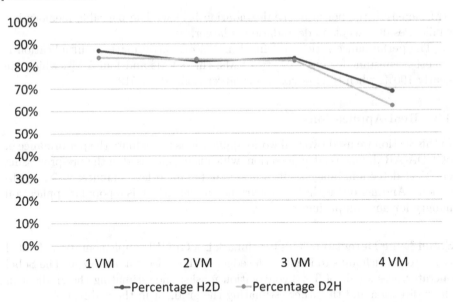

Fig. 9. Bandwidth efficiency of multiple VMs and native CUDA. (pinned memory)

The results in Fig. 10 tell that the larger images, the less performance degradation. Figure 11 displays the stacked percentage of execution time in each parts of edge detection for both native CUDA and qCUDA-ARM. It can be clearly

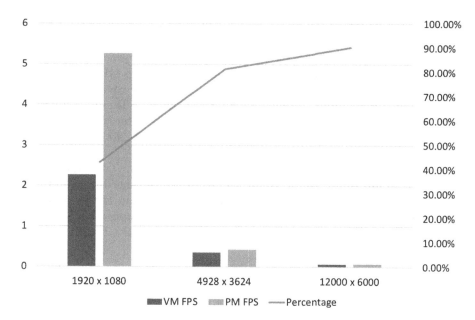

Fig. 10. The Frame per Second of Sobel edge detection on native CUDA and qCUDA-ARM.

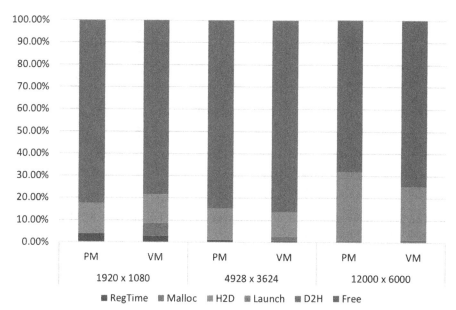

Fig. 11. Profile of the Sobel edge detection execution time for VM and PM.

seen that the Sobel edge detection is an IO bound problem. The bandwidthTest benchmark shows for larger data, the better performance.

Cryptocurrency Miner. The cryptocurrency miner is an application to search the special patterns that can be only discovered by brute-force method. The one we used takes a string of size 20 as the block header and generates Message-Digest Algorithm (MD5) hash code of this string. It utilizes GPU to calculate all possible MD5 in parallel to find an hash that is lower or equal to the target hash. It also takes another variable ACCEPTED_ZEROS to indicate the required number of leading zeros for the calculated hash. The parameter ACCEPTED_ZEROS controls the difficulty of block mining: the larger ACCEPTED_ZEROS is, the more computation is required.

We compared the performance of qCUDA-ARM and native CUDA, and plotted the results in Fig. 12. The X-axis is ACCEPTED_ZEROS, ranged from 25 to 35, and the Y-axis shows the execution time in millisecond and the performance ratio, as defined in (3). The result shows that for such application, qCUDA-ARM can still maintain around 80% performance of the native CUDA.

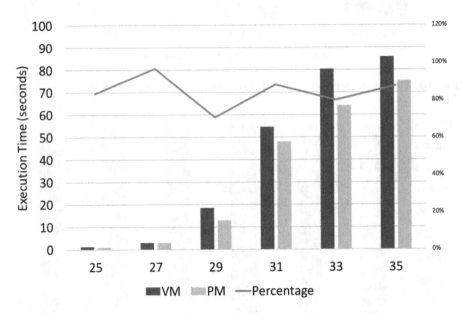

Fig. 12. The execution time of cryptocurrency miner for qCUDA-ARM and native VM, and their performance ratio.

5   Conclusion

In this paper, we presented a GPGPU virtualization solution for ARM architecture, called qCUDA-ARM, which is based on the qCUDA framework. We modified the qCUDA's memory management so that it can be run on ARM architecture. Although we used double sized space for pinned memory, the performance can be improved significantly. We evaluated qCUDA's performance using three benchmarks and two real world applications. For bandwidth test, qCUDA-ARM can achieve up to 90% of the native CUDA on TX2 for pinned memory. For computation bound applications, such as matrix-matrix multiplication, it can also have near native performance.

Since this is the first work to virtualize the GPU on ARM architecture, there are still many future directions to explore. First, for pinned memory, our solution, although having good performance, is not memory efficient. Better solutions should be researched and developed. Second, for IOT applications on edge nodes, light weight virtualization method should be investigated. For heterogeneous systems, this remains an open problem. Last, more tests on real IOT applications and their concurrent execution on single edge node should be conducted to reveal the properties of edge computing, from which new generation of architecture can be built.

References

1. CUDA toolkit document 5.9 memory management. https://docs.nvidia.com/cuda/cuda-runtime-api
2. Mediatek Helio. https://en.wikichip.org/wiki/mediatek/helio
3. Programming guide: CUDA toolkit documentation. https://docs.nvidia.com/cuda/cuda-c-programming-guide/index.html/
4. Amert, T., Otterness, N., Yang, M., Anderson, J.H., Smith, F.D.: GPU scheduling on the NVIDIA TX2: hidden details revealed. In: 2017 IEEE Real-Time Systems Symposium (RTSS), pp. 104–115. IEEE (2017)
5. Bonomi, F., Milito, R., Zhu, J., Addepalli, S.: Fog computing and its role in the internet of things. In: 2012 First Edition of the MCC Workshop on Mobile Cloud Computing, pp. 13–16 (2012)
6. Celesti, A., Mulfari, D., Fazio, M., Villari, M., Puliafito, A.: Exploring container virtualization in IoT clouds. In: 2016 IEEE International Conference on Smart Computing, pp. 1–6 (2016)
7. Duato, J., Peña, A.J., Silla, F., Mayo, R., Quintana-Ortí, E.S.: rCUDA: reducing the number of GPU-based accelerators in high performance clusters, pp. 224–231 (2010)
8. Giunta, G., Montella, R., Agrillo, G., Coviello, G.: A GPGPU transparent virtualization component for high performance computing clouds. In: D'Ambra, P., Guarracino, M., Talia, D. (eds.) Euro-Par 2010. LNCS, vol. 6271, pp. 379–391. Springer, Heidelberg (2010). https://doi.org/10.1007/978-3-642-15277-1_37
9. Gottschlag, M., Hillenbrand, M., Kehne, J., Stoess, J., Bellosa, F.: LoGV: low-overhead GPGPU virtualization. In: 2013 IEEE 10th International Conference on High Performance Computing and Communications and 2013 IEEE International Conference on Embedded and Ubiquitous Computing, pp. 1721–1726 (2013)
10. Gubbi, J., Buyya, R., Marusic, S., Palaniswami, M.: Internet of things (IoT): a vision, architectural elements, and future directions. Future Gener. Comput. Syst. **29**, 1645–1660 (2013)
11. Guo, C., et al.: BCube: a high performance, server-centric network architecture for modular data centers. In: Proceedings of the ACM SIGCOMM 2009 Conference on Data Communication (2009)

12. Hsu, H.C., Lee, C.R.: G-KVM: a full GPU virtualization on KVM. In: 2016 IEEE International Conference on Computer and Information Technology, pp. 545–552 (2016)
13. Jones, R.W.: Optimizing QEMU boot time. http://oirase.annexia.org/tmp/paper.pdf
14. Kato, S., McThrow, M., Maltzahn, C., Brandt, S.: Gdev: first-class GPU resource management in the operating system. In: Proceedings of the 2012 USENIX Conference on Annual Technical Conference, USENIX ATC 2012, p. 37. USENIX Association, Berkeley (2012)
15. Tian, K., Dong, Y., Cowperthwaite, D.: A full GPU virtualization solution with mediated pass-through. In: USENIX ATC 2014 Proceedings of the 2014 USENIX Conference on USENIX Annual Technical Conference, pp. 121–132 (2014)
16. Tong, L., Li, Y., Gao, W.: A hierarchical edge cloud architecture for mobile computing. In: The 35th Annual IEEE International Conference on Computer Communications, pp. 1–9 (2016)
17. Morabito, R., Kjällman, J., Komu, M.: Hypervisors vs. lightweight virtualization: a performance comparison. In: 2015 IEEE International Conference on Cloud Engineering, pp. 386–393, March 2015. https://doi.org/10.1109/IC2E.2015.74
18. Markthub, P., Nomura, A., Matsuoka, S.: mrCUDA: low-overhead middleware for transparently migrating CUDA execution from remote to local GPUs. In: Presented at the SC15 Conference (2015)
19. Russell, R.: Virtio: towards a de-facto standard for virtual I/O devices. In: ACM SIGOPS Operating Systems Review - Research and Developments in the Linux Kernel, pp. 95–103 (2008)
20. Shi, L., Chen, H., Sun, J., Li, K.: vCUDA: GPU-accelerated high-performance computing in virtual machines. IEEE Trans. Comput. **61**(6), 804–816 (2012)
21. Stevens, A.: Introduction to amba® 4 ace™ and big. little™ processing technology. ARM White Paper, CoreLink Intelligent System IP by ARM (2011)
22. Suzuki, Y., Kato, S., Yamada, H., Kono, K.: GPUvm: GPU virtualization at the hypervisor. IEEE Trans. Comput. **65**, 2752–2766 (2015)
23. Suzuki, Y., Kato, S., Yamada, H., Kono, K.: GPUvm: why not virtualizing GPUs at the hypervisor? In: 2014 USENIX Annual Technical Conference, USENIX ATC 2014, pp. 109–120 (2014)
24. Zhu, J., Chan, D.S., Prabhu, M.S., Natarajan, P., Hu, H., Bonomi, F.: Improving web sites performance using edge servers in fog computing architecture. In: 2013 IEEE Seventh International Symposium on Service-Oriented System Engineering, pp. 320–323 (2013)

A Workflow Interoperability Approach Based on Blockchain

Yuchen Fang, Xuanzhao Tang, Maolin Pan[(⊠)], and Yang Yu

School of Data and Computer Science, Sun Yat-sen University, Guangzhou, China
{panml,yuy}@mail.sysu.edu.cn,
{fangych5,tangxzh3}@mail2.sysu.edu.cn

Abstract. Workflow interoperability generally refers to the ability for workflow enactment services to coordinate work. However, the lack of trust is often a roadblock, especially when workflow enactment services interoperate across organizational boundaries. Blockchain technology is a technology for data sharing across a network of untrusted participants. In this paper, we propose a blockchain-based workflow interoperability approach. Workflow enactment services communicate and interoperate with each other via blockchain instead of trusting a central authority, but trust is maintained. Furthermore, blockchain documents interoperation of workflow enactment services, such an audit trail can be used to depict a complete inter-organizational collaboration. Our approach comprises the combination of an interoperability interface and a general interoperability service. Interoperability service runs on a blockchain environment, and workflow enactment services can call interoperability service through their interoperability interface to communicate with each other. We implement the prototype of our approach and demonstrate its feasibility by applying it to an inter-organizational collaboration case. We evaluate our approach mainly via conducting a performance evaluation.

Keywords: Workflow interoperability · Workflow enactment service · Blockchain · Inter-organizational collaboration

1 Introduction

A process represents a coordinated set of process activities to achieve a common goal, and a process instance is one individual enactment of a process. Workflow enactment service (WES), as an essential component of Workflow Management Systems, provides the runtime environment to create, manage, and execute process instances [1]. Many organizations use WES to manage their business process. Considering the suitability, organizations usually select WESs from different workflow vendors. An inter-organizational collaboration always involves multiple business processes, which requires their WESs to communicate and interoperate to coordinate work. In general, WESs of different vendors are diverse, and heterogeneous WESs interoperability remains an important topic.

© Springer Nature Switzerland AG 2020
C.-H. Hsu et al. (Eds.): IOV 2019, LNCS 11894, pp. 303–317, 2020.
https://doi.org/10.1007/978-3-030-38651-1_24

Previous researches about workflow interoperability focus more on interoperability method and communication message exchange format. WESs can request, respond, or notify through a formatted message to complete different interoperation. One weakness of prior research is lack of trust. They do not focus on documenting interoperation of WESs via a trusted approach, nor can they guarantee the indisputable records. However, in a collaboration, tamper-proof and traceable interoperability records facilitate payment under correct interoperation, or penalizing a participant under incorrect interoperation, etc. Another weakness is that WESs directly interoperate in a peer-to-peer way, but it can not depict a decentralized inter-organizational collaboration easily. It is not easy for multiple WESs to establish a centralized control hub, especially when WESs interoperate across organizational boundaries. Furthermore, The quality of service of each WES is uncertain. Blockchain is a technology for decentralized data sharing across a network of untrusted nodes. Through distributed systems, a tamper-proof cryptographic ledger, and distributed consensus mechanisms, the interoperation across WESs can achieve trust. In recent years, Business Process Management explores the suitability of blockchain to integrate into process integration and choreography. However, they mainly propose solutions for high-level modeling while ignoring interoperability details.

This paper proposes a workflow interoperability approach based on blockchain to solve the weaknesses. WESs interoperate and communicate with each other indirectly via blockchain, instead of trusting a central control hub. This interoperability mechanism is more flexible since prior mutual trust is not required for participants on blockchain to interoperate with each other. Blockchain helps to monitor and manage interoperations in case something goes wrong. In this setting, blockchain serves as an immutable shared database, to store and forward interoperation message with access permission. It creates an immutable audit trail for the interoperation of WESs. The audit trail can be used to depict the realization of a decentralized inter-organizational collaboration, since the interoperation of each process instance is tamper-proof and traceable.

Our contribution is that we propose a blockchain-based workflow interoperability approach. We implement its prototype by which WESs can coordinate with each other, using the Hyperledger Fabric blockchain. We apply it to two inter-organizational collaboration to demonstrate its feasibility. We evaluate the approach mainly in performance analysis.

The remainder of the paper is organized as follows: Sect. 2 discusses the background, especially the related work, to show the limitations of existing approaches. In Sect. 3, we introduce the blockchain-based workflow interoperability approach. Afterwards, we evaluate the approach in Sect. 4. Finally, we conclude the paper with Sect. 5.

2   Background

This section discusses related work, the challenges of workflow interoperability, and the blockchain technology.

2.1   Related Work

In the early research, Workflow Management Coalition (WfMC) put forward various standards to allow workflow systems produced by different workflow vendors to interoperate. [1] described a workflow reference model (WRM), which standardizes components and interfaces of Workflow Management Systems. Basing on the WRM, WESs may interoperate with each other via a crucial interoperability interface, so-called WfMC's Interface 4. Then [2] defined the functionality to support the WfMC's Interface 4, as described in [1]. After that, [3] was put up to model the data transfer requirements set forth in [2]. [3] was based on eXtensible Markup Language (XML) and some specifications [2, 4–6]. Workflow information could be described in XML, enabling Workflow Management Systems of different enterprises to share workflow information, by parsing XML to facilitate interoperability of these systems. Those interoperability specifications standardized the peer-to-peer communication of different WESs, including exchanging data and control information via WfMC's Interfaces 4. They employed an interface-based architecture to interoperability, which made modeling inconvenient. The Workflow Management System might utilize Message-oriented middleware to improve the convenience of modeling dramatically. However, to solve the transparency problem of WESs, different organizations need to use the same Message-oriented middleware for communication, which was unrealistic [7].

Later, with the development of web technology, some more abstract interoperability standards such as Wf-XML2.0 [8], BPEL4WS [9] and its successor WS-BPEL [10] were put forward. In those specifications, a process could be invoked as a web-service, which made interoperability more flexible. However, the sequence of information passed during the interoperation of two WESs should be ordered and complete, while Wf-XML 2.0 lacked a way to maintain a chain of data. Although BPEL uses the Service-Oriented Architecture for process integration, it requires different organizations to identify the central control node, which is often unrealistic. Confronted with cross-organizational border collaboration, those standards based on web service were still deficiencies.

Nowadays, A high-level modeling language BPMN 2.0 [11] uses choreography to formalize business process integration and masks the interoperability details of WESs by using high-level modeling of graphical symbols. However, choreography lacks the central control hub of an inter-organization process, which often leads to trust issues [12] that hamper inter-organizational collaboration [13]. Since Nakamoto et al. [14] proposed a peer-to-peer electronic currency trading system, Blockchain technology has received extensive attention and discussion in the field of workflow and BPM [15]. Blockchain technology has been tried to solve the trust problem in process integration. [16] proposed a method for monitoring and coordinating business processes based on blockchain technology. This approach ensures the credibility of collaboration but remains low flexibility. Each time the collaboration process changes, it needs to be remodeled. [17] made improvements in terms of throughput, and latency, etc. based on the research [16]. In runtime verification for choreography, [18] proposed to use the blockchain to monitor and verify the runtime process instance.

2.2   Challenges of Workflow Interoperability

As shown in Fig. 1, Multiple WESs interoperate constitutes an open distributed system, which is inherently dynamic, highly autonomous, and open. Such a system lacks centralized control mechanisms, interactive security, and guaranteed service quality. Without modeling and management of interoperability message sequences, that interoperability messages are tamper-proof can not be guaranteed. So lack-of-trust problem with interoperability possibly exists, especially when confronted with inter-organization collaboration. Anyway, in multi-organizational collaboration, a tamper-proof message sequence is helpful to monitor and manage problems that may arise in collaboration.

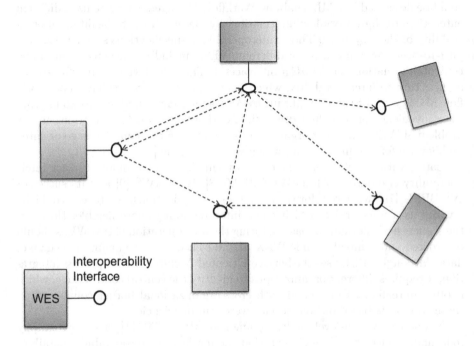

Fig. 1. Multiple WESs interoperate in a peer-to-peer way

Meanwhile, most of the existing process integration research mainly discussed and modelled from the theoretical level, and rarely focus on the interoperability implementation level. Furthermore, the combination of blockchain and process collaboration has not been studied from the interoperability implementation level.

2.3   Blockchain Technology

The blockchain concept stems from Bitcoin [14], an electronic cryptocurrency system of anonymous peer-to-peer transaction. Blockchain essentially is a continuously growing public distributed ledger that is maintained by multiple parties.

Blockchain technology refers to a solution of diverse technologies, including distributed consensus mechanisms, cryptographic algorithms, etc. Numerous nodes on the blockchain network maintain data through a consensus mechanism, and all these nodes can obtain a data backup. This distributed storage mechanism provides the integrity and consistency of the data. The blockchain uses a time-stamped and chained block structure to store data, ensuring the traceability and verifiability of the data. And cryptography and consensus mechanisms ensure that the data is tamper-proof and confidential.

Some blockchain platforms such as the Ethereum and the Hyperledger Fabric provide a Turing-complete scripting language to create smart contracts [19] and provide a trusted execution environment for smart contracts. A smart contract running on a blockchain is an event-driven program and automatically processes assets, data, or value based on preset conditions [20]. Furthermore, Hyperledger Fabric provides some characteristics, such as membership services, restricted public access to data, high-performance scalability, encryption of transaction data. We decided to utilize Hyperledger Fabric because it is more suitable for our interoperability approach.

3 Blockchain-Based Workflow Interoperability Approach

3.1 Conceptual Solution

As shown in Fig. 2, WES interoperate with each other via the Hyperledger Fabric Blockchain. The characteristics of the Fabric Blockchain help to share data between multiple organizations in a decentralized mode. The use of the Fabric Blockchain to model and manage interoperability messages will enable the interoperability records of WESs are traceable and trusted.

Collaboration between organizations requires interoperation between WESs. Each WES only needs to focus on the other WES that directly interoperates with itself, and does not need to know the existence of the third-party WES. WESs only need to expose the necessary business process nodes to each other to a minimum extent and interoperate through these process nodes. When a process instance of a WES executes to a specific node, it can trigger an event and post a notification to the collaborator.

Since the data transmitted via the interoperability interface is closely related to the execution of the internal process instance of the collaborator, it is necessary to record the data. The record of the data must be tamper-proof, which can help to track the process when the process collaboration is wrong. We use the blockchain technology to store data transmitted via interoperability interfaces. Nodes on a blockchain may not belong to the same organization and do not need to trust each other. All nodes jointly maintain data on the blockchain, and each node maintains a complete record copy.

The WES sends messages over a blockchain on a particular process node. When WESs interoperate, they view and update the process instance interoperability status on the blockchain. Changes of the interoperability status of process instances on the blockchain can notify the collaborators promptly. Furthermore,

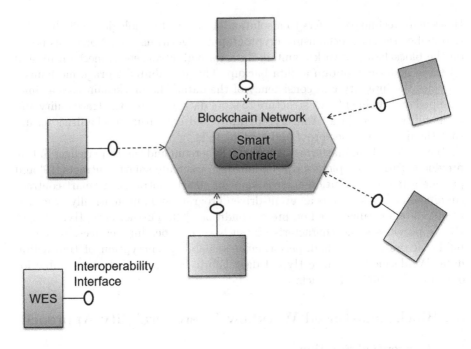

Fig. 2. Multiple WESs interoperate via blockchain

the data transmitted via the interoperability interface will be stored distributedly through the consensus algorithm of the blockchain technology, which ensures the integrity and consistency of the data. The tamper-proof nature of the blockchain guarantees traceability and security of the data.

Process interacts through events, and the communication message between processes allows WES to execute pre-defined internal logic. WES manages the interoperation records of each process instance, maintaining credibility Interoperability history. This interoperability method requires some concepts to support, as shown below:

- **Interoperability Message (IM):** IM is the message exchanged between WESs when they interoperate with each other. IM should include data that is required for the interoperation of WESs, such as workflow relevant data, application data, and workflow control data [1]. The IM can be used to request another WES to create a process instance or to request a process instance to perform a specific task and the like.
- **Interoperability Event (IE):** IE is the pre-announced node of a process. The internal processes in WES interoperate with external processes through such process nodes. Usually, a process has more than one IE. IE can influence the execution of the process. If a WES sends an IM at the IE, it affects the enactment of process instances of other WESs. If a WES receives the IM at the IE, it will affect the enactment of the process instance of its own WES.

– **Process Instance Interoperability Status (PIIS):** PIIS represents the status of a process instance after it completes the interaction with other process instances. A PIIS of a process instance can explain interoperation involves which pair of process instances, and the communication utilizes which couple of IEs to exchange IM.
– **Process Instance Interoperability Status Sequence:** This sequence is capable to express the transition of PIIS of a process instance's in its lifecycle.

Here we explain those concepts by Fig. 3. This Figure depicts a supply chain process adapted from [16], with five organizations participating in a collaborative process. We assume that each organization in the supply chain has a WES to manage its internal processes. The internal processes of each organization are similar to a black box for other organizations. To facilitate communication between WESs, the organization exposes some process events to the direct collaboration parties for interaction before collaboration.

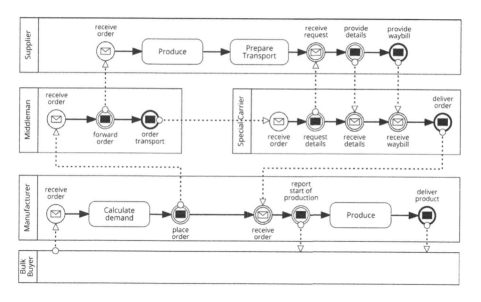

Fig. 3. Supply chain scenario adapted from [16]

Here we focus on how the Supplier's WES interoperates with other WESs and hides some of the details of the collaboration that are invisible to the Supplier, as shown in Fig. 4. In general, a process instance of Supplier will interact with Middleman's process instance and Special Carrier's process instance four times during its life cycle. In the first interaction, the Middleman throws a message through its "forward order" event in its process. Then the Supplier captures the message through its "receive order" event, and executes its internal logic. Such events are IE, and such messages are IM.

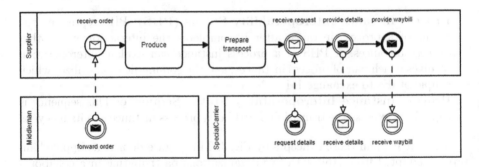

Fig. 4. Supplier's WES interoperate with Middleman's and Special Carrier's

After the Supplier's WES interoperates with other WES through the blockchain, it stores its PIIS in the blockchain. Similarly, other WES can maintain their PIIS sequence. Suppose that in Fig. 4, the Supplier, Middleman, and Special Carrier each runs a process instance, we can get the PIIS sequence diagram shown in Fig. 5. A collection of a certain number of PIIS sequences can express a complete multi-party collaboration process.

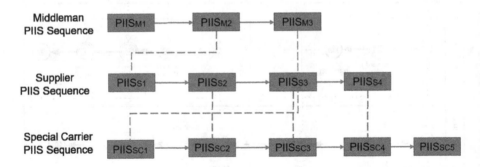

Fig. 5. Section of the supply chain (among Supplier, Middleman and Special Carrier)

3.2 Interoperability Approach Framwork

As shown in Fig. 6, our interoperability method uses the "use of a shared data store" interoperability strategy [6]. This strategy is a form of store-and-forward mechanism that enables WESs to transfer work items through a shared database. In our approach, the blockchain plays such a shared database role, and the WES can communicate and interoperate indirectly through the blockchain. We focus on the management of PIIS. The WES can publish IM or PIIS to the blockchain and add access rights for other WESs to listen. All WESs do not need to interoperate with each other peer-to-peer, while only need to join the blockchain, driven by changes of IM or PIIS on the blockchain.

Our approach is primarily supported by the following two components:

- **Interoperability Service** runs on a blockchain network. Smart contracts are the core of interoperable services. They are an essential component of most types of blockchains and can be automatically executed according to preset conditions. Interoperability services enable direct manipulation of data on the ledger by using smart contracts. At the same time, the interoperability service can also interact with the external world of the blockchain. In this paper, the interoperability service interacts with the WES.
- **Interoperability Interface** connects the WES to the blockchain network. It can call the API to request the interoperability service to update the IM and PIIS on the blockchain, and can also receive timely information from the interoperability service to know the status of the change of the ledger.

3.3 Interoperability Interface

Before WESs interoperate, they need to communicate with each other in advance to agree on necessary IEs and attributes of IM. The specific process of interoperation is that the WES invokes the interoperability service through the interoperability interface, and then the interoperability service operates the data on the blockchain. The change in the status of blockchain can also notify the WESs via Interoperability Service. To support the blockchain-based interoperability method, we need to improve the interoperability interface to a certain extent, so that it can call the interoperability service to exchange messages.

The interoperability interface is supposed to provide six kinds of functions for WESs, namely, send IM, send PIIS, receive IM, receive PIIS, query IM, and query PIIS:

- **Send IM**: The WES throws an IM at the IE, and WES stores the IM on the blockchain via the Interoperability Service. By using data access permission, the IM can be set to be read by the specified WES. Then the IM can be used to require another process to create process instances or perform its specific activities.
- **Receive IM**: The WES uses the Interoperability Service to monitor the status changing of blockchain, and WES receives the specific IM on the blockchain via the Interoperability Service. The IM can be used by the recipient to create a process instance or perform a particular activity in the process instance.
- **Send PIIS**: The WES stores PIIS on the blockchain through the Interoperability Service. The PIIS can be set to be read by some specified WESs.
- **Receive PIIS**: The WES uses the Interoperability Service to monitor the status changing of blockchain, and to read PIIS on the blockchain. The receiver can use such a PIIS to know the completion of interoperation with the other processes.
- **Query IM**: The WES queries the IM record through the Interoperability Service. It can be used to trace and verify in inter-organizational collaboration.

- **Query PIIS**: The WES queries the PIIS record via the Interoperability Service. It can be used to trace and verify in inter-organizational collaboration.

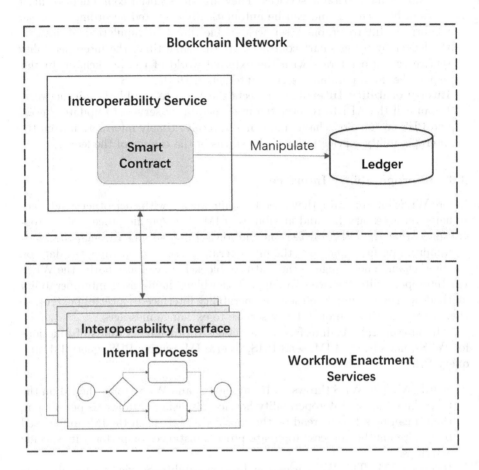

Fig. 6. Overview of our approach

3.4 Interoperability Service

Each WES can join the blockchain and become a blockchain node. The WES cannot directly interact with the blockchain. The interoperability service is equivalent to a connector in the middle of the WES and the blockchain. We need to use smart contracts to set the corresponding business logic for different functions of the interoperability interface so that interoperability services operate on PIIS and IM on the blockchain. As shown in Fig. 7, there are five kinds of functionalities provided by Interoperability Service:

- **Publish Data**: The WES stores data on the blockchain. It will change the status of blockchain.
- **Access Control**: When WES publishes IM, it can set the data to be read or subscribed by the specified collaborator.
- **Subscribe**: WES subscribes to events on the blockchain. When the status of blockchain changes, the WES can receive its target data.
- **Unsubscribe**: WES no more need to pay attention to the events occurring on the blockchain, no more care about the changing status of the ledger, and stop receiving its target data.
- **GetHistory**: WES can read historical self-related interoperability records, which consists of IM Sequence and PIIS Sequence.

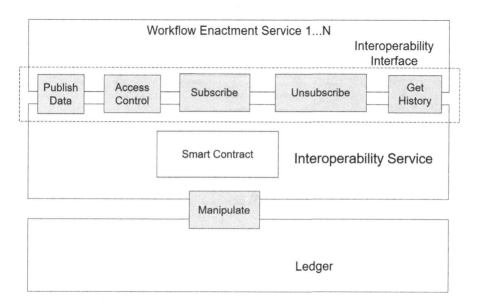

Fig. 7. WESs call Interoperability Service via Interoperability Interface

4   Evaluation

4.1   Experimental Setup

To evaluate the feasibility of the interoperability approach presented in this paper, we implemented an interoperability service prototype. The prototype was implemented by using Hyperledger Composer and Hyperledger Fabric. Figure 8 described the implementation framwork of Interoperability Service. We mainly utilized the Hyperledger Composer tool to build a business network model, using the concepts of Interoperability Services. Then the business network model was

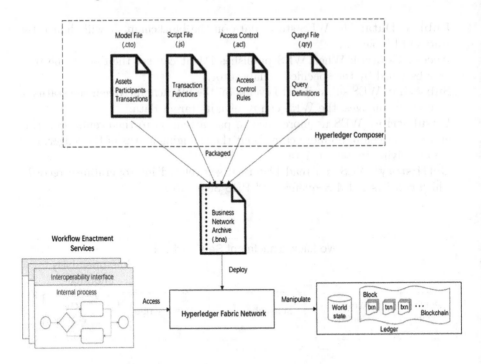

Fig. 8. Implementation Framwork of Interoperability Service

deployed on the Hyperledger Fabric. WESs can interoperate with each other via Hyperledger Fabric.

Then we took the supply chain as the use case process, and we used the Zeebe workflow engine to manage the process. An overview of latency measurements is shown in Fig. 9. In Hyperledger Fabric Blockchain setting, we achieved a median latency of 53 s. Without blockchain, the median latency reached 17 s. Workflow Management is highly tolerant of real-time performance in seconds level. The experimental results show that utilizing the blockchain to interoperate shares one order of magnitude with not-utilizing blockchain to interoperate. So it's acceptable to apply blockchain into workflow interoperability.

4.2   Discussion

Trust. Blockchain technology is used for data sharing across a network of untrusted participants. The traceable and trustworthy PIIS record is helpful to inter-organizational collaboration, especially when something goes wrong in the collaboration, and every organization may come into conflict and hard to reach a consensus with each other.

Flexibility. In fact, the business environment may change dynamically. It's necessary to model a collaborative process in more flexible way. Our solution

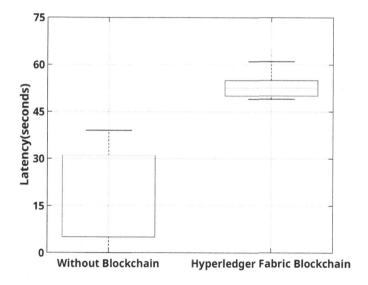

Fig. 9. Latency in seconds, with/without blockchain (box plot)

is flexible enough to meet this requirement. It focuses on interoperation via blockchain. When an enterprise joins or quits a collaboration, all the participants in the collaboration does not need to negotiate specifications and terminology again. Without modeling a whole cross-organizational process again, it only causes partial adjustment of the process collaboration, which cost less.

Privacy. An internal process of an organization is a black box for another organization. They mask most parts of their internal processes, and only expose some IEs to facilitate collaboration across organizational boundaries. At the same time, IM and PIIS are supposed to be read under authorization. With data access permission management, the privacy of the information on the blockchain can be guaranteed. Furthermore, each company does not have the right to monitoring a collaboration, nor can they control the entire cross-organizational process by themselves.

5   Conclusion

By using this method, WESs can interoperate in a trusted manner. Our approach ensures IM sequence and PIIS sequence not only permanently stored in the shared database, but also traceable and tamper-proof. So the lack-of-trust problems of interoperability can be solved. A WES can manage multiple process instances. Each process instance has a PIIS sequence, and a WES can maintain multiple PIIS sequences. In our approach, the blockchain is a tamper-proof data storage that distributes PIIS and IM among WESs. Meanwhile, blockchain also maintains PIIS sequences and IM sequences, generated by all WESs. Each WES can read several PIISs through access permissions. A certain number of

PIIS sequences on a blockchain can show all transitions of the interoperability status of process instances. So the blockchain-based approach could model an inter-organizational collaboration more flexibly.

Acknowledgements. This work is Supported by the National Key Research and Development Program of China under Grant No. 2017YFB0202200; the National Natural Science Foundation of China under Grant Nos. 61972427,61572539; the Research Foundation of Science and Technology Plan Project in Guangzhou City under Grant No. 201704020092.

References

1. Hollingsworth, D., Hampshire, U.: Workflow management coalition: the workflow reference model. Document Number TC00-1003, vol. 19, p. 16 (1995)
2. WfMC, I.: 4–interoperability–abstract specification, WFMC-TC-1012. Technical report (1996)
3. WfMC: Workflow standard-interoperability wf-xml binding (wfmc-tc-1023, version 1.1) (2001)
4. Joint Submitters: Workflow management facility, Revised Submission, OMG Document Number: bom/98-06-07 (1998)
5. W. W. S. Interoperability, Internet e-mail mime binding, document number wfmc-tc-1018
6. Swenson, K.: Simple workflow access protocol. US Patent 6,574,675, 3 June 2003
7. Aldred, L.J.: Fundamentals of process integration, Ph.D. dissertation, Queensland University of Technology (2011)
8. Swenson, K.D., Pradhan, S., Gilger, M.D., Zukowski, M., Cappelaere, P.: Wf-xml 2.0 xml based protocol for run-time integration of process engines, Workflow Management Coalition (2004)
9. Andrews, T., et al.: Business process execution language for web services (2003)
10. Jordan, D., et al.: Web services business process execution language version 2.0, vol. 11, no. 120, p. 5, OASIS standard (2007)
11. BPMN, O.: Business process model and notation (bpmn) (2009)
12. Fdhila, W., Rinderle-Ma, S., Knuplesch, D., Reichert, M.: Change and compliance in collaborative processes. In: 2015 IEEE International Conference on Services Computing, pp. 162–169. IEEE (2015)
13. Panayides, P.M., Lun, Y.V.: The impact of trust on innovativeness and supply chain performance. Int. J. Prod. Econ. **122**(1), 35–46 (2009)
14. Nakamoto, S., et al.: Bitcoin: a peer-to-peer electronic cash system (2008)
15. Mendling, J., et al.: Blockchains for business process management-challenges and opportunities. ACM Trans. Manag. Inf. Syst. (TMIS) **9**(1), 4 (2018)
16. Weber, I., Xu, X., Riveret, R., Governatori, G., Ponomarev, A., Mendling, J.: Untrusted business process monitoring and execution using blockchain. In: La Rosa, M., Loos, P., Pastor, O. (eds.) BPM 2016. LNCS, vol. 9850, pp. 329–347. Springer, Cham (2016). https://doi.org/10.1007/978-3-319-45348-4_19
17. García-Bañuelos, L., Ponomarev, A., Dumas, M., Weber, I.: Optimized execution of business processes on blockchain. In: Carmona, J., Engels, G., Kumar, A. (eds.) BPM 2017. LNCS, vol. 10445, pp. 130–146. Springer, Cham (2017). https://doi.org/10.1007/978-3-319-65000-5_8

18. Prybila, C., Schulte, S., Hochreiner, C., Weber, I.: Runtime verification for business processes utilizing the bitcoin blockchain. Future Gener. Comput. Syst. (2017)
19. Szabo, N.: The idea of smart contracts, Nick Szabo's Papers and Concise Tutorials, vol. 6 (1997)
20. Omohundro, S.: Cryptocurrencies, smart contracts, and artificial intelligence. AI Matters **1**(2), 19–21 (2014)

Air Pollution Forecasting Using LSTM-Multivariate Regression Model

Satheesh Abimannan$^{(\boxtimes)}$, Yue-Shan Chang, and Chi-Yeh Lin

Galgotias University, Greater Noida, Uttar Pradesh, India
satheesha23@gmail.com, ysc@gm.ntpu.edu.tw,
s710783104@webmail.ntpu.edu.tw

Abstract. There are two kinds of air pollutants, such as primary and secondary. Primary pollutants are emitted straight by vehicles such as CO, CO_2, SO_2, NO, NH_3, NO_2, PM10 and PM2.5. Secondary pollutants happen when communicating with each other in the environment. Atmospheric particles or particles, including carbon, sulfur, nitrogen and metal compounds, may be small components or liquid in the environment and consist of hundreds of separate chemicals. Researchers use different machine learning algorithms and struggle to get PM10 and PM2.5 more precise. In this paper, we suggest a regression model for LSTM/Multivariate Variate to predict the more precise PM2.5 value during summer and cold sessions. Finally, the LSTM/MVR model is compared to the LSTM and the outcome demonstrates that the suggested technique efficiently predicts a next one-hour PM2.5 mistake relative to the LSTM error.

Keywords: Air pollution forecasting · LSTM · LSTM-MVR · PM2.5

1 Introduction

Particulate matter (PM) is a term used to define the atmospheric combination of strong particles and fluid droplets. These subtypes are classified by size by scientists. Classified as PM10 are coarse particles with a diameter less than 10 (μm). PM2.5 is categorized as fine particles with a diameter of 2.5 μm or less. The particulate matter measuring unit is microgram per cubic meter. These fine particles are less than 1–28th of a human hair's diameter [1].

Taiwan's air quality has had a severe impact in recent years with fine particulate matter (PM2.5). Fine particulate matter, as illustrated in many studies, presents a significant danger to human health as it causes lung-related diseases [2]. Thus, Taiwan's Environmental Protection Administration (EPA) has created a standard with an average annual PM2.5 concentrations of 15 μg/m^3 and an average 24-hour concentration of 35/μg m^3 [3, 4].

There are two particular sources of PM2.5 pollutions:

i. Primary source is issued by vehicle, truck and other cars directly. Furthermore, retrained from materials discovered on the road (typically referred to as fugitive dust)

© Springer Nature Switzerland AG 2020
C.-H. Hsu et al. (Eds.): IOV 2019, LNCS 11894, pp. 318–326, 2020.
https://doi.org/10.1007/978-3-030-38651-1_25

ii. Secondary Source is the formation that happens owing to atmospheric chemical reaction, usually downwind from a certain distance from the initial source of emission. Precursor emissions like sulfur dioxide (SO_2), nitrogen oxides (NO_x), unstable organic compounds (VOCs) and ammonia (NH_3) are present in secondary formation [5].

PM2.5's chemical structure is Sulfate (24%), Nitrates (13%), Ammonium (13%), Black Carbon (10%), Organic Carbon (27%), Soil (7%), Others (6%) [5].

The research paper [5] demonstrates that the proportion of PM2.5 produced from the primary source is between 10% and 70% and that the secondary source is between 11% and 41%. This finding has been recognized from the United States. However, these main source and secondary source percentage values differed across distinct areas.

Four variables depend on the creation of PM2.5 from organic compounds:

i. Atmospheric abundance
ii. Chemical activity
iii. The availability of oxidants,
iv. Volatility of the products.

All of these variables lead to response times, but volatility plays a major part as extremely volatile chemicals like alkanes and alkenes with less than six carbon atoms are unlikely to form PM2.5.

Measured levels of nitrogen dioxide (NO_2) and carbon monoxide (CO) from Zhangjiakou City play the most significant role in predicting levels of PM2.5. The most immediately relevant influencing variables for the forecast of suspended particulates in local pollutant components are PM2.5 and PM10 levels of the past day [6].

In various seasons, the chemical composition of PM2.5 in a region diverse. For instance, inorganic ions, heavy metals, and organic compounds in PM2.5 have usually been smaller in summer, and sulfates, Al, As, Cr, Cu, and Zn are richer in summer than winter [7–11] XRF assessment revealed levels of 25 components because components such as Sc, Co, Ga, Se, Y, Nb, Mo, Pd, Ag, Cd, In, Sb, Cs, La, Ce, Sm, Eu, Tb, Hf, Ta, Wo, Ir, Au, Hg, Tl, and U were rarely identified at levels greater than three times their corresponding minimum detectable limits [8].

Figure 1 Correlation matrix shows that the positive correlation is PM10, SO_2, O_3, NO_2, NO_x, CO, season and hour, and the negative correlation of PM2.5 is rain, wind speed, temperature, month and week. Therefore, as inputs for the suggested scheme, we use in this paper is PM10, SO_2, O_3, NO_2, NO_x, and CO.

The remainder of the sections will be organized as follows. Section 2 provides the background and work associated with it. The suggested LSTM-MVR technique is described in Sect. 3 and Sect. 4 provides the conclusions of the work.

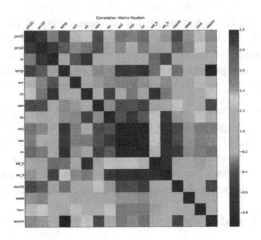

Fig. 1. Correlation matrix of PM2.5

2 Methodology

2.1 Data Source

This research work gathers information from an open database maintained by the Taiwan Government; this data is collected from over 70 air quality-monitoring sites in various Taiwanese regions via the EPA, and publishes sensitive air data every hour through an open web database. Also, the Central Weather Bureau (CWB) has built an automatic weather station in terms of weather data and the information is available every hour. In this work, we combine the three sub-trainings, namely local data, near station data, Chimney and abroad data using 17 dimensions of data and 67 stations. The 17 dimensions of each location are used as training data between 2013 and 2016 and as test data in 2018. The following sub-sections discuss the three categories of the dataset which we used in this research work.

2.2 Data Sample

The local data are collected from EPA and CWB. Table 1 shows the data fields used in the data set of the local station. The data is 17 dimensions of which 13 dimensions such as PM2.5, PM10, SO_2, O_3, NO, NO_2, NO_x, CO, Rainfall, Data time, Month, Weekday, and Hour are from EPA station data, three dimensions are from time data, and the remaining is from CWB station data such as Temperature, Humidity, Wind Speed and Wind Direct.

The concentration value of PM2.5 over the year is shown in Fig. 2. It indicates the PM2.5 concentration information from the twelve months of Hualien. Hualien is Taiwan's eastern part, while the amount of sectors is very small compared to other locations. Figure 2 therefore indicates that the highest PM2.5 value is 30 $\mu g/m^3$. On November, December, January and February, the levels of PM2.5 are very high.

Table 1. Local dataset

Variables	Unit
Real-time concentration	
PM2.5, PM10	$\mu g/m^3$
SO_2, O_3, NO, NO_2, NO_x	ppb
CO	ppm
Sea level pressure atmosphere	Pa
Temperature	°C
Humidity	%
Hour mean concentration	
Wind speed	m/sec
Wind direct	degrees
Hour accumulated concentration	
Rainfall	mm
Date time	
Month	1 to 12
Weekday	0 to 6
Hour	0 to 23

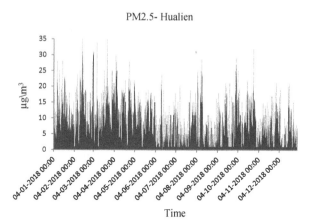

PM2.5- Hualien

Fig. 2. Eastern part of Taiwan

2.3 LSTM-MVR Model

Long Short-Term Memory (LSTM) can almost seamlessly model problems with different input factors. LSTM has an enormous benefit in time series forecasting, where traditional linear methods are difficult to adapt to multivariate or multiple input forecasting problems. In this paper, we adopted LSTM model for multivariate time series forecasting in the Keras deep learning library to forecast the PM2.5 value.

2.3.1   Multivariate Regression Model

Multiple linear regression is the most common form of linear regression analysis. As a predictive analysis, the multiple linear regression is used to explain the relationship between one continuous dependent variable and two or more independent variables.

Let x be the set of independent variable and r be a set of dependent variables denoted by:

$$x = \{x_1, x_2, \ldots x_n\} \tag{1}$$

$$r = \{y_1\} \tag{2}$$

The general regression equation is,

$$y_1 = a_0 + a_1 x_1 + a_2 x_2 + \ldots + a_n x_n \tag{3}$$

Where $a_1, a_2, a_3, \ldots a_n$ are the coefficients.

Table 1 demonstrates the LSTM/MVR model's R^2 value. Eastern Taiwan's R^2 value is 65%. Which is less of the other portion of Taiwan compared to the other portion of Taiwan, the R^2 value of which is above 75%, the analysis part is not included in this paper.

2.4   Error Measurements

Mean absolute error (MAE), root mean square error (RMSE) are used to evaluate the performance of the proposed hybrid model. The MAE value reveals the average deviation between the actual data and forecasting data. The RMSE is sensitive to the relatively close to the ground and carrying a lot of weight error and reflects refined average departure from the norm of forecasting data. MAE and RMSE defined as in (4) and (5),

$$\text{MAE} = \frac{1}{N} \sum_{n=1}^{N} |f_n - R_n| \tag{4}$$

$$\text{RMSE} = \sqrt{\frac{1}{N} \sum_{n=1}^{N} (f_n - R_n)^2} \tag{5}$$

Where, N is the number of data, f_n is the forecast value of the model and R_n is real value.

3   Case Study

The input information from 67 surveillance stations in Taiwan since 2013 are gathered in this research work. It is considered to be a collection of training information in 2013 to 2018. We have categorized the information set into two categories (i) season wise (Summer and Cold) (ii) region wise. In the existing work, many machine learning algorithms are using by the scientists to predict the PM2.5 value. One of the finest algorithms in existence is LSTM. We are therefore benchmarking the suggested LSTM-MVR algorithm with LSTM in this research paper.

A. *Forecasting Result and Analysis on Cold Season (Jan'18–Feb'18)*

The proposed LSTM-MVR algorithm is benchmarking with LSTM on cold season. The Fig. 3 shows that the LSTM and LSTM-MVR are compare with the real value on eastern part of Taiwan. The PM2.5 value is minimum on eastern part of Taiwan (shows in Fig. 3, the number of factories are lower in eastern part compared to other parts. In this paper, forecasting the PM2.5 value using LSTM and LSTM-MVR for one hour to next 24 h. The result shows that the PM2.5 increases continuously every hours ups and downs moderately. The forecasting of the LSTM algorithm is not closely matched to the actual value, but the predicted value of the LSTM-MVR algorithms is closer to the actual value. The real value and the LSTM-MVR value are discovered to be more precise in the 9th and 15th hours. The LSTM forecast value after 11th hour is somewhat near (Fig. 3).

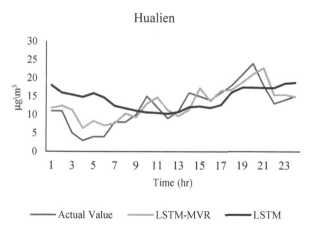

Fig. 3. PM$_{2.5}$ actual value compared to LSTM and LSTM-MVR on cold season in Hualien

B. *Forecasting Result and Analysis on Summer Season (July 2018–August 2018)*

Figure 4 demonstrates the comparison of PM2.5's real value with LSTM and LSTM-MVR forecasting. Figure 4 indicates the summer season PM2.5 value for eastern Taiwan. PM2.5's minimum and maximum value is 0 µg/m^3 and 10 µg/m^3. The minimum value of PM2.5 in the cold season is 10 µg/m^3 and the highest value is 25 µg/m^3. In this paper, only the July 2018-month information is considered. The outcome of the forecast may vary considering the entire summer and cold season.

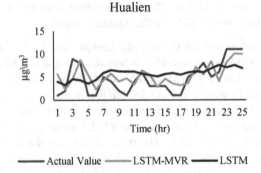

Fig. 4. PM$_{2.5}$ actual value compared to LSTM and LSTM-MVR on summer season in Hualien

C. *Error Measures*

Figures 5 and 6 shows the summer and cold season MAE of the eastern part of Taiwan. The measurement of efficiency is likened between one and eight hours. LSTM's output is very poor in the first hour compared to LSTM-MVR. LSTM-MVR delivers well over 50% effectiveness compared to LSTM. The output of LSTM and LSTM-MVR is more comparable in the 5th to 7th hour. The LSTM-MVR works better than LSTM in the ongoing period from 1st to 8th hour.

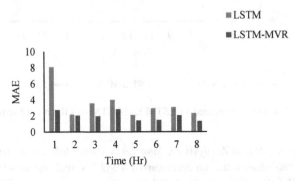

Fig. 5. Hualian MAE summer season

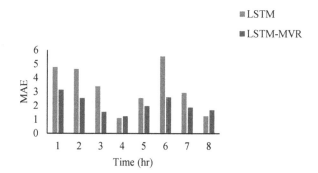

Fig. 6. Hualian MAE cold season

4 Conclusion

We have suggested the LSTM-MVR model in this research paper to enhance air pollution forecast, especially PM2.5 and to compare it with LSTM. The suggested model of LSTM-MVR can efficiently decrease error rate on MAE and RMSE as compared to LSTM. LSTM-MVR model has dramatically enhanced the forecast of air pollution, although there is still space for enhancement. However, air pollutant concentration continues hard to estimate due to the multiplicity of sources and complexity of physical and chemical processes that affect the formation and transportation of air pollutants. In our future work, we need to concentrate on new techniques of anticipating PM2.5 and PM10 levels to overcome the experience of difficulty in this study.

Acknowledgment. This work was partially supported by Ministry of Science and Technology of Taiwan, Republic of China under Grant No. MOST 106-3114-M-305-001-A and MOST 108-2119-M-305-001-A and by National Taipei University under Grant No. 106-NTPU_A-H&E-143-001, 107-NTPU_A-H&E-143-001 and 108-NTPU_A-H&E-143-001. And we are grateful to the Taiwan Environmental Protection Administration and Taiwan Weather Bureau for providing the monitoring data used in this study.

References

1. https://pm25.lass-net.org/
2. Betha, R., Balasubramanian, R.: Corrigendum to "PM2.5 emissions from hand-held sparklers: chemical characterization and health risk assessment" Aerosol Air Qual. Res. 14:1477–1486]. Aerosol Air Qual. Res. **18**(2), 560–563 (2018)
3. Lee, K.L., Lee, W.J., Mwangi, J.K., Wang, L.C., Gao, X., Chang-Chien, G.P.: Atmospheric PM2.5 and depositions of polychlorinated dibenzo-p-dioxins and dibenzofurans Kaohsiung area, Southern Taiwan. Aerosol Air Qual. Res. **16**(7), 1775–1791 (2016)

4. Lu, H.-Y., Wu, Y.-L., Mutuku, J.K., Chang, K.-H.: Various sources PM2.5 of and their impact on the air quality in Tainan City, Taiwan. Aerosol Air Qual. Res. **19**(3), 601–619 (2019)

5. Hodan, W.M., Barnard, W.R.: Evaluating the contribution of PM2.5 precursor gases and re-entrained road emissions to mobile source PM2.5 particulate matter emissions (2004)

6. Mahajan, S., Liu, H.-M., Tsai, T.-C., Chen, L.-J.: Improving the accuracy and efficiency of PM2.5 forecast service using cluster-based hybrid neural network model. IEEE Access **6**, 19193–19204 (2018)

7. Zhang, H.-H., et al.: Physical and chemical characteristics of PM2.5 and its toxicity to human bronchial cells BEAS-2B in the winter and summer. J. Zhejiang Univ.-SCI. B (Biomed. Biotechnol.) **19**(4), 317–326 (2018)

8. Cheng, Y., et al.: PM2.5 and PM10-2.5 chemical composition and source apportionment near a Hong Kong roadway. Particuology **18**, 96–104 (2015)

9. Lang, J., et al.: Trends of PM2.5 and chemical composition in Beijing, 2000–2015. Aerosol Air Qual. Res. **17**, 412–425 (2017)

10. Jiang, N., Guo, Y., Wang, Q., Kang, P., Zhang, R., Tang, X.: Chemical composition characteristics of PM2.5 in three cities in Henan, Central China. Aerosol Air Qual. Res. **17**, 2367–2380 (2017)

11. Ge, X., et al.: Characteristics and formation mechanisms of fine particulate nitrate in typical urban areas in China. Atmosphere **8**(3), 62 (2017). pp. 1–12

Human-Centered Design Tools
for Smart Toys

Anna Priscilla de Albuquerque[1]($\boxtimes$) [iD], Judith Kelner[1] [iD],
and Patrick C. K. Hung[2] [iD]

[1] Federal University of Pernambuco, Recife, PE 50740-560, Brazil
`{apa,jk}@cin.ufpe.br`
[2] Ontario Tech University, Oshawa, ON L1G 0C5, Canada
`patrick.hung@uoit.ca`

Abstract. The smart toy industry faces challenges to achieve Hardware and Software (H&S) integration since numerous products are not generating enduring value propositions to the consumers. It is possible to achieve better H&S integration by following suitable design practices. Here, we propose four Human-Centered Design (HCD) tools for the development of smart toys solutions. The four HCD tools intervene on idea generation, data collection planning, and both low and high-fidelity prototyping of the solutions. The aim is to assist designers, developers, and engineers in producing better H&S integrated solutions by offering tools that meet HCD principles. The primary usage of the HCD tools with 27 graduate students assisted these multidisciplinary teams in creating five prototypes that were positively evaluated by end-users. Technical evaluation checks for the integrity of the prototypes after testing and results show comparative data on battery consumption and list potential privacy and security vulnerabilities. Improvements include adapting ideation tool to incorporate marketing-oriented strategies, authentication and data encryption for the toolkit, and assessing the tools with professional teams of the industry.

Keywords: Smart toys · Rapid prototyping · Human-centered design

1 Introduction

Toys are products designed for leisure and social play activities. Today, toys increasingly incorporate *Hardware and Software* (H&S) computation. Often, toys connect with online services and other computing devices like smartphones and game consoles, thus referred to as "smart toys". Smart toys solutions may appear in various shapes, such as a plush toy, a doll, a ball, a companion robot or a wearable gadget, and can use different computing technologies to obtain real-time data from their users (e.g., geolocation, relative positioning, bio-information, among the tracking of other physical activities) [1]. Computing technologies for smart toys vary since *Augmented Reality* (AR) applications to advances in

© Springer Nature Switzerland AG 2020
C.-H. Hsu et al. (Eds.): IOV 2019, LNCS 11894, pp. 327–343, 2020.
https://doi.org/10.1007/978-3-030-38651-1_26

robotics, wireless connectivity, *Artificial Intelligence* (AI), speech recognition, and location-based applications. Smart toys are a recent design trend, and toy companies still struggle on how to understand the integration of their H&S components. As a result, many solutions are not generating significant new benefits for the consumers (i.e., children and parents) [8]. Toy companies are holding onto the novelty factor of these smart toys, while these products need to create enduring *Unique Selling Propositions* (USP) for the consumers. USP must offer a better user experience than the user can get by using each of the H&S components individually. Meanwhile, toy companies continue looking for best design practices to deliver better H&S integrated solutions [24].

Technical teams usually apply design practices of other general-purpose toys to design smart toys. In general, those teams have none or little expertise in *Information Technology* (IT), such as information security [21]. Thus, they may not fully understand potential security risks and other IT aspects to address them throughout the product's life cycle. As a consequence, several toy companies are relying on third-party licensing technologies to develop their H&S integrated solutions. For instance, the French company *Volumique* supports technology licenses for several smart toys in the industry. In May 2019, the startup *PullString*, which was acquired by *Apple Inc.*, has announced the discontinuity of their speech processing license services for *Mattel* smart toys. It will lead to the deletion of the smart toys' connected application, including all collected and stored user data on their servers. Sensitive cases like this one may suggest that neither the toy companies have enough specialized technical teams or knowledge to design their H&S integrated solutions. Companies can benefit from investing in in-office multidisciplinary technical teams to produce better H&S integrated solutions. Researchers must supply these technical teams with appropriate tools, specifically intended for the design of smart toys. It is likely that such tools to consider the H&S integration aspects since the product's early stages.

Aiming to meet those needs, we propose four tools for the design of smart toys, which relies on *Human-Centered Design* (HCD) approach [10]. These HCD tools suit for planning and implementing of new H&S integrated solutions by intervening on ideation, data collection, and both low and high-fidelity prototyping of the smart toys. A group composed of 27 graduate students experienced the four HCD tools in a 16-week class assessment. Students had a multidisciplinary background in Computer Science, Design, and Engineering. As a result, they successfully generated, selected, planned, and implemented five smart toy solutions that were positively evaluated by end-users in playtesting sessions. We conducted a technical assessment to check for battery consumption and the physical integrity of the toolkit components after play-testing. Besides, we carried a vulnerability analysis for data security and privacy [21] by simulating attacks on the *Bluetooth Low Energy* (BLE) and *Near-Field Communication* (NFC) modules. Security strategies from the literature may solve the identified vulnerabilities [6]. Future evaluation of the tools will incorporate a list of improvements to assist professionals from the smart toy industry.

2   Related Work

Standard design practices for smart toys are mostly marketing-oriented, such as gender-oriented practices and the licensing of transmedia contents from franchises like *Star Wars* and *Marvel*. A common practice is to price the H&S components separately since most of the smart toys offer digital contents for purchase in their connected applications [8]. UK-based marketing group, *Juniper Research*, issued a report which estimates that the purchase of in-app contents will reach 25% of the total revenue of this sector (17.7 billion USD) by 2023 [18]. Usually, these marketing-oriented practices guide the technical teams through the entire design process, which may suggest that H&S components are often planned to support independent play experiences. For instance, the smart toy *Hasbro's Furby Connect* and its mobile application allow parallel playtime using only one of the H&S components. There is little information about the use of specific design tools by toy companies that support H&S integration [24]. While, in related literature, researchers are addressing specific design tools for H&S integrated solutions and the *Internet of Things* (IoT) related applications. Design tools cover everything since ideation tools to interaction models, including low and high-fidelity prototyping tools.

Ideation tools facilitate group discussion, supports the fast development of new ideas, and facilitates collaboration in the brainstorming sessions. Note that card set is a recurrent approach used by related literature. Hornecker proposes card sets to stimulate group discussion during brainstorming sessions [11]. Each card set represents one aspect of her *Tangible User Interface* (TUI) framework, namely: tangible manipulation, spatial interaction, embodied facilitation, and expressive representation. She experimented the card sets with professionals and students during ten workshops. Inspired by her work, the *Internet of Tangible Things* (IoTT) card set consists of 16 cards; 8 cards represent TUI properties and another 8, the IoT properties [3]. The card set was used by 21 participants to help them in the planning of interactivity properties of both low and high fidelity prototypes, the last using the prototyping board *Kniwwelino*. Another study, which was based on related work [16], used card sets and gamification to assist engineers in assembling IoT properties [22]. The authors also conducted workshops with master's students in Electrical and Computer Engineering and other related areas to evaluate their ideation tool.

Schneider advocates that prototypes support the extraction of valuable information for the product's implementing cycles [20]. Either low or high fidelity prototypes can present explorative, experimental, or evolutionary purposes, and all of them enable to elicit general and specific requirements for the desired solution. Rapid prototyping tools can make high-fidelity prototyping of smart toys faster and easier for creators than using custom hardware solutions for each design. They offer more freedom on the editing and testing of play and interface features during both planning and implementing design cycles. We can classify existing rapid prototyping tools for smart toys into smart devices, AR-based platforms, mobile-based platforms, and hardware toolkits. Each prototyping tool approach has its advantages and disadvantages. First, smart devices can be considered smart toys themselves [14,15,23]. They are ready to use and play, and usually promotes inter-device connection and embodied interplays. However, they present fixed interface features, which limit creators to only editing the play features. For instance, *Sifteo Cubes* are modular cubic displays. They can transfer data from one to another and allow touchscreen and natural gesture interactions (e.g., shaking and flipping the cubes) that enable prototyping of closed rules solutions [15].

Second, AR-based platforms use cameras to detect objects (e.g., tokens, cards, and toys) by using either marker-based and markerless recognition techniques (i.e., recognition of shape, color, lighting, saturation, texture, and other image descriptors) [9,13]. In addition to cameras, AR-based approach often requires complex setup to support detection and displaying virtual contents, such as mobile devices, *Head-Mounted Displays* (HMD), and *Infrared* (IR) tabletops. Note that AR-based platforms may expose the user's privacy due to the collection of personal data such as facial pictures or videos of the players manipulating the toys. Mobile-based platforms explore multi-touch, conductive materials, or contactless technology to detect objects using smartphones or tablets [4,19]. This approach reduces setup complexity and privacy issues when compared with the AR-based one. However, these platforms are also limited to promote token-tabletop interaction (e.g., placing tokens on the touchscreen). Finally, hardware toolkits, usually modular pieces, consist of a collection of sensors, actuators, communicators, and other electronic circuits that are reprogrammable [12]. They offer more freedom to the editing of both play and interface features since they permit creators to select components that best fit their projects. Still, the level of programmability, size, and distribution of hardware components can limit its adaptability features. Thus, adequate H&S integration is essential when implementing a hardware toolkit. Achieve better H&S integration, we propose three planning tools to guide the technical teams from the initial concepts until the high-fidelity smart toy solutions. In the next section, we detail how the four tools meet HCD principles and the context of use for H&S integration.

3   Human-Centered Design Tools

HCD practices for interactive systems are defined by the international standard ISO 9241-210:2019 [10]. ISO provides recommendations to employ HCD principles throughout the life cycle of computer-based interactive systems. It is concerned with ways integrated H&S components can enhance human-system interaction. This article proposes to employ HCD practices as a strategy to develop better H&S integrated smart toys. Note that once employing HCD practices does not dismiss the usage of traditional marketing-oriented practices (e.g., gender-oriented and transmedia contents). The goal here is to provide a set of practical tools that can assist the technical teams in developing better H&S integrated solutions. Is expected that the HCD approach can lead to a positive impact on the product's USP. According to ISO, H&S integrated systems designed by HCD practices offer a set of qualities. It increases productivity and operational efficiency, are easier to understand and use, reduce training and support costs, enhance usability to a broader audience and can promote accessibility, improve user experience, reduce discomfort and distress, provide competitive advantages, and contribute towards sustainability objectives. The HCD approach should meet the following principles. First, the design must rely on a clear understanding of the context of use, which covers the user's needs, the interaction environment, and all involved stakeholders. Users must take part in the design and development steps, which must be iterative and driven by user-centered evaluations. The design process must account the whole user experience, and a multidisciplinary team with complementary skills and perspectives must convey it.

In the present article, we propose four design tools that aim to improve H&S integration of smart toys. To adequately relate the HCD principles with the context of use of smart toys, we performed a content analysis of 297 smart toys from the systematic mapping of literature and industry [1]. The content analysis consisted of observing the following aspects: (a) what are the H&S components and how do they interact and connect? (b) what types of data are gathered and exchanged among these H&S components? (c) how do the play rules and dynamics regulate the data sharing, storage, and individual behaviors of each H&S component? (d) how does the user experience occurs with these H&S components during play, and which approaches are adequate to evaluate such experience? Hence, the content analysis supported us to summarize the context of use for smart toys into the following principles.

1. Smart toy solutions must combine physical and social play experiences.
2. User interface setup must be ready to play and reduce complexity.
3. Data collection must prioritize the user's privacy.
4. Play activities must be suitable for both indoors and outdoors.
5. User experience must integrate a multi-target audience.

The five principles above, helped us to propose the four HCD tools. Moreover, content analysis also permitted us to establish *Data Collection Patterns* (DCP) and a list of *Prototyping Requirements* (PR) that support the data planning tool and both low and high-fidelity prototyping tools. First, DCP items classify how data are gathered and exchanged among the H&S components and how play rules regulate data sharing, behavior, and storage [2]. Second, the PR items define what type of data should be collected by the smart toys and how occurs the data processing in the interface components. The DCP and PR items are listed below.

- *DCP1.* Data sharing modalities should regulate all play behaviors: Sharing patterns are namely, "replicate," "extend," and "replace" (e.g., the smart toy extends its motion tracking data to a virtual prefab in the connected application).
- *DCP2.* Individual data behaviors should respect the play rules: Behaviors patterns classifies into "create," "destroy," and "transform" (e.g., the smart toy transforms the color of the virtual prefab from green to red when shaken in the Z-axis).

- *DCP3*. Data storage should support selected data behaviors: Storage patterns comprise "update," "activate," and "augment" (e.g., the smart toy updates its state from green to red when shaken in the Z-axis).
- *PR1*. Prototyping should support adaptability: H&S components should be selected according to the needs of each design, and these components should be fitting for toys of different physical shape, materials, and size.
- *PR2*. Prototyping should support distributed data collection and processing: Smart toys should support connectivity and interoperability of communication protocols for transferring data between the H&S integrated components.
- *PR3*. Prototyping should support multimodal user feedback: Adequate multimodal user feedback can mix visual, auditory, and tactile modalities.
- *PR4*. Prototyping should support different play features: Smart toys can fully or partially regulate the play rules. Open-ended rules permit the players to add or edit new dynamics through play while closed rules are pre-set and can follow progressive challenges through structured level design.
- *PR5*. Prototyping should limit personal data collection: Smart toys should only collect non-personal data [2] from the users while personal information must be retrieved and processed by the secure connected devices.

Furthermore, to fully meet the HCD principles, the four tools must support an iterative and user-centered evaluation design process. According to content analysis and related works, adequate user-evaluation tools for smart toys must meet a set of practices. First, it must combine qualitative and quantitative approaches, and the evaluation instruments must meet the target-audience needs (i.e., children and adults). Evaluation protocols must pass through a pilot assessment, which includes specialists, and it must assess the usability and enjoyment of user experiences. Finally, the HCD tools aim at multidisciplinary. The teams must have complementary backgrounds of at least two of these subjects: Design or Arts, Computer or Electronic Engineering, and Computer Science (i.e., computer programmers). Also, specialists' backgrounds may include relevant fields in Education, Health, Science, and Sports. The following sub-sections describe the proposed HCD tools.

3.1   Brainstorming Toy

Inspiration to create new concepts for H&S integrated smart toys can derive from observing children playing with traditional toys and digital games [13]. Here, we propose the *Brainstorming Toy* as the first HCD tool. It uses various traditional toys along with a set of play rules cards to help creators in generating concepts for smart toys. The goal is to stimulate them to create ideas by assembling the interface features (of the toys) with digital or traditional play features (of the games). Traditional toys set includes everything since balls, Frisbee, hula hoop, toy cars, dexterity toys, sword, figurines of animals (e.g., sea animals, mammals, and insects), dominos, chessboard, and so on. Play rules cards include short descriptions for closed rules (e.g., runner and tower defense) and open-ended rules (e.g., hide and seek, tag, and hotchpotch). Besides, this HCD tool aims to mediate the communication between the multidisciplinary teams, which still is challenging. It supports group discussion by involving all participants since the early concepts – by not separating designers and programmers and by providing means so that they can express themselves better. Its structure is based on *Discussion 66* technique [7]. The original technique consists of distributing participants into small groups so that they can discuss ideas following a sequence of statements or questions. It proposes shifting the participants in the groups to stimulate an exchange of views and to avoid creators to fixate on a single idea.

The *Brainstorming Toy* is performed in groups of 3–5 participants and by exchanging both creators and toy resources within the groups. Short sessions include a 15 min opening session, three or more exchanging sessions (5 min), and a 10 min closing session (that reunites the initial group). After the timing, one or two participants, along with one or two toy resources, are exchanged. Exchanges in the groups must follow simple rules (e.g., professional background, age, or gender). In the short sessions, the entire group discusses one toy at each time, by following a structured paper sheet. The paper sheet contains sections to detail both play and physical aspects of the toy (e.g., "how does one play with this toy?" "what are the toy's materials?"). After describing the toy sample, the group should sort one or more play rules cards to generate ideas. One creator, assigned as the "reporter," has to write down all requested contents in a legible form on the backside of the sheet.

After the closing session, all paper sheets must be collected and grouped by assembling sheets of the same toys. At that moment, the groups receive these sheets to the recycling ideas session. The goal of this session is to improve the quality of ideas by applying creative constraints to them. Creative constraints consist of ten items based on the context of use defined in the previous section. Items include "the idea uses two different physical interactions," "it promotes tangential learning," "it includes two age groups of end-users," "it collects only two types of data," "it has two toy components in the interface," "promotes therapy or rehabilitation," "it supports at least two social interaction modalities," "offers accessibility," "it has a toy component with attachable parts," and "it is gender-neutral." Recycling occurs by adding to the ideas at least one or two constraints. In a marketing-oriented context, the list of creative constraints can add or replace specific items related to transmedia characters, themes, educational topics, among other marketing indicators.

Fig. 1. Hula Hoop Hero concept generated by the students in brainstorming.

All original and recycled ideas serve for the final selection. Each creator selects one up to three preferred ideas to detail them using a slide presentation template. The detailing consists of defining the expected H&S components for the interface and setting the core play rules. Note that if creators pick an original idea, they have to apply the constraints to improve it before detailing. The final idea selection takes part in the *Data Collection Planning* tool. Figure 1 illustrates an example of the *Brainstorming Toy* results. The *Hula Hoop Hero* concept, produced by the students, combines a traditional hula hoop toy with the "rhythm games" card. This H&S integrated solution uses the smart toy to measure the physical movements, and the BLE connected the application to keep the score of the player's performance, display the next movements, and play the songs.

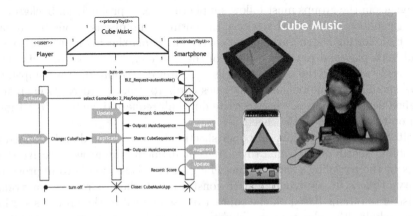

Fig. 2. Cube Music's data collection plan diagram

3.2   Data Collection Planning

UNICEF issued the *Memorandum on Artificial Intelligence and Child Rights* in 2019. It includes the topic named *Children's Rights at Play*, which aims to guarantee the right of privacy by international frameworks for children through the development and marketing of smart toys solutions [25]. The *Data Collection Planning tool* aims to minimize selecting ideas that can potentially introduce threats to children's privacy in the implementing phase. It comprises of two parts. The first part consists of each creator to choose one or two ideas from the *Brainstorming Toy* to pick what type of data they expect that the idea will collect. A paper sheet organizes these types of data into three groups. (A) Non-personal data collection includes non-personal identification, unidentifiable positioning systems, and motion tracking information [2]. (B) Personal-data collection covers data like voice, facial pictures, and other user profile information (e.g., full name, e-mail address, and billing information). (C) Sensitive data collection includes multimedia files related to objects (e.g., pictures or videos of markerless or marked objects with fiducial markers or QR codes).

Often, smart toys, especially those with connected applications, tend to gather unnecessary personal information that may not be relevant for playing time [6,21]. If any personal or sensitive data type is selected; the creator has to pick an alternative for non-personal data to use it instead. In that way, they can reflect if collecting personal information is essential or not to their concepts. Only similar concepts pass for the second part of the planning (i.e., same idea or different ideas related to the same toy component). Participants can exchange ideas if they wish to do so. They can pick-up other concepts to work, only if the idea not expects to collect any personal data. The second part of the *Data Collection Planning* tool consists of the diagram sheet—the diagram uses UML-like notations inspired by the class, sequence, and activity UML diagrams [2]. In the diagram, the creators can plan the data collection exchanges and processing among the H&S components. The diagram relates three entities based on the *Toy User Interface* (ToyUI) interaction model [1]; these are the user, the primary ToyUI (i.e., the smart toy), and the secondary ToyUI (i.e., the connected components). It uses the data collection patterns described in the previous section (i.e., replicate, create, update) along with other UML-like notations. The goal of this diagram is to plan, according to the defined play rules, how will occur the data sharing among each component, including the individual behaviors and appropriate data storage.

After completing the diagram, all planned ideas are assembled and listed for 3-choice voting. After choosing the best-rated ideas, the multidisciplinary teams are set based on the profile of the creators and their preferences. Teams use the planning diagrams as a guide to building both the low and high-fidelity prototypes. Figure 2 shows another of student's projects. The *Cube Music* uses the BLE module to connect to a music application. The data collection diagram uses the "replicate" data sharing pattern to governs all behaviors. The app plays a sequence of music notes which are associated with geometric shapes and colors. Then, the player memorizes the sequence and replay it by flipping the cube. It uses the "transform" pattern to describe the cube's behaviors. The upper face is selected by the application to validate the sequence at each time. All storage patterns are necessary due to the defined play rules (i.e., activate, update, and augment).

3.3 I/O Stickers

The low-fidelity prototyping practice combines traditional toys with office and crafting materials like papers, colored pens, scissors, tapes, and cardboard. To facilitate the practice, the *I/O Stickers* represent different sensors, communication protocols, types of inputs and outputs, displays, and data storage behaviors. The goal of this HCD tool is to simplify technological and interactive aspects to help the teams in first prototyping the interface setup. In that way, by attaching one sticker to a toy component, it may help them to plan and test the concepts.

For example, the motion tracking sensor sticker attached to a toy can mean that the toy component can collect 3D positioning and orientation. Figure 3 shows the *Zombie Tag* low and high-fidelity prototypes. Students defined three interface components for setup: the smart toy is a zombie glove, and two secondary components are the bracelets and game cards. The selected stickers for the smart glove are short-range communication, audio output, single input, and user profile and data. The *I/O stickers* chosen for the bracelets are the single input and user profile and data; the game cards use the multimedia output sticker to represent the play contents. Note that the teams successfully represented all planned behaviors using the *I/O stickers*, and they used it as a reference to develop the Zombie-tag's high-fidelity prototype.

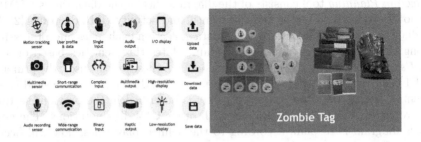

Fig. 3. I/O stickers and the Zombie Tag's low and high-fidelity prototypes.

3.4   IoT4Fun Toolkit

The fourth HCD tool is *IoT4Fun Toolkit*; it allows wireless connectivity via BLE and NFC to support distributed data collection and processing. It collects only non-personal data of both objects and users using a motion-tracking sensor and supports the design of visual, auditory, and tactile feedback. The toolkit uses the *Arduino IDE* to supports the programming of either open-ended or closed play rules and behaviors. Finally, it was manufactured using a modular *Printed Circuit Board* (PCB) approach to improve adaptability. Modularity makes the toolkit fitting for the design of smart toys of different shapes and sizes. The toolkit consists of eight modular PCBs attached to individual hardware components. All modules are attachable to a hub module using plug-and-play flat flex ribbon cables. The hub module contains a central unit, which is an *Arduino Mini-pro* with 16 MHz crystal oscillator, and a 10 DOF IMU motion tracking sensor. The BLE module is a 2.4-GHz BLE, and the NFC module operates at 13.56 MHZ. The visual output module consists of 3 RGB LEDs, the auditory module is a 2 1 W 8OHMS speaker, and the tactile module is a vibrator motor. A polymer li-ion battery module powers the hub module and all connected modules. The toolkit includes a USB recording module that permits ease updating of programmed behaviors of all connected modules. In Fig. 4, we show how the modular toolkit offers adaptability for different "toy-shells." First, the students distributed the components through the *Cobi's* body. They placed the NFC module in the bottom of a cardboard ramp to read the cookie disks. Then, the visual feedback module locates at the top of the body to simulate the eyes, and milk acrylic amplifies the LEDs intensity. Diversely, the *Magic Potato* team assembled most of the toolkit components inside a plastic ball. Except for the visual feedback module, which passes through a leash of the plush toy to simulate the bomb's wick.

Fig. 4. IoT4Fun Toolkit adapted by the Cobi and Magic Potato teams.

4   HCD Tools Results

The four HCD tools assessment occurred during coursework of the graduate program in Computer Science in the *Federal University of Pernambuco* (UFPE), in Brazil. The coursework lasted for 16 weeks between August to December 2018. A group of 27 creators participated in this assessment, among 15 master students and 12 doctorate students with multidisciplinary backgrounds on Computer Science, Engineering, Design, and related areas. The smart toy solutions were named: *Hula-hoop Hero, Cube Music, Zombie-tag, Cobi,* and *Magic Potato*. First, both *Hula Hoop Hero* and *Cube Music* explore the classic H&S integration setup. The two smart toys use the BLE module to connect with their respective mobile applications. Diversely, both *Cobi* and *Zombie-tag* use the NFC module to connect with secondary toy components (i.e., cookie disks and bracelets, respectively). Only the *Magic Potato* prototype did not explore connectivity – it uses the motion tracking sensor to collect positioning information to adapt its behavior through play. Thus, the last three projects do not fully meet the expected setup for H&S integration since they do not present mobile apps. Additional features could justify the need for this classic H&S integration. For example, apps are suitable to keep track of the player's performance and scores, and they allow the editing features, such as selecting play modes or customizing the rules. However, in all three projects, they were not essential.

Different group of users evaluated all prototypes during playtesting sessions. The teams used usability questionnaire adapted from the *System Usability Scale* (SUS) [5], 5-points *Likert* scale likeability questionnaire based on the work of [26], and additional qualitative instruments (i.e., semi-structured interviews, group discussion, observation, and video analysis). First, technical specialists tested all prototypes, which helped the teams to overcome technical and design issues and to make general improvements. Second, teams went on the field to test their prototypes with end-users, preferably with those from the intended target audience. Not all groups managed to assess the prototypes with children. For instance, the *Cobi* team tested their prototype with two children; the girl aged 2 and the boy 4. *Magic Potato* team tested the prototype with two girls (6 and 10 years old). *Cube Music* tested the toy with one boy aged 6 and *Zombie-tag* team tested with three children from 11 to 13 years old (two boys and one girl). All collected user data received written parental consent before testing.

Finally, during a playtesting event on UFPE campus, 40 students of the *Physical Education and Sports Department* were invited to play. They presented a high level of interest in physical activities and sports, which were an adequate fit for the intended target audience. User profile summary consisted of 23 males, and 17 females and age ranged from 18 to 23 years old, while one participant was aged 50. Teams collected data from 8 to 15 participants each, and they analyzed results separately – 26 participants played with at least two prototypes. All smart toys worked adequately and presented as robust enough to allow 90-120 min of playtesting sessions. The public positively evaluated them all, according to the user evaluation instruments used by the teams (i.e., SUS scores $\geq 71.7 \leq 87$, likeability average values $\geq 3.5 \leq 4.5$, purchase intent average values $\geq 3.5 \leq 4.3$, and positive qualitative information). All smart toy solutions presented adequate H&S integration and promoted enjoyable experiences to their users. As an outcome of this event, they applied a shortlist of improvements for their final solutions.

4.1 Technical Assessment

There were reports from the teams about malfunctions of the *IoT4Fun Toolkit* modules during the playtesting sessions. The technical assessment consisted of three types of testing: functional integrity, battery consumption, and data security and privacy vulnerabilities. First, functional integrity tests used the *Arduino IDE* to check core functionalities of each module, and when necessary, a multimeter checked for punctual malfunctions of the PCBs. All original hardware components are fully working after the playtesting sessions. However, some parts of the PCB modules attached to these components suffered damage after testing. It may happen due to collisions during playtime, or by the way that teams handled the modules during development. Damages in the PCBs appears in two visual feedback modules, one auditory module, and one BLE module. It may suggest that the PCB manufacture should be better performed to conquer adequate robustness. In that sense, the future versions of the toolkit cab benefit from professional manufacturing by a third party. Moreover, protective cases can help to secure the modules and other components. Cases can use hard-plastic, acrylic, or flexible materials to reduce external impact during collisions.

Second, the battery consumption tests look to estimate the battery autonomy of each solution to support further improvements in the toolkit.

The instantaneous current analysis was performed using the current shunt method [17]. It consists of measuring the current of consumption, second by second, and according to the working time of each solution. The sensor ACS 712 5 A was attached in series to the toolkit to measure its current circuit. Once knowing the average consumption, it is possible to estimate the battery autonomy of each solution in Table 1. Battery autonomy calculation consists of the relation between 80% of the total battery capacity and the average battery consumption. The 80% rate simulates the behavior of a lithium polymer battery since generally in this type of battery, the circuit stops running before the voltage is entirely over. The total capacity of the battery module is 350 mAh. It uses the battery LP702035 3.7 V. Results suggests that battery consumption relates to how the teams implemented the solutions. *Cobi* and *Magic Potato* use the visual and auditory modules; however, the second solution requires more battery consumption than the first one. To circumvent this issue, note that the *Magic Potato* uses an adapted battery module with six batteries working in parallel; thus, its estimated capacity is 2100 mAh. Hence, better programming practices must be employed to improve battery autonomy in future assessment.

Table 1. Battery autonomy results.

Smart toy	Battery consumption	Battery autonomy
Hula Hoop Hero	33.5 mA	501'
Cube Music	55 mA	305'27"
Zombie-tag	98 mA	171'25"
Cobi	80 mA	210'
Magic Potato	168 mA	600'

Finally, vulnerability analysis points out the main risks for data security and privacy of each solution. A vulnerability taxonomy for smart toys connected to mobile applications classifies threats into physical, nearby, and remote access types [21]. According to it, the toolkit is sensitive to *Unauthorized-config-physical* threats since it offers a USB recorder to update the hub module. It is intended to make the programming and updating of contents faster and easier, but it can be used for malicious configuration since it does not require authentication. The other types of threats are dependent on the toolkit implementation. For example, the toolkit can be sensitive to the *Unauthorized-config-nearby* threat, but both implemented mobile applications do not support configuring their smart toys through them. However, none of the solutions employ security standards to support *local data protection*, and the two connected applications permit both *tampering* of information and *denial of service* threats. Vulnerability items do not cover scenarios that use NFC communication, in which the exchange of data among two toy components (e.g., *Cobi* and the cookie's disks) occurs. Thus, the present article adds a new item named *Insecure-NFC-practice* to the taxonomy, which is alike to the *Insecure-Bluetooth-practice*. The *Unencrypted-comm-channels* item was also adapted to cover NFC communication. Hence, to make the vulnerability analysis comprehensive, it includes testing the security of both BLE and NFC modules. First, the *Android* app, named *BLE Console*, was used to examine the security of the BLE connection. Parameters for a secure BLE connection consider if it requires user authentication and if the MAC address dynamically changes. As a result, both *Cube Music* and *Hula-hoop Hero* pairs without authentication and present fixed MAC addresses. The *BLE Console* app allows accessing of smart toy information. Information includes all data sent by the serial port, among manufacturer's information such as model, serial number, and firmware revision. Likewise, the *NFC Tools* app supports to examine the security of the NFC connection. Although NFC is a safer technology than other protocols for authentication, it still opens the potential for breaches for data disclosure. Neither *Cobi* nor *Zombie-tag* projects encrypted the NFC communications. It allows the attacker to get information from the tags or the reader. Using the *NFC Tools* app, one can access all recorded data on the NFC tags, including rewriting the tag information to limit further readings.

To improve reliability and circumvent the identified vulnerabilities, we select the following data *Security Requirements* (SR) for smart toys, which were proposed by [6]. First, communication between physical toy and mobile device must use a protocol that allows authentication and authorization mechanisms (SR5). Configuration file integrity must be maintained and verified in every mobile app play session (SR7). Every communication in toy computing environment must use cryptography mechanisms (SR8). The mobile app must monitor and limit database growth (SR15). The DNS must provide security mechanisms against external modification of stored data (SR10). Finally, the smart toy should avoid exposing unnecessary information once implemented (SR21). Note that once again, those requirements apply for smart toys connected to mobile applications. Thus, we adapted the SR5 item to cover NFC communication. It may suggest that a taxonomy of vulnerabilities and its security requirements must be expanded to cover a broader range of smart toy solutions. In future assessment of the toolkit is essential to ensure security standards for data encryption and build access control mechanisms, including parental control and management of privacy policies.

5   Conclusion

Toy companies are struggling with H&S integration to deliver products that offer better USP for the consumers. Here, we proposed four HCD tools to assist the companies' multidisciplinary technical teams in creating adequate H&S integrated solutions. All combined, the HCD tools assisted 27 graduate students in ideation, planning, and prototyping of five smart toy solutions. All HCD tools adequately meet the context of use for H&S integration, which was defined based on the content analysis of smart toy solutions from literature and industry. First, the *Brainstorming Toy* tool assisted the teams in creating solutions that combine physical activities with social play modalities, which include direct or parallel competition. Second, the *I/O Stickers* helped them to define interface setups that are simple to use and ready to play. As a direct result of the *Data Collection* tool and the *IoT4Fun Toolkit*, all developed solutions prioritized the user's privacy by limiting the data collection to non-personal information (i.e., motion tracking information). Besides, all solutions are suitable for play in both indoors and outdoors, and playtesting results suggest that they are enjoyable for multi-target audience groups.

More user feedback is needed to improve the HCD tools. Preferably, the next assessment of the HCD tools will occur in a cross-cultural scenario since personal experience may influence the results. Ideation may depend on the personal knowledge of the creators about the toys and how people can play with them. Is expected that by assessing these tools with creators from different cultures can turn results more suitable for a worldwide audience. Ideation can benefit from incorporating marketing-oriented strategies to increase its acceptance by the toy companies. Furthermore, the technical assessment results suggest the need for improvements in the *IoT4Fun Toolkit* on robustness, access control, data encryption, and other reliability aspects. Therefore, it is essential to build a reliable development framework to assist the creators in delivering the *IoT4Fun Toolkit* best potential. Until now, we cannot state conclusive findings for how the perceived H&S integration can impact the USP of the solutions. Research evidence resumes to the positive user evaluation results and cannot infer acceptance of the created solutions by this market niche. Although the HCD tools presented satisfactory results, the benefits of employing these HCD tools with the toy companies are unclear since the assessment happened with 27 graduate students. Future opportunities include reaching out for toy companies and professionals who are active in the industry for more comprehensive assessment of the tools.

References

1. de Albuquerque, A.P., Kelner, J.: Toy user interfaces: systematic and industrial mapping. J. Syst. Architect. **97**, 99–106 (2018)
2. de Albuquerque, A.P., Kelner, J.: Non-personal data collection for toy user interfaces. In: Proceedings of the 52nd Hawaii International Conference on System Sciences (2019)
3. Angelini, L., Mugellini, E., Couture, N., Abou Khaled, O.: Designing the interaction with the Internet of Tangible Things: a card set. In: Proceedings of the Twelfth International Conference on Tangible, Embedded, and Embodied Interaction, pp. 299–306. ACM (2018)
4. Appert, C., Pietriga, E., Bartenlian, E., González, R.M.: Custom-made tangible interfaces with touchtokens. In: Proceedings of the 2018 International Conference on Advanced Visual Interfaces, p. 15. ACM (2018)
5. Brooke, J., et al.: SUS-A quick and dirty usability scale. Usability Eval. Indu. **189**(194), 4–7 (1996)
6. de Carvalho, L.G., Eler, M.M.: Security requirements for smart toys. In: ICEIS, vol. 2, pp. 144–154 (2017)

7. Denton, D.K., Denton, R.A.: The Toolbox for the Mind: Finding and Implementing Creative Solutions in the Workplace. McGraw-Hill (1999)

8. Dhar, T., Wu, T.: Mobile computing toys: marketing challenges and implications. In: Hung, P.C.K. (ed.) Mobile Services for Toy Computing. ISCEMT, pp. 39–49. Springer, Cham (2015). https://doi.org/10.1007/978-3-319-21323-1_3

9. Gohlke, K., Hlatky, M., de Jong, B.: Physical construction toys for rapid sketching of tangible user interfaces. In: Proceedings of the Ninth International Conference on Tangible, Embedded, and Embodied Interaction, pp. 643–648. ACM (2015)

10. Group, B.: Ergonomics of human-system interaction: human-centred design for interactive systems: Iso 9241–210. BSI Standards Publication (2019)

11. Hornecker, E.: Creative idea exploration within the structure of a guiding framework: the card brainstorming game (2010)

12. Kazemitabaar, M., McPeak, J., Jiao, A., He, L., Outing, T., Froehlich, J.E.: MakerWear: a tangible approach to interactive wearable creation for children. In: Proceedings of the 2017 Chi Conference on Human Factors in Computing Systems, pp. 133–145. ACM (2017)

13. Marco, J., Cerezo, E., Baldassarri, S.: Tangible interaction and tabletops: new horizons for children's games. Int. J. Arts Technol. 5(2–4), 151–176 (2012)

14. Márquez Segura, E., Waern, A., Moen, J., Johansson, C.: The design space of body games: technological, physical, and social design. In: Proceedings of the SIGCHI Conference on Human Factors in Computing Systems, pp. 3365–3374. ACM (2013)

15. Merrill, D., Sun, E., Kalanithi, J.: Sifteo cubes. In: CHI 2012 Extended Abstracts on Human Factors in Computing Systems, pp. 1015–1018. ACM (2012)

16. Mora, S., Gianni, F., Divitini, M.: Tiles: a card-based ideation toolkit for the Internet of Things. In: Proceedings of the 2017 Conference on Designing Interactive Systems, pp. 587–598. ACM (2017)

17. Nakutis, Z.: Embedded systems power consumption measurement methods overview. MATAVIMAI 2(44), 29–35 (2009)

18. Juniper Research: Why evolution is key to consumer robotics' survival. Technical report, August 2019

19. Schmitz, M., Steimle, J., Huber, J., Dezfuli, N., Mühlhäuser, M.: Flexibles: deformation-aware 3D-printed tangibles for capacitive touchscreens. In: Proceedings of the 2017 CHI Conference on Human Factors in Computing Systems, pp. 1001–1014. ACM (2017)

20. Schneider, K.: Prototypes as assets, not toys: why and how to extract knowledge from prototypes. In: Proceedings of the 18th International Conference on Software Engineering, pp. 522–531. IEEE Computer Society (1996)

21. Shasha, S., Mahmoud, M., Mannan, M., Youssef, A.: Playing with danger: a taxonomy and evaluation of threats to smart toys. IEEE Internet Things J. 6(2), 2986–3002 (2018)

22. Sintoris, C., Mavrommati, I., Avouris, N., Chatzigiannakis, I.: Out of the box: using gamification cards to teach ideation to engineering students. In: Kameas, A., Stathis, K. (eds.) AmI 2018. LNCS, vol. 11249, pp. 221–226. Springer, Cham (2018). https://doi.org/10.1007/978-3-030-03062-9_17

23. Soute, I., Vacaretu, T., Wit, J.D., Markopoulos, P.: Design and evaluation of rapido, a platform for rapid prototyping of interactive outdoor games. ACM Trans. Comput.-Hum. Interact. (TOCHI) 24(4), 28 (2017)

24. Tyni, H., Kultima, A.: The emergence of industry of playful hybrids: developer's perspective. In: Proceedings of the 20th International Academic Mindtrek Conference, pp. 413–421. ACM (2016)

25. UNICEF Innovation, Human Rights Center, U.B.: Memorandum on artificial intelligence and child rights. Technical report, May 2019
26. Zaman, B., Abeele, V.V.: Laddering with young children in user experience evaluations: theoretical groundings and a practical case. In: Proceedings of the 9th International Conference on Interaction Design and Children, pp. 156–165. ACM (2010)

Edge Service Migration for Vehicular Networks Based on Multi-agent Deep Reinforcement Learning

Haohan Zhang[✉], Jinglin Li, and Quan Yuan

The State Key Laboratory of Networking and Switching Technology,
Beijing University of Posts and Telecommunications, Beijing, China
{hhzhang, jlli, yuanquan}@bupt.edu.cn

Abstract. To meet the increasing resource demand of intelligent driving, roadside infrastructure is used to provide communication and computing capabilities to vehicles. Existing studies have leveraged deep reinforcement learning to perform small-scale resource scheduling for vehicles. It is critical to implement large-scale resource scheduling to deal with the high mobility of vehicles. However, this large-scale optimization is confronted with huge state and action space. To overcome this challenge, we propose an edge resource allocation method based on multi-agent deep reinforcement learning to reduce system cost while guarantee the quality of intelligent driving. The proposed method considers both immediate and long-term resource status, which helps to select appropriate base stations and edge servers. Trace driven simulations are performed to validate the efficiency of the proposed method.

Keywords: Internet of Vehicles · Multi-agent reinforcement learning · Edge computing · Resource allocation

1 Introduction

Intelligent transportation system is purposed to reduce traffic accidents and congestion. Being a significant infrastructure of our modern intelligent transportation system, as shown in Fig. 1, Internet of Vehicles (IoV) mainly provides two kinds of services. One is to increase driving safety and reduce congestion; the other is to provide recreation for passengers. A larger quantity of hardware, which is equipped in cars, is needed to meet the increasing resource demand of vehicle applications. Vehicles, acting as nodes, connect with the others and the whole network. At the same time, onboard computing resources enable the vehicles to understand and react to the environment correctly. However, inevitable disadvantages are found in this way. Deploying a lot of hardware increases the cost and a large amount of resources are idle while our cars are not in use. Moreover, due to the limited space and energy provided in the vehicle, equipment is difficult to meet our ever-changing demand for on-board applications. Although IOV based on cloud computing is able to unload hardware from vehicles, cellular network connecting the data center to the mobile vehicles causes long delay, which is not conducive to grasp real-time status of connected cars and control their current behavior

© Springer Nature Switzerland AG 2020
C.-H. Hsu et al. (Eds.): IOV 2019, LNCS 11894, pp. 344–352, 2020.
https://doi.org/10.1007/978-3-030-38651-1_27

on cloud. Deploying computational resources in roadside units to provide resources directly is able to reduce vehicle communication overhead and optimize vehicle network resources effectively.

More and more researchers are also concerned about using roadside units to improve IOV performance. However, previous studies are more likely to focus on single resource optimization, without the consideration of the characteristics of IOV services. Meanwhile, the scalability of roadside units serving vehicles has been neglected for a long time. The number of vehicles in an area and their demand for resources may change dramatically over time. Previous methods usually require the full amount of information on the road. Due to the requirement of computing power and time delay, these methods work roughly in IOV's large-scale scenario.

In this paper, we propose a multi-agent deep reinforcement learning based edge resource allocation method to select right roadside unit for the vehicle to improves the performance of vehicle network, and the main contributions are as follows:

- Various costs on accessing resources from roadside units considering real driving situations are investigated.
- We explored the impact of vehicle dynamic changes, vehicle travel trajectory, and timeliness of decision-making on the allocation strategy so as to select appropriate roadside units for each vehicle.
- We propose a multi-agent reinforcement learning based resource optimization scheme to select appropriate roadside unit for each vehicle to optimize the system cost of vehicular network.

2 Related Works

Researches based on roadside unit have been developed for many years. Zhang et al. [1] studied the planning of heterogeneous IOV, which is composed of traditional macro base stations and roadside units with the function of buffering and renewable energy collection to minimize the cost of network deployment by jointly optimizing roadside cell density, buffer size and energy collection rate. Wang et al. [2] proposed a computational unloading strategy in mobile edge computing, which can make unloading decisions based on the local computing cost estimated by all user devices and the unloading cost estimated by mobile edge computing server. Zhang et al. [3] studied the use of base station cache to store content with high hit rate to reduce file transmission delay and network load. He proposed a greedy content placement algorithm to achieve near optimal delay performance with low computational complexity. Wu et al. [4] studied the deployment of roadside units in similar highway scenarios. Considering the characteristics of roadside unit access, wireless interference, vehicle distribution and vehicle speed, a new method is proposed, which requires only a small amount of roadside units to realize an efficient deployment strategy with larger network throughput. He et al. [5] proposed an integrated framework that achieves a dynamic schedule on network, cache and computing resource to improve the performance of the next-generation IOV. Using this framework, a resource allocation strategy based on single agent deep reinforcement learning is proposed to maximize joint revenue, but the scenario of large-scale vehicles has not been discussed.

To some extent, the above schemes improves the quality of roadside units on providing resources and services for vehicles, and reduces costs on accessing related resources. However, these algorithms have some limitations. They often focus on the single resource of the vehicle network, or on the joint optimization of multiple resources in a small scale. Yet, the problem becomes quite complex, talking about allocating appropriate roadside unit resources for larger quantities of vehicles and a wider-area IOV.

Therefore, we proposed an algorithm based on multi-agent deep reinforcement learning, which can make decision quickly and has an excellent performance in dealing with complex problems. It significantly reduce network communication delay, improves the quality of IOV services, and optimizes IOV resources.

3 Resource Optimization Scheme for IOV

3.1 System Model

Based on the characteristics of existing traffic roads and communication methods, we construct a road traffic model on the basis of vehicle network. The scene is mainly composed of base stations and vehicles. The base station has computing power which can provide computing services to the vehicle by communicating with them. The resource pool of each base station is limited, and the resource pool as well as communication cost of each base station varies. Multiple vehicles may travel simultaneously on the road. The vehicle needs to select a suitable base station to use its resources. During the entire driving process, the vehicle will always communicate with the base station to obtain relevant resources, as shown in Fig. 1. The base station can undertake the limited resource requirements of vehicles. We introduce a concept called virtual vehicle, which represents the data stored by the vehicle in the base station and the unit occupying the base station resources. When the agent selects the base station, the corresponding virtual vehicle is generated on the base station subsequently. As the vehicle switches to a new base station that provides the resource service, the virtual vehicle migrates to the corresponding base station as well.

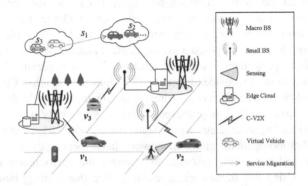

Fig. 1. An example to demonstrate the edge computing assisted intelligent driving.

3.2   Resource Cost Model

Communication Cost Model: Vehicles acquire resources by communicating with base stations. When the distance between the vehicle and the base station is far, communication delay will be caused, and the quality of service of the low-latency application cannot be guaranteed. Ideally, the vehicle will pick the nearest base station to obtain resource. Nevertheless, if a large number of vehicles gather in the same area to select the nearest base station, it may lead to a situation that the base station will be overload. In our proposed communication cost model, the cost of vehicle-to-base communication is as follows.

$$E_c = \left((x_p - x_v)^2 + (y_p - y_v)^2 \right) * w_c, \tag{1}$$

where E_c represents the communication cost between the vehicle and the virtual vehicle. (x_p, y_p) represents the location of the vehicle, (x_v, y_v) represents the location of the virtual vehicle, w_c represents the weight that reflects the impact of communication costs on acquiring resources.

Resource Competition Cost Model: The base station has limited hardware resources. When a base station undertakes too many resource requests and exceeds the resources of the base station, the resources allocated for each vehicle may not be sufficient to support the normal use of the vehicle application. Meanwhile, the base station needs to communicate frequently with a large number of vehicles, which may result in a decline in vehicle network service performance. The resource request undertaken by each base station should match its own capability. If the current resource request does not exceed the capacity of the base station, the resource requirements of each vehicle can be fully satisfied. We propose a resource competition cost model to characterize the ability of a base station resource to meet vehicle demand as follows.

$$E_r = \begin{cases} 0, & if \ \sum_{v \in b} r_v \le c_b \\ \left(\frac{c_b - \sum_{v \in b} r_v}{c_b} \right)^2 * w_r, & otherwise \end{cases} \tag{2}$$

where E_r represents the cost of competing resources for the vehicle to obtain resources, c_b represents the capability of the computing resources of the base station b, $v \in b$ represents the virtual vehicle deployed on the base station, r_v represents the resources occupied by the virtual vehicle v, w_r represents the weight that reflects the impact of resource competition costs on acquiring resources.

Migration Cost Model: The position of the vehicle in motion will change constantly. When a vehicle moves from the coverage of one road-side unit to the coverage of another Road-Side Unit, the vehicle should consider whether to change the road-side unit. However, when the road-side unit is switched, the data of the vehicle is still stored in the original road-side unit and the data needs to be migrated to the next road-side unit. We propose a migration cost model to characterize the cost of vehicle data migration.

$$E_t = \begin{cases} 0, & \text{if virtual vehicle is not migrated} \\ w_t, & \text{otherwise} \end{cases} \tag{3}$$

Where E_t represents the cost of virtual vehicle migration.

System Cost Model: The system cost of the vehicle which obtains the resources per unit time is the sum of communication cost, resource competition cost, and migration cost. The goal of our proposed edge resource allocation method is to minimize the system cost of all vehicles by allocating appropriate roadside units to vehicles.

$$E = E_c + E_r + E_t, \tag{4}$$

3.3 Analysis of Factors Affecting Allocation Strategy

The optimization of IOV resources is mainly to optimize the resource competition cost, migration cost and communication cost by assigning appropriate road-side unit to the vehicles. We need to consider the impact of multiple factors on the allocation strategy.

Vehicle Dynamic Changes: In an area, some vehicles may be starting to drive or entering the area at any time, others may be stopping driving or exiting the area. Therefore, the requirements of resources for road-side unit in an area are constantly changing. The algorithm for assigning a road-side unit to a vehicle would consider the spatial position of each vehicle and the distribution of the road-side units in the entire area. Furthermore, the algorithm should have good extensibility and can deal with resource allocation problems of a large number of vehicles.

Vehicle Travel Trajectory: When allocating the road-side units to the vehicle, the vehicle travel trajectory should be fully considered. If the road-side unit corresponding to the vehicle is located in front of it, the vehicle can use the services from road-side unit for a long time. Conversely, if the assigned road-side unit is located behind the vehicle, the distance between the vehicle and the road-side unit may become very far in a short time, which force the vehicle to switch the road-side unit.

Timeliness of Decision-Making: The constant change of the vehicle's spatial position causes the vehicle's state to change frequently. If it takes a lot of time to run the algorithm, the state of the actual vehicle may be completely different from the state acquired by the algorithm, and the decision of the algorithm will not be right and causes a significant drop in the performance of IoV. Therefore, the allocation algorithm would make quick decisions based on the changing state of vehicles.

When designing the allocation algorithm, it is indispensable to fully consider the influence of all above factors, which guarantees the performance of the optimization algorithm in the actual scene.

3.4 Roadside Unit Resource Allocation Algorithm Based on Multi-agent Deep Reinforcement Learning

The number of vehicles in an area and the states of all vehicles are changing at any time, which requires the proposed algorithm to respond quickly and have excellent scalability. Traditional reinforcement learning is limited to small action and state space, and is used in a discrete context. However, the more complex tasks that are closer to the actual situation often have large action and state space. Traditional reinforcement learning is difficult to deal with those problems. Deep reinforcement learning combines high-dimensional input of deep learning with reinforcement learning. Good performance in dealing with complex issues. In Multi-Agent Reinforcement learning, each vehicle acts as an agent. The agent chooses the appropriate base station to request resources according to his own observation. Multi-agent reinforcement learning has obvious advantages. First of all, the amount of data calculated by each agent in multi-agent reinforcement learning is only related to the scope of its own observation. The agent does not care about the state and cost of other agents. The computational cost of a single agent is small, and the running time of the algorithm is short, which meet the low latency requirements of the vehicle network. Secondly, the participation and exit of each agent in the system is not directly related to the decision of other agent. The agents in the system can be added or cancelled at any time. The algorithm proposed by us has excellent scalability.

Considering the characteristics of traffic roads and vehicle network, an independent DQN model is used to realize the roadside unit resource allocation algorithm. The reinforcement learning model is defined as follows:

Agent: Each vehicle is regarded as an independent agent. The agent would select the appropriate base station to obtain relevant resources.

State: The state of the agent includes the distance between the selected base station and the vehicle, the load status of the base stations near the vehicle, the distribution of the surrounding vehicles of the base stations near the virtual vehicle, the vector between the current vehicle position and the destination position, etc. The state we define takes into account the factors affecting the performance of allocation strategy.

Action: For an agent, its action space is to select the base station around the virtual vehicle as the target of the migration.

Reward: The cost of acquiring the base station resource for each vehicle is closely related to the capacity of the base station in the entire area and the distribution of the vehicle. A fixed reward cannot accurately indicate the correctness of the algorithm's decision-making. The reward should be related to the overall cost of vehicles. Based on this point of view, we propose a reward model.

$$\text{Reward} = \begin{cases} 0, & \text{if } abs(E_{ave} - E)/E_{ave} \leq 0.2 \\ E_{ave} - E, & \text{otherwise} \end{cases} \tag{5}$$

where E_{ave} is the average cost of acquiring resources for vehicles in the current area.

The process of the algorithm is as follows:

Algorithm 1: Road Unit Resource Allocation Algorithm Based on Multi-Agent Deep Reinforcement Learning

---

Input: Driving route of vehicles, location of road base station resources, Episodes: number of algorithm iterations.

Output: Optimal action of each vehicle in its current state

01:    Initialize multiple DQN network parameters and replay memory according to different attributes of the vehicles. The same kind of vehicles use the same DQN network

02:    **for** each episode in Episodes:

03:    Initialize the base station status

04:        **for** each step of an episode **do:**

05:            **for** each vehicle **do:**

06:                The vehicle selects an action from its own corresponding DQN according to the current state s.

07:                The virtual vehicle is migrated according to the action a, the next state s' is obtained, and the cost of acquiring the resource in the state s' is calculated, and the reward generated by the current decision is calculated according to formula (4).

08:                This experience s, s', a, reward is stored in the replay memory of the vehicle corresponding DQN.

09:            **end for**

10:            **for** each DQN:

11:                Models are trained using data from replay memory

12:            **end for**

13:            **if** a vehicle arrives at the end, **then:**

14:                break;

15:            **end if**

16:        **end for**

17:    **end for**

---

4   Evaluation

We experimented in a square area in which 10*10 base stations were arranged evenly. We have placed 4 types of cars, each with 100 vehicles, and each type of vehicle can adopt different strategies for base station selection. During training, the overall cost of the vehicles in our approach is declining and we compare our approach with random approach, as shown in Fig. 2.

According to the experimental data, we can find that the moving vehicle can select the appropriate base station, mainly in the following two aspects. First, as the vehicle moves, the virtual vehicle corresponding to the vehicle will follow the vehicle for migration, thus ensuring that the vehicle takes low communication cost to obtain resources. However, simply considering the communication cost will cause vehicles in one region to get resources from the same base station. Our algorithm takes the

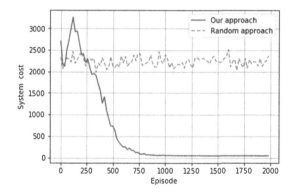

Fig. 2. Performance evaluation on system cost.

competition cost into consideration, which makes the vehicle select the base station with lower load and closer when the vehicle finds that the nearest base station has no remaining resource.

5 Conclusion and Future Works

In order to meet the increasing resource demand of vehicle usage, roadside units are used to provide services. However, due to the mobility, the changing number of vehicles, and the limit of roadside unit resources, it is quite a complicated problem to select suitable roadside units for the vehicle. We proposed a road unit resource allocation algorithm based on multi-agent deep reinforcement learning. This algorithm takes a variety of factors into account, which help us select appropriate base stations. Our algorithm can significantly reduce the network communication delay and improve the service quality of vehicle network applications, and optimize vehicle network resources. Furthermore, our future work mainly includes optimizing the network structure to improve the performance of the algorithm.

Acknowledgment. This work was supported in part by the Natural Science Foundation of China under Grant 61876023 and Grant 61902035, and in part by the Natural Science Foundation of Beijing under Grant 4181002.

References

1. Zhang, S., Zhang, N., Fang, X., Yang, P., Shen, X.S.: Cost-effective vehicular network planning with cache-enabled green roadside units. In: 2017 IEEE International Conference on Communications (ICC), pp. 1–6. IEEE (2017)
2. Wang, C., Yu, F.R., Liang, C., Chen, Q., Tang, L.: Joint computation offloading and interference management in wireless cellular networks with mobile edge computing. IEEE Trans. Veh. Technol. **66**(8), 7432–7445 (2017)

3. Zhang, S., He, P., Suto, K., Yang, P., Zhao, L., Shen, X.: Traffic steering assisted mobile edge caching: exploiting spatial content diversity gain. In: 2017 IEEE Global Communications Conference, GLOBECOM 2017, pp. 1–6. IEEE (2017)
4. Wu, T.J., Liao, W., Chang, C.J.: A cost-effective strategy for road-side unit placement in vehicular networks. IEEE Trans. Commun. **60**(8), 2295–2303 (2012)
5. He, Y., Zhao, N., Yin, H.: Integrated networking, caching, and computing for connected vehicles: a deep reinforcement learning approach. IEEE Trans. Veh. Technol. **67**(1), 44–55 (2018)

A Road Traffic Guidance Service Based on Deep Reinforcement Learning

Kaihui Chen[✉], Zhihan Liu[✉], Jinglin Li[✉], and Quan Yuan[✉]

State Key Laboratory of Networking and Switching Technology,
Beijing University of Posts and Telecommunications,
Haidian District 100876, People's Republic of China
{kayc,zhihan,jlli,yuanquan}@bupt.edu.cn

Abstract. The development of Internet of vehicle (IOV) and autopilot technology indicates the coming of smart traffic and automatic unmanned era. The promotion of networking and intelligence not only provides a rich source for urban traffic data, but also provides an efficient and direct way to solve urban traffic problems. With the help of deep learning and reinforcement learning technology, we propose a model to mine the urban traffic rule from the travel history of urban travelers, and utilize it achieving better allocation of traffic resources by providing a traffic guidance service, finally realize the system optimal traffic travel.

Keywords: Cloud service · Deep learning · Reinforcement learning · Traffic guidance

1 Introduction

The route selection of urban travelers have personal habits and preferences, and the travelers also have a certain preference in selecting. In the meanwhile, due to the deviation between the travelers' perception and the actual travel time cost, it result in user optimization (UO) in the utilization process of traffic road resources, but not achieve the system optimization (SO). It makes the excessive competition of road resources in certain areas, resulting in the imbalance of traffic flow and jam, but the other areas are empty, which is a waste. If the travelers are reasonably guided, the problem of route selection imbalance can be solved. It can be solved by the traffic assignment algorithm, however, the scalability of the traditional traffic assignment algorithm is limited.

With the development of edge computing, vehicle networking, and autopilot technology, the problem can be solved in a highly connected and intelligent environment. Specifically, utilize deep learning, it fits and learns an urban traffic rule from the traffic flow from a global point of view, and utilizes deep reinforcement learning to give the best guidance to the travelers under the current

This work was supported in part by the Natural Science Foundation of China under Grant 61876023 and Grant 61902035, and in part by the Natural Science Foundation of Beijing under Grant 4181002.

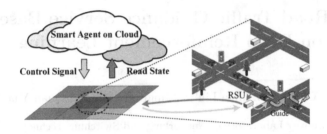

Fig. 1. System architecture.

traffic condition. For travelers' view, as shown in Fig. 1, a center-based traffic guidance service is provided, travelers upload vehicle information through the urban roadside unit (RSU) and send travel route requests, center smart agent on cloud generate traffic guidance decisions based on global information, finally, the travel route is then returned to the roadside unit to guide the vehicles.

The structure of this paper is as follows: the second section introduces the related work, the third section introduces the structure of the proposed model, the fourth section gives the experimental results, and the last section summarizes the work.

2   Related Work

This problem is the traffic assignment problem essentially. The traffic flow assignment model can be traced back to Beckmann et al. [1] In 1956, a nonlinear programming model of traffic flow assignment satisfying the first principle of Wardrop was proposed. LeBlanc et al. [2] successfully solved the model with the Frank-Wolfe algorithm. Smith and Dafermos et al. [3–5] proposed more generalized nonlinear congruence model and variational inequality model.

Merchant et al. [4] put forward the concept of dynamic traffic flow assignment for the first time. The macroscopic model then takes the whole vehicle flow as the research object and analyzes the traffic flow characteristics macroscopically, such as METACOR model of Diakaki et al. [6].

The traffic flow assignment models of now can be divided into 3 types. for traditional part, Zhou et al. [7] proposed the congestion-based C-logit SUE model, they provide two equivalent variational inequality formulations and solved it. For the game-based part, Messmer et al. [8] propose a method based on feedback dynamic traffic assignment (DTA) strategy. For the artificial intelligence part, Varia et al. [9] used the technique of genetic algorithms (GAs) to minimize the global travel cost in the network, and Hongwei et al. [10] used a random multidimensional mutation particle swarm optimization algorithm (RMMPSO) to solving the problem.

Table 1. Symbol definition.

Table 1. Symbol definition.

Symbol	Definition
N	Set of nodes
A	A set of directed arcs (segments)
R	A set of origin nodes of demand, $R \subseteq N$
F	A set of destination nodes of the demand, $F \subseteq N$
r	A origin node, $r \in R$
s	A destination node $s \in F$
q_{rs}	Travel demand between starting and ending points of OD
x_a	Traffic flow at segment a
t_a	Traffic impedance of segment a, where $a \in A$
$K^{r \cdot s}$	OD pair for the set of all paths between r - s, where $k \in K^{r \cdot s}$
$f_k^{r \cdot s}$	OD to the traffic flow of path k in r - s
$\delta_{a,k}^{r \cdot S}$	The correlation between the road section and the path in r - s of OD pairs, where $\delta_{a,k}^{r \cdot s} = 1$, then the section a is on the path $\delta_{a,k}^{r \cdot s} = 0$, indicating t the section a is not on the path k
D_a	Reduction rate of section a

3 Proposed Method

3.1 Problem Definition

Target Function. Similar to Beckmann et al. [1] constructed a mathematical programming model of wardrop. Our Target function is as follow:

$$\min Z(x) = \sum_a x_a t_a (x_a) \tag{1}$$

it means minimize the time costs of all cars. Around this goal, we decide to change the probability of path travelers selection, to minimize global costs. The probability of travelers selection is expressed as follows, where P_k^{rs} is the probability choosing path k of OD pair r-s:

$$P_k^{p^{r s}} \cdot q_{rs} = f_k^{rs} \tag{2}$$

$$\sum_{k \in K^{rs}} f_k^{rs} = q_{rs} \tag{3}$$

The traffic flow of a single road segment a is calculated as follows:

$$x_a = \sum_{rs} \sum_k f_k^{rs} \delta_{a,k}^{rs} \tag{4}$$

The initial user routing ratio is:

$$P_k^{rs} = \Pr\left(C_k^{rs} \le C_l^{rs}\right) \tag{5}$$

where, C_k^n, C_l^{rs} is travel time estimation of the route k, l of traveler.

We also divide urban areas into the grids for reducing the complex of the problem, when a traveler passing through the target grid will be guided. In this paper, grid size is set contains 3–5 roads. When conducting the calculation of route probability, the reduction rate D_k is given according to the traffic load between the nearby regions, as shown in the following formula:

$$D_a = \gamma \cdot \frac{AVG\left(x_l\right)}{AVG\left(x_k\right)} \tag{6}$$

where k is the roads in the target grid, l is all the roads in the nearby grids. The way of the decay rate take effect is selecting the maximum decay rate of a road in the path, as the decay of this path, then the selected probability of this path will decay by this rate, such as:

$$f_i^{rs} = \frac{D_i \cdot f_i^{rs}}{\sum_{k \in K^{rs}} D_k \cdot f_k^{rs}} \tag{7}$$

The guidance decision based on the cloud agent is to decide when and which grid to calculating the decay. The agent finally learns the transform function:

$$T\left(S_t\right) \xrightarrow{a} S_{t+1} \tag{8}$$

where S_t represents the global condition, t represents the time, and a represents the guide action on the target region.

3.2   Model Structure

To obtain the decision under the current traffic condition, the input of the model is the current traffic condition, and the output is a action of guidance. It is divided into three parts: convolution neural network, Monte Carlo search, and simulator.

Convolution Neural Network Part. CNN part is used to evaluate the situation from a global perspective. The structure of the network is divided into 3 layers and 2 heads, 3 layers are $5 \times 3 \times 3 \times 32$ filter, $32 \times 3 \times 3 \times 64$ filter, and $64 \times 3 \times 3 \times 128$ filter, 2 heads are 2 fully connected layers down sample to 10 and 1 dimension, for policy and value head respectively. The input of CNN is a traffic condition representation, which is a tensor of W*H*5, it stores the speed value in a period t of all road. W and H represent the number of the grid, and 4 represents the nearest four timeslots. From it can mine the rule of urban traffic. At the last dimension, represent the current guided state, formatted as W*H*1 [11].

Then the training data is organized as (s_t, π_t, z_t) for all the time t during simulating, and the new neural network $f_{\theta_i}(s)$ is trained and used for the next

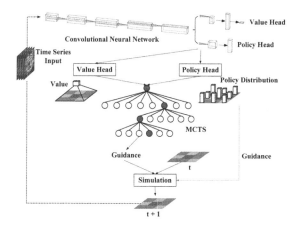

Fig. 2. Model architecture.

simulation round. The network parameters are trained by gradient drop, and the objective function is as follows (Fig. 2):

$$l = (z - v)^2 - \pi^{\mathrm{T}} \log p + c\|\theta\|^2 \qquad (9)$$

It is the sum of the root mean square and cross-entropy. where c is a parameter controlling the level of L2 weight regularization used to prevent overfitting [12, 13].

The Monte Carlo Part. The output of CNN part be used to help to search traffic state in the Monte Carlo part. In Specifically, each edge (s, a) in the search tree stores a prior probability $P(s, a)$, a visit count $N(s, a)$, and an action value $Q(s, a)$. [12, 13]. Each rollout starting from the root node, three steps are then carried out: the guidance selection, the situation expanding and updating the Monte Carlo tree are performed.

The guidance selection depends on the edge value $Q(s, a) + U(s, a)$ with the maximum criteria.

$$U(s, a) = c_{\mathrm{puct}} \cdot P(s, a) \frac{\sqrt{\sum_b N(s, b)}}{1 + N(s, a)} \qquad (10)$$

Each time a node is traversed, the count of the node is added, and the action value Q (s, a) of the node is updated with the action value $Q(s, a) = 1/N(s, a) \sum_{s'|s, a \to s'} V(s')$. When the terminal node is reached (simulation 1.5 h in this paper), the action value is updated by back propagation, $W(s_t, a_t) = W(s_t, a_t) + v$, $Q(s_t, a_t) = W(s_t, a_t)$. After the simulation is over, the final guide action selection is made, that is,

$$\pi(a|s_0) = N(s_0, a)^{1/\tau} / \sum_b N(s_0, b)^{1/\tau} \qquad (11)$$

4   Experiment

4.1   Simulator Setting

The simulator is designed for simulating the dynamic traffic flow, user road selection, and road congestion. Details include building road topology, defining lane capacity, setting steering wait, setting exceed waiting of road capacity. The traffic flow model used is the BPR function:

$$t_d^n = t_0^n \left[1 + \alpha \left(\frac{q_n}{C_n} \right)^\beta \right] \tag{12}$$

To perform the horizontal comparison, we selected a relatively small urban area to experiment, the size of the area is 6 km * 4.8 km to reflect the effect of the algorithm on congestion avoidance and balanced utilization of traffic resources, the simulation time lasts 1.5 h. In the road network structure, origin as the starting point is shown as the white circle in Fig. 3, intersection of the road as a black circle, link as a black line segment, green triangle as the main travel endpoint placed on the edge, where origin acts as the vehicle emission point. 80% of the travel endpoint is at the green triangle, the remaining 20% are randomly distributed on the black circle Intersection point.

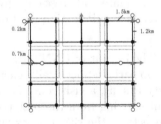

Fig. 3. Traffic network. (Color figure online)

The total duration of the simulation is 90 min, each origin output 20 cars per minute, the total number of cars is 18,000 (Fig. 4).

4.2   Result Analysis

There are four different models in our experiment, the average selection model, distance weighted selection model, game-based model Bang-bang [8], and deep reinforcement learning model DRLTraffic (ours), the result of model are shown in Table 1. In terms of the execution efficiency of the model, we can see that in a certain scale of the urban area, the DRLTraffic model benefits from the advantages of GPU and shows the real-time performance, while the shortest path and random routing model do not need additional computation, so it is

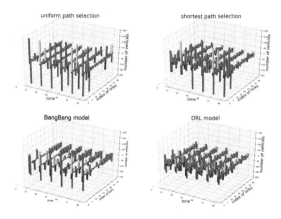

Fig. 4. Model result campare.

also very fast. On the other hand, the Bang-bang model needs to solve the Nash equilibrium every time, and the speed is relatively slow. In terms of guidance effect, we can see that there is no guidance in the shortest path selection and random selection model, resulting in local congestion and imbalance of resource utilization, so the average traffic time and throughput are worse than the other two methods. The Bang-bang model aiming at user optimization without using global information, but still gets good results. The DRLTraffic model aiming at global load balance, finally achieve the highest throughput and the shortest average traffic time (Table 2).

Table 2. Model performance & result.

Model name	Execution time(/ms)	Average travel time(/secs)
Random selection (uniform distribution)	46.66	800.92
Shortest selection (weighted distribution)	33.33	521.94
Bang-bang	16.601	440.40
DRLTraffic (ours)	32.16	415.66

5 Conclusion

This paper introduces a region-based deep reinforcement learning and Monte Carlo tree search method to provide center-based user travel guidance cloud services. With the help of the Monte Carlo tree search, the global optimal travel route can be solved, and achieved the global road load balance state. The experiment results shows, due to the generalization ability of the deep learning model, the deep learning model has more robustness and optimization performance in large-scale computing tasks, it gains the good result.

Acknowledgement. This work was supported in part by the Natural Science Foundation of China under Grant 61876023 and Grant 61902035, and in part by the Natural Science Foundation of Beijing under Grant 4181002.

References

1. Beckmann, M., McGuire, C.B., Winsten, C.B.: Studies in the economics of transportation, Technical report (1956)
2. LeBlanc, L.J., Morlok, E.K., Pierskalla, W.P.: An efficient approach to solving the road network equilibrium traffic assignment problem. Transp. Res. **9**(5), 309–318 (1975)
3. Smith, M.J.: The existence, uniqueness and stability of traffic equilibria. Transp. Res. Part B: Methodol. **13**(4), 295–304 (1979)
4. Dafermos, S.: Traffic equilibrium and variational inequalities. Transp. Sci. **14**(1), 42–54 (1980)
5. Dafermos, S.: An iterative scheme for variational inequalities. Math. Program. **26**(1), 40–47 (1983)
6. Diakaki, C., Papageorgiou, M., McLean, T.: Simulation studies of integrated corridor control in Glasgow. Transp. Res. Part C: Emerg. Technol. **5**(3–4), 211–224 (1997)
7. Zhou, Z., Chen, A., Bekhor, S.: C-logit stochastic user equilibrium model: formulations and solution algorithm. Transportmetrica **8**(1), 17–41 (2012)
8. Messmer, A., Papageorgiou, M.: METANET: a macroscopic simulation program for motorway networks. Traffic Eng. Control **31**(9) (1990)
9. Varia, H.R., Dhingra, S.L.: Dynamic optimal traffic assignment and signal time optimization using genetic algorithms. Comput.-Aided Civil Infrastruct. Eng. **19**(4), 260–273 (2004)
10. Hongwei, G., Qiaoxia, Z., Fan, W.: Solving traffic assignment problem by an improved particle swarm optimization and a segmented impedance function. In: Park, J., Kim, J., Zou, D., Lee, Y. (eds.) Information Technology Convergence, Secure and Trust Computing, and Data Management. LNEE, vol. 180, pp. 76–86. Springer, Dordrecht (2012). https://doi.org/10.1007/978-94-007-5083-8_12
11. Zhang, J., Zheng, Y., Qi, D.: Deep spatio-temporal residual networks for citywide crowd flows prediction. In: Thirty-First AAAI Conference on Artificial Intelligence (2017)
12. Silver, D., et al.: Mastering the game of go with deep neural networks and tree search. Nature **529**, 484–489 (2016)
13. Silver, D., et al.: Mastering the game of go without human knowledge. Nature **550**, 354–359 (2017)

expanAI: A Smart End-to-End Platform for the Development of AI Applications

Yongmei Wei[(⊠)] and Jia Xin Low

Nanyang Polytechnic, 180 Ang Mo Kio Avenue, Singapore, Singapore
Sophia_wei@nyp.edu.sg

Abstract. Building Modern Artificial Intelligence (AI) applications is a complicated process involving data preparation, model selection, and intensive training over large-scale data. It usually requires expertise in various domains, namely resource management, distribute storage, parallel computing, machine learning and deep learning. Acquiring all these skills for many small and medium companies to build an efficient AI application can be extremely hard. ExpanAI is proposed as a smart end-to-end platform for building efficient AI applications. ExpanAI provides a set of microservices to abstract away low-level implementation, like infrastructure and resource management, from the end users. Frequently used middleware, such as Spark, Kafka, Cassandra, etc., are first-class residences in the ExpanAI and are always available to users. Furthermore, ExpanAI introduces a smart interpreter to provide easy-to-use interface to execute data-intensive jobs. This interpreter automatically optimizes the execution plans according to the profile of the data and available resources. Lastly, a workflow optimization recommender is also proposed to conduct self-analysis over all jobs and automatically generates reports to suggest ways to improve performance or to avoid failures.

Keywords: Artificial intelligence · End-to-end · Optimization · Workflow

1 Introduction

The creation and consumption of data continues to grow by leaps and bounds. To harvest the value brought by the Big Data, however, there are many challenges.

Firstly, Building AI applications is a complicated process. A typical AI workflow starts from building proper infrastructure, followed by managing various resources. Data preparation including cleansing then can be conducted by using various tools/systems. After data preparation, AI applications are developed through applying different algorithms to model the data. Each stage in the AI workflow requires different tools and skillsets.

Secondly, it is challenging to build AI applications with high efficiency. A data scientist may not be able to efficiently utilize the dataset prepared by data engineers, if he/she is not aware the impact of the underlying data format on the chosen model. While, when data engineers work on their data pipelines, they may not know what data format that data scientists actually need. Although the world has witnessed a large proliferation of tools/system [2–8] for different steps in developing AI applications, the industry still lacks a platform to merge the gap between multiple data teams.

© Springer Nature Switzerland AG 2020
C.-H. Hsu et al. (Eds.): IOV 2019, LNCS 11894, pp. 361–365, 2020.
https://doi.org/10.1007/978-3-030-38651-1_29

In this paper, we present expanAI, a platform to ease the AI application development. ExpanAI divides the platform into three layers: Resource management layer, service layer, and optimization layer. By applying automation and machine learning techniques, expanAI let users to focus more on the Please note that the first paragraph of a section or subsection is not indented end results rather than the cluster management and job optimization. The detailed design of ExpanAI is presented in Sect. 3.

2 Related Work

In both academia and industrial worlds, tremendous effort has been put to address the challenges raised by Big Data processing A number of cloud-based services or platform [2, 3] has been developed. For example, Amazon Web Service (AWS) launched Elastic MapReduce (EMR) to provide managed Hadoop framework [4] to make Hadoop platform instantly available to its users. Big Data companies such as Cloudera and Hortonworks expanded rapidly in the past several years and standardized the big-data systems across multiple industries. IBM launched Data Science Experience (DSX) in 2016. DSX integrates with tools from different domains such as RStudio, Spark, Jupyter notebook.

The existing platforms do not provide any tools to automatically improve the efficiencies of the AI applications built. The existing solutions heavily rely on the experience of the users. If the users lack experience handling large scale data sets, the performance of the AI application developed would be largely affected. The focus of ExpanAI is on the "efficiency" side. ExpanAI takes the following approaches elaborated in Sect. 3 to simplify the development process and improve the efficiency of the end products.

3 Approach

Figure 1 shows the system architecture of the proposed platform. ExpanAI contains three layers, namely resource management layer, service management layer and optimization layers. Each layer contains a few microservices.

3.1 Resource Management

Resource management layer manages raw resource. Raw resources refers to physical servers or virtual instances from Cloud providers, and special computing devices like GPUs. The mission of the resource management is to simply the work of IT and Data engineers.

Kubernetes [3] is used here to dynamically group available raw resources into manageable resources. Microservices based on Ansible [7] are deployed in this layer, which is responsible to scale up and down the cluster and manage system configurations. Kubernetes standardized most of the traditional IT tasks, like monitoring,

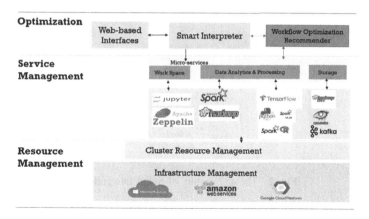

Fig. 1. Architecture of ExpanAI platform

logging, and alerting, as well as modern service management [3]. These standard tools and systems considerably lowered the effort to build an autonomous and self-healing platform.

3.2 Service Management

Service management layer has three types of operators.

- Workspace operators: Provide workspace environment to users. Users interact with other ExpanAI service via web-based UIs (Jupyter Notebook and Zeppelin). For the user workspace, the docker image is pre-populated with popular machine learning and deep learning library/software packages, such as Pandas, Scikit-learn, and TensorFlow.
- Data analytics and Processing operators: Provisioning data processing systems like Spark and Hadoop.
- Storage operators: Exposing shared storage system like HDFS and Kafka to users. With the help of these operators, ExpanAI can almost instantly provide a working environment with pre-configured connectors to various sub-systems to users.

3.3 Optimization Layer

Optimization layer is composed of two microservices, one is Smart Interpreter which does job-level optimization, and the other is Workflow Optimization Recommender that focus on analyzing the entire workflow and giving tuning advices.

Smart Interpreter

Figure 2 shows the components of Smart Interpreter. ExpanAI uses SQL as the main interface for user to describe their data processing and modeling logics. ExpanAI takes one step further to extend standard SQL with machine learning functions. Such extension allow user to use one standard approach to handle both ETL and modeling jobs, without shifting among various tools.

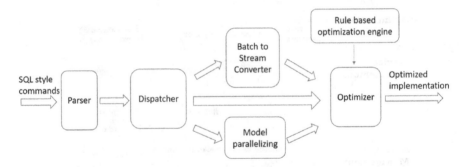

Fig. 2. The architecture of Smart Interpreter

Figure 2 shows the components of Smart Interpreter. expanAI uses SQL as the main interface for user to describe their data processing and modeling logics. ExpanAI takes one step further to extend standard SQL with machine learning functions. Such extension allow user to use one standard approach to handle both ETL and modeling jobs, without shifting among various tools.

With the extended SQL functions, a new parser is developed to translate the extended SQL function to platform specific implementation. In ExpanAI, Spark is integrated in the first phase and the extended SQL function is planned to execute as Spark jobs. expanAI identified a few optimization scenarios: Model Parallelizing, Batch-to-Stream Converter and Rule-based optimization.

Model Parallelizing is required when massive models are required to be trained. In nature, the big data processing platform such as Spark enables the parallelism on massive data, Unfortunately, the parallelism does not happen naturally if massive number of models are required to be trained parallelly. The proposed Model Parallelize utilizes the vectorized User Defined Functions (UDFs) [8] to allow training massive number of models efficiently.

Batch-to-Stream Converter is applied to applications dealing with time series data. This is because there are many cases, time series are often stored in block files where records are sorted by timestamp. If users are not aware of this case and use batch query to process the data, they would not be able to utilize the sorted data efficiently.

Rule-based optimization is to incorporate best practices. The best practices included in the initial phase is the data shuffling management. One key factor in big data processing is shuffling efficiency. The statistics of the data and the types of operations on the data both influence the final performance. ExpanAI applies pre-proven rules to take care of data shuffling. In the future, another key factor to select proper machine learning algorithmic implementation will also be incorporated as it has been shown in [1] that different implementation of machine learning algorithms to realize the same purpose can exhibit significant performance difference for various data set.

Workflow Optimization Recommender

Figure 3 shows the architecture of Workflow Optimization Recommender. There are two major components – self discovery and self analysis. The self-discovery component is responsible for discovering different aspects of the involved data and required

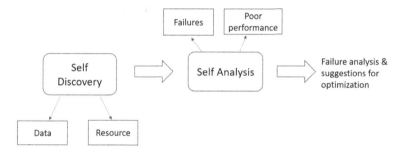

Fig. 3. The architecture of workflow optimization recommender

resources, generating profiles. With this information, together with job status, the self-analysis component automatically analyzes the reasons of failures and/or cause of poor performance.

4   Conclusion

ExpanAI is proposed to provide an easy-to-use end-to-end AI workflow management platform. The low level details on the infrastructure and resources management have been abstracted way. Optimization is also provided to ensure the efficiency of the AI applications developed.

References

1. Evan, R.S., Shivaram, V., Tomer, K., Michael, J.F., Benjamin, R.: KeystoneML: optimizing pipelines for large-scale advanced analytics. In: IEEE International Conference on Data Engineering (2017)
2. Apache Spark. http://spark.apache.org/
3. Kubernetes. https://kubernetes.io/
4. TensorFlow. https://www.tensorflow.org/
5. Helm. https://helm.sh/
6. Practical advice for analysis of large, complex data sets. http://www.unofficialgoogle datascience.com/2016/10/practical-advice-for-analysis-of-large.html. Accessed 31 Oct 2016
7. Venezia, P.: Review: puppet vs. chef vs. ansible vs. salt
8. http://www.infoworld.com/article/2609482/data-center/data-center-review-puppet-vs-chef-vs-ansible-vs-salt.html
9. Lijin: Introducing pandas UDF for pySpark. https://databricks.com/blog/2017/10/30/introducing-vectorized-udfs-for-pyspark.html

Smoke and Stress Tests for Travel Service Applications via LoadRunner

Chau-Yi Chou[✉], Yu-Bin Fang, Shuen-Tai Wang, and Fang-An Kuo

National Center for High-Performance Computing, Hsinchu, Taiwan
cychou@nchc.narl.org.tw

Abstract. The web applications have now become one of the most important parts of people's life. It entered the time-to-market age, that is, the faster released the products, the more the chances that it will increase the company potentialities. System stability test plays an important role of improving the service quality and developing these web applications. There were three well-known strategies to solve this problem: developing application program interface to measure the response time, through open source softwares (e.g. Jmeter), and via the commercial packages (e.g. LoadRunner). LoadRunner is an industry-standard package that has the advantages of graph-based analysis, statistical analysis of the measured data, service-level agreement, and the loading analysis for the client end compared with other strategies. This paper demonstrated that it monitored the service quality of web applications using the smoke and stress tests for travel service applications via LoadRunner. And we proposed a strategy for on-line web server testing. We hope that the practical experience and the information are useful for researchers.

Keywords: Smoke test · Stress test · System stability test · LoadRunner · Web application

1 Introduction

We enjoy the benefits of convenience via web applications, for example, on-line shopping web service, social network (Facebook, Line, Twitter, etc.), virtual group on-line games, data process (upload/download/editor) via cloud, mail service, and so on. It entered the time-to-market age, that is, faster released the products more potentially. System stability test [1] plays an important role of improving service quality and developing these web applications. Programmers easily understood the user-friendly of the web applications from the viewpoint of end-users, clear measured the transaction time (Application Program Interface Response time), and employed the stress tests. That is, do our developing web applications inherit the user-friendly characteristics, completeness, usefulness, and stability? There are well-known strategies to discover this problem. Developing programmers implemented the application program interface (API) to measure the elapsed time between the client HTTP request and the server response, for example, NCHC TWCC-CLI [2]. The open-source software may be often adopted, for example, Jmeter [3]. Moreover, we should employ the commercial packages, such as LoadRunner [4].

© Springer Nature Switzerland AG 2020
C.-H. Hsu et al. (Eds.): IOV 2019, LNCS 11894, pp. 366–373, 2020.
https://doi.org/10.1007/978-3-030-38651-1_30

The researchers [5–12] show that the commercial package (LoadRunner) is an industry-standard software. This package has the advantages of graph-based analysis, statistical analysis of the measured data, service level agreement (SLA), and the loading analysis for the client end compared with other strategies. LoadRunner contains three main modules to simulate different user behavior, for example, via different brewers, different think time, and various request options. VuGen module created the working scripts (programs) each virtual user (Vuser). Controller module created the executing scenarios which decide the number of the virtual users, performed period, the Vuser behavior, and so on. Finally, analysis module presented graph-based analyzing tools.

Furthermore, the recorded scripts could be modified by VuGen GUI or C or JavaScript programming for various heavier; for instance different request option, different think time, adjustable parameters, and programmable for dynamic web response. Controller module defined the number of virtual users, Vuser behavior (the models of the virtual users entered/left computation and the interval between two virtual users), the number of execution or the period of execution, the service level agreement, and so on.

The replay environment parameters let us simulate the user behavior, for example, random think time, the number of iterations, the type of network, the executing program modules, standard or more detail output for debugging the bugs, etc. The working script with the replay environment parameters became the cornerstone of the controller module. This module presented interactive monitor tools at running status, such as the status (initial/running/stop/fail) of virtual users, error messages and the related documents, hits per second, throughput, the overloading of the client ends, and so on. The analysis module generated these graph-based and statistical reports for service level agreements, the transaction response time, hits per second, throughput, etc.

Niranjanamurthy and co-researchers [9] compared the functionality of Loadrunner with JMeter. Aggarwal and Solanki [8] employed the parameterization and customization features of VuGen GUI to conveniently manage various scripts. Khan and Amjad [6] presented the performance evaluations of Loadrunner and CA Wily for the number of hits per second and throughput on different the number of the virtual users. This paper demonstrated that it monitored the service quality of web applications using the smoke and stress tests for travel service applications via LoadRunner. And we proposed a strategy for on-line web server testing. We hope that the practical experience and the information are useful for re-searchers.

2 Testbed

We adopted the testbed which consisted of the Intel Core i5-6500 CPU (Central Processing Unit) running at 3.2 GHz, 4 cores shared 8 GB memory and 1 TB hard disk, and Windows 10 Pro operator system. Web Tours 1.0 with strawberry-perl-5.10.1.0 [13] is our web tours sample application system. We employed the LoadRunner 12.60 trial version, that is, the controller module was limited in 50 Vusers simulation.

Figure 1 depicted the LoadRunner flowchart. First of all we installed these packages and planned the anchors and service agreement levels, then we recorded the script and set anchors via VuGen (Virtual User Generator). If it failed, it finished this job. That is, LoadRunner did not measure this web site; for instance AWS portal systems. We repeated the replay function (with different environment parameters, programming, and parameterization via GUI) of VuGen until met our plans. This scripts and their replay environment setting were cornerstones for entering the controller module. We defined the scenarios including the number of the virtual users, performed period, the Vuser behavior, the service level agreements (SLAs), etc. On executing phase we monitored the interactive status via GUI. It included the initial/running/stop/fail status of virtual users, error message and the related documents, hits per second, throughput, the overloading of the client ends, and so on. Finally, analysis module presented graph-based reports for service level agreements, the transaction response time, hits per second, throughput, etc.

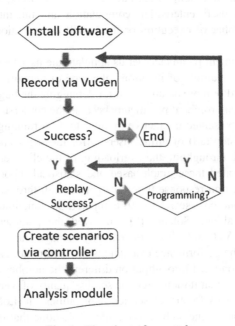

Fig. 1. Flowchart of our study.

3 Smoke Test

We defined 6 anchors (check points) for web application performance evaluations, transaction response time and service level agreements. C program was written as

```
lr_start_transaction...
        HTTP request and response...
lr_end_transaction...
```

Figure 2 depicted the login anchor for simulating the system stability when multiusers entered the system simultaneously. The logout anchor was order to measure the transaction response time on multiusers exited the system at the same time. The Lunch, booking, and itinerary anchors presented the web service preparation time, response time for user booking, and itinerary response time, respectively.

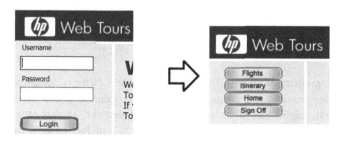

Fig. 2. Login anchor.

We defined the "search flights button" anchor as the web service response time of the left-hand-side sub-figure of Fig. 3 after pushed the "continue" button. The right-hand-side sub-figure of Fig. 3 demonstrated a search for the ticket from Los Angeles to Paris on 10 July 2019 with a person, Coach, none seat preference, and a single trip.

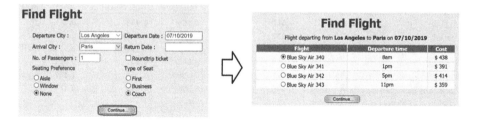

Fig. 3. Search flights button anchor.

Table 1 showed the results on 1 virtual user (Vuser). The Lunch anchor spent the longest time than other anchors. The Lunch response time was around 2 times of login (the second place). The logout and itinerary presented near response time.

4   Stress Test

We simultaneously employed 50 virtual users to use the travel service applications during 1 h for stress tests. It was random allowed to simulate the different browsers, for example, IE, Chrome, Firefox, and so on, seat preference (Window, Aisle, None), departure/return date, types of seat (first, business, coach), single trip or roundtrip, etc. We also defined the service level agreements (SLAs) as any the transaction response time of anchors less than 10 s.

Table 1. Results on 1 virtual user.

Anchor (check point)	Transaction response time (sec.)
Lunch	0.361
login	0.182
Search flights button	0.122
Booking	0.113
Itinerary	0.146
Logout	0.159

Figure 4 demonstrated the results on 50 virtual users (Vusers) simultaneously. We assumed that the maximal transaction response time occurred in the stress tests. Two anchors (Lunch, login) failed at service level agreement, that is, the transaction response time of the two anchors were more than 10 s. It mainly because that 50 virtual users simultaneously employed the travel service applications caused the web service to spend more time for the web service preparation time and login the web site. Form these statistical analysis (the average, standard deviation, and 90%) we found that only few failed the service level agreements. The transaction response time of the two anchors (logout and booking) were big more than 1 Vuser. Figure 5 depicted the loading of the web site near at 750 KB/s of throughout.

Transaction Name	SLA Status	Minimum	Average	Maximum	Std. Deviation	90 Percent
booking	✔	0.057	0.19	4.566	0.405	0.211
itinerary	✔	0.057	0.193	3.542	0.395	0.163
login	✗	0.105	0.686	13.757	1.817	1.16
logout	✔	0.094	0.439	5.542	0.831	1.082
Lunch	✗	0.101	0.627	24.589	2.336	0.592
Search Flights Button	✔	0.106	0.144	2.391	0.108	0.174

Service Level Agreement Legend: ✔ Pass   ✗ Fail

Fig. 4. Results (SLA Status) on 50 virtual users.

5   A Strategy for on-Line Web Service via LoadRunner

Smoke tests are to define the anchors while stress tests are for the web service benchmarks via heavy loading. The stress test was suitably applied to off-line servers. It is mainly because that the servers significantly decrease service quality and even crash. Therefore, the stress test was not suitable for an on-line server. We proposed a strategy for on-line servers via LoadRunner. As shown in Fig. 6, we suppose that the simulation required around 300 s each iteration, the interval time = 10 s and the maximal transaction response time occurred in the stress tests. It spent 600 s for two iterations; therefore, every anchor was performed at least once during heavy loading. On the other hand, the on-line servers will be significantly a decrease in loading.

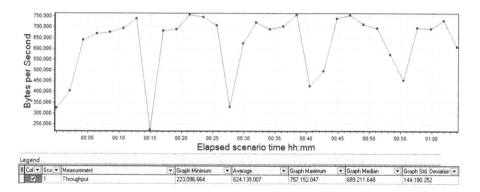

Fig. 5. Throughout on 50 virtual users.

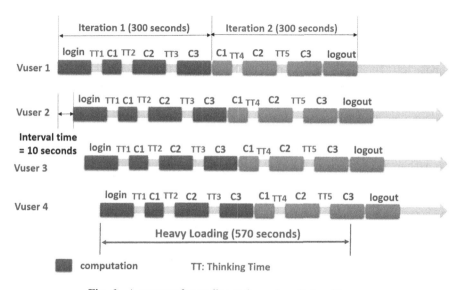

Fig. 6. A strategy for on-line web service via LoadRunner.

LoadRunner defined the parameter (Think Time) to simulate the thinking time while the end-users used web applications. We recommended the random value between a half and 2 times of recorded one. Figure 7 illustrated the results of an on-line web service application for our proposed strategy. The abnormal phenomenon occurred at 10 virtual users.

What is different the numbers of iterations on replay environment settings of the VuGen module from the interval at controller execution settings? Assume a job spent 5 min each iteration. Case1: VuGen defined 2 iterations with exit after complete jobs via controller modules. Case2: VuGen defined 1 iteration with a scenario of 10 min of the execution interval. If they were successfully performed, the both cases showed the same simulations. But they failed, Case1 performed 2 iterations and finished; Case2 was repeatedly executed 10 min and caused the on-line web service a big loading.

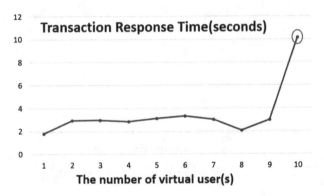

Fig. 7. Results of an on-line web service application.

6 Conclusion

We defined 6 anchors (Lunch, login, booking, itinerary, Search Flights Button, logout) at smoke test. The Lunch anchor spent the longest time than other anchors. The second place occurred at the login anchor. We employed 50 of virtual users at 1 h execution interval for stress tests and defined the service level agreement as the transaction response time of anchors less than 10 s. It simulated the different browsers, for example, IE, Chrome, Firefox, and so on, seat preference (Window, Aisle, None), departure/return date, types of seat (first, business, coach), single trip or roundtrip, etc. Two anchors (Lunch, login) failed at service level agreement. It mainly because that 50 virtual users simultaneously employed the travel service applications caused the web service to spend more time for the web service preparation time and login the web site. Form these statistical analysis (the average, standard deviation, and 90%) we found that only few failed the service level agreements. The transaction response time of the two anchors (logout and booking) were big more than 1 Vuser. We also proposed a strategy for on-line web server testing. We hope that the practical experience and the information are useful for re-searchers.

References

1. Prasad, K.V.K.K.: Software Testing Tools: Covering WinRunner, SilkTest, LoadRunner, JMeter, TestDirector and QTP with Case Studies. Dreamtech Press (2007)
2. NCHC TWCC-CLI. https://github.com/TW-NCHC/TWCC-CLI
3. Kaur, N., Bahl, K.: Performance testing of institute website using Jmeter. Int. J. Innov. Sci. Eng. Technol. 3(4), 534–537 (2016)
4. Zhang, H., Zhang, S., Li, X., Zhang, P., Liu, S.: Research of load testing and result application based on LoadRunner. In: ITCS 2012 (2012)
5. Fang, Y.-B., Chou, C.-Y., Kuo, F.-A., Wang, S.-T.: Loading analysis of cloud computing platforms. In: TANET 2019 (2019, in press)
6. Khan, R., Amjad, M.: Web application's performance testing using HP LoadRunner and CA Wily introscope tools. In: ICCCA 2016, pp. 802–806 (2016)

7. Khan, R., Amjad, M.: Performance testing (load) of web applications based on test case management. Perspect. Sci. **8**, 355–357 (2016)
8. Aggarwal, J., Solanki, A.: Performance testing on web application through HP loadrunner with parameterization and customization. J. Web Eng. Technol. **3**, 1–14 (2016)
9. Niranjanamurthy, M., Kiran, M.S., Anupama, S., Dharmendra, C.: Comparative study on performance testing with JMeter. IJARCCE **5**, 70–76 (2016)
10. Erinle, B.: Performance Testing With JMeter 2.9. Packt Publishing (2013)
11. Meier, J.D., Farre, C., Bansode, P., Barber, S., Rea, D.: Performance Testing Guidance for Web Applications. Microsoft Corporation (2007)
12. Fahrurazi, F., Ibrahim, S., Suffian, D.: The design and execution of performance testing cloud-based system. IJSET **1**, 19–25 (2014)
13. Web Tours Sample Application. https://marketplace.microfocus.com/appdelivery/content/web-tours-sample-application

Privacy-Preserving Content-Based Publish/Subscribe Service Based on Order Preserving Encryption

Mingdong Li[1], Qifeng Luo[2], Lu Wang[1], Ruisheng Shi[2(✉)],
and Jinqiao Shi[2]

[1] Aisino Corporation, Beijing, China
{limingdong, wanglul}@aisino.com
[2] Beijing University of Posts and Telecommunications, Beijing, China
{luoqifeng, shiruisheng, shijinqiao}@bupt.edu.cn

Abstract. The publish/subscribe model offers a loose-couple communication paradigm for large-scale distribute applications. Content-based publish/subscribe system allows publishers send events with attributes to admin sever, which are called broker, and subscribers can send subscriptions with attributes' constraints to broker. The brokers can match the events with subscriptions and then forward the events to the matched subscriptions' sender depends on the results of matching. However, subscriptions reveal subscriber's privacy information and subscribe strategy, the events also include valuable information. And to reduce the cost, the broker might be deployed on third party's servers where server owners or malicious entities may access the subscriptions and events, and then may lead to the leakage of privacy information. In this paper, we propose an event matching approach based on order-preserving encryption. The experiments show that our approach privacy-preserving event matching performance significantly.

Keywords: Publish/subscribe system · Order-preserving encryption · Privacy-preserving

1 Introduction

The publish/subscribe system is a loose-couple communication paradigm. The senders i.e. publishers and the receivers i.e. subscribers exchange the message through the overlay network. Publishers do not send the messages called events directly to the subscribers, but send the events to the interconnected brokers and let them forward the events to the subscribers depends on the result of matching the events with subscriber's interests. Subscribers also send their interests, which are called subscriptions to the broker instead of the publishers directly. So, in the publish/subscribe system, publishers

This work is supported by Key Research and Development Program for Guangdong Province under grant No. 2019B010137003, the Fundamental Research Funds for the Central Universities (Grant no. 24820192019RC56).

The original version of this chapter was revised: The Grant no. should be "24820192019RC56", not "2018RC56". This has now been corrected. The correction to this chapter is available at https://doi.org/10.1007/978-3-030-38651-1_33

C.-H. Hsu et al. (Eds.): IOV 2019, LNCS 11894, pp. 374–381, 2020.
https://doi.org/10.1007/978-3-030-38651-1_31

don't know which subscribers will get the events and subscriber don't know which publisher will send events to them and only broker know where the subscriptions or events will be sent.

However, to save the cost, the broker might be deployed on the third party's server, the server owners and malicious entities may access the subscriptions and events in the brokers and then causing the leakage of information. The subscriptions may include the sender's subscribe strategy and the events might also include valuable information as well. For example, in a stock system, the subscriptions may include the investors' investment strategy, when malicious entities access the brokers, they can get the subscriptions from investor, know which stock has a good Appreciation space, and then cause economic loss to the investors.

So, it's important to protect the confidentiality of events and subscriptions. It's a challenge to let broker operate encrypted message. When values are encrypted, the order and arrange of values is removed as well and it's hard for broker to match the events with subscriptions' filter without accessing the original value.

Many researches have already given some solutions to the privacy protection in publish/subscribe system. Choi et al. [1] present an encrypt algorithm called Asymmetric Scalar-product Preserving Encryption (ASPE). Although ASPE can do strict order-preserving range queries, it spends too much time on matching operation because ASPE changed the attribute's value, for example an integer value into a 2*2 matrix and then increase the program complexity. For broker need to handle millions of matching processes, the time cost of event matching process increases significantly. Barazzutti et al. [2] use bloom-filter as the pre-filter to decrease the invoke frequency of ASPE. However, the pre-filter can only process the "equality" constraints.

In this paper, we propose a privacy-preserving event matching approach based on OPE for content-based publish/subscribe systems. Order-Preserving Symmetric Encryption (OPE) [3] is an encryption algorithm that not only encrypt the data but also allows indexing and query processing to be done exactly and as efficiently as for unencrypted data. Our approach can protect the confidentiality of subscription and publication messages and keep the efficiency of matching operation as well.

2 Design and Implementation

The main Idea of Order-Preserving Symmetric Encryption (OPE) is that if $x < y$, then $E_{key}(x) < E_{key}(y)$, where E is the OPE algorithm, key is a symmetric encryption key [3]. About the system, we use PADRES [4] as the test pub/sub system. Because there's no difference between publisher and subscribers in PADRES, we set a default symmetric encryption key in the clients. When the filter's attribute's value's type is integer, it's easy to use OPE to encrypt the data and broker can match the events with subscriptions as matching unencrypted data.

Algorithms 1 and 2 gives the process of encrypting the subscriptions and events. The predicateMap is a key-value data structure, the key is attribute's name and the value is a data structure which include attribute's value and attribute's operator (equality, greater, lower, etc.); the pairMap is a key-value data structure in events, where the key is attribute's name and the value is attribute's value.

Algorithm 3 gives the process of decrypt the events. We didn't give the decrypt algorithm of subscriptions because in the whole overlay network, neither broker nor client needs to know the original message of subscriptions except the subscription's creator. What brokers need to do is matching the events with subscriptions in the cipher environment.

Algorithm 1 Encrypt subscriptions

Input $predicateMap,key$
Output encryptPreMap

1: encryptPreMap $\leftarrow \phi$
2: $preKeySet = predicateMap.getKeyset()$
3: **for** each $attriName$ in $preKeySet$ **do**
4:     $pre \leftarrow PredicateMap.get(attriName)$
5:     Create new Predicate $encPre$
6:     $encPre.op \leftarrow pre.op$
7:     $encPre.value \leftarrow$ OPE.encrypt($pre.value, key$)
8:     $encryptPreMap.put(attriName, encPre)$
9: **end for**

Algorithm 2 Encrypt events

Input $pairMap,key$
Output encryptPairMap

1: encryptPairMap $\leftarrow \phi$
2: $pairKeySet = pairMap.getKeyset()$
3: **for** each $attriName$ in $pairKeySet$ **do**
4:     $encryptPairMap.put(attriName,$OPE.encrypt($pairMap.get(attriName), key$))
5: **end for**

Algorithm 3 Decrypt events

Input $encryptPairMap,key$
Output pairMap

1: pairMap $\leftarrow \phi$
2: $pairKeySet = encryptPairMap.getKeyset()$
3: **for** each $attriName$ in $pairKeySet$ **do**
4:     $pairMap.put($
5:     $attriName,$OPE.decrypt($pairMap.get(attriName), key$))
6: **end for**

When the type is String, we change the string data into a key-value data structure. The key is a long type value and it's equal to the combination of the string's letters' ASCII code. The value is an array form constructed by ASCII code. For example, when the string is "test", the string's value is [116,101,115,116] where each integer is the ASCII code corresponding to each letter, and the string's key is "116101115116" and then the subscriber encrypts both string's key and string's value by OPE. Even when the filter's attribute's constraint is "prefix equal", "suffix equal". It's also easy for brokers to match the events with the subscriptions.

The matching process works as shown in Algorithm 4. Predict is a data structure in the subscriptions which include attribute's value: the key-value data structure of the string and attribute's operator (equality, prefix, suffix, etc.) and StringMap is the key-value data structure of the original string in the event. When the attribute's constraint is "equality", broker just to compare if the string's key in subscription is equal to the string's key in event and this process's algorithmic complexity is much lower than original process of string matching. If the attribute's constraint is "prefix" or "suffix", then we can check if the string's value in subscription is prefix array or suffix array of the event's string's value array. What we should notice is that all the data has already encrypted by OPE.

For OPE do not change the attribute's form like ASPE and the encryption process can be done in publishers and subscribers, it is easy to see that the efficiency of matching operation when use OPE is almost the same as not using any encryption algorithm.

Algorithm 4 Match String type attribute

Input $predicate, StringMap$
Output result

 1: $eventStrArray \leftarrow StringMap.get(StringArray)$
 2: $eventStrlong \leftarrow StringMap.get(Stringlong)$
 3: $preStrArray \leftarrow predicate.getValue().get(StringArray)$
 4: $preStrlong \leftarrow predicate.getValue().get(Stringlong)$
 5: **if** $predicate.op = $ "equality" **then**
 6:     **if** preStrlong $=$ eventStrlong **then**
 7:         result $\leftarrow true$
 8:     **else**
         result $\leftarrow false$
 9:     **end if**
10: **end if**
11: **if** $predicate.op = $ "prefix" **then**
12:     //Only Prefix match
13:     **for** $i = 0; i < eventStrArray.length; i + + $ **do**
14:         **if** $eventStrArray[i] = preStrArray[i]$ **then**
15:             continue
16:         **else**
             result $\leftarrow false$
17:         **end if**
18:     **end for**
19:     result $\leftarrow true$
20: **end if**
21: **if** $predocate.op = $ "suffix" **then**
22:     // Only suffix match
23:     **for** $i = eventStrArray.length - 1; i >= 0; i - - $ **do**
24:         **if** $eventStrArray[i] = preStrArray[i]$ **then**
25:             continue
26:         **else**
             result $\leftarrow false$
27:         **end if**
28:     **end for**
29: **end if**

---

3 Experiment Results

3.1 Workload

We used PADRES in JAVA as the Content-based publish/subscribe system (CBPSS). For we just compare the difference of time consumption of forwarding encrypted message and unencrypted message, there's only 1 broker, 1 subscriber and 1 publisher. We use uniform distribute subscription dataset with 4, 6, 8 attributes respectively. We built events dataset with 4, 6, 8 attributes. All the attributes' type is long. To test matching time cost, the events dataset was tested with the subscription dataset which has the same number of attributes with the events dataset.

The test device is OMEN by HP laptop, with Intel Core i7-7700HQ, 16 GB RAM, Windows 10 1083. The JAVA version is JAVA 1.8.0_141.

3.2 Time Cost of Sending Subscriptions

We test the subscriber sent 10000, 20000, 30000, 40000, 50000 subscriptions to broker with different number of attributes in each subscription.

The Fig. 1 shows how long the time cost in sending subscriptions with different number of subscriptions and different number of attributes. With the increasing of the number of attributes, the time cost of sending plaintext does not change too much, however when sending 50000 subscriptions and encrypted by OPE with 6 attributes and 8 attributes, the time increase 23.23% and 49.63% respectively compare with sending subscriptions with 4 attributes, when sending 50000 subscriptions and encrypted by ASPE with 6 attributes and 8 attributes, the time increase 17.04% and 31.45% respectively.

What we should note is that in real situation, one subscriber will not send too many subscriptions at one time, and for the average time cost of sending subscription with 8 attributes, the time cost is 0.519 ms in OPE per subscription, 0.348 ms in ASPE per subscription and 0.243 ms in plaintext per subscription and we think the time cost compromise is acceptable.

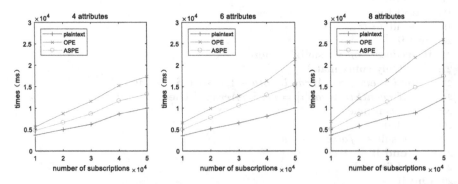

Fig. 1. Time cost of sending subscriptions

3.3 Time Cost of Insert and Delete Subscriptions

The Fig. 2 shows the time cost of inserting subscriptions in broker and we can see that because OPE does not change the type of attributes and allow the system to insert the subscription in original way, the time cost of inserting subscription with OPE is close to the time cost of inserting subscription in plaintext.

However, when inserting subscription with ASPE, the system spends more time than OPE and plaintext. Different from subscriber sends subscriptions to broker, broker always need to handle amount of subscriptions, so it's important for CBPSS to insert the subscription without too much time. and CBPSS with OPE meet the requirement.

Figure 3 shows the time cost of deleting subscription. For the algorithm the PADRES use in deleting subscriptions depend on total number of subscriptions rather than the attributes type and attribute's value. So, there is not too much change in plaintext, OPE and ASPE.

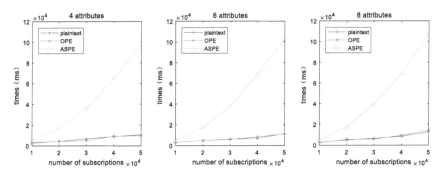

Fig. 2. Time cost of inserting subscriptions

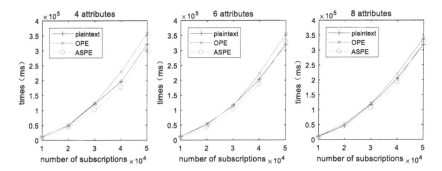

Fig. 3. Time cost of deleting subscriptions

3.4   Time Cost of Event Matching

The time cost of event matching is shown in Fig. 4. We can see that when the number of subscriptions increased, the time cost of plaintext and OPE are less than the time cost of ASPE, and time cost of plaintext and OPE is almost same.

When the number of attributes is increased, the time cost of matching with ASPE is decreased, that is because the events have higher probability to meet the un-match subscriptions and can break the match process more quickly.

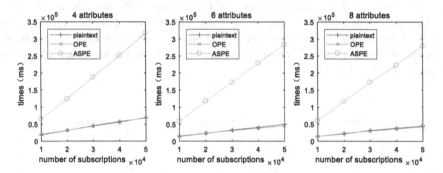

Fig. 4. Time cost of matching subscriptions

4   Limitation of PUB/SUB System with OPE

Although OPE allow efficient range queries, it's not secure when the attribute's domain is small, especially when the server owner or malicious entities know the plaintext's domain. Reference [5] introduce an algorithm called modular order-preserving encryption to improve the security of OPE, but it's no longer strictly order-preserving and so not suitable for pub/sub system unless the system user accepts false positive or false negative.

From now on we are finding a way to improve the security of OPE also keep the strict order-preserving. The second limitation of pub/sub system with OPE is that current program can only handle the integer type's data, we will find a way to do range queries when the attribute's type is float or double and other types in the future.

5   Conclusion

In this work, we use OPE as the pub/sub system's encryption algorithm, and show the feasibility of publish/subscribe system with OPE by experiments and the results show that OPE can not only encrypt the message but also keep good efficiency when broker does match operations than ASPE. We give an implementation of how to match the message when the attribute's type is string. In further work, we will find a way to not only keep the efficiency of range queries, but also improve the security of OPE when the attribute's value domain is small.

References

1. Choi, S., Ghinita, G., Bertino, E.: A privacy-enhancing content-based publish/subscribe system using scalar product preserving transformations. In: Bringas, P.G., Hameurlain, A., Quirchmayr, G. (eds.) DEXA 2010. LNCS, vol. 6261, pp. 368–384. Springer, Heidelberg (2010). https://doi.org/10.1007/978-3-642-15364-8_32
2. Barazzutti, R., Felber, P., Mercier, H., Onica, E., Rivière, E.: Thrifty privacy: efficient support for privacy-preserving publish/subscribe. In: Proceedings of the 6th ACM International Conference on Distributed Event-Based Systems, New York, pp. 225–236. ACM (2012)
3. Boldyreva, A., Chenette, N., Lee, Y., O'Neill, A.: Order-preserving symmetric encryption. In: Joux, A. (ed.) EUROCRYPT 2009. LNCS, vol. 5479, pp. 224–241. Springer, Heidelberg (2009). https://doi.org/10.1007/978-3-642-01001-9_13
4. Jacobsen, H.A., et al.: The PADRES publish/subscribe system. In: Principles and Applications of Distributed Event-Based Systems, pp. 164–205. IGI Global (2010)
5. Boldyreva, A., Chenette, N., O'Neill, A.: Order-preserving encryption revisited: improved security analysis and alternative solutions. In: Rogaway, P. (ed.) CRYPTO 2011. LNCS, vol. 6841, pp. 578–595. Springer, Heidelberg (2011). https://doi.org/10.1007/978-3-642-22792-9_33

Improve the House Price Prediction Accuracy with a Stacked Generalization Ensemble Model

Shilong Xiong$^{(\boxtimes)}$ (ID), Qibo Sun, and Ao Zhou

State Key Laboratory of Networking and Switching Technology,
Beijing University of Posts and Telecommunications, Beijing, China
279642779@qq.com

Abstract. House price prediction plays an important role in estate mar-
ketplace. Prediction future house price accurately can provide decision
making support for home buyers. With the development of machine
learning and AI technology, different machine learning models are proposed for house price prediction. However, the prediction accuracy is still
not very high. Model ensembling is a very powerful technique to increase
the accuracy of a variety of machine learning models. To address this
issue, we propose a stacked generation model which consists of various
regression models to predict house price. The experiment results show
that the stacked model performs better than traditional machine learning
models.

Keywords: House price prediction · Machine learning · Ensemble
learning

1 Introduction

It is traditionally a challenge for home buyers to make decision on real estates
investment [2,6]. House price prediction can provide decision making support
for home buyers, Machine learning and AI technology have made great progress
recently [1]. Many researchers try to exploit machine learning models to predict
the future house prices [2,4].

However, the performances of these methods are still limited, and numerous
factors make house price prediction a challenging problem [3,5]. The house price
differs with time, location and many other factors. Therefore, a large amount
of features are constructed for price prediction. Traditional machine learning
algorithm is easy to overfit when a large amount of features are adopted. In
addition, it is hard to optimize the proposed model with popular methods such
as grid search or random search.

This research is supported in part by the National Natural Science Foundation of China
under Grant No. 61571066, No. 61602054, (NSFC, 61571066, 61602054).

C.-H. Hsu et al. (Eds.): IOV 2019, LNCS 11894, pp. 382–389, 2020.
https://doi.org/10.1007/978-3-030-38651-1_32

To address the above issues, the paper proposes a stacked generalization model, which can improve the accuracy of house price prediction. Meanwhile, tuning parameters is tedious and trivial when training a large amount of house data. Therefore, Beyesian optimization is introduced to configure our models automatically. We conduct experiments on real world dataset. The experiment results show that the stacked model performs better than other models.

This paper is organized as follows. Section 2 shows the technical details of our stacked generalization method. Experiment results are illustrated in Sects. 3 and 4 concludes this paper.

2   The Method Proposed for House Price Prediction

This section consists of two parts: tuning hyperparameters based on Bayesian optimization, and house price prediction based on model stacking. We combine multiple base learners into a two-layer integrated model based on the model stacking strategy, in which each learner uses the Bayesian optimization to automatically configure corresponding model.

2.1   Prediction Based on Model Stacking

Model stacking is a mechanism that tries to leverage the benefits of a group of base models while disregarding their disadvantages. Details of stacked generalization are described in Algorithm 1. Our stacked generalization model consists two layers. In the first layer, each model makes predictions separately. Then, their output becomes the input of the second layer. Based on the predictions of the base learners, the second layer calculates the final result with higher accuracy and smaller error.

Algorithm 1. Stacked Generalization Algorithm

Input: Train set $D_{train} = \{X_{train}, Y_{train}\}$, test set X_{test}, baseline models $\Phi_1, \Phi_2, ..., \Phi_k$, meta model Φ
Output: prediction results on test set Y_{pred}
1: Split D_{train} into disjoint sets: $D'_{train}, D'_{holdout}$
2: Split D'_{train} into $D_1, D_2, ..., D_k$
3: **for** $i = 1 \rightarrow k$ **do**
4:    $C_i = D_{train} - D_i$
5:    Train Φ_i with C_i
6:    Use Φ_i to make predictions for $X'_{holdout}$ and obtain Y_i
7: **end for**
8: Use the predictions $\{Y_1, Y_2, Y_3, ...Y_k\}$ as the inputs, and $Y'_{holdout}$ as the outputs to train Φ
9: Use Φ to predict X_{test} and obtain Y_{pred}
10: Return Y_{pred}

2.2   Tuning Parameters Based on Bayesian Optimization

Bayesian optimization is a well-established method for the global optimization of expensive black-box functions. More specially, we assume the problem is to maximum an costly function $f : \chi \to \mathbb{R}$

$$x_{opt} = \arg\max_{x \in \chi} f(x) \tag{1}$$

within a domain $\chi \subset R^d$, which is a bounding box.

In our work, we build a Bayesian optimization model with the commonly used GP-based approach, which uses a GP surrogate and a acquisition function to optimize the parameter tuning process. For the hyperparamters Θ of the surrogate model,we adopt $\sigma^2(x; \Theta) = \Sigma(x, x; \Theta)$ as the marginal predictive variance of the probabilistic model, and adopt $\mu(x; X, \theta)$ as the predictive mean. The acquisition function is defined as follows:

$$\gamma(x) = \frac{f(x_{optimal}) - \mu(x; X, \theta)}{\sigma^2(x; X, \theta)} \tag{2}$$

where $f(x_{optimal})$ is the lowest observation. The expected improvement criterion is defined as

$$\alpha_E I(x; X, \theta) = \alpha(x; X, \theta)[\gamma(x)\phi(\gamma(x)) + \psi(\gamma(x); 0, 1)] \tag{3}$$

It is worth noting that Bayesian optimization strategy can be effective even if the underlying function being optimized is stochastic, non-convex,or even non-continuous.

3   Experiment

In this section, we comprehensively evaluate the performance of our stacked generalization ensemble model with six baseline models.

3.1   Experiment Setup

Dataset Description. We experiment on two datasets: the Melbourne Regional Information Dataset and the Victorian Regional Information Dataset. The Melbourne Regional Information Dataset contains house purchase transactions from 2015 to 2019. The Victorian Regional Information Dataset contains the related house purchase information of 8245 suburbs in Vic, Australia. The features in each transaction are shown in Table 1.

Data Preprocessing. Because part of the values in the dataset are missed, we fill the missing value by the mean value for numerical variables. Moreover, the mean value of categorical variables cannot be calculated directly, so we convert them to numerical variables with One-Hot Encoding. Figure 1 show that

Table 1. Description of features

Feature name	Description	Type
House Type	Type of the sale house	Categorical
Sale Date	Date of the sale house	Numerical
Distance	Distance to CBD	Numerical
Bedroom	The number of bedrooms	Numerical
Bathroom	The number of bathrooms	Numerical
Car Space	The number of parking spaces	Numerical
Build Year	The year of house built	Numerical
Land Size	The overall size of land	Categorical
Floor Size	The overall size of floor	Categorical
Suburb Area	The suburb the house located in	Categorical
Median Price	The median price of the suburb	Numerical
Property Count	The count of houses in the suburb	Numerical

the distribution of sale price is right skewed. As linear models prefer normally distributed data, we use the function $y = \log 1 + x$ to make the values more approximate to normally distributed. After transformation, the frequency distribution law of the prices is shown as Fig. 2.

Due to the large scale of the datasets, the cost of model training becomes very high. To reduce the training cost, we adopt the Bayesian optimization to auto-adjust hyperparameters, which is more efficient than random search and grid search.

3.2 Evaluation Metrics

The two metrics that are the commonly used in evaluation are root mean square error (RMSE) and absolute mean error (MAE). RMSE and MAE are calculated as follows:

$$RMSE = \sqrt{\frac{1}{N}\sum_{i=1}^{N}(y_i - \hat{y}_i)^2} \tag{4}$$

$$MAE = \frac{1}{N}\sum_{i=1}^{N}|y_i - \hat{y}_i| \tag{5}$$

$y_i, \hat{y}_i$ are the actual house price and the predicted house price, respectively. N denotes the number of house purchase records. However,these two indicators will bring a problem that errors in predicting expensive houses have higher influence than the cheap ones.

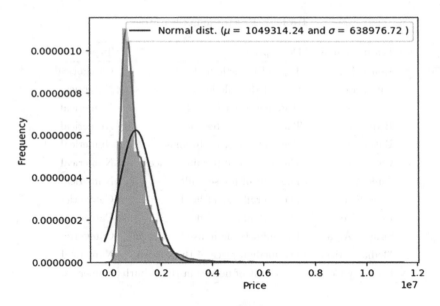

Fig. 1. The frequency distribution of price before transformation.

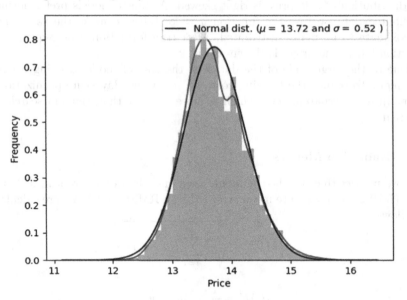

Fig. 2. The frequency distribution of price after transformation.

In order to avoid this condition, we propose two new indicators that are calculated as follows:

$$RMSE = \sqrt{\frac{1}{N}\sum_{i=1}^{N}\left(\log y_i - \log \hat{y}_i\right)^2} \tag{6}$$

$$MRE = \frac{1}{N}\sum_{i=1}^{N}\frac{|y_i - \hat{y}_i|}{y_i} \tag{7}$$

3.3   Experiment Results Under Different Parameters Tuning Strategies

We use scikit-learn library to implement the following six baseline models: Lasso Regression, Elastic Net Regression, Random Forest, Gradient Boosting, Extra Tree and XGBoost. Then, we investigate the performance of those models when different parameter tuning strategies are adopted.

Table 2. Number of hyperparameters.

Model	Number of parameters
Lasso	1
Elastic Net	2
Extra Tree	7
Random Forest	7
GDBT	11
XGBoost	10

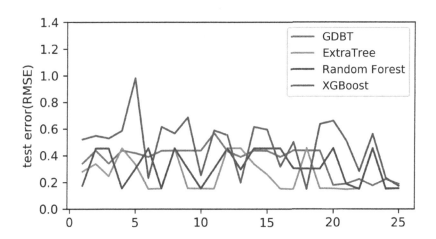

Fig. 3. RMSE on test set of each iteration.

There are various parameters and options in each model. The comparison between manual configuration and automatic configuration for all models is shown in Table 2. * denotes that the hypeparameters of those models are tuned by Bayesian optimization.

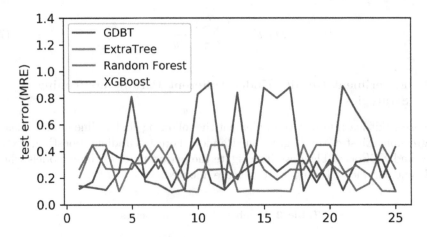

Fig. 4. MRE on test set of each iteration.

From Table 3, we can observe that models configured by Bayesian optimization obviously have a better performance. Figures 3 and 4 display the test error in each iteration. We can find that Bayesian optimization can find a good combination of hyperparamters in less iterations, which is of significance in training the dataset with large size.

Table 3. RMSE and MRE for baseline models.

Model name	RMSE	MAE
Lasso	0.3829	0.2219
Elastic Net	0.3797	0.2279
Random Forests	0.1960	0.1657
ExtraTree	0.1883	0.1513
Xgboost	0.1864	0.1540
GDBT	0.1866	0.1548
Random Forests*	0.1735	0.1404
Extra Tree*	0.1736	0.1413
Xgboost*	0.1702	0.1390
GDBT*	0.1675	0.1343

3.4 Experiment Results Under Different Base Models

This section explores the performance of various stacking models by combining different base learners. Table 4 shows the values of RMSE and MRE for all stacked generation models. From the experimental results, we can observe that:

(1) Stacking strategy has a positive effect in improving the accuracy of prediction. (2) When more base models and more powerful algorithms are employed, the final stacking model will have better performance on house price prediction.

Table 4. RMSE and MRE for models ensembled by stacking strategy.

Model name	First stage models	Meta model	RMSE	MAE
STACK_2MODEL_1	Lasso,Elastic Net	XGBoost*	0.2222	0.1874
STACK_2MODEL_2	Lasso,XGBoost*	Elastic Net	0.1691	0.1391
STACK_2MODEL_3	Elastic Net,XGBoost*	Lasso	0.1685	0.1386
STACK_3MODEL_1	ExtraTree*,GDBT*,XGBoost*	Lasso	0.1631	0.1334
STACK_3MODEL_2	ExtraTree*,GDBT*,XGBoost*	Elastic Net	0.1632	0.1334
STACK_3MODEL_3	ExtraTree*,GDBT*,XGBoost*	Random Forest*	0.1702	0.1395
STACK_4MODEL_1	ExtraTree*,GDBT*,XGBoost*,RandomForest*	Lasso	0.1626	0.1327
STACK_4MODEL_2	ExtraTree*,GDBT*,XGBoost*,RandomForest*	Elastic Net	0.1629	0.1327
STACK_5MODEL_1	ExtraTree*,GDBT*,XGBoost*,RandomForest*Lasso	Elastic Net	0.1626	0.1327
STACK_5MODEL_2	ExtraTree*,GDBT*,XGBoost*,RandomForest*Elastic Net	Lasso	0.1624	0.1325

4 Conclusion

In this paper, we introduce a stacked generalization strategy to established a integrated model for house price prediction. To reduce the cost of model configuration, we employ the Bayesian optimization to automatically tune hyperparameter of baseline models. Experimental results on real world datasets show that our model outperforms other model in prediction accuracy.

References

1. Anifowose, F., Labadin, J., Abdulraheem, A.: Improving the prediction of petroleum reservoir characterization with a stacked generalization ensemble model of support vector machines. Appl. Soft Comput. 26, 483–496 (2015)
2. Antipov, E.A., Pokryshevskaya, E.B.: Mass appraisal of residential apartments: an application of random forest for valuation and a cart-based approach for model diagnostics. Expert Syst. Appl. 39(2), 1772–1778 (2012)
3. Doumpos, M., Zopounidis, C.: Model combination for credit risk assessment: a stacked generalization approach. Ann. Oper. Res. 151(1), 289–306 (2007)
4. Gao, G., et al.: Location-centered house price prediction: a multi-task learning approach. arXiv preprint arXiv:1901.01774 (2019)
5. Wolpert, D.H.: Stacked generalization. Neural Netw. 5(2), 241–259 (1992)
6. Worzala, E., Lenk, M., Silva, A.: An exploration of neural networks and its application to real estate valuation. J. Real Estate Res. 10(2), 185–201 (1995)

Correction to: Internet of Vehicles

Ching-Hsien Hsu, Sondès Kallel, Kun-Chan Lan, and Zibin Zheng(iD)

Correction to:
C.-H. Hsu et al. (Eds.): *Internet of Vehicles*,
LNCS 11894, https://doi.org/10.1007/978-3-030-38651-1

In the version of these papers that was originally published, the Grant no. should be "24820192019RC56", not "2018RC56". This has now been corrected.

The updated version of these chapters can be found at
https://doi.org/10.1007/978-3-030-38651-1_19
https://doi.org/10.1007/978-3-030-38651-1_31

Author Index

Printed in the United States
By Bookmasters